Sexual Harassment:
Communication Implications

SCA Applied Communication Publication Program

Gary L. Kreps, Editor
Northern Illinois University

The SCA Program in Applied Communication supports the Speech Communication Association mission of promoting the study, criticism, research, teaching, and application of artistic, humanistic, and scientific principles of communication. Specifically, the goal of this publication program is to develop an innovative, theoretically informed, and socially relevant body of scholarly works that examine a wide range of applied communication topics. Each publication clearly demonstrates the value of human communication in addressing serious social issues and challenges.

Sexual Harassment: Communication Implications

Edited by
Gary L. Kreps

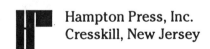

Hampton Press, Inc.
Cresskill, New Jersey

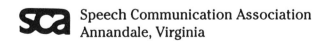

Speech Communication Association
Annandale, Virginia

Printed in the United States of America

Library of Congress Cataloging-in-Publication Data

Sexual harassment : communication implications / edited by Gary L. Kreps.
    p. cm. -- (SCA applied communication publication program)
    Includes bibliographical references and indexes.
    ISBN 1-881303-44-6 (cloth). -- ISBN 1-881303-45-4 (paper)
    1. Sexual harassment. 2. Sexual harassment in universities and colleges. 3. Interpersonal communication. 4. Communication in organizations. 5. Sexual harassment--Prevention. I. Kreps, Gary L. II. Series: Speech Communication Association/Hampton Press applied communication program.
    HD6060.3.S5 1993
331.4'133--dc20   92-38370
                                                   CIP

Hampton Press, Inc.
23 Broadway
Cresskill, NJ 07626.

▼ *Contents*

SECTION III: SEXUAL HARASSMENT ON THE COLLEGE CAMPUS

SECTION IV: RESPONDING TO HARASSMENT

▼*About the Authors*

Jill Axelrod (B.A. Politics and Government, Ohio Wesleyan University) will earn an M.A. in Public Communication from The American University when she completes her Master's project on sexual harassment and sex-role stereotypes. Before returning to graduate school, she worked for Disclosure Incorporated in Bethesda, MD for four years in marketing communications.

Thomas W. Benson (Ph.D., Cornell University) is Edwin Erle Sparks Professor of Rhetoric in the Department of Speech Communication at Penn State University.

Cynthia Berryman-Fink (Ph.D., Bowling Green State University) is Professor of Communication at the University of Cincinnati. She has published three books and over 20 articles on gender issues in language, organizations, and relationships; management communication; and education. She has served as a consultant to 25 organizations.

Judith K. Bowker (Ph.D., University of Oregon) is Assistant Professor of Interpersonal Communication at Oregon State University with specialities in family and gender. She writes and speaks on topics of family environment, gender and intimacy, education, and health issues related to cancer patients.

Mark J. Braun (Ph.D., University of Minnesota, Twin Cities) is Assistant Professor of Speech and Communication Studies at Gustavus Adolphus College, Saint Peter, MN, and is currently a Visiting Lecturer in the Department of Speech Communication at the University of Minnesota. He specializes in broadcast regulation and policy and is the author of a forthcoming book on the FCC's controversial AM Stereo decision. His dissertation was awarded the Kenneth Harwood Award by the Broadcast Education Association in 1990 and was cited for honorable mention by the Mass Communication Division of the International Communication Association in 1992.

Mary Helen Brown (Ph.D., The University of Texas at Austin) is Associate Professor and Graduate Program Officer in the Department of Communication at Auburn University. Research interests include organizational stories and narrative forms of expression. She gratefully acknowledges the assistance of Andrea Baldwin in arranging the interviews.

Robin P. Clair (Ph.D., Kent State University) is Assistant Professor in the Communication Department at Purdue University. The author's primary teaching and research interest is organizational communication; specific areas of interest include alienation, hegemony, feminism, and racial and gender-related social problems.

Chris J. Foreman (M.A., University of Kentucky) is a doctoral student in the Department of Communication at the University of Kentucky. Her research interests include cultural analyses of communicative processes in an organizational context, with emphases on storytelling, leadership, organizational change, and organizational subcultures.

Kathleen M. Galvin (Ph.D., Northwestern University) is Associate Dean and Professor in the School of Speech and a member of the Counseling Psychology faculty at Northwestern University. She has authored or co-authored six books and numerous articles on the role of communication in classrooms and families.

Mary M. Gill (Ph.D., University of Nebraska-Lincoln) is Assistant Professor at Buena Vista College. Her primary research program focuses on interpersonal dynamics within classrooms with a special emphasis on the effects of accents on comprehension. She has presented and published several articles addressing topics such as the effects of national accents in classrooms, sexual harassment in academia, people problems in organizations, forensic education, and religious rhetoric.

Gail Armstead Hankins (Ph.D., University of Florida) is Assistant Professor of Communication at North Carolina State University. Her research emphasis is in interracial and business communication and in gender.

Susan Jarboe (Ph.D., University of Wisconsin) is Assistant Professor of Speech Communication at Pennsylvania State University. Her research interests center on problem-solving communication, emphasizing analytic procedures and communicative behaviors that enhance decision effectiveness. She is also interested in the study and application of communication theory to professional relationships, work groups, and organizations.

Gary L. Kreps (Ph.D., University of Southern California) is Professor of Communication Studies and a member of the Gerontology Faculty (Social Science Research Institute) at Northern Illinois University. He has published 15 books and more than 100 articles and chapters examining the role of communication in organizational life, health promotion, and education.

Rebecca Leonard (Ph.D., Purdue University) is Associate Professor of Communication and Assistant Provost at North Carolina State University.

She has published on issues of gender and diversity and directs *The First Year Experience* program.

Laura Carroll Ling (M.A., University of New Mexico) has served as Visiting Lecturer at North Carolina State University and as Director of Publications for the North Carolina Symphony.

Carol H. Maidon (M.S., North Carolina State University) former Assistant Affirmative Action Officer, is currently Assistant Director of the University Undesignated Program at North Carolina State University. She is currently pursuing a Ph.D. in Science Education. Her research interests include the underrepresentation of women and minorities in math and science and methodology of science teaching at the elementary level.

Michael J. McGoun (M.A., Cleveland State University) has research interests that include mass media, popular culture, media preferences and personality traits, and social problems (especially racial and gender-related issues).

Robert Miller (B.S. Electrical Engineering, University of Kentucky) is a graduate student in the Department of Communication at the University of Kentucky. His research interests include gender differences and similarities in organizational and interpersonal communication contexts.

Anne M. O'Leary-Kelly (Ph.D., Michigan State University) is Assistant Professor of Management at Texas A & M University, specializing in the areas of organizational behavior and human resource management. Her research interests include issues related to women in organizations, organizational justice, group motivation, and employee training.

Ramona L. Paetzold (J.D., University of Nebraska; D.B.A., Indiana University) is Assistant Professor of Management at Texas A & M University. She currently publishes in areas relating to employment law and human resources management, with primary emphases on discrimination law, women and law, and law and statistics.

Kay E. Payne (Ph.D., Vanderbilt University) has focused her studies on organizational communication. She has a special interest in gender studies, family communication, and applied communication. She presently occupies a position on the faculty of Western Kentucky University in Bowling Green, KY.

Gerald M. Phillips (Ph.D., Western Reserve University) is Professor Emeritus of Speech Communication at Pennsylvania State University. He is author of 44 books and more than 200 articles. He is currently working as a freelance medical writer and editor. He is also editor of *IPCT-J: An Electronic Journal for the Twenty-First Century.*

Paul F. Potorti (M.A., Western Virginia University) is Visiting Lecturer emphasizing interpersonal and relational communication at North Carolina State University.

Jan Rogers (M.A., Michigan State University) will soon complete a Doctoral Degree in Counselor Education at North Carolina State University. Her areas of research interests include violence against women, female psychological development, and issues of gender and racial equity.

Leonard J. Shedletsky (Ph.D., University of Illinois) is Professor of Communication at the University of Southern Maine. His research has examined cognitive aspects of communication, focusing upon memory and language. He carried out his dissertation research on clause variables and memory-scanning as a Visiting Scholar at Columbia University. He has been a Visiting Research Fellow at the University of Sussex and University of London. He is author of the book, *Meaning and Mind,* numerous journal articles, and two chapters on intrapersonal communication.

Melissa M. Spirek (A.B.D., Purdue University) has recently accepted a position in the Telecommunications Department at Bowling Green University. Her research interests are the social and psychological effects of mass media and social problems.

Vincent R. Waldron (Ph.D., Ohio State University) is Associate Professor in the Department of Communication, Arizona State University—West. His research program examines strategic communication in organizational and interpersonal settings. His recent work includes studies on upward influence, conflict, and the acquisition of socially sensitive information. He has published his research in such journals as *Communication Monographs, Human Communication Research*, and *Management Communication Quarterly.*

Hal R. Witteman (Ph.D., University of Wisconsin) is Assistant Professor of Speech Communication at The Pennsylvania State University. He has published articles examining the processes of problem solving and conflict management in interpersonal relationships and small groups.

Julia T. Wood (Ph.D., Pennsylvania State University) is Professor of Speech Communication at the University of North Carolina at Chapel Hill. Specializing in interpersonal relationships, communication, gender and culture, and feminist theory, she has published five books, edited two others, and written over 100 articles and papers.

▼ *Foreword*

Thomas W. Benson
The Pennsylvania State University
University Park, PA

The 1991 Senate confirmation hearings of Supreme Court Justice Clarence Thomas made the issue of sexual harassment a topic of reflection and discussion throughout the United States. In schools, workplaces, and families, people asked themselves what they could do to better understand and cope with the problem of sexual harassment. The Speech Communication Association has commissioned this book as part of its contribution to understanding and combatting sexual harassment. This volume represents the findings of a diverse group of scholars on the communicative dimensions of sexual harassment—legal and sociological definitions, the communicative contexts and manifestations of harassment, and advice on how individuals and institutions can deal with the subject in their own practices.

In his chapter in this volume, Hal Witteman cites the definition of sexual harassment established by the Equal Employment Opportunity Commission: "unwelcome sexual advances, requests for sexual favors, and other verbal or physical conduct of a sexual nature, when followed by any of the following facts: (a) Submission to the conduct is made a condition of employment; (b) Submission to or rejection of the conduct is made the basis for an employment decision; and (c) The conduct seriously affects an employee's work performance, or creates an intimidating, hostile, or offensive working environment." A growing body of research, fundamentally extended and refined in this volume, indicates that sexual harassment is a serious and pervasive problem.

The reports gathered here are written at a variety of levels of academic formality and employ a variety of methods, which are probably real strengths in the case of this complex and conflicted phenomenon, which is itself shifting in definition and has a powerfully stigmatizing potential for all who become embroiled in it as victims or alleged perpetrators.

The volume editor, Gary Kreps, has organized the book in such a way as to define the nature and scope of sexual and gender harassment, to evaluate various communicative strategies for responding to sexual harassment, to present a variety of case studies, and to propose strategies for eliminating sexual harassment.

Students, scholars, and administrators will find in this book much that challenges long established organizational practices and much that offers hope for a way through the conflicts of organizational life.

Readers may find that they do not agree with all the positions advanced here—that, at least, has certainly been my own experience in reading these chapters, which are, by turns, hardheadedly practical, deeply idealistic, and, in at least one case, savagely cynical. But the turmoil thus constituted in the text, mirroring the conditions and moral agonies of the society, will surely stimulate useful discussion and research, and some of the advisory chapters will be of immediate use to women and men dedicated to eliminating sexual harassment from school and workplace.

Thomas W. Benson
February, 1993

Introduction: Sexual Harassment and Communication

Gary L. Kreps
Northern Illinois University
DeKalb, IL

 RATIONALE

Sexual harassment is a serious and pervasive problem in modern organizational life, with both the targets of sexual harassment and those who are accused of sexual harassment (falsely or not) suffering personal anguish and dehumanization. Human communication performs a central, yet complex, role in sexual harassment. Communication is the primary medium through which sexual harassment is expressed; it is the means by which those who are harassed respond to harassment, and it is also the primary means by which policies for eliminating sexual harassment in the workplace can be implemented.

This book is designed to carefully evaluate the nature of sexual harassment from a communicative perspective, to help increase understanding of this disturbing social phenomenon and improve the quality of organizational life by identifying effective strategies for confronting and preventing this problem. The chapters in this book review and demystify the powerful role human communication performs in sexual harassment by:

1. providing in-depth examinations of the communicative bases of sexual harassment from a variety of different organizational perspectives;
2. evaluating the ways that communication has been used and can be used to respond effectively to sexual harassment;

1

3. describing and analyzing relevant case studies of the role communication has performed in instances of sexual harassment;
   and
4. proposing specific communicative strategies for minimizing and
   ultimately preventing sexual harassment in modern organizational life.

BACKGROUND

This book is the product of a special jointly sponsored project of the
Speech Communication Association's (SCA) Applied Communication
Publication Series and the SCA-sponsored *Journal of Applied
Communication Research*. In an attempt to focus concerted attention on
the issue of sexual harassment, two related projects were developed.
One, a special issue of the *Journal of Applied Communication Research*
(*JACR*), which devoted a section to presenting and analyzing "Personal
Narratives About Sexual Harassment," was coordinated by Julia Wood
and *JACR* Editor Bill Eadie. This special issue was designed to describe
the very private and personal individual perspectives on the experience
of being sexually harassed that are rarely shared in a public forum.
Building upon this important special issue, this book was designed to
provide a more detailed analytic forum both to examine the role of communication in sexual harassment and to suggest communicative strategies for responding effectively to harassment in the workplace.

Calls for papers and paper proposals were published in SCA's
newsletter *Spectra*, the *Journal of Applied Communication Research*, and
on numerous e-mail computer networks (such as CRTNET and COM-
SERVE) inviting submissions for this book and for the special section of
JACR. More than 30 interesting chapter proposals were submitted for
review for this volume. Of those excellent submissions, 15 were selected
for this volume based on their particular relevance and far-reaching
insights into this important topic. In reading these chapters you will note
that no single political, methodological, or philosophical orientation was
mandated for this book. The chapters represent a broad range of different approaches for examining sexual harassment and communication.
The book's chapters represent the perspectives of those who have been
sexually harassed, those who have been accused of sexual harassment,
and those whose job it is to respond to claims of sexual harassment and
to prevent sexual harassment in their organizations. The influences of
communication on sexual harassment are analyzed in the book from
interpersonal, group, organizational, societal, and mediated perspectives. Furthermore, the analytic methods used in the chapters include

theoretical overviews, empirical studies, policy proposals, and strategic plans for organizational intervention to prevent sexual harassment.

ORGANIZATION AND OVERVIEW OF THE BOOK

This book is organized into four major parts. The first part, "Communication and Sexual Harassment," frames sexual harassment as a communication event, providing a theoretical and pragmatic overview of the relationships between sexual harassment and communication. Following the brief introduction provided here, in Chapter 1, Julia Wood presents a more detailed review of current knowledge about sexual harassment, examines the ways that sexual harassment is communicated, and suggests several fruitful directions for studying the role of communication in sexual harassment. Hal Witteman builds on Wood's review of sexual harassment and communication in Chapter 2 by contrasting the expression of sexual harassment with the expression of organizational romance, identifying how sexual harassment might be understood as incompetent attempts to initiate romance. In the final chapter in this part, Chapter 3, Ramona Paetzold and Anne O'Leary Kelly examine some of the legal aspects of sexual harassment, describing how a hostile work environment can influence sexual harassment and identifying implications from workplace sexual harassment law for organizational communication.

In the second part of the book, "Communicating About Sexual Harassment," the conceptual overview of the role of communication in sexual harassment provided in the first section is applied by describing and analyzing specific instances in which sexual harassment has been communicated and communicated about in the workplace. For example, in Chapter 4, Leonard Shedletsky provides a very personal account of a situation in which he had been accused of sexual harassment, examining the influences of the accusation on his life and relationships and examining the communicative options available to those who are accused. In Chapter 5, Mark Braun recounts and analyzes a dramatic story of how a very successful advertising agency suffered significant loss of income and reputation as a result of public outrage about the incredibly rude and harassing way they responded to a letter of complaint (about an instance in which the agency used sexist messages) from a female professor. In Chapter 6, Jill Axelrod examines how the portrayal of sexual harassment in popular movies encourages public legitimation of sexual harassment, actually promoting the expression of sexual harassment in the workplace. In the final chapter in this part, Chapter 7, Mary Helen Brown vividly illustrates women's concerns about and experiences with sexual harassment by ethnographically recounting the conversation of a group of professional women communicating about sexual harassment.

The third part of the book, "Sexual Harassment on the College Campus," describes the expression of sexual harassment in a specific organizational context, academe, clearly illustrating the pervasive influences of sexual harassment in modern organizational life. In the first chapter in this part, Chapter 8 Kay Payne examines four cases in which male professors sexually harassed female students (reported in *The Lecherous Professor*, Dzeich & Weiner, 1984) in light of Social Judgment-Involvement theory, illustrating how the students' communication about the incidents demonstrates the influences of power myths and the use of persuasion in sexual harassment. In Chapter 9, Mary Gill reports and discusses the implications of a survey of male and female professors' and students' perceptions of sexually harassing behaviors, which indicates that subjects were more likely to recognize overt rather than subtle forms of harassment, with females more likely than males to recognize subtle forms of harassment. In Chapter 10, Rebecca Leonard and a group of her colleagues at North Carolina State University report the results of a large survey of female students, staff, and faculty members' experiences with sexual harassment at that institution, identifying implications from the survey for university policy and practices regarding sexual harassment. In the final chapter in this part, Chapter 11, Judy Bowker addresses the delicate issues of deciding whether or not to report and how to report sexual harassment.

The last part of this book, "Responding to Harassment," examines the short- and long-term effectiveness of different communicative responses to sexual harassment, as well as the development of proactive strategies to prevent and eliminate sexual harassment in the workplace. In the first chapter in this part, Chapter 12, Robin Clair and two colleagues report a survey of the experiences of a sample of working women with sexual harassment, with close to half of the respondents reporting that they had been harassed and describing the specific strategies they used to respond to harassment. In the next chapter, Chapter 13, Vincent Waldron and two colleagues present a study examining the differences in the ways male and female subordinates define and maintain their relationships with their supervisors, describing strategic ways relational communication can be used to prevent sexual harassment and gender bias. In Chapter 14, Kathleen Galvin describes a pilot program used at Northwestern University to proactively prevent sexual harassment by educating faculty about the nature of sexual harassment and helping them develop strategies for creating a hospitable academic environment. Similarly, in Chapter 15, Cynthia Berryman-Fink describes a training program, this time focusing on gender communication, to prevent sexual harassment by encouraging employees to develop an organizational culture characterized by equality and professionalism. In Chapter 16, Gerald Phillips and Susan Jarboe provide a unique, irreverent, and unsettling description of sexual harassment as a natural and irreversible primeval predisposition of men to sexually dominate and subordinate women, suggesting that the most viable techniques available to women to prevent sexual harassment involve strategic servility and obsequiousness. In the concluding chapter, Chapter 17, I rebut Phillips's and Jarboe's conclusions, describing a sociocultural evolutionary model for preventing sexual harassment through the use of meta-communication.

REFERENCES

Dziech, B. W., & Weiner, L. (1984). *The lecherous professor.* Boston: Beacon Press.

Communication and Sexual Harassment

▼Chapter 1

Naming and Interpreting Sexual Harassment: A Conceptual Framework for Scholarship

Julia T. Wood
The University of North Carolina
Chapel Hill, NC

"The limits of my language are the limits of my world."
–Wittgenstein

The Hill–Thomas hearings simultaneously enhanced the salience of sexual harassment to the general public and directed scholars toward sexual harassment as an issue that merits sustained, serious research. While isolated research on sexual harassment has punctuated academic publications for some time (for example, see Dziech & Weiner, 1984; Lott, Reilly, & Howard, 1982; Winks, 1982), only since the fall of 1991 has this issue emerged as a focus of substantial research.

In the wake of the Hill–Thomas hearings, scholars of Speech Communication responded quickly and impressively. As early as November 1991, Strine (1991), for instance, offered an incisive analysis of some of the psychodynamics evident in textual accounts from the Congressional hearings. Since then the *Journal of Applied Communication Research* featured a symposium titled *Telling Our Stories* in which individuals who had been sexually harassed narrated their experiences, which were then critically interpreted by Conrad

(1992) and Strine (1992).[1] This book represents another effort by communication researchers to increase understanding of sexual harassment by inquiring into its communicative dimensions. As this volume goes to press, yet another communication-focused collection of studies is being edited (Bingham, in press).

There are good reasons why sexual harassment is a particularly compelling topic for scholars in Speech Communication. Whatever else sexual harassment may entail—power issues, psychological motives and dysfunctions, cultural constructions including gender roles—it is undeniably a communication phenomenon. It is so in at least two ways. First, the existence and meaning of sexual harassment are constructed symbolically both through culturally formed and legitimated definitions and through the processes whereby individuals interpret experiences. Second, sexual harassment and the responses to it are enacted through communication. While many of the chapters in this volume focus on the second way in which sexual harassment is a communicative phenomenon, this chapter addresses the first. My purposes are to look more closely at the ways in which sexual harassment has—and has not been—constructed and, following that, to elaborate the unique strengths of critical and interpretive research approaches for increasing understanding of this pervasive and persistent problem in the workplace.

UNNAMED AND UNSEEN:
THE HISTORY OF SEXUAL HARASSMENT

While sexual harassment may have only recently entered the general vocabulary of our society, it certainly is not a new phenomenon. Much like other long performed and little discussed sexist practices such as date rape and spouse abuse, sexual harassment is thoroughly ensconced in our society. Historically, none of these practices has received substantial public acknowledgment, much less concern and censure. Only very recently has discussion of these topics punctuated civic life, finding its way into social, professional, institutional, and legal discourses.

Phenomena that are unacknowledged are not (at least, not fully) recognized; thus, of course, they cannot be studied. It is not surprising, then, that for so long sexual harassment went undocumented and uninvestigated. In one of the earliest statements about sexual harassment, the Project on the Status and Education of Women noted that "prior to

---

[1]This chapter is an extension and revision of the article I wrote to introduce the symposium, "Telling Our Stories," in *The Journal of Applied Communication Research* (in press). Permission granted by *JACR*.

1976, there were few reliable statistics on the incidence of sexual harassment" ("Sexual Harassment" 1978, p. 2). Throughout the 1970s research remained less than vigorous and only in the 1980s did a sizable body of findings document the extensiveness and consequences of this pattern of (mis)conduct.

Once attention was paid to sexual harassment, initial reports[2] unequivocally and consistently verified its pervasiveness. In one of the first national studies, *Redbook's* 1976 survey of 9,000 clerical and professional women found that fully 92% had experienced some form of sexual harassment on the job (Safran, 1976). In 1987, the U.S. Merit Systems Protection Board discovered that 42% of the women working for the federal government (ironically including those very agencies specifically charged to protect civil rights) reported having been sexually harassed in the workplace (Edmunds, 1988). According to other surveys, sexual harassment had been experienced by 70% of the women in military service and 50% of the women working in congressional offices (Fairhurst, 1986; "Sexual harassment", 1991). Studies of academic environments revealed that they too had a disturbingly high incidence of sexual harassment: Up to 50% of students and up to 30% of faculty members reported they had been sexually harassed (Blum, 1991; Jaschik & Frentz, 1991; McMillen, 1991; Rubin & Borgers, 1990). Once inquiry was made into the incidence of sexual harassment, then, it became abundantly clear that the problem was–and is–of enormous proportions. In transcending lines of class, ethnicity, sexual preference, race, age, and profession, it affects a substantial portion of the contemporary workforce.

Growing awareness of sexual harassment, precipitated largely by feminist efforts, led to legal and institutional measures to address the problem. Jurisprudential action followed documentation of the extensiveness of the problem, yet it moved at a rather laggardly pace. Only in 1964, with the passage of the Civil Rights Act, was sexual harassment legally acknowledged as unconstitutional, but that alone promoted neither substantial awareness in the minds of the general public nor reform in institutional policies and practices. Eight years later when Title IX of the Education Amendments of 1972 became law, educational institutions were formally bound not to discriminate on the basis of gender, yet sexual harassment still remained nonsalient in the priorities of most administrators and educators.

Perhaps the watershed moment in taking sexual harassment seriously came more than a decade later when the Supreme Court ruled in *Meritor Savings Bank v. Vinson* (106 S. Ct. 2399; 1986) that sexual

[2]The first wave of reports appeared almost exclusively in popular magazines rather than academic journals. Only after public attention was at least minimally captured did academic research on sexual harassment emerge as a substantial voice.

harassment is a form of sexual discrimination and, as such, workers are granted legal protection from it. Most recently, in February 1992, the Supreme Court rendered a unanimous decision that victims of sexual harassment within educational institutions may bring suit and collect damages, a right not explicitly granted by Title IX itself. That move, a surprise to many, granted victims the right to sue for both compensatory and punitive damages, thereby creating what is probably, albeit unfortunately, a necessary condition for taking something seriously in a capitalist society.

With the enactment of laws, professional organizations and educational institutions, not previously motivated by philosophical and moral arguments, were forced to address the problem in order to protect themselves against litigation. Researchers offered a wealth of advice (see the discussion of this in Chapter 16) to organizations designed to help them deal with harassment, from defining it to providing sample company policy statements. Across the United States, campuses and businesses designed educational and training programs to inform participants in those organizations what constitutes sexual harassment, what responsibilities obtain to which members, what consequences may follow charges and findings of harassment, and what avenues of redress are available to victims. Policies were instituted; organizational units and roles were created to educate, monitor, receive, and investigate complaints about sexual harassment; and grievance procedures were devised. With these developments, sexual harassment, long dismissed and denied, finally gained at least limited institutional and public recognition.

NAMING SEXUAL HARASSMENT

During most of Western history there was no appropriate name to refer to unwanted and unwelcome sexual advances in professional settings. They occurred; in fact, from all reports they did so with alarming frequency. Yet, as long as such advances were not defined as sexual harassment, they weren't generally seen as such. Eventually, feminists coined the term "sexual harassment" to label behavior that objectifies and humiliates women (Wise & Stanley, 1987, p. 19). A full understanding of sexual harassment, however, must be predicated on realizing that historically it has not been a term with currency in either legal or general discourse.

What are the implications of not naming something? Mead (1934) and those who have extended his work, notably Blumer (1969), would argue that the importance of naming is that we lift something out of the "booming, buzzing confusion" and isolate it for attention: In naming we argue that something merits our notice. Conversely, when we do not name things, we argue—at least implicitly—that they do not merit recognition. In her classic essay, "Defining Reality: A Powerful Tool," Spender (1984) maintained that to not name something is to negate it, to make it invisible, to deny it exists or matters. Naming, she insists, defines reality—defines what it is we recognize as constituting the world and our experiences in it.

But who gets to do the naming of the world? Germinal work by a number of scholars including Spender (1980, 1984), Daly (1973, 1978), Ardener (1975), Kramarae, Thorne, and Henley (1978), and Rich (1979), among others, underscores the relationship between language and power: Those who have power have the prerogative of naming the world. Invariably—and perhaps unavoidably—they name it from their perspectives, ones that inevitably are less than fully cognizant of standpoints outside of their own. Understanding the naming process and its intimate linkage with power sheds light on the long history of silence surrounding sexual harassment—the not naming of it. Because it was experienced primarily by women (Winks, 1982) and, not coincidentally, persons with low power including the power to name, it was not a significant concern of those in power who, again not coincidentally, were primarily men. Sexual harassment's low salience to those with the power to confer name and legitimacy left it unrepresented in the language they generated to represent their experiences of the world. From the perspective of individuals who were not adversely affected by sexual harassment, it was not worth naming; it didn't exist. (Later in this chapter I return to discuss in greater detail the critical role of perspective in naming the reality of sexual harassment).

Not naming sexual harassment had specific, predictable consequences. Like victims of date rape, persons who were sexually harassed had no publicly legitimated way to label what happened to them, much less to talk with others about this "problem that had no name." Each incident was isolated from the web of social interaction out of which consensual recognition and meaning arise. Each individual victim (though, of course, not defined by others or her or himself as such) struggled alone to make sense of her or his[3] experience. Individuals engaged in this process almost entirely bereft of any culturally legitimated interpretive screens that might have defined the harasser as wrong and the victim as both not to blame and not solitary in the situation. Because it had no name, sexual harassment could not be lifted from the flow of events in the world to isolate it as a focus of attention. There was no socially legitimated vocabulary

---

[3]Although all available evidence suggests women are disproportionately the victims and men disproportionately the perpetrators of sexual harassment, there are cases in which men, both gay and heterosexual, have been harassed. Thus, I use the constructions "her or his" and "she or he" to avoid a falsely generic "she." When I use only "she" or "her," my referent is exclusively female.

to describe the feelings such incidents evoked, and there were no words to depict sexualized interactions that transpired out of the contexts conventionally associated with sexuality. Thus, it was not much discussed. Even in their internal efforts to construct meanings, victims were restricted to existing language, which necessarily denied, distorted, misrepresented, and/or minimized the nature of sexual harassment.

Resorting out of necessity to the only language that did exist for representing sexual encounters invoked (mis)representations, whereby harassers might be labeled merely "forward" or "pushy," harassment was understood as "just something they are going to do" (a description that implicitly condones the behavior and advises victims to tolerate it) or—more strongly—as "going too far." Blatant quid pro quos such as "seduction," and entirely inappropriate requests or demands for sexual favors were called "overtures," "advances," or "passes."

Yet, because these terms were invented for and are associated with dating-romantic situations in social and intimate contexts, they distorted conceptions of behavior that occurs in work environs and humiliates, arises out of power discrepancies, and/or links recognition and rewards to exchanges unrelated to job qualifications and performance. The language of male-female flirtation entails assumptions of an established social-intimate relationship, relatively equal partners who have choices about what to allow or not, and amorous or friendly feelings and motives. Such assumptions are sharply discordant with the dynamics of sexual harassment. None of these terms calls attention to the blatant abuse of power and position that typically characterizes harassment. None defines harassers as unequivocally and inexcusably wrong. None captures the sense of entrapment and powerlessness (Bingham, 1991; Clarke, 1982; Farley, 1978; Wise & Stanley, 1987) that victims report feeling when their jobs, grades, promotions, salaries, or other matters depend on submitting to (or, at the very least, tolerating "with good humor") harassers' behaviors. Instead, terminology derived from romantic relationships crucially misrepresents harassment as a natural, acceptable, and even complimentary way for men to show their "appreciation" of women. Most fundamentally, using terminology associated with amorous contexts obscures the ugliness, unwantedness, violation, repugnance, and sheer darkness of sexual harassment.

The link between naming and recognizing sexual harassment was dramatically demonstrated in a study by Brooks and Perot (1991). Using a questionnaire that asked women faculty and graduate students whether they had ever experienced 31 situations within the legal definition of sexual harassment, Brooks and Perot reported that while up to 88.8% of respondents had experienced some of these, only 5.6% of faculty and 2.8% of graduate students answered affirmatively to the single question that asked directly if they had been sexually harassed.

As Brooks and Perot's research reveals, without a recognized name, sexual harassment is not identified as such.[4] As long as the only available language (mis)represented sexual harassment within the framework of romantic and social interaction, it could not be conceived in alternative ways—ones that would define it as abuse of power, wrongdoing, violation, or in other configurations that depict it as unacceptable, even criminal, and most certainly not a form of romantic interaction. For sexual harassment to be understood and subjected to critique, then, it first had to be named.

Naming sexual harassment has been a priority of feminist activists and researchers during recent years. Since 1980, an alternative vocabulary has been created, one that defines unwanted and unwelcome sexual actions in work and educational contexts as "sexual harassment," a term now widely used, if less than consensually understood. Other related phenomena are being correspondingly retitled and, thus, reconstituted: "Objects of attention" are redefined as "victims;" "pushy" or "forward" individuals are now named "harassers" and, ultimately, "defendants;" and "going too far," "seduction," and "advances" are renamed "violations of individual rights." Consistent with its fundamental power to shape perceptions, this new language has begun to reform attitudes toward the behaviors comprising sexual harassment so that it is decreasingly widely expected, tolerated, or shrugged off. Naming sexual harassment in ways that call attention to its violence and wrongness is an achievement of critical importance. The emergence of sexual harassment as a recognized phenomenon highlights the pivotal power of naming. In turn, attention to the significance of naming, as I suggest later, reveals key directions for continuing scholarship and activism by professionals in communication.

TRANSFORMING MEANING:
DIRECTIONS FOR RESEARCH AND SOCIAL CHANGE

Recent efforts to name sexual harassment as such and to instill new meanings for the behaviors comprising it have not, of course, effected an overnight transformation in public attitudes. It would be both naive and imprudent to assume that people in general recognize, much less accept, the meanings that recently have been proffered both by jurisprudential actions and educational efforts. Ongoing vigilance and effort are required for the extended process of attempting to establish and legitimate new names and, with them, new understandings of sexual harassment.

---

[4]This, of course, suggests that studies of sexual harassment, especially early ones, were conservative in their estimations of how frequently it occurs. Since many people did not label their experiences as "sexual harassment," we must infer that it has been underreported, perhaps dramatically so.

Agents of Social Change

At this moment in history the meaning of sexual harassment remains contested–new definitions exist in tension with long established and still widely endorsed views that hold sexual advances are a male preroga- tive, should be understood as harmless flirtation, and can be stopped by any woman who simply says "no." Gaining adherence for newer views of sexual harassment, then, is one priority for communication profession- als. In a number of ways we can contribute to the emergent effort to name sexual harassment as wrong and unacceptable and to lodge responsibility with the harasser rather than the victim. Professionals trained in communicative understandings and skills are particularly well suited to further the process of naming sexual harassment through their work as educators, sought-after speakers for various organizations, and consultants. Each of these roles provides opportunities to advance awareness of what constitutes harassment, what responses are legally allowable, and why victims often do not feel able to stop harassment in forceful, assertive ways.   Many of the chapters in this volume point to ways that communication specialists can contribute to naming and reducing sexual harassment in the workplace.

Directions for Scholarship

Turning now to communication-focused scholarship on sexual harass- ment, it is useful to recall Kelly's (1955) critical insight that if you want to understand people's behavior, you must first discover how they repre- sent their circumstances to themselves. This suggests that perhaps the most foundational issue for research on sexual harassment is increasing understanding of alternative ways in which various behaviors are con- strued by different individuals. We know, for instance, that women and men tend to perceive sexually related behaviors differently and to have distinct understandings of their own roles in sexualized situations (Fitzgerald & Ormerod, 1991; McKinney, 1990). Yet, we need to know considerably more about these demonstrated differences.

Two promising lines of inquiry are suggested by existing knowl- edge of gender-based differences. One is to track the implications of divergent views and meanings generally characteristic of women and men: What does each construal invite and preclude as courses of action (e.g., types of responses viewed as possible and desirable), images of self, and views of the other and the relationship with her or him? Are some construals of sexually harassing situations more "healthy" or empowering than others?

A second line of inquiry is to resist the essentializing implications of research that demonstrates generalizable differences between women's and men's perceptions of sexualized interactions. Without denying that gender-linked patterns exist, it is possible to push beyond this to explore differences *within* each gender's representations of sexual advances and responses to them. The patterns that have been reported, while important, have the potential to obscure equally important divergencies among the meanings and feelings women and men experience (Harding, 1991). Understanding why different women and men interpret the "same" behaviors quite differently might provide us with important insights into a number of influences on symbolic constructions of sexual harassment.

Both theory and practice would benefit by more in-depth knowledge of conditions and personal qualities–both between and within the genders–that tend to give rise to alternative ways of conceiving harassing situations. Such knowledge could inform efforts to design effective educational programs and intervention strategies. In short, we need to know a great deal more about why individuals initiate, tolerate, and/or resist sexual harassment, what professional, psychological, and cognitive consequences (both "payoffs" and problems) it entails, and what conditions in individuals, relationships, organizations, and culture legitimate, perpetuate, and sometimes promote it. Insight into these issues is prerequisite to any informed effort to empower victims and eliminate–or at least reduce–the incidence of occurrence. Discovering alternative and potentially interactive ways of conceiving sexual harassment and assessing the implications of each provides a strong foundation for designing effective personal, organizational, and societal strategies of intervention.

Recognizing the Situatedness of Experience

Whatever else it may be, sexual harassment is a range of personal experiences, each of which is situated in particular historical and social moments. Given this, efforts to unravel its genesis, dynamics, and meaning should be informed by close attention to the actual experiences of participants in sexually harassing situations. From studies of individuals' descriptions of sexual harassment, scholars can inductively derive powerful conceptual frameworks consonant with the real, lived experiences of those involved. In turn, this fosters the likelihood that whatever knowledge is generated will be theoretically sound and pragmatically germane and useful.

Contemporary scholarship spanning most of the social sciences and humanities is increasingly influenced by postmodern views of knowledge (Gergen, 1991), which have precipitated what has been called "the interpretive turn." Cognizant of the failure of grand theorizing, a number of scholars have urged recommitment to studying concrete experiences in their richness, complexity, and particularity. Strine, for instance, argues that with research topics "to set goals or questions without benefit of the contextualized understandings that such in-depth interpretive accounts afford would be premature, reductionist and misleading" (1991, p.1). Out of careful interpretation of situated narratives, grounded theories can be derived to account for phenomena within a limited sphere. Geertz (1973), among others (Jameson, 1981; Johnson, 1986/87; Scott, 1991; Strine, 1991), advocates scholarship that engages in "thick descriptions" of richly detailed texts of particularly situated, lived experiences. The task of the scholar confronting these narratives is to interpret them within the horizons of their historical, social, political, and personal location and to do so in ways that illuminate the meanings of the texts as socially and historically encumbered constructions. This approach understands both meanings of experiences, such as sexual harassment, and the subjective identities of individuals as being formed in and through social interaction.

Within postmodernist thinking *situated knowledge* (Haraway, 1988) emerges as a key term, one that would be oxymoronic within the frameworks of prior world views. According to postmodernity, all knowledge, all experience is necessarily situated and, thus, can be understood only in light of its unique historical location. Caricatures of postmodern scholarship notwithstanding, acknowledging the situatedness of all experience does not reduce us to a restrictive and restricting concentration on spontaneous, individual interpretations. Such a focus would be solipsistic and certainly not very epistemologically heuristic. What recognition of the situated character of knowledge does do is to provide a counterpoint to the positivistic thrust of traditional science, which assumes a transhistorical kind of truth. Its value, then, lies in introducing a tension between efforts to respect the unique historicity of experience and the need to generalize beyond individual lives.[5]

Interpretive and critical scholarship will not lead us to the kinds of knowledge traditionally sought by the sciences and, indeed, that goal is part of what is contested by interpretive and critical theories. Interpretive

---

[5]As my discussion makes clear, abandoning grand theorizing generates dilemmas of its own. A particularly troublesome issue is the relationship between experience and knowledge. On the one hand, postmodern theories call for respecting the specificity of situated experience; on the other hand, there is a need to realize that, to use Harding's phrase (1991), experience can lie. Experience is a basis of knowledge, yet like the "view from nowhere," it can be limited and parochial, not to mention atypical of others in one's social group.

scholarship, instead, promotes distinct and distinctly valuable insights. A first outcome is that in place of *truth*, we are led to recognize that a number of legitimate truths may emanate from different voices speaking about disparate experiences in particularly located, concrete moments. Recognizing that validity is variable and contingent on contexts, including mediated and symbolic representations that shape meanings, explodes stable, static views of what things, and even individuals, are. All become evolving, changing, processual phenomena whose nature is inextricably tied up with culture, placement, practices, and production.

This insight, in turn, leads us to focus more closely on cultural conditions themselves as ones which create social groups and, within them, individual lives and, within those, predispositions toward particular ways of understanding oneself, others, and a range of situations and actions. Contemporary theorists, such as Harding (1991), explore standpoint theory's potential to promote understanding of how specific cultural processes, practices, and structures create social conditions that, in turn, allow and withhold certain experiences and legitimize and disallow sundry proclivities for interpreting them. The shift from looking at individual lives to the social conditions that create those lives invites uncustomary and valuable insights into structural characteristics and their implications.

Researchers who operate out of interpretive frameworks are from the outset open to multiple potential enactments and meanings of sexual harassment as they occur in contexts which, by nature, are unstable and variable. Given this starting point, researchers inquire first into how sexual harassment is actually experienced by a variety of victims who exist and whose identities arise in a range of symbolic and material environments.

Precisely this approach was embraced in a symposium on sexual harassment published in The *Journal of Applied Communication Research* (1992). Featured in that issue were the stories of individuals who had been sexually harassed. To preserve the coherence of the account as it was experienced, each story was told in the narrator's own words without any editing. Following the texts from individuals were critical interpretations by Professors Mary Strine (1992) and Charles Conrad (1992). Both scholars' analyses not only provided insights into sexual harassment, but also offered excellent illustrations of research that relies on "thick descriptions" as the basis for theorizing. Strine focused her interpretation particularly on the psychodynamic aspects of sexual harassment as revealed in the stories. This angle of analysis clarified

---

Articulating a stance that respects the specificity of experience while avoiding its potential for parochialism is a primary focus of current efforts to develop postmodern theories, including notably standpoint theories. I discuss conceptual, methodological, and ethical challenges confronting researchers of sexual harassment more fully in a chapter in a forthcoming book (Bingham, in press).

some of the personal and psychological issues entailed in incidents of sexual harassment.

Taking a more macro approach in his analysis, Conrad emphasized ways in which organizational and cultural constructions influence both the likelihood of sexual harassment and the meanings that will be attached to it. In arguing that sexual harassment is primarily an issue of power, Conrad probes the ways in which power is granted or withheld by organizational cultures and broadly held social values in which both individuals and organizations are embedded. He also turns our attention to the important issue of the means of resisting dominant power formations. This suggests a compelling focus for future scholarship aimed at contributing to social change.

The critical readings of texts by Conrad and Strine functioned to pry open narrative accounts in ways that illuminated a range of means in which victims and larger social systems construct meanings of harassment as well. In addition, these analyses disclosed larger patterns and practices that, deliberately or not, legitimize and sustain sexual harassment. By grounding itself in actual experiences as they are situated and enacted within social, political, economic, and historical contexts, a critical approach furthers both theoretical and practical interests in the interpretive processes entailed in sexual harassment.

This brings us back to the issue of perspective, upon which I touched earlier. What phenomena are recognized to exist and what meanings are attributed to them issue always from some perspective that is constituted by its particular social, political, economic, and personal situation. Harding (1991, p. 14) contends that to have integrity, any effort at theorizing must take into account particular historical intersections of race, class, and culture, which are regarded as primary aspects of situatedness. Applying this insight to sexual harassment suggests that within any interaction there will be inevitably, necessarily multiple perspectives, each representing a specific view of what transpires as well as what it means and doesn't mean. Not only would we expect different perspectives from those labeled "victims" and "harassers," but also among different "victims" and "harassers."

Consider a concrete example of how perspectives emerge out of particular locations and shape what an experience means. Case One involves a young woman named Emily, who is unsure of her sexual attractiveness and value since she has received almost no attention from males in her social group. Given the value her culture places on attractiveness in a woman, lack of responsiveness from males whose attention she desires has led Emily to a generalized low self-concept. Currently, she has no boyfriend and is investing her energy and dreams into her major field of study in which she hopes to do graduate work. Case Two is a highly attractive, very confident, young woman named Erica.

Accustomed to attention from men from an early age, Erica is quite sure of both her attractiveness and her overall value. This base of self-esteem has encouraged her to develop considerable assertiveness and a clear sense of her rights as well as infringements upon them. Erica is engaged to a young professional man and much of her time during her senior year is devoted to planning her wedding. She chose her major rather carelessly and feels no particular commitment to it since she plans to be a homemaker and mother after graduating. Both Emily and Erica are propositioned by Dr. Smith, a professor in their major field of study and someone widely known to be very influential throughout his field.

While we cannot know how any individual will interpret an incident, it is plausible that Emily might see it as confirming, at least in some ways, since Dr. Smith's attention can be interpreted as evidence she has not before received that she meets the image of a desirable female as defined by her culture. Further, regardless of how Emily construes her professor's behavior, she is limited in the personal confidence and skills necessary to resist advances from men. Compared to Erica, Emily is far less experienced in receiving and fending off inappropriate sexual advances, and she has a less finely developed sense of her rights than does her more socially secure counterpart. In short, Emily appears vastly more vulnerable by virtue of her particular situation. Differences in the historicity–the social situatedness–of these two victims make it likely that they will bring different perspectives to bear on what happens. As this illustration suggests, because perspectives are situated and multiple, a critical initial focus of research on sexual harassment is to learn more about diverse perspectives and the locations that inform them. We need to discover patterns of thought and social conditions that ground various understandings of behaviors (both harassment and responses to it) and guild them with the patina of reasonableness, at least in the thinking of those who hold them.

Ethical Issues in Research on Sexual Harassment

While ethical issues must be considered in designing and conducting any type of study, special considerations are germane to research on sexual harassment. The topic itself is controversial and volatile. It can and often does arouse strong reactions including offense, embarrassment, anger, depression, and shame. Even what appears to be a relatively harmless procedure, such as having participants in research read a hypothetical case study, may provoke strong responses, particularly if participants have been involved as perpetrators or victims in sexually harassing situations. For this reason it is prudent to fortify the standard informed-consent form, now required by most universities. Researchers might consider including in requests for participation statements that acknowledge the potential for psychological harm as well as ones that actively invite participants to cease participating at any point in the research process. Cautionary statements such as these both protect researchers from recriminations if participants do experience unanticipated harm and provide appropriately ample warnings to participants themselves.

Related to the foregoing is the need for researchers to recognize and respect the substantial personal (and, sometimes, professional) costs that may be entailed in participation in certain kinds of research on sexual harassment. For example, studies based on actual accounts of sexual harassment require individuals to recall and revisit what had to be an extremely disturbing incident in their lives. When I served as guest editor for the symposium, *Telling Our Stories*, I was deluged by calls from women who were considering writing about their experiences with sexual harassment. From those conversations I realized with new intensity the range of fierce emotions recalling sexual harassment evokes–from shame and feeling wrong or stupid, to feeling violated, to guilt about *allowing* it to occur, to entrapment with no viable alternatives, to anger at being impotent to stop harassment.

In recalling incidents from their past, these feelings were revived and had to be reconfronted and reconfigured. Remembering them is typically accompanied by a painful return to a former self who was dependent, powerless, and trapped–a self whose existence may now evoke shame. Because it is so disturbing to recall a traumatic event and to encounter a less able self, to do so requires courage. To be willing to share the memory with others, to expose a less able self to others, and to speak in public about what has for so long been unspeakable demand even more courage. More than is usually the case in research, then, those who study sexual harassment from the perspective of victims need to be especially aware of the costs of participation. Further, given the burdens participants assume, researchers might appropriately extend more than the pro forma expressions of gratitude to those generous enough to share their experiences in order to contribute to the ongoing process of naming sexual harassment in ways that discourage its being inflicted on the next generation of professionals.

SUMMARY

In this chapter I attempted to call attention to the crucially important and powerful process of naming. I argued that while sexually harassing behaviors have long polluted the workplace, only recently have they been labeled sexual harassment; and only with that name can we fully recognize the behaviors comprising sexual harassment. Naming stimulated legal and institutional measures to address the problem, and those continue as our jurisprudential system considers cases and issues rulings that alter what is and is not allowable and that determines the kinds of penalties that obtain to unacceptable practices.

Yet, naming is an extended process. Especially in the area of sexual harassment where old meanings of sexually provocative behavior define it as flirtation, complimentary, and "natural," arguments for new definitions of it as unwanted, unwelcome, unprofessional, and unacceptable must be persistently asserted in professional contexts. It is a process we have only just begun and must continue to engage in until reformed understandings of sexual harassment are more broadly held in the culture at large.

As we continue to put forward newer definitions and to educate colleagues and the public about sexual harassment, one of the strongest foundations for our efforts will be grounded understandings of sexual harassment as it is experienced. Thus, in this chapter I urge researchers to study sexual harassment as it is perceived and constructed by those who have endured it. Because this kind of scholarship requires participants to revisit painful, often traumatic, incidents in their lives, as researchers we need to exercise keen sensitivity to the feelings of participants in our studies. A primary way that scholars can make it worthwhile for people to suffer the trauma of discussing sexual harassment and compensate them for their courage and generosity in telling us about their experiences is to employ our most incisive critical lenses to pry open their accounts and mine them with all of our resources in order to develop theories that reflect how social actors define behaviors, themselves, and their options for responding to sexually harassing situations. By engaging in critical research that starts from the perspective of individuals' lives, we move ourselves toward strong theories that reflect lived experiences and that, in time, can inform efforts to reduce the frequency of sexual harassment and to increase the options victims recognize and employ in responding to it.

REFERENCES

Ardener, S. (1975). Sexual insult and female militancy. In S. Ardener (Ed.), *Perceiving women* (pp. 29-54). London: Malaby Press.

Bingham, S. (1991). Communication strategies for managing sexual harassment in organizations: Understanding message options and their effects. *Journal of Applied Communication Research*, 1 and 2, 88-115.

Bingham, S. (in press, 1992). *Conceptual approaches to scholarship on sexual harassment* (tentative title).

Blumer, H. (1969). *Symbolic interactionism: Perspective and method.* Englewood Cliffs, NJ: Prentice-Hall.

Blum. D. E. (1991, October 9). Environment still hostile to women in academe, new evidence indicates. *Chronicle of Higher Education*, 38 (1), 20.

Brooks, L., & Perot, A. (1991). Reporting sexual harassment: Exploring a predictive model. *Psychology of Women Quarterly*, 15, 31-47.

Clarke, E. (1982). *Stopping sexual harassment: A handbook* (2nd ed.). Detroit, MI: Labor Education and Research Project.

Conrad, C. R. (1992, in press). *Journal of Applied Communication Research*, 20.

Daly, M. (1973). *Beyond God the Father*. Boston: Beacon.

Daly, M. (1978). *Gyn/Ecology: The metaethics of radical feminism.* Boston: Beacon.

Dziech, B. W., & Weiner, L. (1984). *The lecherous professor: Sexual harassment on campus*. Boston, Ma: Beacon Press.

Edmunds, E. (1988). Unwelcome advances. *Atlanta Magazine*, pp. 90-93 and 120-126.

Fairhurst, G. T. (1986). Male-female communication on the job: Literature review and commentary. In M. McLaughlin (Ed.), *Communication yearbook 9* (pp. 83-116). Beverly Hills, CA: Sage.

Farley, L. (1978). *Sexual shakedown: The sexual harassment of women on the job*. New York: McGraw-Hill.

Fitzgerald, L. F., & Ormerod, A.J. (1991). Perceptions of sexual harassment: The influence of gender and academic context. *Psychology of Women Quarterly*, 15, 281-294.

Geertz, C. (1973). *The interpretation of cultures*. New York: Basic Books.

Gergen, K. (1991). *The saturated self: Dilemmas of identity in contemporary life*. New York: Basic.

Haraway, D. (1988). Situated knowledges: *The science question in feminism* and the privilege of partial perspective. Signs, 14, 575-599.

Harding, S. (1991). *Whose science? Whose knowledge? Thinking from* women's lives. Ithaca, NY: Cornell University Press.

Jameson, F. (1981). The political unconscious: Narrative as a socially symbolic act. Ithaca, NY: Cornell University Press.

Jaschik, M. L., & Frentz, B. R. (1991). Women's perceptions and labeling of sexual harassment. Sex Roles, 25, 19-23.

Johnson, R. (1986/87). What is cultural studies anyway? Social Text, 16, 38-80.

Kelly, G. A. (1955). The psychology of personal constructs. New York: Norton.

Kramarae, C., Thorne, B., & Henley, N., (1978). Perspectives on language and communication. Signs, 5, 638-51.

Lott, B., Reilly, M. E., & Howard, D. R. (1982). Sexual assault and harassment: A campus community case study. Signs: Journal of Women in Culture and Society, 8, 296-319.

McKinney, K. (1990). Sexual harassment of university faculty by colleagues and students. Sex Roles, 23, 421-438.

McMillen, L. (1991, October 23). A mixed message for campuses seen in Thomas hearings. Chronicle of Higher Education, 38, 1 & 14.

Mead, G. (1934). Mind, self, and society. Chicago: University of Chicago Press.

Rich, A. (1979). On lies, secrets and silence: Selected prose: 1966-78. New York: Norton.

Rubin, L.J., & Borgers, S. B. (1990). Sexual harassment in universities during the 1980s. Sex Roles, 23, 397-411.

Safran, C. (1976, November). What men do to women on the job: a shocking look at sexual harassment. Redbook 24-27.

Scott, J. (1991). The evidence of experience. Critical Inquiry, 17(4), 773-97.

Sexual harassment: A hidden issue (1978). Project on the status and education of women. Washington, DC: Association of American Colleges.

Sexual harassment: Gender gap on capitol hill.(1991, November 17). Parade Magazine, p. 8.

Spender, D. (1980). Man made language (esp. Chap. Two, pp. 52-75). London: Routledge and Kegan Paul.

Spender, D. (1984). Defining reality: A powerful tool. In C. Kramarae, M. Schultz, & W. O'Barr (Eds.), Language and power (pp. 9-22). Beverly Hills, CA: Sage.

Strine, M. (1991). Bodies/subjects and the contemporary public sphere: Preliminary reflections on the interdependence of communication, power and order. Paper presented at 1991 Speech Communication Association Convention, Atlanta, GA.

Strine, M. (1992, in press). Journal of Applied Communication Research, 20.

Telling our stories. (in press). Special symposium in Journal of Applied

Communication Research.

Winks, P. L. (1982). Legal implications of sexual contact between teacher and student. *Journal of Law and Education*, 11, 437-478.

Wise, S., & Stanley, L. (1987). *Georgie porgie: Sexual harassment in everyday life.* New York: Pandora Press.

Wood, J. T. (1992, in press). Telling our stories: Narratives as a basis for theorizing sexual harassment. *Journal of Applied Communication Research*, 20.

▼Chapter 2

The Interface Between Sexual Harassment and Organizational Romance

Hal Witteman
The Pennsylvania State University
University Park, PA

▼ An incredible variety of interpersonal relationships exist in organizations. They result from intermittent face-to-face interaction between interdependent members (Hinde, 1979). Concerns of control, affect, and intimacy characterize them, and indeed, the communication that develops them (see Berger, 1985; Danzinger, 1976; Wish, Deutsch, & Kaplan, 1976). Two kinds of interpersonal relationships receive attention in this chapter: those involving sexual harassment (RSHs) and organizational romances (ORs). In the former, interactants have unequal organizational status and differ with respect to levels of sexual attraction and expressions of intimacy and affect. ORs, like RSHs, reflect unequal organizational status. However, unlike RSHs, ORs are characterized by relatively high levels of mutual intimacy and sexual attraction.[1]

The objectives of this chapter are threefold. The first is to outline the interface between ORs and RSHs. The second objective is to discuss organizational policies for managing cross-gender[2] relationships in which

---

[1]This chapter primarily focuses on relationships between men and women in which women have lower organizational status. Still, "sexual harassment" is conceptualized such that it may occur in relationships in which the male member has lower status than the female, both have equal status, and/or both are of the same gender. Also, "organizational romance" is defined such that romances involving members of equal status and the same gender are possible.
[2]While it is clear that same-gender relationships occur in organizations, this

27

intimacy and affect are issues of concern. The examination of the policy to stop and prevent such interpersonal relationships is central to this objective. A description of a general organizational strategy for dealing with ORs, RSHs, and problems resulting from them is the third objective.

Specifically, this analysis answers a number of key questions: (a) What is sexual harassment? (b) What is an organizational romance? (c) What is the association between RSHs and ORs? (d) Do RSHs and ORs cause interpersonal and organizational problems? (e) What are these problems? (f) Do RSHs and ORs exist in sufficient numbers to warrant a policy for the management of interpersonal relationships? (g) Should RSHs and ORs be stopped and/or prevented? (h) Can RSHs and ORs be managed effectively? (I) What is an effective management strategy?

ANALYSIS

What is Sexual Harassment?

The Equal Employment Opportunity Commission guidelines define illegal sexual harassment as unwelcome sexual advances, requests for sexual favors, and other verbal or physical conduct of a sexual nature, when followed by any of these facts: (a) submission to the conduct is made a condition of employment; (b) submission to or rejection of the conduct is made the basis for an employment decision; and (c) the conduct seriously affects an employee's work performance, or creates an intimidating, hostile, or offensive working environment. Hadjifotiou (1983, p. 9) synthesizes a number of definitions of harassment and defines harassment as:

> all those actions and practices by a person or group of people at work which are directed at one or more workers and which: are repeated and unwanted; may be deliberate or done unconsciously; cause humiliation, offense, or distress; may interfere with job performance or create an unpleasant working environment; comprise remarks or actions associated with a person's sex; and emphasize a person's sexuality over her role as a worker.

In general, there are two main types of sexual harassment: quid pro quo (i.e., you give me this, I'll give you that), and that which results in a hostile work environment (Aggarwal, 1987; Neville, 1989). These two conditions, however, are not entirely exclusive.

chapter will focus on the more numerous cross-gender organizational relationships.

There are many different reasons why one sexually harasses others (Neville, 1989). Two reasons frequently mentioned involve power and affect. One may harass for the sake of having power and control over another person or because he or she is genuinely attracted to another.

Harassment is most prevalent for women who are under the age of 35 (Gutek, 1985), have some college education, have a nontraditional job, and/or work in a predominantly male environment (U.S. Merit Systems Protection Board, 1981). Also, women experiencing harassment tend to be younger than the man, never married, or divorced (Lafontaine & Tredeau, 1986). While most harassment presently occurs in relationships composed of female harassees and male harassers (Hadjifotiou, 1983), men are also victims of harassment (Backhouse & Cohen, 1981). Female initiators are younger and less likely to be married than the average working woman (Meyers, Berchtold, Oestreich, Collins, & Chaddock, 1981).

Fitzgerald (1990) synthesized the work of Till (1980) and defined five progressively more severe levels of harassment: gender harassment, seductive behavior, sexual bribery, sexual coercion, and sexual impositions. Gender harassment refers to sexist remarks and behavior not necessarily designed to elicit sexual cooperation. Inappropriate and offensive sexual advances that do not explicitly attach a penalty to an unfavorable response by the harassee reflect seductive behavior. Sexual bribery refers to solicitation of sex-linked behavior or sexual activity. Sexual coercion occurs when a threat or punishment is associated with the solicitation. Finally, a physical assault is sexual imposition. Hence, on the basis of this conception, harassment varies in terms of severity.

Interpersonal problem conception of harassment. Inherent to the interactive processes characterizing relationships in organizations is interpersonal conflict. Conflict interaction results when one person perceives that his or her goals are unmet and views another as interfering with the achievement of them (Putnam & Poole, 1987). Fundamental to any interpersonal conflict is the perception of an interpersonal problem (Witteman, 1988). An interpersonal problem is defined to exist when one perceives a difference between a desired state of affairs involving another with whom he or she has an interpersonal relationship and a present state of affairs involving the other. Sexual harassment exists when a member's (i.e., harasser) communication with another (i.e., harassee) incorporates a level of affect or intimacy that is greater than that desired by the other.

Mild and severe harassment. For the purposes of this chapter, sexual harassment is defined as an interpersonal problem that varies from being mild to severe. Several qualities characterize this continuum.

The first is the perceived size (as perceived by the harassee) of the difference between the level of intimacy or affect expressed by the harasser (i.e., the present state of affairs) and the level desired or expected by the other (i.e., the desired state of affairs). The second quality is the degree to which the harassee perceives that the harasser will be instrumental in creating negative consequences for the harassee in the organization if he or she does not respond favorably to the intimate communication of the harasser. The frequency of occurrence with which the harassee perceives the undesired communication is the third quality.

A harassee experiencing severe harassment perceives: (a) an extreme violation of intimacy or affective expectancies as a result of communication with the harasser; (b) a high possibility that negative consequences will accrue if her or his response to the harasser is unfavorable; and/or (c) a relatively high frequency of occurrence of undesired communication interactions. While any of these perceptions reflect severe harassment, the most severe kind occurs when all of these perceptions are extreme. On the other hand, when one perceives (a) a minor or trivial violation of expectancies, (b) no possibility of negative consequences if he or she does not respond favorably, and (c) infrequent occurrences or a single instance of an undesirable communication, then mild harassment exists.

Since harassment-related perceptions may vary from person to person, different individuals may have different perceptions of similar situations and behaviors. For example, behavior perceived by a harassee as a gross violation of her or his affective expectancies may not be perceived as extreme by another, if at all (Hadjifotiou, 1983). Also, harassees may differ in their perceptions of the favorableness of their response to the harasser, the likelihood of negative consequences if their behavior is not favorable, the negativity of the consequences, and the frequency of occurrence of harassment. Furthermore, perceptions of the harassee and the harasser may differ. It is possible that well-intended gestures and remarks of friendship and affect may be perceived as harassment (Aggarwal, 1987).

Obviously, since harassment involves perceptions, a consensual operationalization of harassment is difficult to obtain (Fitzgerald, 1990; Hadjifotiou, 1983; Meyers et al., 1981). One method of assessing harassment is to compare its behaviors to the typical limits of usual social interaction (Aggarwal, 1987). Accordingly, harassment is a behavior or set of repeated actions that any "reasonable" person should have known was unsolicited and unwelcome.

Secondary perceptions resulting from harassment. Since harassment is by definition an interpersonal problem, other problem-related perceptions likely occur when a person experiences harassment (see

Witteman, 1988). These have the potential to influence the harassee's response to the harasser. One is the degree of goal-path uncertainty or doubt the harassee has about what should and/or can be done to manage or resolve the problem. The second perception reflects causal attribution processes. Whenever one experiences an interpersonal problem, one is likely to seek the cause of the problem. The degree to which a harassee attributes cause to the harasser represents one type of attribution likely to occur in a harassment situation. The degree to which the harassee has negative feelings for the harasser is the third perception.

Research examining interpersonal problem solving indicates that these perceptions are related to several management styles (Witteman, 1988, 1992). Findings show that goal-path uncertainty is positively related to avoidance, a general withdrawal away from any discussion about the problem. Both causal attributions to the other and negative feelings for the other are positively related to distributive communication, an active style characterized by high concern for oneself but low concern for the thoughts and feelings of the other. These results suggest that a harassee may experience incompatible behavioral tendencies: (a) to engage the harasser in active and possibly angry discussion about the problem, and (b) to avoid any problem-related discussion with the harasser.

Avoidance of discussion. Generally, harassees utilize avoidance, often in the hope that harassment will go away (Conte, 1990; Hadjifotiou, 1983). For example, Gutek (1985) reported that less than 20% of those surveyed reported the incident to someone in authority. Also, harassee responses reflect a more general avoidance: taking time off work, transferring to another job, and leaving the job (Alfred Marks Bureau, 1982; NALGO Research Section, 1980). Hence, while the harassee may attribute blame to the harasser and feel angry, he or she often avoids discussing the problem. Unfortunately, evidence indicates that when the harassment is ignored, it tends to worsen (Conte, 1990; Farley, 1978). Also, relentless repeaters tend to be in the majority (Backhouse & Cohen, 1981).

What promotes avoidance rather than active problem discussion? A variety of unique factors associated with the phenomenon of harassment, when compared to other kinds of interpersonal problems, may be responsible. They may act individually or in combination to create uncertainty in a harassee's mind about how to manage the situation and the necessity of avoiding problem-related discussion. One factor is the relatively higher organizational status of the harasser. The harassee may find it difficult to complain when the harasser has power over her or his job (Backhouse & Cohen, 1981; Hadjifotiou, 1983). A second related factor is the harassee's perception of the harasser's ability and/or willingness to provide negative consequences. Many women report being fearful that they might be blamed, ridiculed, and/or terminated if they do not respond favorably or openly acknowledge the problem (Backhouse & Cohen, 1981; Gutek, 1985; Meyers et al., 1981). A third factor is the humiliation and guilt felt by the harassee (Backhouse & Cohen, 1981; Conte, 1990). Fourth, victims of harassment often feel that complaints would be futile (Backhouse & Cohen, 1981; Conte, 1990). Lack of experience in actively managing harassment problems is a fifth factor. Finally, many women feel that it would take too much time and effort to discuss the problem (Gutek, 1985; Meyers et al., 1981).

Co-worker discussion of harassment. While harassees often avoid discussing harassment with the harassers and members in positions of authority, they may inform some co-workers of the harassment (Meyers et al., 1981). Indeed, Gutek (1985) found this to be the case 23% of the time. Research examining interpersonal conflict shows that the perception of goal-path uncertainty is positively related to communication with a third party, one who has neither formal outcome nor process control in the problem-management process (Witteman, 1991). Communication with co-workers provides the harassee with an outlet for her or his problem-related thoughts and feelings, thereby enabling her or him to receive validation. Also, people use such interaction to acquire advice on how to manage the problem.

Discussion of the problem with co-workers represents a first step in a process by which members of the organization become aware of the harassment. Also, such interaction may function to warn other members that certain relationships have the potential to be RSHs (Neville, 1989). Hence, informal communication networks in an organization may be used to exchange information about sexual harassment. As a result, many members may be aware of specific RSHs.

In sum, sexual harassment is an interpersonal problem. While it varies from being mild to severe, people may differ in the severity they ascribe to the same "harassing" behavior. Hence, what one member perceives as harassing, another may not. Since sexual harassment is an interpersonal problem, several problem-related perceptions may influence a harassee's management response to the problem. While a harassee may blame the harasser for intentionally engaging in harassment and be quite angry, she or he often does not engage the harasser nor those in positions of authority in discussion about the harassment. This behavior is characteristic of one who perceives relatively high levels of goal-path uncertainty. Several factors may promote such perceptions of uncertainty: the relatively higher status of the harasser, fear of punitive responses by the harasser, and lack of experience in actively managing such problems. Still, some harassees engage fellow co-workers in a discussion of the harassment. This is the first step in the process of informing many members of the harassment. Any organizational policy for managing sexual harassment must account for all of these perceptual and behavioral consequences of harassment.

What is an OR?

Dillard and Miller (1988) define an organizational romance as an intimate interpersonal relationship between employees of the same organization that can be characterized by a substantial degree of mutual sexual attraction. On the basis of this definition, heightened degrees of mutual intimacy and mutual sexual attraction differentiate ORs from RSHs.

Those involved in ORs enact communication enabling co-workers to know they exist before romance participants publicly acknowledge them (Anderson & Hunsaker, 1985; Mainiero, 1986; Quinn, 1977). When this finding is combined with the possibility that members are aware of RSHs, member awareness of any relationship involving concerns of intimacy and affect is possible.

What is the Association between RSHs and ORs?

Mild forms of sexual harassment are natural consequences of the formation and ever-changing nature of cross-gender relationships in organizations. Indeed, both the experiencing and managing of affect or intimacy-related problems reflect the natural development of interpersonal relationships.

Self-disclosure and RSHs and ORs. Self-disclosure, or the intentional sharing of intimate information about oneself with others, is characteristic of almost all interpersonal relationships (Hinde, 1979; Knapp, 1984). People tend to self-disclose to those who are self-disclosing and tend to self-disclose roughly at the same level of intimacy as the other (Altman, 1973; Archer, 1979; Cappella, 1981; Dindia, 1985; Feigenbaum, 1977; Jourard, 1959; Kleinke, 1979). Self-disclosure is governed by norms of reciprocity and developmental propriety (Berger, Gardner, Clatterbuck, & Schulman, 1976; Bradac, Tardy, & Hasman, 1980; Chaikin & Derlega, 1974; Gouldner, 1960). Such patterns of reciprocity often appear within the first minutes of interaction (Kohen, 1975). It is through this reciprocal process that ORs develop.

The reciprocal nature of self-disclosure may have one person leading the other into deeper levels of intimacy. However, when one does not reciprocate another's more intimate self-disclosure, the other may end further attempts at reaching the more intimate level of self-disclosure. In this way, the accepted level of intimacy in a relationship is negotiated. While both men and women generally self-disclose more to

women, a number of studies have demonstrated that men may sometimes disclose information earlier in the development of the relationship
than do women (Berger et al., 1976; Derlega, Winstead, Wong, &
Hunter, 1985; Gilbert & Whiteneck, 1976). Hence, it may be the male
member of the organization, more often than not, who initiates the self-
disclosure process.

While self-disclosure tends to be reciprocal, some compensatory
findings do exist. For example, Archer and Berg (1978) note that compensatory disclosure may occur in a lower number of words, even
though the level of intimacy remains the same. Baxter (1979) notes that
people are less willing to disclose when attempting to disengage from a
relationship. The depth of disclosure dimension reveals the greatest
reversal of disclosure (Baxter, 1983). Hence, in normal interaction
between superiors and subordinates, it may be the high status male who
initiates self-disclosure and the lower status woman who limits self-disclosure and ends the process.

While much self-disclosure does not directly reflect one's affect
for another nor have sexual overtones, inevitably, some may. It is also
likely that one may sometimes feel uncomfortable reciprocating disclosure. Hence, experiencing intimacy or affective problems is almost
inevitable. Further, lower status women may experience more of these
problems than men. According to the general notion of sexual harassment brought forth earlier, any problem arising from such self-disclosure
represents sexual harassment, albeit a mild form. Hence, affect and intimacy-related problems may, on the one hand, reflect severe forms of
sexual harassment, and on the other hand, represent normal occurrences in the development, maintenance, and negotiated definition of
the state of a cross-gender relationship.

In the cases of severe forms of harassment, self-disclosure at
nonnegotiated levels of sexual intimacy occur and persist. For example,
a severe harasser self-discloses at a much deeper level than that
desired by another. A severe harasser asks the other to divulge highly
intimate information. Even when the harassee does not reciprocate such
self-disclosure nor respond to overly personal questions, the severe
harasser may continue to self-disclose or continue to ask for highly intimate information (Hadjifotiou, 1983). The harasser, by such actions, dis-
regards the negotiable quality of intimacy in interpersonal relationships.

Relational and communicative competence. Frequent occurrence and persistence of self-disclosure at nonnegotiated levels of sexual
intimacy, however, do not necessarily reflect intentional displays of power
nor objectively severe harassment. Instead, they may reflect the unintentional behavior of a well-meaning person who is interpersonally and/or
communicatively incompetent. Indeed, research indicates that appropri-

ate self-disclosure is one dimension of perceived communication competency and one ability related to communication adaptability (Duran, 1983). While moderate self-disclosure generally results in positive outcomes, a great deal of it is perceived as inappropriate (Lombardo & Wood, 1979) and characteristic of one who is less competent (Jones & Brunner, 1984). Hence, some people may simply be unaware of the inappropriate intimacy of their communication and the problems they cause.

Behaviors indicating sexual harassment and relationship development. Research indicates that a variety of verbal and physical behaviors may be perceived as harassing (e.g., Alfred Marks Bureau, 1982; Gutek, 1985; Hadjifotiou, 1983; Loy & Stewart, 1984; Neville, 1989; U.S. Merit Systems Protection Board, 1981). Verbal forms include: unwelcome remarks, jokes that cause awkwardness or embarrassment, innuendoes or taunting, gender-based insults or sexist remarks, displays of pornographic or other offensive or derogatory pictures, and telephone calls with sexual overtones. Physically, the employee may be the victim of: pinching, grabbing, hugging, patting, leering, brushing against, touching, and kissing. Further, both physical and verbal behaviors may be included in a relentless proposal of intimacy.

Inspection of such lists of behaviors indicates that some behaviors characterized as harassing are similar to those representing normal relational interaction. For example, in one study, the most frequently mentioned social-sexual behaviors experienced in past or present jobs by women were (Gutek, 1985) complementary comments, complementary gestures, nonsexual touching, sexual touching, insulting comments, and insulting looks and gestures. All of these were reported by more than 20% of the respondents. Behaviors experienced and labeled as sexual harassment by women were complementary comments, insulting comments, complementary looks, gestures, insulting looks and gestures, sexual touching, and expected socializing. Such behavior was mentioned more than 10% of the time.

In sum, while sexual harassment is widespread, it is not always easily distinguished from mutually entered social-sexual exchanges (Gutek, 1985). Behaviors taken as instances of severe harassment by some may be perceived by others as relatively normal behaviors. Hence, it is unclear where harassing communication begins and a communication reflecting the natural development of cross-gender friendships and ORs end.

Secondary problem-related perceptions. The experiencing of even mild harassment is likely to create perceptions reflecting some degree of goal-path uncertainty, causal attribution to the other, and negative feelings for the other. Relatively low levels of uncertainty, a lack of attributing intent to the other, and little or no negative feelings are likely to be perceived in the case of mild harassment. In normal day-to-day cross-gender interaction outside of the organization, such perceptions are likely to result in the trivializing or smoothing of the problem and/or the integrative management of it (see Witteman, 1988). However, in the organizational context, the harassee may avoid any discussion with the harasser about the small problem. She or he may be uncertain in knowing how the higher status harasser may react to open-ended discussion. Without receiving an indication that his or her behavior is somewhat problematic, a mild harasser, even though he or she is not attempting to exert power over the other, may continue to create problems for the harassee.

In sum, the perception and reaction to affect or intimacy-related behaviors reflects the natural development of all cross-gender relationships. It is basic to self-disclosure. Inevitably, such behavior results in interpersonal problems. Behaviors that are most frequently mentioned as harassing are also those likely to occur as friendships and organizational romances develop. Even when people perceive mild harassment, perceptions of goal-path uncertainty, causal attribution to the other, and negative feelings for the other influence their behavioral response to it. While the occurrence and persistence of severe harassment communication may be indicative of a need to show power, it may also reflect the relatively natural behavior of someone who is unaware that the other is perceiving a problem. Further, such communication may reflect the unintentional behavior of someone who is communicatively incompetent. Hence, not all expressions of sexuality in the workplace can be called sexual harassment (Gutek, 1985). Any organizational policy of managing interpersonal relationships, including ORs and RSHs, must account for these possibilities.

Do RSHs and ORs Cause Interpersonal Problems?

Three factors suggest that a variety of task and social problems frequently occur in any type of interpersonal relationship in an organization. One factor is basic human nature. Humans are problem solvers (Witteman, 1988). They have goals, continually perceive problems, and manage them. Also, humans are social beings who belong to organizations and develop interpersonal relationships in them. Inevitably, humans experience and cope with interpersonal problems. Also, sex is a basic human drive. While not all interpersonal relationships in organizations involve members of the opposite sex, and while not all relationships with the opposite sex involve concerns of intimacy, some invariably do. Since interpersonal relationships in organizations exist, and since humans are problem solvers, most if not all organizational members are likely to perceive interpersonal problems.

A second indication that interpersonal relationships create difficulties derives from the influences that relationships have on the perceptions and behaviors of other organizational members. With the formation and change of any relationship arrives new interpersonal goals for a person and his or her assessment of the degree to which these goals are being met. With such comparisons come new behaviors. These behaviors, however, do not occur in a vacuum. Rather, because an organization is composed of interdependent members, these new behaviors also influence his or her relational partner's perceptions and behaviors. Further, the perceptions and behaviors of the partner change as he or she senses new problems and responds to them. In turn, these actions may cause additional problems for the person and promote a never ending cycle of problem perception and behavioral change. Hence, with the existence of interpersonal relationships in organizations comes perceptual and behavioral changes that make interpersonal problems almost inevitable. (For a discussion of a control system perspective of interpersonal problem solving, see Powers, 1973.)

A third factor is the ongoing clash between private and public or interpersonal and organizational forces. (For a discussion of the struggle between private and public forces over the definition of interpersonal intimacy, see Gadlin, 1977.) In the organization, there is an ongoing struggle between the individual and the organization over the definition of intimacy, the normative level of expressed intimacy, and in general, the very nature of interpersonal relationships. For example, each member has behavioral preferences for how to conduct his or her interpersonal relationships within the organization. Also, there are members who instantiate organizational preferences and/or norms regarding the conduct of interpersonal relationships. These members may actively sanction such behavior and punish others who violate norms. Inevitably, some individuals' preferences and behaviors will be different than those expected by the organization and enacted by some of its members. Hence, a variety of interpersonal problems, including sexual harassment, may result.

In sum, as long as organizations provide an arena in which individual and organizational preferences for interpersonal behavior clash, as long as people retain a sexual drive, and as long as humans are motivated to perceive and resolve problems, a variety of interpersonal problems will be perceived. Because RSHs and ORs exist in any organization, those involved in them and all other members are likely to experience a variety of interpersonal problems related to them. Hence, any policy for the management of interpersonal relationships in organizations must account for this inevitability.

What are the Interpersonal Problems Caused by the Existence of RSHs and ORs?

Several methods of categorizing interpersonal problems resulting from ORs and RSHs have theoretical utility. These illustrate the fact that while different types of relationships generate them, both sets of problems are quite similar.

One method of categorizing problems resulting from the existence of harassment and ORs is based on the organizational member who perceives them. For example, problems may be perceived by the harassee, the harasser, romance participants, and other organizational members including co-workers and managers. Another scheme dichotomizes problems into task and social types. When a person confronts an incompatibility involving his or her assigned job or that of another member, he or she perceives a task-related problem. If it involves the nature of the interpersonal relationship or another's relationship with still another member, it is a social problem. A third method utilizes preinvolvement and postinvolvement categories. People experience preinvolvement problems when they anticipate experiencing negative consequences resulting from the formation or continuation of an interpersonal relationship (i.e., OR and RSH), while concern with the consequences of an existing relationship (i.e., OR and RSH) signifies postinvolvement problems. These schemes also may be combined.

Problems perceived by the harassee. The following are task-related problems involving supervisors: threats or denial of job-related benefits (i.e., denial of raise, benefits or promotions, and loss of existing benefits), retaliation in terms of being overly critical, negative job evaluations, and poor references (Aggarwal, 1987; Hadjifotiou, 1983). Social problems reflect the notion that the job and working environment may become poisonous (Aggarwal, 1987). These include expressions of hostility by one's supervisor and co-workers and the social isolation of the harassee.

A harassee may have psychological and health-related problems that can influence task and social activity (Aggarwal, 1987; Backhouse & Cohen, 1981). Psychologically, victims may experience decreased ambition, a dread of going to work, and a loss of self-confidence and self-esteem. Koss (1990) suggests that the sequence of psychological consequences of harassment includes confusion and self-blame, fear and anxiety, depression and anger, and finally disillusionment. Gutek (1985) notes that the two strongest emotional reactions are disgust and anger. Physically, harassment could create loss of sleep and ill-health (Gutek, 1985). Hence, a harassee may experience a variety of psychological and physical difficulties as a result of harassment.

One set of task and social problems is related to the discussion of the problem with others in the organization. For example, a harassee may want to discuss the issue of sexual harassment with the harasser and/or other members of the organization. However, she or he may fail to do so in anticipation of the negative consequences that such a discussion may have on her or his relationships with them. She or he may fear that disclosure will promote an unfair accusation by others of the use of sexual leverage for personal organizational gain. She or he may also fear that such discussion may negatively impact on her or his ability to perform work-related duties, advance in the organization, and/or maintain her or his employment.

A harassee may also experience such negative consequences after interacting with another, and hence, experience postinvolvement problems. For example, those who act unfavorably may experience the harasser's retaliation. Retaliation may take many forms and create both social and task problems. For example, Hadjifotiou (1983) lists the following retaliations: verbal abuse, noncooperation from male co-workers, poor personal recommendations/references, poor job evaluation/bonus rating, impossible performance standards, refusal to offer overtime, demotion or downgrading, transfer to less satisfactory work, worsening of working hours, and termination of employment.

Another set of problems focuses on the nature of the harassee if she or he continues to work with the harasser. For example, a harassee may want to continue working with the harasser in order to perform her or his job, but not be able to do so in anticipation of the continuation of harassment, negative feelings that may result from continued interaction with the harasser, and/or negative impacts on job performance. Again, a harassee may experience such negative consequences when she or he continues to work with the harasser.

Problems perceived by the sexual harasser. In the literature on harassment, interpersonal problems faced by the harasser do not receive much attention. Still, the harasser may experience a variety of social and task-related problems. These also reflect preinvolvement and postinvolvement types.

One set of problems may result from the harassee's indication that the harasser's communication is unwelcome. For example, once the harassee informs the harasser of her or his perceptions of harassment, he or she may want to continue interaction with the harassee, but anticipate undesirable changes in the relationship and a negative impact on his or her work performance. Also, a harasser may experience such negative consequences and experience postinvolvement problems.

A second set of problems results from an awareness that other organizational members know of the harassment. For example, a harasser may want to continue interacting with other members of the organization, but anticipate unwelcome changes in his or her interpersonal relationships with others or a negative impact on his or her ability to accomplish work. Again, a harasser may experience such negative consequences.

One factor that may influence the harasser's experiencing of problems is his or her communicative incompetence. He or she may experience a problem with the harassee and other organizational members because his or her well-meaning and unintentional actions were perceived as harassment. He or she may not know why others react differently to him or her. Even if one becomes aware that others perceive of him or her as acting improperly, he or she may not know how to respond to the accusations.

Problems perceived by OR participants. The problems experienced by those involved in a romance may be social and task-related, as well as preinvolvement and postinvolvement. Most of the research literature, however, emphasizes postinvolvement problems in which co-workers or managers become barriers. For example, participants may perceive task-related problems that involve narrowing job prospects and career advancement (Horn & Horn, 1982). Concern about "loose gossip" (Horn & Horn, 1982) is a social problem that also arises.

Similar to harassees, participants in romances often attempt to keep them secret (Quinn, 1977). This action may reflect a variety of fears. Primarily, social fears involving co-workers and management top the list: fear of violating implicit rules against fraternization, fear that disclosure could lead to punishment, fear of gossip, fear of general disapproval (Quinn, 1977), and fear of an unfair accusation of the use of sexual leverage to attain higher power (Anderson & Hunsaker, 1985).

Also, people who are sexually attracted to one another may experience preinvolvement problems. People may avoid working with one another because they fear that continued interaction may result in postinvolvement romantic problems (Driscoll & Bova, 1980). Research indicates that women who anticipate working in organizations have such anxieties more than men (Powell, 1986).

Problems may occur in any organizational romance as the relationship disintegrates. Disintegration is characterized by a lessening of mutual sexual attraction and intimacy. For example, one person may not like this disintegration and sexually harass the other in an attempt to keep the relationship as intimate as it previously had been (Bureau of National Affairs, 1988). Such harassment may be mild or severe. Hence, severe sexual harassment may become characteristic of relationships that were once romantic or contained relatively high levels of intimacy.

RSH-related problems perceived by co-workers. The problems perceived by co-workers as a result of sexual harassment exist. They are likely to be the result of direct communication by the harassed person or of the sharing of information by co-workers. These problems may also be task and social, as well as preinvolvement and postinvolvement.

Co-workers may desire not to interact with or work with the harasser or harassee, even though the harasser and harassee desire such interaction. Co-workers may anticipate negative consequences for the relationship they have with the harasser or harassee and their ability to perform their job if they interact with them. They may also experience such problems when they do interact.

One set of problems reflects the co-worker's desire to tell the harasser or harassee that they are aware of the harassment and how it should be resolved. However, they may be uncertain about the consequences of such action, at both the interpersonal and task levels.

Another set of problems is related to the act of communicating awareness of the harassment to fellow co-workers, supervisors, and/or affirmative action representatives. For example, a co-worker may want to discuss the harassment situation with these people, but may be afraid of the negative consequences that might accrue in the relationships he or she has with them. Similarly, a co-worker may anticipate that such discussion may create task-related problems. Again, a co-worker may experience such negative consequences.

OR-related problems experienced by co-workers. Problems perceived by co-workers receive more attention in the literature than those perceived by participants (e.g., Anderson & Hunsaker, 1985; Quinn, 1977). Most listings in the literature emphasize postinvolvement problems with the participants being seen as a barrier to goal accomplishment (i.e., Anderson & Hunsaker, 1985; Quinn, 1977). For example, co-workers report having problems involving a participant's quantity of work, quality of performance, general competence, speed of decision making, and redistribution of work. Also mentioned are the participant's acts of favoring the partner, covering mistakes of the partner, arriving late, leaving early, failing to meet commitments, missing meetings, making costly errors, ignoring complaints, isolating the partner from co-workers, and generally jeopardizing unit effectiveness. Social problems mentioned by co-workers involve lowered organizational morale, loss of respect for participants, participant preoccupation with the partner, and participants' inaccessibility to the co-workers. In addition, researchers not surveying large samples mention other problems reflecting the job-related consequences of a romance: change of the existing power hierarchy (Driscoll & Bova, 1980; Jamison, 1983), loss or gain of promotions through sexual favoritism, and loss of respect for participants' judgments (Clawson &

Kram, 1984; Collins, 1983; Spellman & Crary, 1984). Violations of sexual morality (Jamison, 1983), uncomfortableness at work due to enforced closeness of participants when the romance ends, the act of having to choose sides when participants break up (Horn & Horn, 1982), and fear of "pillow talk" or the sharing of secrets by participants (Collins, 1983) represent some of the social problems that also have been identified.

RSH-related problems perceived by managers. Managers are likely to perceive the same problems as co-workers. These may be task and social, as well as preinvolvement and postinvolvement.

In addition, supervisors may have difficulties resulting from a lack of knowledge and uncertainty about how to manage the problems. Even if a policy for the management of sexual harassment is formally outlined, uncertainty may occur when the problem is moderately severe. It is here that the difference between behaviors representing sexual harassment and normal interpersonal interaction, including the unintentional and well-meaning actions of someone who is incompetent, becomes most unclear.

Another set of problems managers are likely to face involve the proliferation of sexual harassment accusations. Once a manager becomes aware of the existence of severe harassment, he or she may anticipate that others in the organization will discuss the harassment, devalue the harassee or harasser, and/or come forth with complaints of their own. Further, the manager may anticipate negative consequences for his or her own job or interpersonal relationships with others if such activities occur and are not properly managed. Of course, the manager may observe such behavior and experience such negative consequences.

Finally, managers may anticipate perceiving or perceive task or social problems with people external to the organization (Meyers et al., 1981), such as stockholders and customers. For example, managers may anticipate that people external to the organization will react negatively if word of harassment gets out. Again, they may suffer from negative reactions.

OR-related problems perceived by managers. The existing literature suggests that managers perceive basically the same problems as do co-workers. There are, however, several notable additions to the list.

One is the co-worker-related problem of illegitimate reactions (Anderson & Hunsaker, 1985; Quinn, 1977). For example, managers often foresee problems involving disruptive or inappropriate reactions of co-workers to the romance: blackmail, sabotage, ostracism, and threats.

Another problem, romance proliferation, deserves mention because of its significance for those interested in a policy of stoppage and prevention. For example, managers may feel that the mere presence of a romance has a legitimizing effect that promotes co-worker experimentation with similar behavior (Quinn & Judge, 1978). Quinn's (1977) research supports this possibility.

A third problem involves the manager's relationship with people external to the organization. For example, Jamison (1983) notes that managers may face a problem of organizational image in which people outside of the organization believe management is not in control because of the existence of office romance.

In sum, any organizational policy for the management of interpersonal relationships within organizations will have to account for a wide variety of social and task-related problems. Some may result because of the existence of ORs. Others may result from RSHs involving either mild or severe harassment. Those task and social problems experienced by organizational members as a result of an OR resemble those that occur as a result of a RSH. Any policy that attempts to manage problems resulting from ORs could also be used to manage those resulting from the existence of RSHs. Indeed, a policy set up to manage problems caused by ORs may have to manage sexual harassment, since this is one type of problem that may occur as ORs disintegrate. Hence, any attempt to manage intimacy and attraction in the workplace automatically has direct implications for the management of all interpersonal relationships and interpersonal problems occurring in the organization.

Perceptual Biases in the Perception of Interpersonal Problems

The relative status and gender of those involved in interpersonal relationships may influence the perception of interpersonal problems. Whenever this occurs several biases may result. Such biases may promote sexual discrimination.

One implication of a status-based categorization of problems is that the lower-status individual in most ORs (Anderson & Hunsaker, 1986; Dillard & Miller, 1988; Dillard & Witteman, 1985; Quinn, 1977) and RSHs is female. A related implication is that the behavior of females is perceived more negatively than that of males. Indeed, existing research suggests that organizational members perceive the behavior of female members of ORs more negatively than those of males (Anderson & Hunsaker, 1985). The same may hold when evaluating the behavior of those in RSHs. For example, rather than attributing blame to the man in a relationship for harassment, the woman may be seen as responsible, or at least partially responsible, for the problem. Further, organizational members may perceive the harassment by a male harasser as less severe than it is perceived by the female harassee. One reason for such attributional biasing may be widely held stereotypes of masculine and feminine traits in our society. For example, men are believed to be more achieving, active, striving, intelligent, powerful, and independent than women (see Broverman, Vogel, Broverman, Clarkson, & Rosenkrantz, 1972).

Further, gender-related stereotypes are reflected in several common misconceptions regarding sexual harassment (Hadjifotiou, 1983; Neville, 1989, pp. 144-145): (a) "Nice women don't get harassed;" (b) "Women ask for it;" (c) "Sexual harassment happens only to promiscuous and willing women;" (d) "Sexual harassment exists only in the minds of women who have overactive imaginations;" (e) "Only uptight and maladjusted women with sexual and social hang-ups claim to have been harassed;" (f) "Troublemakers use claims of harassment to retaliate against a supervisor or co-worker;" (g) "People who are incompetent and fear the loss of their jobs hide under the discrimination umbrella and claim that they are being harassed in order to save a job they otherwise wouldn't be able to hold onto;" or (h) "The issue of sexual harassment is raised to mask a communication problem between a manager and a subordinate." Other common and unfounded myths mentioned are (Backhouse & Cohen, 1981; Quina, 1990): (a) Women who object have no sense of humor; (b) A firm "no" is enough to discourage any man; (c) Middle-and upper-class women do not suffer from sexual harassment; (d) Women often make false accusations of sexual harassment; (e) Women secretly want to be forced into sex; or (f) Women do not tell the truth.

Women involved in ORs and RSHs may be aware of these biases. Because of their often lower status in romances, and because the risks of becoming involved in organizational romances are greater for the lower status person, females, as opposed to males, perceive higher levels of risk associated with involvement in ORs (Collins, 1983; Mainiero, 1986, 1989; Powell, 1986). The same perceptions of risk hold for the act of complaining to others about sexual harassment. For example, a female harassee may anticipate that her chances for career advancement may suffer more than those of her male harasser if she discusses the harassment with other members of the organization.

Even though woman are aware of these biases as they relate to their own behaviors, many women act as if they are unaware of them when analyzing other women's organizational behavior (Gutek, 1985). For example, while women report they are personally insulted by sexual advances, they also believe that other women are flattered and complimented. Hence, if sexual advances occur, female members, like males, tend to believe that the recipients probably welcomed them and certainly could have prevented them. Also, both men and women tend to place blame or put responsibility on the recipient rather than attribute sexual advances to some nebulous force like sex-role expectations.

Do RSHs and ORs Exist in Sufficient Numbers in Organizations?

RSHs and ORs are and will continue to be pervasive. Those conditions that give rise to ORs are also those that permit sexual harassment. The more people come into contact, the greater the potential for expressions of sexuality, especially if women continue to join organizations in positions of relatively low status and low power (Gutek, 1985). Hence, interpersonal problems arising from ORs and RSHs also are likely to be pervasive.

Present pervasiveness of RSHs and ORs. Studies indicate that between 42% and 90% of women in organizations experience harassment (Aggarwal, 1987; Gutek, 1985; Safran, 1976; U.S. Merit Systems Protection Board, 1981, 1988). Of course, harassment is not limited to just women. Gutek (1985) found, for instance, that over 27% of the men surveyed indicated they experienced definite or probable harassment.

Dillard and Miller (1988) established the pervasiveness of romances by examining the results of five studies (i.e., Anderson & Hunsaker, 1985; Dillard & Witteman, 1985; LoVette, 1987; Miller & Ellis, 1987; Quinn, 1977). They noted that over two-thirds of the respondents observed at least one romantic relationship and that almost one-third of those surveyed had themselves been participants.

Future pervasiveness of RSHs and ORs. Demographic, personal, and organizational factors indicate that ORs and RSHs will continue to be pervasive. First, ever-increasing numbers of women are entering the labor market and remaining in it (Crary, 1987; U.S. Bureau of the Census, 1984). Also, since 1970, nearly half of the increase in the female labor force is among women between the ages of 25 and 34 (Neville, 1989). While many of them initially seek employment out of economic necessity (Matlin, 1987), most prefer to continue working, even if it becomes unnecessary (Crowley, Levitin, & Quinn, 1973). Hence, the number of females in future organizations should be sufficient to continue the development of ORs and RSHs.

Second, most humans have an interest in interacting more freely in matters involving sex (Jamison, 1983). Current social norms reinforce this new freedom, and the situation is not likely to change in the near future (Mainiero, 1989).

Finally, members of organizations spend and are likely to continue to spend much time working in close proximity with members of the opposite sex. The likely consequences of this are heightened interaction (Huston & Levinger, 1978), increased levels of knowledge about others, the creation of shared work goals (Jacobs, 1981), and the development of a commitment for prolonged interaction (Anderson & Hunsaker, 1985). These factors positively relate to interpersonal attraction. Indeed, many researchers stress that working in close proximity fosters interpersonal attraction (e.g., Anderson & Hunsaker, 1985; Collins, 1983; Dillard & Witteman, 1985; Jamison, 1983; Mainiero, 1989; Quinn, 1977). While factors within the organization such as size (Dillard & Witteman, 1985) and formalization (LoVette & Canary, 1987) act to limit the development of interpersonal intimacy among employees, and while people do not always become sexually attracted to others who work in close proximity, future organizations will likely satisfy the proxemic requirements for a continuation of a substantial amount of ORs and RSHs.

Should Sexual Harassment and OR be Stopped and/or Prevented?

Like sexual harassment, organizational romance is a phenomenon of continuing concern for interpersonal, management, and organizational researchers (Dillard & Miller, 1988; Mainiero, 1986, 1989; Neville, 1989). Two research rationales emerge from their work. One stresses that romance should be examined because it impacts on the organization and this influence is not well understood (e.g., Burrell, 1984; Chatov, 1981; Dillard & Miller, 1988; Dillard & Witteman, 1985; Mainiero, 1986; Quinn, 1977). Researchers using this justification assume that romances are pervasive and occur at all levels of most organizations. A second rationale is concerned with discovering and outlining the strategies of stopping and preventing romances (i.e., policy of stoppage and prevention). Those utilizing this rationale accept what the first group does, but further emphasize that romances negatively influence organizations by causing problems which severely undermine workplace dynamics and organizational productivity (e.g., Collins, 1983; Quinn, 1977; Quinn & Judge, 1978)[3].

The same two rationales reflect the interests of researchers and managers who are concerned with sexual harassment. Aggarwal (1987) notes that within organizations, traditionally, feelings of attraction have been looked upon with disfavor and as a source of a variety of problems. In the past, these conditions generally discouraged the employment of women. Currently, there are two different points of view on how far management should go to prohibit sexual relations in the workplace. One is that sexual relations have no place in the workplace because they drain employees' energy and cause a loss of production. A complete ban on sexual relations in the workplace is therefore needed. By having a complete ban, employees will be protected from sexual harassment and the

---

[3]Other researchers (e.g., Clawson & Kram, 1984; Dillard & Miller, 1988) imply that romances need examination because they may negatively impact on those romantically involved.

organization will be protected from legal and financial liability. Indeed, harassment is costly to the organization in other ways such as employee morale, reduction in worker productivity, and increased rates of absenteeism. Further, many people choose to quit rather than fight or endure the harassment. Higher rates of employee turnover promote all the associated costs of training new employees and lost production.

The other view is that organizations are well on their way to replacing the family as a source of affection, community, and support. People spend more time in the company than at home. It is natural for people to turn to the office to fulfill affection and inclusion needs. Relationships developing in organizations that are based on mutual understanding and willingness neither harm working relationships nor productivity (Horn & Horn, 1982). Hence, rather than promoting a policy of stoppage and prevention, management should help people sort out feelings of attraction, as well as aid those experiencing actions which they consider harassing. Hence, organizations should not be designed to restrict normal social interaction (Aggarwal, 1987).

The policy of stoppage and prevention is not justifiable for at least four reasons. Both ORs and RSHs are pervasive. Prevention of them would be costly. Both ORs and relationships involving mild harassment may have positive consequences for members of these relationships, as well as for the organization. Further, the policy of stoppage and prevention may involve sexual discrimination.

Pervasiveness of ORs and RSHs. As previously mentioned, interpersonal relationships incorporating affective or intimacy components are pervasive and likely to remain so. Researchers and managers need to assess the degree to which prevention is even possible before they promote a policy of stoppage and prevention. Previous discussion suggests that prevention of ORs and RSHs is nearly impossible.

Cost of prevention. The policy of stoppage and prevention of all relationships that involve intimacy and affect-related concerns may be more costly for members than less-restrictive policies. For example, explicit use of the policy of stoppage and prevention signals members that they must limit their emotional and interpersonal involvement with fellow workers (Bradford, Sargent, & Sprague, 1975). Member acquiescence may produce interpersonal anxiety, distance, and formality in the organization and, in general, prevent the emergence of fulfilling interpersonal relationships. In addition, the policy may have a decremental impact on productivity in organizations in which informality and close working relationships enhance organizational morale and productivity. It may also lead to a loss of training and development resources (Driscoll

& Bova, 1980) because it may require that one or both participants in a relationship involving inappropriate levels of intimacy leave the organization or change jobs. Resources are also expended because replacement personnel require new training and development.

Before researchers and practitioners call for a policy of stoppage and prevention, research must determine both the interpersonal and organizational costs of a policy of prevention and stoppage. In addition, these costs need to be compared with those of other less-restrictive policies. These determinations and comparisons require the objective measurement of both the interpersonal and organizational costs and benefits of a variety of policies.

Positive consequences of interpersonal relationships involving intimacy. ORs may have a positive or, at least, no impact on workplace dynamics and organizational productivity (Anderson & Hunsaker, 1985; Clawson & Kram, 1984; Collins, 1983; Dillard, 1987; Horn & Horn, 1982; Jacobs, 1981; Jamison, 1983; Leighton, 1984; Mainiero, 1989; Neugarten & Shafritz, 1980; Quinn, 1977). Specific improvements involve greater coordination, lower tensions, heightened teamwork, and improved work flow. In another study, observers noted that in some instances romance participants were easier to get along with, more productive, and changed for the better (Quinn, 1977). The same results should apply for relationships involving mild forms of harassment since they are inevitable in the development and maintenance of cross-gender relationships.

While several surveys imply that the negative impact of ORs outweighs the positive (e.g., Anderson & Hunsaker, 1985; Dillard, 1987; Quinn, 1977), these self-reports may reflect a negativity bias in which research participants are more conscious of and better able to report on the negative effects of ORs. In fact, Mainiero (1986) stresses that the negative impact of ORs may be exaggerated.

Sexual discrimination. A policy of stoppage and prevention may be sexually discriminatory (Jamison, 1983). For example, those espousing it for ORs and relationships involving mild harassment may conclude that females cause more intimacy-related problems and/or problems of greater severity than males. This line of argument further suggests that women should be kept out of organizations or isolated from men in order to prevent such problems from occurring. For example, some may stress, as Collins (1983) does, that romances should be treated as conflicts of interest and resolved by having the least effective member of the relationship leave the organization. Present demographic data indicate that in a significant majority of cases, the female would be the one asked to leave. While Collins (1983) claims that this policy is not sexist because it utilizes the criterion of organizational effectiveness, it would discriminate against females. It would insure that females remain in positions of lower status. For example, the person asked to change jobs or leave the organization is not likely to be given a higher status job in the same organization nor find a new job in another that has more status.

Can Sexual Harassment and Romance-Related Problems be Managed Effectively?

While many authors stress the need for policies on the issue of organizational romance (e.g., Collins, 1983; Gutek, 1985; Jacobs, 1981; Jamison, 1983; Leighton, 1984; Mead, 1978; Neville, 1989; Spruell, 1985), disagreement persists about whether organizations should support, ignore, or punish romantic involvement (Mainiero, 1986). Presently, no objective evidence indicates the relative costs or benefits of management strategies in dealing with such relationships or relationships involving mild forms of harassment, nor does research on the organizational conditions in which each strategy would be most effective exist. Hence, a policy of "problem management" rather than one of stoppage and prevention appears to be the most logical one to pursue. It has the potential to energize members of the organization and increase organizational effectiveness (Jamison, 1983).

Specifically, this policy reflects the notion that romances and interpersonal relationships involving harassment are pervasive, and therefore, prevention may be impossible. It assumes that romances and relationships involving mild forms of harassment should at times be supported or ignored, because they may have a positive effect on organizational productivity, workplace dynamics, and the well-being of members. It assumes that all members may perceive intimacy-related problems in relationships, but that most problems can be effectively managed without outside intervention. Further, it attempts to account for perceptual biases that may promote sexual discrimination.

Policy for the Effective Management of Interpersonal Relationships

A policy for the effective management of interpersonal relationships and problems in the workplace should specifically address the existence of ORs and RSHs. Such a focus should examine what they are, what problems result from them, and how they can be managed by all members of the organization. Aggarwal (1987) notes that any policy should contain three elements: communication, education, and training. First, policy should be clearly and precisely communicated to members, along with documentation. It should have an awareness component, one in which members become more aware of sexuality, interpersonal relationships, and interpersonal problems in the workplace. Third, it should have a behavioral component, one in which members receive training in interpersonal skills, such as assertiveness training, decision making, problem solving, conflict resolution, and stress management (see Hadjifotiou, 1983; Meyers et al., 1981; Rabinowitz, 1990). In this way, all organizational members can be encouraged to perform behaviors that limit the negative consequences of ORs and RSHs and promote positive ones.

In general, all members of the organization should be aware of the policy and enact it (Aggarwal, 1987; Meyers et al., 1981; Neville, 1989). All members should agree that they have a responsibility to review their behavior and that of co-workers in light of the information they have gained. Both the organization and its members should be committed to learning new behavioral techniques.

Ideally, all members of the organization should assist in the development of such a policy. Employees might help management develop a clear set of norms and expectancies regarding organizational romances (Quinn & Judge, 1978), sexual harassment, and methods of dealing with interpersonal problems through the discussion of hypothetical cases. Managers cannot merely legislate "solutions" to organizational romance (Crary, 1987) and mild forms of sexual harassment and/or make rules that prohibit them.

Many authors discuss exactly what elements should be included in that aspect of the policy which deals with severe and potentially illegal harassment (see Aggarwal, 1987; Meyers et al., 1981). However, what follows is a discussion of what members should be aware and specific actions managers, co-workers, harassees, and participants in ORs can do to manage ORs, RSHs, and the problems arising from each.

Awareness of interpersonal relationships in organizations. Members should be aware of a variety of things. Shared awareness can provide a commonality of understanding in the organization (Meyers et al., 1981). First, organizational members need to be aware that interpersonal relationships involving the concerns of affect and intimacy are natural occurrences in organizations. Managers should freely acknowledge ways in which sexuality may be expressed in the office (Anderson & Hunsaker, 1985; Bradford et al., 1975). Second, members must be cognizant of the fact that ORs and both social and task-related problems arising from them occur. Third, sexual harassment, ranging from mild to severe, is a likely occurrence (Aggarwal, 1987). Fourth, both men and women may harass and experience harassment (Meyers et al., 1981). Fifth, interpretations as to what is sexually harassing may depend on the individual. Sixth, problems resulting from the existence of RSHs are likely. Seventh, those experiencing interpersonal problems, whether or not they result from ORs or RSHs, may fail to engage in the active management of interpersonal problems because of uncertainty regarding what management strategies to employ and what impact such discussion might have on their interpersonal relationships and job. Eighth, members need to be aware that status and gender-related stereotypes may influence the perception of interpersonal problems. Such awareness will enable them to be more objective in perceiving them. If active intervention in a problematic situation becomes necessary, then a manager who is at least aware of such stereotypes can be more objective than one who is not.

Finally, members should be aware that problem situations can and often do escalate. Members need to be conscious of this so that they can prevent escalation. Once it occurs, dysfunctional or negative consequences for individuals, interpersonal relationships, and organizational productivity may result. With escalation, social bonds that once included positive attitudes for others, respect for others, friendship with others, perception of common group membership, and a shared perception of the future become strained and broken (Deutsch, 1973; Folger & Poole, 1984; Pruitt & Rubin, 1985).

Pruitt and Rubin (1985) indicate several transitions through which perceptions and behaviors pass when problem situations escalate. While these do not always occur at the same time, organizational members should be aware of these transitions because they signify the development of dysfunctional conflict. Such transitions indicate the need for active intervention by third parties.

The first transition is from light to heavy. When one experiences a problem, he or she often attempts to resolve it by using a variety of persuasive strategies. Often, the initial strategies are "light" in that they involve hints, direct requests, and/or open-ended discussions of the problem. When these do not work, the person may employ "heavier" strategies represented by demands and/or threats. A similar transition reflects changes in a person's motivations from wanting to win to wanting to hurt the other.

A small-to-large transition represents the move from the perception that a problem involves one issue to the belief that many issues are problematic. Another transition is from specific to general. It represents a movement from concern over one specific behavior to general concern about the nature of the other. This transition resembles the small to large transition except that the focus shifts from one specific behavior to the general nature of the person perceived to be responsible for the problem.

The next transition, from a few to many, represents a movement from a problem situation involving a few parties to one involving many. In the case of sexual harassment, knowledge of the harassment may quickly move from being restricted to one organizational member to many. As this occurs many people may realize that they and/or others have been involved in a relationship with the harasser. Also, many people may begin to realize that many individuals in the organization enact a variety of harassment activities.

Manager's management policy. In addition to being aware in the ways previously discussed, managers must be actively involved in setting a clear policy regarding the management of interpersonal relationships and problems. They must enact it consistently and insure that members are aware of it. The first step to managing interpersonal problems is to determine whether or not an interpersonal problem exists, and if it does, to identify it. In the case of reported harassment, the manager needs to determine its severity, determine who is responsible for the problem, and assess its impact on job-related performance. Finally, he or she needs to assess the problem situation's escalation potential. It is in the assessment process that people must account for status and gender-related biases in the isolation of problems and in the making of causal attributions.

While Mainiero (1986) stresses that the job-related performance of romance participants should be the key criterion of any organizational intervention into organizational romance problems, I extend this criterion. For example, the performance of any organizational member should be the key criterion for intervention into most problematic situations. This criterion suggests that the assessment of problems involving other members not directly involved in ORs and RSHs is possible. If no problem situation exists, or if one exists but does not have a severe impact on job-related performance, is not escalating, and does not involve severe sexual harassment, then toleration of the problem situation seems to be most appropriate. In other words, for relatively minor interpersonal problems, the avoidance of active intervention seems to be the best strategy. It lets others manage their own problems.

On the other hand, if a problem situation has a negative impact on organizational productivity and involves severe harassment, then more active managerial strategies are warranted. Two active reactions of managers to romances emerge from research: integrative discussion and punitive action (Anderson & Hunsaker, 1985; Quinn, 1977). The strategy that managers should employ first is to integratively discuss the problem with those responsible for it. More specifically, when organizational members' behaviors are problematic, managers should approach each separately, strive to be nonjudgmental, encourage them to see sexual attraction as something positive, talk about the disruption, outline its effect on the organization, indicate how careers could be affected, and stress superordinate goals that participants have in common with other organizational members (Jamison, 1983). This strategy should be employed whether or not those directly involved in the problematic situation are romance participants, members of RSHs, or other members of the organization.

Punitive actions by management include giving warnings, reprimands, and/or termination (Collins, 1983; Quinn, 1977). Use of these strategies for problems not involving severe sexual harassment, especially before attempting integrative discussion, ignores the facts that sexual attraction is natural and that ORs and relationships involving mild harassment are pervasive and likely to remain so. Also, such use discounts the possibility that the existence of such relationships may have positive consequences for the organization. In general, punitive strategies are measures of last resort for managing interpersonal problems because they may be sexist, have hidden costs for both the organization and its members, and promote further escalation. At least until research isolates the conditions under which punitive strategies are effective and nonsexist, managers should respond punitively only after isolating an interpersonal problem, identifying those responsible for it, assuring its negative impact on job performance, and using integrative management strategies.

Co-worker management policy. In addition to being aware of interpersonal relationships in the organization, co-workers themselves should have a policy of managing problems stemming from the existence of ORs and RSHs. Training and/or workshops in conflict resolution and problem-solving may be useful for giving workers the necessary skills (Neville, 1989). Such skills are necessary to prevent the escalation of the problem situation. Beyond developing interpersonal skills, constraint should exist on dictating what problem-solving behaviors workers use to manage interpersonal problems. This gives members of the organization the freedom to actively participate with others in the natural development of interpersonal relationships. However, if the problem situation negatively impacts on organizational productivity, is escalating, and/or results from severe sexual harassment, then co-workers should actively seek third-party intervention. This is where educational sessions may be used to develop consensus in the organization regarding what severe harassment is and what responsibilities organizational members have when they become aware of such harassment. Such sessions should help prevent a lack of response by co-workers after observing severe harassment.

Relationship member management policy. As with all other members of the organization, participants in ORs and RSHs should be aware of those elements previously mentioned. Also, they should have gone through the same training as other members of the organization. Such training should help them express how they feel and know when and how to involve third parties in the problem management process. In essence, it should help reduce the uncertainty they are likely to feel regarding how to manage problems and what might result from engaging members in the organization in active discussion of problems. Also, such workshops may be employed to educate and protect those who truly are interpersonally and communicatively incompetent.

In addition to these suggestions, the literature cites several other ways in which participants in romances, especially romantically involved managers, may help prevent the perception and escalation of a problem situation. In general, participants should keep interpersonal and organization roles separate in the work setting. Specifically, participants should take co-workers to lunch, circulate with them, share personal information with them, let them witness the skills or quality of the lower status partner, avoid extended after-hour meetings with the partner, use consistent language for all workers including the partner, and schedule meetings with the partner well in advance (Clawson & Kram, 1984). These activities should impede others from losing respect for the participants' judgments, automatically assuming that a participant favors the partner over co-workers, and becoming demoralized when acts occur that seemingly favor one participant. As Mainiero (1989) notes, the best defense is a good offense. Participants should anticipate potential problems and maintain excellence in work performance.

Those experiencing harassment may perform several actions to avoid future harassment (Backhouse & Cohen, 1982; Hadjifotiou, 1983): have a dress code, keep the relationship with the harasser at a professional level, work late only when others are working late, leave doors open, avoid asking for special treatment, refuse to discuss any personal problems with the harasser, refrain from drinking or socializing alone, and create a protector. Once harassment occurs, harassees may take several actions in the following order (Backhouse & Cohen (1981): pretend not to see or hear the harasser, directly confront him or her, and move from being low-key and diplomatic to taking a more blunt approach.

DISCUSSION

Sexual harassment and romance are pervasive in organizations. There are three reasons why this condition is likely to continue well into the future. First, women are likely to remain in organizations in large numbers, if indeed, they do not soon become more numerous than men. Second, humans have an inherent interest in sexual relationships. This is not likely to change. Finally, conditions fostering attraction and interaction in most organizations are not likely to change. Members are likely to continue to interact in close proximity with others. Indeed, organizations may be well on their way to replacing the family as the context in which a person's social needs are met.

RSHs and ORs are similar in that they involve concerns of intimacy and affect. Organizational members are both interested and aware of such relationships. Such interest and awareness is not likely to abate in the near future. The self-disclosure process both characterizes and develops RSHs and ORs. Many behaviors indicative of harassment also function productively in the normal development of friendships and romances. Indeed, sexual harassment varies from being mild to severe, and people differ in what they perceive as harassment.

The existence of both RSHs and ORs may cause both social and task problems. The experiencing of interpersonal problems in organizations is inevitable for several reasons. First, humans are basically problem solvers who have social goals, sense when their goals are unmet, and become motivated to achieve them. In addition, interpersonal problems are inevitable since people are interdependent and have constantly changing goals, perceptions, and behaviors. The perception of either mild or severe harassment promotes secondary perceptions of the problem situation, as does the perception of any interpersonal problem. Some of these perceptions may be biased in that they promote a negative evaluation of women. Women even display these biases when assessing the behavior of other women. When such biases influence the organization's response to problems, sexual discrimination may result. Further, perceptions of uncertainty about what to do and how others will respond to one's actions may promote the avoidance of problem-solving discussion.

A policy of problem management should reflect all of these conclusions. One policy that does not is the policy of stoppage and prevention. It would be nearly impossible to implement. Even if this was possible, it would be very costly for the organization to maintain. Further, it ignores the positive impact that ORs and relationships involving mild sexual harassment have on the organization. Also, such a policy, once enacted, may be sexually discriminatory.

A policy for the management of interpersonal relationships is offered as the most effective strategy. It contains communication, awareness, and behavioral components. In general, the policy accepts the existence of interpersonal relationships and problems in organizations. It reflects an attempt to make all members aware of both interpersonal relationships and problems and to have all of its members actively involved in the productive management of them.

One method of concluding this chapter is to compare the characterization of interpersonal relationships and harassment inherent in this chapter with theoretical perspectives used to characterize and explain harassment. Gutek (1985) outlines four general characterizations and four specific explanations of harassment. The four characterizations reflect feminist, legal, and two managerial perspectives of harassment.

From a feminist perspective, sexual harassment reflects the more general status of women in society. Harassment represents a societal condition in which men have more power than women. Harassment constitutes economic coercion and threatens women's economic livelihood. Further, this perspective suggests that harassment is an attempt by men to assert the traditional role of women into their work role.

From a legal perspective, harassment reflects an unequal power relationship that is exploitive. Harassment influences both implicit and explicit terms of employment. A person's gender and the reactions of one gender to the other are used as a basis for employment decisions.

From the first managerial perspective, sexual harassment is an interpersonal phenomenon. It consists of misperceptions or misunderstandings of a person's intent. Often, harassment is a "love affair" gone sour. Harassment and interpersonal relationships are the business of the individuals and not the organization. Hence, harassment is normal behavior at work that sometimes gets out of hand.

Like the first managerial perspective, the second views harassment as an interpersonal phenomenon. However, unlike the first, it stresses that it is improper for one to use organizational power to extort sexual gratification. As such, harassment is coercive, exploitive, and improper. In essence, the second managerial view takes harassment more seriously than the first.

Inherent within these perspectives are explanations of why sexual harassment occurs (Gutek, 1985). None of these explanations, however, receives complete support. One explanation for harassment is biological. A natural/biological model pinpoints harassment within the individual rather than in a situation or social structure (Tangri, Burt, & Johnson, 1982). For example, sexual attraction is natural. Sexual expressions are simply manifestations of the natural attraction between two people.

The organizational explanation asserts that sexual harassment results from the opportunities presented by power and authority relations in the organization. These relationships are derived from the hierarchical structure of organizations. In essence, the institutional hierarchy provides the opportunity structure that makes sexual harassment possible. Hence, sexual harassment is seen as an issue of organizational power. This explanation underlies the legal and the second managerial perspective described earlier.

The sociocultural explanation argues that sexual harassment reflects the larger society. Specifically, sexual harassment is only one manifestation of the much larger patriarchal system in which men are the dominant group. Harassment is often an example of men asserting power based on gender. This argument is basic to a feminist perspective.

Gutek and Morasch (1982) propose the sex-role spillover model. This explanation suggests that basic gender-role stereotypes carry over into the workplace and characterize members' expectations and behavior. Hence, gender-based roles, usually irrelevant in the organization, tend to manifest themselves at work. This explanation is compatible with the sociocultural model.

The view of sexual harassment used in this chapter is broader than any one of these characterizations or explanations. This chapter attempts to place sexual harassment, RSHs, ORs, and the interpersonal problems arising from these relationships into a more general framework. As such, this chapter does not favor one perspective or explanation over another. Instead, it accepts the basic tenets of each. For example, interpersonal behavior in organizations is influenced by biological factors, broad social factors, gender-role stereotypes, the hierarchical structure of the organization, and legal constraints. Indeed, a complete explanation of interpersonal behavior in organizations, one that includes RSHs, ORs, and interpersonal problems arising from such relationships, must account for all these factors.

REFERENCES

Aggarwal, A. P. (1987). *Sexual harassment in the workplace*. Toronto: Butterworths.

Alfred Marks Bureau. (1982). *Sex in the office – An investigation into the incidence of sexual harassment*. London: Statistical Services Division.

Altman, I. (1973). Reciprocity of interpersonal exchange. *Journal for the Theory of Social Behavior, 3*, 249-261.

Anderson, C., & Hunsaker, P. (1985). Why there's romancing at the office and why it's everyone's problem. *Personnel, 62*, 57-63.

Archer, R. L. (1979). Role of personality and the social situation. In G. J. Chelune & Associates (Eds.), *Self-disclosure* (pp. 28-58). San Francisco: Jossey-Bass.

Archer, R. L., & Berg, J. H. (1978). Disclosure reciprocity and its limits: A reactance analysis. *Journal of Experimental Social Psychology, 14*, 527-540.

Backhouse, C., & Cohen, L. (1981). *Sexual harassment on the job: How to avoid the working woman's nightmare*. Englewood Cliffs, NJ: Prentice-Hall.

Baxter, L. A. (1979). Self-disclosure as a relationship disengagement strategy. *Human Communication Research, 5*, 215-222.

Baxter, L. A. (1983). Relationship disengagement: An examination of the reversal hypothesis. *Western Journal of Speech Communication, 47*, 85-98.

Berger, C. (1985). Social power and interpersonal communication. In M. L. Knapp & G. R. Miller (Eds.), *Handbook of interpersonal communication* (pp. 439-499). Beverly Hills, CA: Sage.

Berger, C. R., Gardner, R. R., Clatterbuck, G. W., & Schulman, L. S. (1976). Perceptions of information sequencing in relationship development. *Human Communication Research, 3*, 29-46.

Bradac, J. J., Tardy, C. H., & Hasman, L. A. (1980). Disclosure styles and a hint at their genesis. *Human Communication Research, 6*, 228-238.

Bradford, D. L., Sargent, A. G., & Sprague, M. S. (1975). The executive man and woman: The issue of sexuality. In F. E. Gordon & M. H. Strober (Eds.), *Bringing women into management* (pp 39-58). New York: McGraw-Hill.

Broverman, I. K., Vogel, S. R., Broverman, D. M., Clarkson, F. E., & Rosenkrantz, P. S. (1972). Sex-role stereotypes: A current appraisal. *Journal of Social Issues, 28*, 59-78.

Burrell, G. (1984). Sex and organizational analysis. *Organizational Studies, 5*, 92-118.

Bureau of National Affairs, Inc. (1988). *Corporate affairs: Nepotism, office romance, and sexual harassment.* Washington, DC: Bureau of National Affairs, Inc.

Cappella, J. N. (1981). Mutual influence in expressive behavior: Adult-adult and infant-adult dyadic interaction. *Psychological Bulletin, 89*, 101-132.

Chaikin, A. L., & Derlega, F. J. (1974). Liking for the norm-breaker in self-disclosure. *Journal of Personality, 42*, 117-129.

Chatov, R. (1981). Cooperation between government and business. In P. C. Nystrom & W. H. Starbuck (Eds.), *Handbook of organizational design* (Vol. 1, pp. 487-502). New York: Oxford University Press.

Clawson, J., & Kram, K. (1984, May-June). Managing cross-gender mentoring. *Business Horizons*, pp. 22-32.

Collins, E. G. C. (1983). Managers & lovers. Harvard *Business Review, 83*, 142-153.

Conte, A. (1990). *Sexual harassment in the workplace: Law and practice.* New York: John Wiley & Sons.

Crary, M. (1987). Managing attraction and intimacy at work. *Organizational Dynamics, 15*, 26-41.

Crowley, J., Levitin, T., & Quinn, R. (1973). Seven deadly half-truths about women. *Psychology Today, 6*, 94-96.

Danzinger, K. (1976). *Interpersonal communication.* New York: Pergamon Press.

Derlega, V. J., Winstead, B. A., Wong, P. T., & Hunter, S. (1985). Gender effects in an initial encounter: A case where men exceed women in disclosure. *Journal of Social and Personal Relationships, 2*, 25-44.

Deutsch, M. (1973). *The resolution of conflict.* New Haven, CT: Yale

University Press.

Dillard, J. P. (1987). Close relationships at work: Perceptions of the motives and performance of relational participants. *Journal of Social and Personal Relationships, 4,* 179-193.

Dillard, J. P., & Miller, K. I. (1988). Intimate relationships in task environments. In S. Duck (Ed.), *Handbook of personal relationships* (pp. 449-465). Sussex, UK: John Wiley.

Dillard, J. P., & Witteman, H. (1985). Romantic relationships at work: Organizational and personal influences. *Human Communication Research, 12,* 99-116.

Dindia, K. (1985). A functional approach to self-disclosure. In R. L. Street & J. N. Cappella (Eds.), *Sequence and pattern in communicative behavior* (pp. 142-160). London: Edward Arnold.

Driscoll, J., & Bova, R. (1980). The sexual side of enterprise. *Management Review, 69,* 51-62.

Duran, R. L. (1983). Communicative adaptability: A measure of social communicative competence. *Communication Quarterly, 31,* 320-326.

Farley, L. (1978). *Sexual shakedown: The sexual harassment of women on the job.* New York: Warner Books.

Feigenbaum, W. M. (1977). Reciprocity in self-disclosure within the psychological interview. *Psychological Reports, 40,* 15-26.

Fitzgerald, L. F. (1990). Sexual harassment: The definition and measurement of a construct. In M. A. Paludi (Ed.), *Ivory power: Sexual harassment on campus* (pp. 21-44). Albany, NY: State University of New York Press.

Folger, J. P., & Poole, M. S. (1984). *Working through conflict.* Glenview, IL: Scott Foresman.

Gadlin, H. (1977). Private lives and public order: A critical view of the history of intimate relations in the United States. In G. Levinger & H. L. Raush (Eds.), *Close relationships* (pp. 33-72). Amherst, MA: University of Massachusetts Press.

Gilbert, S. J., & Whiteneck, G. G. (1976). Toward a multidimensional approach to the study of self-disclosure. *Human Communication Research, 2,* 327-332.

Gouldner, A. W. (1960). The reciprocity norm: A preliminary statement. *American Sociological Review, 25,* 161-178.

Gutek, B. A. (1985). *Sex and the workplace.* San Francisco: Jossey-Bass.

Gutek, B. A., & Morasch, B. (1982). Sex-ratios, sex-role spillover, and sexual harassment of women at work. *Journal of Social Issues, 38,* 55-74.

Hadjifotiou, H. (1983). *Women and harassment at work.* London: Pluto Press.

Hinde, R. A. (1979). *Towards understanding relationships.* New York:

Academic Press.

Horn, P. D., & Horn, J. C. (1982). *Sex in the office.* Reading, MA: Addison-Wesley Publishing Company.

Huston, T. L., & Levinger, G. (1978). Interpersonal attraction and relationship. In M. R. Rosenzweig & L. W. Porter (Eds.), *Annual review of psychology* (pp. 115-156). Palo Alto, CA: Annual Reviews, Inc.

Jacobs, B. (1981). Sex in the office. *Industry Week, 208,* 32-38.

Jamison, K. (1983). Managing sexual attraction in the workplace. *Personnel Administrator, 28,* 45-51

Jones, T. S., & Brunner, C. C. (1984). The effects of self-disclosure and sex on perceptions of interpersonal communicative competence. *Women's Studies in Communication, 7,* 23-37.

Jourard, S. M. (1959). Self-disclosure and other cathexis. *Journal of Abnormal and Social Psychology, 59,* 428-431.

Kleinke, C. L. (1979). Effects of personal evaluations. In G. J. Chelune & Associates (Eds.), *Self-disclosure* (pp. 59-79). San Francisco: Jossey-Bass.

Knapp, M. (1984). *Interpersonal communication and human relationships.* Boston, MA: Allyn and Bacon, Inc.

Kohen, J. A. (1975). The development of reciprocal self-disclosure in opposite sex interaction. *Journal of Counseling Psychology, 22,* 404-410.

Koss, M. P. (1990). Changed lives: The psychological impact of sexual harassment. In M. A. Paludi (Ed.), *Ivory power: Sexual harassment on campus* (pp. 73-92). Albany, NY: State University of New York Press.

Lafontaine, E., & Tredeau, L. (1986). The frequency, sources, and correlates of sexual harassment among women in traditional male occupations. *Sex Roles, 15,* 433-442.

Leighton, T. (1984). When love walks in. *Canadian Business Journal, 57,* 78-83.

Lombardo, J. P., & Wood, R. D. (1979). Satisfaction with interpersonal relations as a function of level of self-disclosure. *Journal of Psychology, 102,* 21-26.

LoVette, S. (1987). *Applying uncertainty reduction theory to organizational romance: An empirical investigation.* Paper presented at the annual convention of the Western Speech Communication Association, Salt Lake City, UT.

LoVette, S., & Canary, D. J. (1987). *Beliefs and communication strategies associated with organizational romance.* Unpublished manuscript, Department of Communication Arts and Sciences, University of Southern California, Los Angeles, CA.

Loy, P., & Stewart, L. P. (1984). The extent and effect of sexual harassment of working women. *Sociological Forces, 17,* 31-43.

Mainiero, L. A. (1986). A review and analysis of power dynamics in organizational romance. *Academy of Management Review, 11*, 750-762.

Mainiero, L. A. (1989). *Office romance: Love, power, & sex in the workplace.* New York: MacMillan Publishing Company.

Matlin, M. W. (1987). *The psychology of women.* New York: Holt, Rinehart and Winston.

Mead, M. (1978, April). A proposal: We need taboos on sex at work. *Redbook*, pp.31-38.

Meyers, M. C., Berchtold, I. M., Oestreich, J. L., Collins, F. J., & Chaddock, P. (1981). *Sexual harassment.* New York: Petrocelli Books, Inc.

Miller, K. I., & Ellis, B. H. (1987). *Stereotypical views of intimate relationships in organizations.* Paper presented at the annual meeting of the International Communication Association, Montreal, Canada.

NALGO Research Section. (1980). *Equality? Report of a survey of NALGO members.* Cardiff, England: Sociological Research Unit, University College, Cardiff.

Neugarten, D., & Shafritz, J. (Eds.). (1980). *Sexuality in organizations.* Oak Park, IL: More Publishing.

Neville, K. (1989). *Corporate attractions.* Washington, DC: Acropolis Books Ltd.

Powell, G. (1986). What do tomorrow's managers think about sexual intimacy in the workplace? *Business Horizons, 29,* 30-33.

Powers, W. T. (1973). *Behavior: The control of perception.* Chicago: Aldine.

Pruitt, D. G., & Rubin, J. Z. (1985). *Social conflict.* New York: Random House.

Putnam, L. L., & Poole, M. S. (1987). Conflict and negotiation. In F. M. Jablin, L. L. Putnam, K. H. Roberts, & L. W. Porter (Eds.), *Handbook of organizational communication* (pp. 549-599). Beverly Hills, CA: Sage.

Quina, K. (1990). The victimization of women. In M. A. Paludi (Ed.), *Ivory power: Sexual harassment on campus* (pp. 93-102). Albany, NY: State University of New York Press.

Quinn, R. E. (1977). Coping with cupid: The formation, impact and management of romantic relationships in organizations. *Administration Science Quarterly, 22,* 30-45.

Quinn, R. E., & Judge, M. A. (1978). The office romance: No bliss for the boss. *Management Review, 67,* 43-49.

Rabinowitz, V. C. (1990). Coping with sexual harassment. In M. A. Paludi (Ed.),*Ivory power: Sexual harassment on campus* (pp. 103-118). Albany, NY: State University of New York Press.

Safran, C. (1976). What men do to women on the job: A shocking look at sexual Harassment. *Redbook,* 149, 217-224.

Spellman, D., & Crary, M. (1984). Intimacy versus distance: A case of male-female attraction at work. Organizational Behavior *Teaching Review, 9,* 72-85.

Spruell, G. (1985). Daytime drama: Love in the office. *Training and Development Journal, 39,* 20-23.

Tangri, S. S., Burt, M. R., & Johnson, L. B. (1982). Sexual harassment at work: Three explanatory models. *Journal of Social Issues, 38,* 33-54.

Till, F. (1980). *Sexual harassment: A report on the sexual harassment of students.* Washington, DC: National Advisory Council on Women's Educational Programs.

U.S. Bureau of the Census (1984). *Statistical Abstract of the United States, 1982-1983* (103rd ed.). Washington DC: U.S. Government Printing Office.

U.S. Merit Systems Protection Board (1981). *Sexual harassment in the federal workplace. Is it a problem?* Washington DC: U.S. Government Printing Office.

U.S. Merit Systems Protection Board (1988). *Sexual harassment in the Federal Government: An update.* Washington DC: U.S. Government Printing Office.

Wish, M. Deutsch, M., & Kaplan, S. (1976). Perceived dimensions of interpersonal relations. *Journal of Personality and Social Psychology, 33,* 409-420.

Witteman, H. (1988). Interpersonal problem solving: Problem conceptualization and communication use. *Communication Monographs, 55,* 336-359.

Witteman, H. (1991). *Interpersonal conflict and communication with a third party.* Paper presented at the International Communication Association, Chicago.

Witteman, H. (1992). Analyzing interpersonal conflict: Nature of awareness, type of initiating event, situational perceptions, and management styles. *Western Journal of Communication, 56,* 248-280.

▼Chapter 3

Organizational Communication and the Legal Dimensions of Hostile Work Environment Sexual Harassment

Ramona L. Paetzold
Anne M. O'Leary-Kelly
Texas A & M University
College Station, TX

 INTRODUCTION

Sexual harassment continues to be a prevalent and costly form of discrimination within organizations. Increased attention to this form of employment discrimination has resulted from the Senate confirmation hearings regarding Clarence Thomas's nomination to the Supreme Court, as well as from the severity of the consequences for both victims and employers. A majority of sexual harassment victims report detrimental physical and psychological, and/or performance-related effects (Crull, 1982; Jensen & Gutek, 1982); in addition, many victims feel forced to leave their jobs (Crull, 1982; Terpstra & Cook, 1985). Employer organizations suffer from negative reputational effects, lowered employee morale, increased absenteeism and turnover, and possible financial liability (Popovich, 1988). Although the causes of sexual harassment are still debated (e.g., Gutek, 1985; Licata & Popovich, 1987; Rizzo & Brosnan, 1990), there is an increasing focus on prescriptions for "managing" sexual harassment; for example, communication strategies (e.g., Bingham, 1991) and role clarification strategies (Licata & Popovich,

1987) may provide ways for organizations and victims proactively to combat sexual harassment.

This chapter provides a framework for understanding the *legal* dimensions of sexual harassment and the implications that law provides for organizational communication. Since the law of workplace sexual harassment continues to evolve, it is important for all scholars in the communications area who are concerned about sexual harassment in organizations to be aware of recent developments that can have an impact on prescriptions for avoiding, eliminating, or managing the problem. In particular, the primary focus of this chapter is on hostile work environment sexual harassment, since this form of sexual harassment is a more recent, but increasingly prevalent, problem in the workplace. The ambiguous boundaries defining this form of sexual harassment suggest that communications strategies can play an effective role in combating this problem.

We first provide a framework for understanding the legal dimensions of workplace sexual harassment. This framework includes background information involving the identification of sexual harassment as illegal discrimination, current requirements for legally proving that sexual harassment has occurred, and legal remedies available to victims of sexual harassment. Next, we identify the organizational lines of communication that are implicated by sexual harassment law and discuss what the evolving case law currently suggests about the nature of those communication linkages. Finally, we briefly discuss implications of the Civil Rights Act of 1991 for the continued evolution of sexual harassment law.

LEGAL BACKGROUND

Workplace sexual harassment is covered by Title VII of the Civil Rights Act of 1964 (and as later amended), which makes it illegal for an employer

> to fail or refuse to hire or to discharge any individual,or otherwise to discriminate against any individual with respect to his [sic] compensation, terms, conditions, or privileges of employment, because of such individual's race, color, religion, sex, or national origin. (42 U.S.C. § 2000e, 1982)

One form of sexual harassment, quid pro quo sexual harassment, has long been recognized as illegal sexual discrimination and has been analyzed by courts as a form of intentional discrimination. In *quid pro quo* sexual harassment, the victim is required by the harasser to provide sexual favors in exchange for either the retention of a position or the possibility of some employment privilege or opportunity. This threatened loss of economic opportunity—that is, a term, condition, or privilege of employment—made it easy for courts to recognize quid pro quo sexual harassment as a form of illegal sex discrimination. Another theory of sexual harassment—*hostile work environment* sexual harassment—is relatively new and was only endorsed by the U.S. Supreme Court as a form of illegal sex discrimination in 1986. The hostile work environment theory prohibits conduct that "has the purpose or effect of unreasonably interfering with an individual's work performance or creating an intimidating, hostile, or offensive working environment" (EEOC Guidelines, 29 C.F.R. § 1604.11, 1986). In other words, Title VII has been interpreted as being broad enough to guarantee employees a right to a work environment that is free from discriminatory insult, ridicule, or intimidation. (It should be noted that various state and local laws also protect individuals against workplace sexual harassment specifically, or may provide alternative bases for remedying the ill effects suffered as a result of the harassment. Additionally, employees of public employers may enjoy federal and/or state constitutional protections against sexual harassment as illegal discrimination. This chapter focuses on Title VII protections only.)

In *Meritor Savings Bank v. Vinson* (1986), the only Supreme Court case that has addressed hostile environment sexual harassment, the Supreme Court held that Mechelle Vinson's working conditions constituted a hostile work environment that violated Title VII's prohibition on sex discrimination. Her supervisor (a bank Vice President) had repeatedly demanded sexual favors from her, both during the business day and after hours. Although she at first rebuffed his advances, she eventually gave in to them out of fear of losing her job. She admitted having intercourse with him at least 40 times. She also testified that on various occasions at work he had fondled her, exposed himself to her, followed her into the women's restroom, and raped her.

Because the Court was limited in its holding by the facts of this particular case, it could not delineate a complete theory of hostile work environment sexual harassment. It did, however, establish important guidelines for a finding of discrimination based on the hostile work environment theory. First, the Court indicated that *unwelcomeness* was the touchstone of such a case. Whether Mechelle Vinson had "voluntarily" engaged in sexual intercourse with her supervisor was not the appropriate question; instead, courts needed to determine whether the conduct had been unwelcome to the victim. Second, the Court indicated that Vinson could proceed with her claim despite the fact that she had not followed the bank's grievance procedure for reporting the harassment.

Third, the Court indicated that there did not have to be economic loss or detriment to support this type of discrimination claim. Fourth, the Court began to address the issue of employer liability, suggesting that employers should not be strictly liable for hostile work environment sexual harassment by supervisors, but that instead courts should look to "agency principles" to determine the conditions under which an employer could be held liable. The various circuit courts have continued to develop the theory of the hostile work environment, based on the guidelines provided by the Supreme Court.

HOSTILE WORK ENVIRONMENT SEXUAL HARASSMENT

Circuit courts have developed a prototype for the plaintiff-victim's[1] prima facie showing in hostile work environment cases, requiring that the plaintiff prove that:

1. She is a member of a protected class;
2. She was subject to unwelcome harassment;
3. The harassment occurred because of her sex;
4. The harassment affected a term, condition, or privilege of her employment; *and*
5. The employer(s) should be held liable.

The plaintiff must persuade the factfinder by a preponderance of the evidence that all five of these elements are true in order to prevail in her suit.

Protected Class

Protected class membership is readily shown by invoking Title VII's prohibition on sex discrimination; both men and women can claim protection under Title VII. Sex discrimination under Title VII has been held not to include sexual orientation discrimination. Thus, harassment of an individual *because of that individual's sexual orientation* may not satisfy this first element. However, harassment of an individual by a gay co-worker or supervisor may satisfy the first element because the individual is claiming protection from sex discrimination, with the individual's sexual orientation being irrelevant.

---

[1]Since most workplace sexual harassment is of women by men (Riger, 1991), we refer to the victim-plaintiff as being female throughout our discussion.

Unwelcomeness

The "unwelcomeness" aspect of the second element of the prima facie case has been interpreted to mean that the victim cannot have invited or incited the offensive conduct. The Supreme Court had indicated in *Meritor Savings Bank* that aspects of the plaintiff's own conduct or personality should be considered in deciding whether the conduct complained of was unwelcome to the plaintiff. It is not necessary for the plaintiff to communicate directly the undesirability of the conduct to the harasser. Courts have been willing to infer unwelcomeness from the nature of the harassing behavior as well as from the manner in which the victim behaved.

Due to Sex

The harassing conduct cannot be illegal sex discrimination unless it occurs because of the plaintiff's sex. In other words, the conduct must be intentional in the sense that the plaintiff would not have been subjected to the harassment had she been male. The conduct does not have to occur for the purpose of harassing the plaintiff; however, it is enough that it have the effect of harassing her.

A wide variety of behaviors have been found to be unwelcome harassment due to sex in employment relationships. Conduct or language that is explicitly sexual—for example, sexual advances, demands for sexual favors, physical touching such as stroking or fondling, sexual assault, lewd or explicit sexual commentary or gestures—is often found to be unwelcome and is most clearly "due to sex" in the eyes of the courts, probably because of its perceived clear link to a woman's *sexuality*. These behaviors could be unwelcome harassment either because they are directed at the plaintiff herself, or because she witnessed them directed at others. Additionally, use of lewd or insulting graffiti, pornographic or sexually explicit materials, or other forms of pictorial display can be unwelcome and "due to sex." Other behaviors may also be unwelcome sexual harassment if they are insulting or intimidating to women—for example, vandalism of personal belongings or work area, repeated phone calls, staring, following the plaintiff, or pranks. The case is not clear-cut, however; courts must recognize differences between men and women *as gendered* and be aware of the fact that women are exposed to differential threats and fears of violence and intimidation in order to see these behaviors as "due to sex."

Affected Employment Relationship

Since Title VII's prohibition on discrimination is directed at behavior that affects a term, condition, or privilege of employment, plaintiffs must show that the unwelcome sexually harassing conduct is sufficiently severe or pervasive so as to alter the employment relationship. This element typically must be demonstrated both *subjectively* (the plaintiff herself is affected in this manner) and *objectively* (a reasonable person in the plaintiff's position would be affected in this manner). Although there has been a recent movement toward adoption of a "reasonable woman" standard—that is, a standard that would view the harassment from the perspective of the victim—for evaluating the objective aspect of pervasiveness, most courts still use the supposedly neutral "reasonable person" standard.

Courts differ as to their interpretation of this element, although all indicate that they examine the "totality of the circumstances" in deciding whether this element is met. Some courts look more at the *consequences* (for the woman) of the harassing conduct, perhaps influenced by the "sufficiently severe" aspect of the articulated standard. Others look more at the *nature of the harassing conduct* to determine its pervasiveness. Both can be considered together as representing the "totality of the circumstances." Thus, women can satisfy their required showing of seriousness or pervasiveness by demonstrating severe physical or emotional effects that either directly or indirectly affect their ability to perform their jobs. For example, many women report absenteeism caused by harassment. Some women feel compelled to leave their job due to the severity of the harassment, although this economic loss is not necessary to prove liability for a hostile work environment. Women may also meet this element by painting a persuasive picture of their work environment as being so contaminated or poisoned by the harassing conduct that it is impossible to escape from it. In other words, women may succeed on this element by convincing the court that, in the aggregate, the harassment was pervasive. How severe or pervasive the conduct must be depends upon the types of unwelcome conduct that are occurring, so that behaviors seen by courts as being more offensive or outrageous need not occur as frequently as behaviors viewed by courts as being more subtle or less offensive.

Employer Liability

Under the hostile work environment theory, the plaintiff bears the burden of demonstrating that the employer should be held liable. Courts subsequent to the *Meritor Savings Bank* case have articulated this element as requiring that the plaintiff show that the employer *knew or should have known* of the harassing behavior, and *failed to take prompt and appropriate remedial action*. A plaintiff can show that an employer had actual knowledge of the harassment by proving that she reported the problem to management-level or supervisory personnel. Alternatively, she can demonstrate that the employer should have known of the harassment if she can prove that management-level employees would have been aware of the problem had they been reasonably monitoring activities in the workplace. Additionally, she must demonstrate that the employer either failed to act, or acted in a manner that did not end the harassment, but instead allowed the offensive behavior to persist.

Only employers can be liable for sexual harassment in the workplace under Title VII, regardless who the harasser is. Title VII's definition of employer, however, is broad enough to include not only organizations, but also individuals who possess sufficient supervisory authority so as to exercise significant control over important aspects of the plaintiff's job. Thus, when an illegal hostile work environment exists, it is possible for both the organization itself and key supervisory or managerial staff to be found liable. Nonsupervisory co-workers can never be liable under Title VII for their roles in creating a hostile work environment.

Plaintiffs who ultimately succeed in demonstrating illegal hostile work environment sexual harassment can receive a number of remedies. At minimum, the plaintiff can receive an injunction ordering the employer not to discriminate against her in the future. Injunctive relief may also order the employer to adopt a particular sexual harassment policy and grievance procedure (usually one that the plaintiff has played a role in formulating). If the plaintiff has been fired, or felt forced to leave the job, then she can be reinstated, complete with back pay and interest. She can also receive *front* pay if the employer cannot immediately return her to her former position. In addition, the winning plaintiff is usually entitled to an award of her attorney's fees. Under the Civil Rights Act of 1991, winning plaintiffs may also receive compensatory and/or punitive damages from employers who illegally discriminate against them.

ORGANIZATIONAL COMMUNICATION
IMPLICATIONS AND STRATEGIES

The law of hostile work environment sexual harassment has created an external environment that promotes desexualization and degenderization of the workplace. Due to the pervasiveness of sexual harassment (according to the *Houston Post* ("Sexual Harassment," 1991), over 5,000 such charges were filed nationwide in 1990), the nonlegal costs associated with it due to a loss of productivity, and the legal costs of tolerating sexual harassment in the workplace, organizations have an interest in eliminating and/or managing the problem. Although organizations in sectors that have been traditionally male-dominated (e.g., construction) or that involve relationships based upon traditional male-female sex roles (e.g., male boss to female secretary) are disproportionately implicated in reported cases, all types of organizations and organizational relationships are represented among hostile work environment cases (Paetzold & O'Leary-Kelly, 1992).

There are several communication linkages that must be considered in the prevention and management of sexual harassment in organizations (see Figure 1). These linkages involve the three parties relevant to a sexual harassment exchange: the employing organization, the harasser, and the victim. Communications between each of these three parties may have implications for the court's judgment regarding the existence of hostile work environment sexual harassment. The next section discusses existing case law in order to determine the key communication issues relevant to each of these linkages.

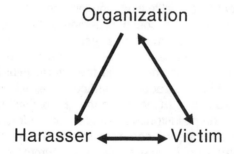

Figure 1. Organizational communication linkages.

Communication from Organization to Harasser

Clearly, workplace conduct and communications must be "desexualized" so that behaviors are not offensive and/or unwelcome to women (or men). A growing recognition by the courts that behaviors need not involve a woman's sexuality to constitute sexual harassment implies that the workplace should become "degendered" as well.

Employers bear the responsibility of communicating a desexualized and degendered culture to their employees. One way to do this is through a sexual harassment policy. Organizations must provide sexual harassment policies that clearly communicate to all employees the wide range of behaviors that cannot be tolerated in the workplace. Since studies show that many women perceive a wider variety of behaviors as harassing and objectionable than do men (Collins & Blodgett, 1981; Gutek, Nakamura, Gahart, Handschumacher, & Russell, 1980; Konrad & Gutek, 1986; Powell, 1986), and since courts seem to be moving toward a reasonable woman standard, the range of behaviors should be inclusive of the types of communication and conduct that women can find offensive. Also, since courts recognize an increasingly greater variety of behaviors as potentially unwelcome and due to sex (e.g., the presence of calendars displaying nude or scantily clad women), it is important that organizations update policies periodically so that they reflect current legal thinking regarding unacceptable behaviors.

The policy should also indicate the variety of ways that a woman can indicate that conduct is unwelcome and offensive. Although some authors have advocated assertive, direct interpersonal communicative strategies for victims (e.g., Bingham, 1991), it is known that many women respond with more self-protective strategies (Tannen, 1990). Men need to know that silence, avoidance, or withdrawal can all indicate unwelcomeness for a woman, and the organization must communicate this.

In addition, sexual harassment policies should communicate clearly the consequences for employees who engage in harassing behaviors. Because an organization can avoid liability by taking prompt remedial action, organizations will want to provide for (a) immediate investigation of all claims, rumors, or allegations of sexual harassment, and (b) some form of immediate intervention to separate the alleged harasser(s) from the victim(s). Employer organizations can avoid liability, for example, by putting an alleged harasser on leave during the course of the investigation. If the organization can substantiate that the harassment has likely occurred, it may have to require training, discipline, or even termination of the harasser. The combination of "prohibition plus penalty" spelled out in a sexual harassment policy can communicate both the seriousness of the problem and the organization's commitment to eradicating it (Kronenberger & Bourke, 1981).

Another way for organizations to communicate to employees that sexual harassment will not be tolerated is via employee training. Organizations should provide training for supervisors and managerial staff to sensitize them to the nature and costs associated with sexual harassment (Kronenberger & Bourke, 1981; Meyers, Berchtold, Oestreich, & Collins, 1981). Training workshops help both to inform personnel of the issues surrounding sexual harassment and to communicate the organization's position in regard to it (Licata & Popovich, 1987). However, since organizations can be liable for harassment committed by co-workers other than supervisors, and since informal organizational power may lead co-workers to engage in harassing behaviors, organizations need to consider more comprehensive workforce training as a way of preventing sexual harassment. Investment in training for all employees communicates more strongly an organization's desire to eliminate harassment from the work environment and may accomplish the goal of reforming the organizational climate so as to eradicate harassment.

Case law consistently indicates that organizations can be held responsible for employee conduct that occurs outside of the workplace. For example, harassers may have direct links with important communication networks that help to promote success in the workplace. Many of these employment-related networking opportunities are social and informal and may take place away from the traditional workplace. Organizations must communicate that these opportunities should also be available to women in a manner consistent with both "desexualized" and "degendered" workplace conduct.

Communication from Organization to Victim

In order to foster a climate intolerant of sexual harassment, employers must also communicate with potential and actual victims. Special reporting or grievance procedures for handling sexual harassment claims should be instituted by organizations, and these procedures should be clearly and effectively communicated to employees. Courts recognize that standard grievance procedures are often unsatisfactory for dealing with sexual harassment because the "chain of command" mandated by the procedures typically requires that an employee first report the incident to his or her supervisor. Supervisors themselves are implicated in nearly two-thirds of recent hostile work environment cases (Paetzold & O'Leary-Kelly, 1992).

Additionally, the immediate power-and-work relationship between supervisor and subordinate may make reporting uncomfortable for the victim of harassment. An EEO or human resources specialist may provide a more appropriate avenue for reporting workplace harassment. The combination of policy and procedure must serve to make the victim aware of her rights and to provide an attractive and comfortable means for the victim to pursue her claim (Robertson, Dyer, & Campbell, 1988).

Organizations must also communicate to victims any actions that are being taken to end reported sexual harassment. Once an organization begins to investigate and/or eradicate an incident of harassment, it is important that the organization report to the victim and provide some assurances that the problem will be eliminated. Recent case law suggests that uncertainty regarding the organization's response (and concomitant uncertainty about the harasser's future conduct) can have the effect of leaving the victim in an illegal hostile work environment.

Thus, organizations that do not communicate their remedial efforts to the victim may leave her in the position of believing that the organization is not responsive to her complaints. She may continue to feel harassed by her environment, even to the point of having to transfer or otherwise separate from her job. Organizations can be liable for the harassment suffered during this time period and if the plaintiff felt forced to resign, may have to reinstate her with backpay.

Communication from Harasser to Victim

Potential harassers may not be aware of the range of communication exchanges that can be found to constitute sex-based harassment. As discussed above, courts have indicated that language or conduct need not be explicitly sexual in nature. Nor must it be specifically directed at the victim in order to constitute illegal harassment. Conduct or language that is aimed at women more generally, or that can be easily viewed or overheard by women who find it offensive, can be considered harassing. In addition, harassment of any woman in the organization may also serve to create a hostile environment for other women who become aware of it.

It is important for potential harassers to be aware that the harassing nature of their behavior must be judged from the victim's point of view. There is considerable evidence that men view behaviors differently from women (Gutek, 1985; Kenig & Ryan, 1986; Konrad & Gutek, 1986) and that men find women at fault for provoking the very behaviors that women find harassing. For example, studies have shown that men may tend to misinterpret a woman's friendliness as sexual interest in him (Saal, Johnson, & Weber, 1989; Shotland & Craig, 1988). However, hostile work environment law indicates that male harassers must consider their victim's point of view. First, the victim's view of what is unwelcome is relevant and courts do not often find harassing behavior to have been provoked. Thus, the potential harasser must learn to put himself in the victim's position to determine what could be unwelcome and offensive to her. Second, the pervasiveness element of the prima facie case involves the victim's perspective. According to the subjective standard, the victim herself must indicate that the behavior was sufficiently offensive to her and/or had severe consequences for her. Additionally, the objective standard is evolving in the direction of a "reasonable woman" or reasonable victim's point of view. Thus, the potential harasser must determine whether it is likely that groups of women could find his behavior unwelcome and offensive and/or could suffer adverse job-related effects as a result of his behavior. The potential harasser should also be aware that even though some women in the workplace may find his language or conduct acceptable, a "reasonable woman" may not agree.

Communication from Victim to Harasser

As previously mentioned, courts have indicated that victims of harassment do not have to communicate directly to the harasser the unwelcome nature of the harassing behavior. Many factors could make direct, interpersonal communication with the harasser difficult for the victim—for example, organizational culture, power differences between harasser and victim, fear of having misperceived the offensive conduct, or fear of reprisal (Bingham & Burleson, 1989; Farley, 1978; MacKinnon, 1979; Riger, 1991). However, unless the conduct is so outrageous that a court can find that virtually anyone would have found the conduct to be unwelcome, the plaintiff is always on safest ground by sending a clear message of unwelcomeness to the harasser.

Courts do suggest that the victim has some communication responsibilities, however. Because unwelcomeness has been interpreted by courts to mean that a victim cannot have invited or incited the harassing behavior, courts have placed a burden on the victim to avoid language, conduct, or appearance that could elicit or provoke the harassment. This is problematic for women in the sense that it fosters a "blame the victim" mentality; however, a review of appellate-level cases indicates that most courts have tended not to view female victims as having elicited their own harassment and have resolved ambiguity in favor of the woman (Paetzold & O'Leary-Kelly, 1992). To date, however, the law has not focused on the range of normal responses of sexual harassment victims, leaving the possibility that a response that is typical for victims may be construed by a court as eliciting further harassing conduct.

Communication from Victim to Organization

In accordance with *Meritor Savings Bank*, hostile work environment law does not require the victim to have reported the harassing, unwelcome behavior to management, or to have availed herself of a sexual harassment grievance procedure, in order to win her lawsuit. Thus, the law recognizes that various gender differences, coupled with the employment relationship itself and the various interpersonal relationships that arise in the workplace, may make it difficult for the victim to report sexual harassment. Hostile work environment law allows the victim to prove instead that the employer *should* have known about the harassment through ordinary day-to-day workplace operations. Thus, to reduce exposure to liability, organizations should try to facilitate both a culture and climate that will encourage women to report the harassment directly, as well as providing a comfortable reporting procedure—it is easier for organizations to respond to *reported* harassment than *inferred* harassment, particularly since an appropriate inference may never be made.

SEXUAL HARASSMENT AND THE CIVIL RIGHTS ACT OF 1991

The new Civil Rights Act does not directly change the law regarding hostile work environment sexual harassment. However, its applications can have a major impact on sexual harassment litigation. As previously mentioned, the new law provides for compensatory and punitive damages for victims of illegal sexual harassment. The availability of a monetary damage award means that plaintiffs have a right to a jury trial, and juries may be more sympathetic to harassment plaintiffs than judges have traditionally been. Both of these factors may imply direct increased exposure for organizations (due to a higher expected award per plaintiff) as well as indirect increased exposure for organizations (due to an anticipated increase in claims filed as a result of more favorable legal outcomes for victims). Thus, organizations today have increased incentives to try to deal effectively with sexual harassment in the workplace.

Additionally, the new Civil Rights Act may help organizations do a better job in preventing or managing sexual harassment. The presence of jury trials will lead to more crystallized standards for factual issues in sexual harassment cases because jury instructions will need to be developed and refined. Well-articulated standards for framing factual issues will aid organizations in framing their communications for both harassers and victims.

CONCLUSION

The law of hostile work environment sexual harassment continues to evolve, delineating a balance between the rights and responsibilities of organizations, harassers, and victims. Communications scholars need to be aware of these legal boundaries because organizational communications play an important role in creating both a culture intolerant of sexual harassment and a climate reflective of workplace equity for men and women.

REFERENCES

Bingham, S. G. (1991). Communication strategies for managing sexual harassment in organizations: Understanding message options and their effects. *Journal of Applied Communication Research, 19,* 88-115.

Bingham, S. G., & Burleson, B. R. (1989). Multiple effects of messages with multiple goals: Some perceived outcomes of responses to sexual harassment. *Human Communication Research, 16* (2), 184-216.

Civil Rights Act of 1964, 42 U.S.C. § 2000e (1982).

Collins, E. G. C., & Blodgett, T. B. (1981). Sexual harassment: Some see it...some won't. *Harvard Business Review, 59* (2), 76-95.

Crull, P. (1982). Stress effects of sexual harassment on the job: Implications for counseling. *American Journal of Orthopsychiatry, 52*, 539-544.

EEOC Guidelines, 29 C.F.R. § 1604.11 (1986).

Farley, L. (1978). *Sexual shakedown: The sexual harassment of women on the job.* New York: McGraw-Hill.

Gutek, B. A. (1985). *Sex and the workplace.* San Francisco: Jossey-Bass.

Gutek, B. A., Nakamura, C. Y., Gahart, M., Handschumacher, I., & Russell, D. (1980). Sexuality and the workplace. *Basic and Applied Social Psychology, 1*, 255-265.

Jensen, I. W., & Gutek, B. A. (1982). Attributions and assignment of responsibility in sexual harassment. *Journal of Social Issues, 38*, 121-136.

Kenig, S., & Ryan, J. (1986). Sex differences in levels of tolerance and attributions of blame for sexual harassment on a university campus. *Sex Roles, 15*, 535-549.

Konrad, A. M., & Gutek, B. A. (1986). Impact of work experiences on attitudes toward sexual harassment. *Administrative Science Quarterly, 31*, 422-438.

Kronenberger, G. K., & Bourke, D. L. (1981). Effective training and elimination of sexual harassment. *Personnel Journal, 60*, 879-883.

Licata, B. J., & Popovich, P. M. (1987, May). Preventing sexual harassment: A proactive approach. *Training and Development Journal*, 34-38.

MacKinnon, C. A. (1979). *Sexual harassment of working women: A case of sex discrimination.* London: Yale University Press.

Meritor Savings Bank v. Vinson, 477 U.S. 57 (1986).

Meyers, M. C., Berchtold, I. M., Oestreich, J. L., & Collins, F. J. (1981). *Sexual harassment.* New York: Petrocelli Books.

Paetzold, R. L., & O'Leary-Kelly, A. M. (1992). *Hostile environment sexual harassment: A review of circuit court cases.* Manuscript submitted for publication.

Popovich, P. M. (1988). Sexual harassment in organizations. *Employee Responsibilities and Rights Journal, 1*, 273-822.

Powell, G. N. (1986). Effects of sex role identity and sex on definitions of sexual harassment. *Sex Roles, 14*, 9-19.

Riger, S. (1991). Gender dilemmas in sexual harassment policies and procedures. *American Psychologist, 46* (5), 497-505.

Rizzo, A-M., & Brosnan, D. (1990). Critical theory and communication dysfunction: The case of sexually ambiguous behavior. *Administration & Society, 22* (1), 66-85.

Robertson, C., Dyer, C. E., & Campbell, D. (1988). Campus harassment: Sexual harassment policies and procedures at institutions of higher learning. *Signs: Journal of Women in Culture and Society, 13,* 792-812.

Saal, F. E., Johnson, C. B., & Weber, N. (1989). Friendly or sexy? It may depend on whom you ask. *Psychology of Women Quarterly, 13,* 263-276.

Sexual harassment in the U.S. (1991, October). *The Houston Post,* p. 1.

Shotland, R. L., & Craig, J. M. (1988). Can men and women differentiate between friendly and sexually interested behavior? *Social Psychology Quarterly, 51,* 66-73.

Tannen, D. (1990). *You just don't understand.* New York: William Morrow & Co.

Terpstra, D. E., & Cook, S. E. (1985). Compliant characteristics and reported behaviors and consequences associated with formal sexual harassment charges. *Personnel Psychology, 38,* 559-574.

Communicating About Sexual Harassment

Chapter 4

Accused of Sexual Harassment

Leonard J. Shedletsky

University of Southern Maine

Gorham, ME

▼ Have you ever been accused of something you did not do? Or, have you ever been accused of an intention that you did not have? I believe that we recall such events with special clarity; they cut deep and the frustration and anger, the hurt are not difficult to recover. I recall a teacher accusing me of cheating on a test on which I did not cheat. That occurred over 30 years ago. Yet, I can recall much about the event, especially how hurt and angry I felt. That was a powerful event for me. The message was: "you are less than you think you are." I wanted to say, "No, I am more than you say," but what an awful position to be in, to have to defend one's worth. When the accusation is aimed at what we value in our selves, and when it works to undermine our belief in the basic fairness of our institutions, it should come as no surprise that being accused is a powerful act of communication.

There are numerous ways in which we encounter inaccurate accusations. Have you ever been told to stop interrupting when you didn't think you were interrupting? Describing such moments in conversation, Tannen (1990) writes: "Being blamed for interrupting when you know you didn't mean to is as frustrating as feeling interrupted. Nothing is more disappointing in a close relationship than being accused of bad intentions when you know your intentions were good" (p. 215). The point I am making here is simply this: Being accused is a significant event.

But the larger point that I wish to develop is that when one is accused formally, it is important that we do not abrogate the freedom of speech of the accused, even when that accusation involves a reference to sexist ideas, or any ideas that the community may abhor. Disempowering a group—the accused—is not the way to provide equality of opportunity.

In addressing just these issues, Haiman (1991) writes:

> There *is* a serious problem of racism and sexism on our college campuses; it *does* cause emotional pain and suffering to its targets; and it may indeed hinder their academic performance and opportunities. The narratives that are told of harassment and victimization cannot be dismissed as lacking in authenticity, nor is the point without merit that intelligent women and men regard racist and sexist ideas as anathema to a civilized society. Where reason breaks down is in the leap to the conclusion that it is freedom of *speech* which is in conflict with equality, rather than the racist and sexist *behaviors* and *practices* that underlie the verbal expression of racial and sexual bigotry.

> Freedom of speech and equality of opportunity are, and always have been, allies, not enemies. We must not allow them to be divided and conquered. What equality we have achieved in this country—for women, for racial and religious minorities, for gays and lesbians, and for the physically handicapped—has been significantly advanced by the exercise of freedom of speech; and freedom of speech, in turn, has been strengthened and enriched by the increased empowerment of previously disempowered groups. (p. 332, emphasis in original)

In short, Haiman makes a passionate plea for hearing everyone's voice, for giving equal weight to the lone dissenter as to the many. In the story of being accused of sexual harassment that I am about to tell, the accused—this writer—was denied freedom of speech in the name of equality of opportunity. Here is my experience with being accused of sexual harassment.

I am a male professor and at the time of my encounter with sexual harassment I was chairperson of my department. A female colleague had come up for the tenure decision. There were two tenured faculty in my department who got to vote on this decision—myself and another male faculty member. The other tenured faculty member wrote a letter recommending her for tenure, and I wrote a letter not recommending her for tenure. While my letter was lengthy and covered much ground, at its core was the clear thesis that in my opinion she had not met the standards required for tenure at our university, nor did I believe that the quality of her academic work put her in a position to meet our standards. In my judgment, she certainly didn't meet my standards for excellence in academic ability.

As it turned out, the dean of our college agreed with me that the applicant should not be recommended for tenure. Similarly, the Provost recommended against tenure. The President concurred, recommending against tenure.

After being notified that she was not recommended for tenure, the applicant appealed the decision with help from our union by initiating a grievance procedure and, in addition, she took her case to the state's Human Rights Commission for a hearing. Her claim to the Human Rights Commission was focused on the accusation that the university, specifically the College of Arts and Sciences, had a history of discrimination against women. She worked through the union grievance process and wrote a statement appealing to a wide range of alleged injustices. Among them was the accusation that I had committed sexual harassment[1]. The accusation about sexual harassment was very briefly stated in the grievance, but it was there. I did not learn of its presence in the document, nor just what was claimed, until much later in the process.

I learned of the accusation against me when I received a phone call from our director of Equal Employment Opportunity. I don't think that I will ever forget this phone call. It came on a Friday, at about four o'clock. The director of Equal Employment Opportunity was calling to tell me that I had been named in the grievance as someone who had committed sexual harassment.

She said that she wanted to help out by having me come in and discuss this matter with her and some others; she wanted to clear the issue up and help me out. I was stunned. Furthermore, by judging from the response on the other end of the phone, I was led to believe that there was something surprising about my being stunned. I was told that this was all more or less routine, and she simply wanted to chat with me and several other people to clear this up.

I asked who else would be there, and I was informed that our director of Labor Relations & Human Resource Info Systems would be. Since she was unable to get him on the telephone for a conference call, I requested to call him and to speak with him. I did get him in and we spoke.

In that conversation it became clear to me that the proposed meeting for the following week was not a chat. The director of Equal

---

[1]Eventually, when I got to speak with a union official about the case, I was told that typically the grievant is advised to make as many charges as possible. I was told not to worry about the accusation made about me, not to take it personally. In my opinion, what this encourages is accusing for strategic reasons, out of the desire to gain tenure in this case, rather than out of the desire to protect a victim of sexual harassment.

Employment Opportunity and the director of Labor Relations were part of a university team to work on such matters. Moreover, the Labor Relations director informed me that he had spoken with the university's lawyer in preparation for this "chat." At some point I came to understand that they were preparing to fight the university's case before the Human Rights Commission.

I called the director of EEO back. I asked her to read to me the accusations made against me. She refused to do that. She said that she didn't want to do that on the telephone. I pointed out that the tenure applicant had been represented by a union official in writing her grievance; the two directors had consulted a lawyer. I was the accused, and I was the only one who was expected to show up unrepresented, without knowing of what specifically I was accused. All of this took place during a period of roughly less than an hour on the telephone late in the afternoon on a Friday. I can still hear the director of EEO saying in a voice that sounded surprised by my shock, "I hope I haven't ruined your weekend." I also recall saying that it was not everyday that I was accused of sexual harassment. Of course, this would ruin my weekend. I was whirling from the accusation, the request that I show up unprepared to discuss serious matters as if they were casual, and the display of surprise that I was wounded by the whole incident. I was wounded by this incident because I had long prided myself on being a fair and honest person. I taught a very successful senior seminar in our department on sex-related differences in communication, I had attended two international congresses on women, and I had been one of the original members of the committee to form the women's studies program at our university. I took pride in the fact that I had published a paper in the journal, *Women's Studies in Communication*. I had long considered myself a supporter of equal rights. I was a loyal husband and the father of a then 6-year-old daughter whom I loved dearly and who was the center of my life. All of this, somehow, seemed to be called into question in that moment of being accused. For me, this was not merely a matter of chat.

Finally, I agreed to attend a meeting with the directors of EEO and Labor Relations under two conditions: first, that it be understood that I was coming to listen, to hear what I was accused of; and second, that I was bringing a union representative with me. I made it clear that I was not coming to answer questions, since I had no specific accusation to think about in advance and to which to respond. The union sent a representative from the central office in the state. We agreed that we were there simply to listen.

When we got into the room, the director of EEO was present, as was the director of Labor Relations. But there was an additional and unexpected person present; the university lawyer. When she introduced herself, I told her that I was present to hear what I was accused of and that I didn't know why she was present. This statement seemed to come as a surprise to her. We proceeded anyway.

The director of EEO hemmed and hawed and apologized profusely when she was called upon to tell me of what I was accused. She said that it was only after many meetings with my accuser that she could get any specific accusation stated. She apologetically told me that the accusation was that five years earlier I had called the woman on the telephone, and I had told her that my wife was out of town. She said that I asked to visit her, that she indicated that she was busy, and that she offered to have me over for a visit the following weekend. (It should be noted parenthetically that at the time of this alleged phone call, my accuser and I were friends; she had had many meals at my house, frequently with one or another of her children. My wife and I also had been to her house on various occasions.) That was it. From this incident, which I do not recall at all, she claimed that my tone of voice indicated a sexual interest, and that when I was "rebuffed," I became biased against her for evermore. That was it. There was a round of laughter from all. My representative and I asked to leave the room to discuss the accusation and to decide whether or not we wanted to discuss this further at that time. We met in a separate room for approximately 10 minutes. Immediately, he informed me that we might as well go back and discuss this further, since the accusation was laughable (although he understood my deep sadness over this and how in the hands of the bureaucracy such matters could become monstrous). We returned to the meeting to talk.

The mood was as follows. All agreed that the accusation was laughable. The university lawyer said that there was nothing here in the way of a charge against me, and that you essentially couldn't accuse people of such things based on your memory of their tone of voice. She also indicated that there would have to be some connection made between my alleged phone call and behavior on my part that showed discrimination against the accuser. There would have to be questions raised about why five years had passed without any mention of this. The director of EEO continued to be apologetic for this whole thing. She said that not only was the accusation weak, but that it took many meetings with the accuser before she would even offer this story of how she was harassed. While the director of Labor Relations played less of a role in this part of the discussion, he too communicated that he saw the accusation as overstepping bounds.

My concern was what does one do who is falsely accused? How do I redress this attack against me? Little was offered in the way of help on that question. Also, the university lawyer commented on the fact that the Human Rights Commission was soliciting from the university all documentation associated with tenure decisions in the College of Arts and Sciences going back five years. The Human Rights Commission was asking for my syllabus for the course, Sex-Related Differences in Communication. She said that, based on her long experience with such cases (in which she specialized), and based on her experience with the Human Rights Commission, she did not know why the Human Rights Commission was making a federal case out of this particular instance. She indicated that they were treating this case with greater intensity than any other they had handled for years. She indicated that she was going to make some phone calls and look into that.

I agreed to dig out every memo I could find from my files to speak to the charge that I might be unfair to any group, especially women, and to send all that material to the university lawyer. I felt strongly that I had an exceptionally good record of treating people fairly. I did that, and I provided the lawyer with a large pile of memos going back years.

Meanwhile, the grievance process was proceeding. The grievance, much like the tenure application itself, had to run its course through specified steps. First, the dean got to respond to the grievance. He rejected the grievance maintaining his stand that the woman should not receive tenure. The Provost also rejected her appeal for changing the decision. Finally, the President, who had recently announced that she would be retiring from our university within the year, reversed her earlier decision and recommended that the applicant be tenured.

After the grievance process reversed the tenure decision, the Human Rights Commission case was dropped. I never got my day in court. The accusation against me was, therefore, never erased. Somewhere the document accusing me still exists.

In the following weeks and months it became increasingly clear to me that no one in the process of seeing this case through was going to do anything to respond to my pain. I made numerous phone calls to our union. I wanted to know how it could be that the union would represent one side of a disagreement between two union members. I wanted to know what the union was now going to do to help me to redress this ugly attack against me. I wanted counsel. I was bounced from one union official to another. No one seemed to know how the decision was made to represent one union member in a case in which two union members were at odds. No one seemed to know how the union could now represent me. No one would respond to my request that the union pay for a private lawyer to represent me. Finally, after many, many phone calls, I got to speak to the union lawyer. He heard me out. He heard my pain. He heard my outrage at being accused and at being left without representation. He called the accusation against me "bullshit." He acknowledged that it was a sham. In the very same breath, he told me the hard facts about life. I would be without counsel, unless, that is, I was willing to pay for a lawyer. His position was:"You weren't fired were you; you haven't been injured by this incident in ways that we can redress."

What a terribly painful lesson to learn. Your feelings hurt, a document to be around forever containing an ugly charge against you, possible rumors in the community—a tinge of doubt that accompanies such accusations—a name called into question. The bureaucracy has closed in further on one's self. This is a form of violation; and the grown-up world of union officials, lawyers, directors of EEO, and Labor Relations, and even some friends and relatives, are saying: "Walk away from it. There is nothing you can do."

The thought of paying for a lawyer added to my pain. But after months of trying to get some help from my union, I decided to call private lawyers. What I learned from my calls was that they too had a similar view. Some were sympathetic. All who I spoke with thought that the charge was vacuous. But no one wanted the case, that is, unless I was willing to pay them lots of money for a case they could not recommend.

Why didn't they want it? Simple—there was no money in it for them. The lawyers wanted to know what would we win if we won. My name, my reputation, justice, fairness—these were not the spoils of war for lawyers; they wanted bucks. If we could sue the union or the university, now that would be worth thinking about; those organizations have money. But when I inquired about the biased way in which the union had treated me, lawyers responded: "That happens every day in unions and there isn't much you can do about it." They generally said they were sorry, but that the law privileged the accuser in such cases. The advice was: Take your lumps.

I want people to understand how destructive this process is to our deeply ingrained sense of right and wrong. Such accusations strike at our core of belief in how things work. This process erodes any sense of security in doing what is right. It opens one to the harshness of a bureaucratic world that could strike at any moment and leave one wounded. It undermines taking responsibility for decisions in an organization. How can I forget that our provost called me to his office, at the president's request, ostensibly to apologize. She had gone off on vacation and left this apology for the provost. (By the way, the president never did speak directly to me about the whole incident, and there was plenty of time after she returned from her vacation.) But I cannot forget that in the course of that conversation, the provost asked me point blank if I had committed sexual harassment. The question itself makes my point: To be accused is to cast enough doubt, so that the question must be asked, if not out loud, then to one's self. He asked me if I could prove I hadn't committed sexual harassment. I pointed out the impossibility of my doing that—how could I prove I hadn't?

I have left out many details along the way: the sleepless nights, the awkward position in which it puts a spouse, the erosion of trust between the individual and the university, the union, the law. The dean told me that he pleaded with the president not to reverse her decision. He too was left in an awkward position, but at least he didn't have to go back to department meetings with this person. (To add injury to insult, the director of EEO informed me that my accuser was now in a position to claim that I am retaliating against her for her accusation, should I do anything she deems a retaliation; in short, I am stripped of any authority as a chair.) The dean told me that since the president was leaving the university, he guessed that she simply didn't want to leave with messy litigation going on, perhaps requiring her to fly back here several times. He presented that to me as if, for him, it justified her reversal. He could understand her motivation and forgive her. I will leave you to imagine what this tenure decision did to the cohesiveness of our department. The dean, of course, being an opportunist, immediately used the vulnerability of the department to undermine us and steal from us. I won't go into that here, only to say that he wasted no time in sending around the message that the Communication people couldn't get along.

Finally, I want people to understand that I am telling my story for reasons that go beyond the relief I gain from the telling. I believe in equal rights. I am not in favor of sexual harassment; that is why, in part, this all hurts so much. But in addition to my feelings, I believe that for equal rights to be furthered and for laws protecting the innocent to be fostered, we must figure out how to enact a process that protects all. Am I wrong to feel that being a male handicapped me in this process? Am I wrong to feel that being the accused handicapped me in this process?

What could we do to improve the situation? I believe that we must operate on the principle that everyone involved—the accuser, the accused, the university lawyer, the university directors of EEO and Labor Relations, the dean, the provost, the president, union officials, and any others—is entitled to an equal right of expression. Clearly, this was not what happened in the case related here. In so many respects, the accused was denied an opportunity to express himself, beginning with one-sided union representation and ending with no opportunity to redress the accusation. The system acted as if it was alright to accuse and made no provision for the accused to respond.

Certainly, we want to aid the victim of sexual harassment to speak out. But such aid must operate within the confines of a principle that safeguards the freedom of expression of everyone involved. Otherwise, I think that we will destroy some cherished principles as we try to live by others. If we don't operate within the limits of respecting the rights of everyone involved, then we risk suppressing voices that may otherwise be heard. I believe that the accused should be given the opportunity to respond; that the accuser should be asked to make a case; and that the record should be set straight in the end if the accusation cannot be adequately supported by evidence. In addition, I believe that a truly independent body of judges must review such cases. Neither the union nor the university, in this case, demonstrated the will to stand for such principles of freedom of expression. Instead, what showed itself at work were the forces of self-interest. To emphasize the point, I will repeat Haiman's (1991) words: "Freedom of speech and equality of opportunity are, and always have been, allies, not enemies. We must not allow them to be divided and conquered" (p. 332).

REFERENCES

Haiman, F. (1991). Majorities versus the First Amendment: Rationality on trial. *Communication Monographs, 58*, 327-335.

Tannen, D. (1990). *You just don't understand: Women and men in conversation*. New York: William Morrow.

Chapter 5

Fallongate: The Ad Agency, the Feminist, and the $10 Million Case of Sexual Harassment

Mark J. Braun

Gustavus Adolphus College
Saint Peter, MN

INTRODUCTION AND REVIEW OF LITERATURE

> And now, I said, let me show in a figure how far our nature is enlight-
> ened or unenlightened:—Behold! human beings living in an under-
> ground den, which has a mouth open towards the light . . . here they
> have been from their childhood, and have their legs and necks
> chained so that they cannot move, and can only see before them. . . .
> Above and behind them a fire is blazing at a distance . . . and they
> see only their own shadows or the shadows of one another, which
> the fire throws on the opposite wall of the cave. . . .To them, I said,
> the truth would be literally nothing but the shadows of the images.

These are the opening phrases of Book VII of Plato's *Republic*. In this
parable, Plato recounts Socrates's tale of a people chained to the walls
of an underground cave. The inhabitants of this cave construct their
"reality" based on only limited knowledge—in this case, the shadows on
the wall in front of them. Socrates argued that once someone escaped
the cave, they were blinded by the outside light, and thus, upon reenter-
ing the cave, could never view their old "reality" the same way. They
rejected, and in turn were rejected by, those who were still chained to
the walls. Morgan (1986, pp. 199-231) suggested that Socrates's allego-

ry represents humankind's construction of reality based on appearances and that the ascent from the cave represents the embrace of knowledge.

Morgan's image of the workplace as "psychic prison" provides an exciting interpretive framework for research on how media organizations continue to propagate sexist images in both programming and advertising production. My thesis in this chapter is that a male-dominated ad agency might best be illustrated as a "psychic prison," with the organizational communication reflecting the culture of the patriarchal family. In this view, the members of the organization become trapped in a world created by their subconscious—and sometimes conscious—denigration of women. This psychic prison can be maintained by a corporate culture in which structural sexism is both established and encouraged by the patriarchy.

Morgan (1986, pp. 201-212) addressed two ways in which organizations may be viewed as psychic prisons. The first he called the "trap of favored ways of thinking," noting that an organization may become trapped by its own success, by the comfort of built-in organizational slack, and by group processes—as seen in Janis's (1972) "groupthink" phenomenon. Second, members of an organization may become trapped by their unconscious, as manifested in situations of repressed sexuality, unconscious anxiety, and organizational patriarchy. It is in this final area, that of organizational patriarchy (Morgan, 1986, p. 210), that I find utility for the psychic prison metaphor as it applies to communication and sexual harassment in the workplace.

The literature supports the structural separation of the feminist experience from the day-to-day activity of the male-dominated business. For instance, Spender (1984, p. 199) noted that, in general, in our culture, "the exclusion of women is structural," and that "the negation of their experience is probably the inevitable outcome of such a structure." Similarly, Hearn and Parkin (1987) documented the structure of sexuality in organizations, noting that most fixed or formal bureaucratic procedures are entangled with what they termed "hierarchic heterosexuality." Brittan (1989, p. 204) concluded that not only are organizations stratified in terms of gender, but that organizations provide "the framework in which men join together to objectify and trivialize women." As demonstrated by countless content analyses conducted over the past 20 years, the mass media play a key role in the objectification and trivialization of women in our society. Interestingly, Butler and Paisley (1980) held that negative mass media portrayals of women are generally the result of informal, rather than formal, policies. Yet, these policies are, because of their informal nature, rarely documented. Perhaps because of the inherently competitive character of the business environments in which they operate, there is little research on the internal communication and decision-making structures of modern media organizations, including advertising agencies. I believe that the case study which follows provides a rich opportunity to document and examine communication in the workplace, which culminated in the sexual harassment of a feminist scholar by a male-dominated advertising agency.

FALLONGATE - A CASE STUDY

One of the most controversial and bizarre incidents on "Madison Avenue" in the past decade did not emerge from Madison Avenue at all, but rather, from Fourth Avenue South in Minneapolis. This fiasco, which came to be called "Fallongate," involved Fallon McElligott, a "hot" Minnesota advertising agency. In the fallout after the scandal broke, Fallon McElligott lost a $10 million client and received a great deal of negative publicity in such national publications as *USA Today, The Wall Street Journal, Time, Newsweek,* and *Advertising Age.*

Fallon McElligott was, in the fall of 1987, a rather small but up-and-coming ad agency which had enjoyed a meteoric rise. The phenomenal success of the young agency was perhaps best demonstrated by the fact that in only six and one-half years of business, Fallon McElligott had racked up an astounding 46 industry-wide Clio awards ("Ad Agency Apologizes," 1988, p.5). Also indicative of its rapid rise, Fallon McElligott was already billing $130 million per year, with major accounts such as Timex, Porsche USA, Lee Jeans, First Tennessee Corporation, Continental Illinois National Bank and Trust, *Rolling Stone* magazine, and *The Wall Street Journal.* The agency's largest client was the Federal Express Corporation (Gibson, 1988, p.18), and Fallon McElligott was, at the time of the scandal, a contender to take over "a $20 million chunk" of General Electric's advertising (Miller, 1988, p. 55).

In October 1987, Dr. Neala Schleuning, director of the Women's Center at Mankato State University—about 80 miles southwest of Minneapolis–attended a two-day marketing conference in the Twin Cities. The conclave, entitled "Telling Our Story Better," was sponsored by the Minnesota State University System. Schleuning attended a workshop at the conference presented by Charles Anderson of the Duffy Design Group, a subsidiary of Fallon McElligott.

Schleuning was offended by parts of Anderson's audiovisual presentation, which she felt were sexist. One such portion featured a Fallon McElligott ad for WFLD-TV to promote the television show *Dynasty.* The ad featured photographs of the program's three female leads, captioned with the phrase "Bitch, Bitch, Bitch." Schleuning also objected to Anderson's use in another portion of the presentation of a cartoon depicting Can-Can dancers, that was captioned "Whores."

Anderson later said that he included the illustration to convey his firm's belief that advertising agencies shouldn't "whore themselves," or sell out for money, but should instead insist on doing quality work for a client (Fink, 1987, p.1). Before the slide show, Anderson had told the audience of State University System professionals that he hoped they wouldn't object to the material and invited them to respond. Schleuning did just that. She decided to write to Anderson to complain about the gender stereotypes in the ad presentation. According to Schleuning, "I've been a feminist for 20 years, and I've never sat down and written a letter about some of the junk you see, but on a scale of one to ten, I was just sort of mildly annoyed" (Kohl, 1987, p.10D). Schleuning wrote the following letter:

Dear Mr. Anderson,

I had the opportunity of sitting in on your presentation at the Minnesota State University System conference on marketing, "Telling Our Story Better."

While I was generally impressed with the creative level and quality of the work of your organization, I would like you to know that I was both annoyed and offended by the persistence of negative stereotypes of women in your AV presentation. I appreciate your personal apologies and discomfort with that material, but it somehow didn't make up for the references to "bitches," and "whores," and, in particular, your company's interest in perpetuating what I will forevermore think of as the male gonad style of doing business.

While you may dismiss my complaints as those of a "feminist," I would also like to point out to you the irony that a company which prides itself on new images and creativity must continue, for some strange reason, to perpetuate such base and offensive stereotypes in its promotional literature. It's a shame that you have to resort to such shop-worn ideas to convince us of your creativity.

Sincerely yours,
Neala Schleuning, Ph.D.
Director, Mankato State University Women's Center

According to Schleuning, "I wrote this time because you don't get in the same room with an ad agency that often. The opportunity to address directly the people making the ads was too tempting to dismiss" (Wascoe, 1988, p. 3D). About a week later, Schleuning received this reply from Charles Anderson:

Dear Dr. Schleuning:

Thank you for your deeply thoughtful and perceptive letter. All of us here at the Duffy Design Group feel embarrassed and properly chastened for our behavior. Based on your insightful comments, we are currently re-examining not only our approach to design, but to life as well.

At the same time, Doctor, something else has come to our attention. Something we all find extremely disturbing on many levels.

As the enclosed photo clearly illustrates, the Dinka tribe of East Africa has a rather barbaric ritual that has apparently been going on for centuries. I know you'll find it as deeply troubling as we do, but I pass it along to you believing that you will be able to deal with these people in the same firm, yet evenhanded manner in which you dealt with us. Won't you please write them (or better yet, *visit* them), and put an end to this horrible practice, Doctor?

Again, thank you for your letter. We will eagerly await to hear your response to the Dinka problem.

Best regards,
Charles S. Anderson

The letter was accompanied by a large color photograph of a naked African boy from the Dinka tribe of the Sudan. The boy in the photo was pressing his mouth against the anus of a cow.

Schleuning said that she couldn't believe the letter and photograph, and her first reaction was to throw them away. She said, "They could have tossed [my letter] in the garbage. They could send a form letter—the kind you hold up to see whether it was signed by a real person. Or they could have sent a response saying, 'We disagree.'" What she did not expect was a violation of what she called "this mutual ground that citizens, business and industry meet on—mutual respect" (Wascoe, 1988, p. 3D). Schleuning noted that the picture sent by the agency was "very racist. It was putting down another culture, making fun of someone's rituals." The boy in the picture was following a practice used by his people to stimulate milk production in their cows, without which they couldn't survive, not engaging in what was implied by the letter to be a sexual act (Menton, 1988, p.9). Schleuning said, "the issue for me is personal: the right to express yourself comfortably in this country. That letter was meant to silence me. It was meant to say 'Shut up, we don't ever want to hear from you again" (Smith, 1988, p. 1B). She also said, "I was so ashamed, I thought, 'how could I share this with anyone. These people have done such a terrible thing.' But then I got mad" (Ugland, 1988, p. 1). The author of the letter, Charles Anderson, responded "I don't think its a women's issue . . . I think she has a problem" (Fink, 1987, p.1). The problem soon became Fallon McElligott's.

Schleuning sent copies of Anderson's letter to the 5,000-member Minnesota Women's Consortium (MWC), an umbrella organization for 170 women's groups. According to Gloria Griffin, MWC coordinator, consumers frequently clip ads they consider to be sexist and send them to the MWC. The consortium then passes the message to the agency responsible for the ads, usually getting a positive reaction. Griffin noted that "in the past, the president or vice-president was always quick to apologize. Companies don't want to offend their customers" (Coleman, 1987, p. 5).

On November 25, the MWC wrote a letter to Fallon McElligott in which Griffin and staff member Kay Taylor sent copies of Anderson's letter directly to agency Chairman Pat Fallon and Creative Director Tom McElligott, asking if Anderson's reply reflected company policy (Geiger, 1988a,). The MWC received no reply (Fink, 1987, p. 1). Instead, Pat Fallon responded directly to Schleuning on December 4:

Dear Dr. Schleuning:

It has come to my attention that Charles Anderson of The Duffy Group sent you a photocopy of the notorious Dinka boy. I am absolutely appalled. The fact that Charles sent you that single photo is, well, nothing less than outrageous.

Charles should obviously have sent you not just one photo, but the *entire* Dinka story. How else could he expect you to be prepared for your trip to the Dinka tribe of East Africa, after all? Moreover, Charles didn't even offer to help defray your expenses, or provide you with a map! Again, I'm appalled. Anyway, on behalf of this entire organization, I'd like to apologize for Charles' behavior, and set things right. Therefore, I have enclosed the *whole* Dinka story (copied from the December 1982 issue of *Life* magazine). I've also enclosed a map of Africa to help you prepare for your trip. And, finally, Dr. Schleuning, realizing that this public service effort on your part will not be cheap, all of us here have agreed to pay half of your travel expenses to Africa (or *full* expenses, one way).

Thank you in advance for your attention to this matter. I do agree with Charles on one thing. You, Doctor, are the person to handle this problem.

Sincerely,
Patrick R. Fallon
Chairman

A few days later, Schleuning received this letter from Creative Director Thomas McElligott:

> Dear Dr. Schleuning:
>
> After reviewing your letter to Charles Anderson, the only thing all of us here know for certain is that your Ph.D. may not be in English. [sic]
>
> In any event, we're all extremely pleased to hear about your gracious offer regarding the Dinka problem. Let's face it, Doctor, the Sudan is not exactly Cannes. Getting volunteers for this mission—*especially* appropriate volunteers—hasn't been easy.
>
> So while last week you may have been just a strange, anonymous person whose amusing letter entertained 150 people around the company bulletin board, today you are our brave missionary to the Dinkas. Needless to say, you've made all of us here very, very happy.
>
> Godspeed, Doctor.
> Sincerely,
> Tom McElligott
>
> p.s. Please accept the enclosed pith helmet and mosquito net as small tokens of our appreciation.

Just as Charles Dickens stressed the necessity of the reader's acceptance that Marley was indeed "dead as a doornail . . .or nothing wonderful can come of the story I am going to relate," for the purposes of this case study, it must be understood from the outset that Fallon McElligott was a male-dominated advertising agency. One of the agency's original founders was a woman: executive art director Nancy Rice. But she left to form a competing agency in 1985, and her departure left a gender gap which was not filled. At the time of the "Dinka" incident in late 1987, there were no female art directors—not even a female copywriter working at the agency. In fact, a woman at a rival agency alleged that the entire incident was a symptom of Fallon McElligott's "hiring bias against women" (Keller, 1991, p. 62).

Morgan's image of the psychic prison predicts that organizational patriarchs may come to the aid of family members in need of "help and protection." Morgan says that this protective role, often portrayed in a mentoring tradition, is one way by which key organizational members "cultivate fatherly roles" (Morgan, 1986, p. 211). The notion of this father-child relationship in the organizational patriarchy of an ad agency is strengthened by the following statement made by an executive from a rival firm: "There's always been a certain adolescent quality about making advertising. The go-for-broke, risky style of advertising and the child-like quality often required in creative thinking would characterize the Fallon shop" (Keller, 1991, p. 62). In the written responses of Patrick Fallon and Tom McElligott, we see examples of organizational "fathers" coming to the aid of their errant son. But rather than offer an apology for the son, or better yet, teach the errant son the harm in his mistake and draw forth from the boy a sincere apology, they trivialize and objectify the source of irritation in an effort to defend the misdirected son. Brittan wrote that the reason people in power tend to oppress and dominate is because of a fear of the implicit "human potency" in the threat. Thus, according to Brittan (1989, p. 204), "men oppress women because they have an intuition of their potency, their potential and actual power." It could very well be that subconsciously the "fathers and sons" at Fallon McElligott feared the power of Schleuning.

In any event, the letters jolted Schleuning. "All I did was share my impressions with them. Is this their typical response to any kind of public input? It was such a personal assault" (Fink, 1987, p. 1). Schleuning said that she gained a greater appreciation for the creative genius that made Fallon McElligott a prestigious, award-winning agency. "They're very good at words and pictures," she said. "The letters did exactly what they were intended to do. They hurt" (Kohl, 1987, p. 10D).

In her book on evil and women, Noddings (1989, pp. 225-226) writes of both "the universal psychological abuse that every society holds ready to ensure conformity," and "the abuse that individuals visit on one another." In describing psychologist M. Scott Peck's perspective on the "way people inflict pain in the name of good" and on the twisted relationship sometimes seen between control and autonomy, domination and hate, love and destruction, Noddings makes the powerful observation that some unfortunate people "have no real feelings for those close to them...They make these decisions from a perspective of righteousness; that is, the doer of great harm acts in the name of good." It seems reasonable to presume that Fallon and McElligott, acting *in loco parentus* as organizational patriarchs, tried to hurt Schleuning in order to scare her off–thus protecting their metaphorical "son," Charles Duffy.

As for the Fallon McElligott response? Fallon's defensive strategy was to point out that his company had produced campaigns specifically aimed at promoting women, including a media campaign for the Minnesota Women's Fund. In addition, Fallon claimed that the letters he and McElligott sent to Schleuning weren't supposed to be taken seriously. "Somewhere along the line, a sense of humor doesn't hurt," said Fallon. "People need a release" (Fink, 1987, p. 1). Overall, the literature predicts such a response on the part of organizational image builders, as exemplified by Hewes and Graham's (1989, p. 213) observation that "governments, corporations, the mass media and individuals try to conceal their mistakes or present themselves to others in an unduly positive light. They often hold unwarranted beliefs that they unknowingly inflict on others."

But rather than own up to the mistake and attempt to correct it, Patrick Fallon compounded the error by asserting that "We received what we thought was an insulting and inappropriate letter from her, and we felt it deserved an inappropriate response . . . our hurt and insult was just as deep" as Schleunings's. We simply do not do antifeminist advertising" (Fink, 1987, p. 17). This attempt to explain away the actions of the men at Fallon McElligott lies in the void known as the "victimization thesis." This early subject in the male studies popular press stated that men were not to blame for the evils identified by feminists. Instead, according to Brod (1987, pp. 12-13), men were described by the victimization thesis as "passive victims of impersonal socializing forces, often in defensive reaction against overly voluntarist interpretations they found in some feminist writings." Yet, Brod tells us why this thesis fails: "Academically, lacking a complementary group to identify as victimizers, the analysis was vague, and glossed over too many issues, particularly issues of power." Thus as Brittan (1989, p. 195) noted, "the 'victimization thesis' gave men an opportunity to deny their responsibility for oppression. It allowed men to be seen as being equally oppressed with women. In its extreme form it seemed to suggest that the man who attacked a woman was somehow . . . more to be pitied than condemned." Of course, we know this thesis to be wanting; nonetheless, it is clear in this case study that the victimization of the ad agency is what its patriarch would have us believe.

RESPONSE BY WOMEN'S GROUPS

Official reaction by spokespersons for women's groups was predictable. "It's really explosive," said Dixie Riley, a local National Organization for Women (NOW) board member. "We're going to make sure that people know about it. You'd think they'd be smart enough not to offend half of the population. Women *are* consumers nowadays." Likewise, MWC coordinator, Gloria Griffin stated "It's so shocking to find these guys acting like little kids...Everyone I show it to feels it's total insulting to women" (Fink, 1987, p. 1). Griffin's simile depicting the ad agency patriarchs as acting like "little kids" is especially telling, not only because of the earlier discussion of "fathers and sons," but in light of the link Morgan sketches between the human subconscious and the organization as a psychic prison, pointing out that in Freudian and neo-Freudian psychology, regression is seen as just one of several unconscious defensive reactions. Regression is defined as the adoption of behavior patterns which one found satisfying in childhood in order to reduce the present demands on one's ego (Morgan, 1986, exhibit 7.1; see also Hampden-Turner, 1981, p. 40-42; Klein, 1980, p. 1-24). Morgan (1986, p. 205) asserted that Freud's theory of human personality emphasizes that character traits in adult life emerge from "the way the child manages to reconcile the demands of his or her sexuality and the forces of external control and constraint." The case study clearly illustrates the regressive behavior of the Fallon McElligott patriarchs. Indeed, the letters resemble cruel notes passed secretly between elementary schoolchildren, except for their inventive maliciousness which could only be the product of an adult mind.

Outraged by the responses of Fallon and McElligott, the Minnesota Women's Consortium, assisted by the Twin Cities chapter of the National Organization for Women (NOW), sent packets of the correspondence to politicians, media representatives, and other advertising agencies. They enclosed a letter which asked, "Is there a way that you can help Fallon McElligott realize how this reflects on their agency and their clients?" (Coleman, 1987, p. 5). The women's groups then mailed 35 copies of the series of letters to a select group of four Fallon McElligott clients; Federal Express Corporation, U.S. West Communications, *The Wall Street Journal*, and Wolverine World Wide (Geiger, 1988a).

When Patrick Fallon learned of the MWC's actions, he phoned its office to assure the MWC that the conflict was between the agency and Schleuning and did not involve the women's groups. Such a move is consistent with what Gerbner (1978, pp. 46-50) described as the media's "isolating" tactic. This method, one of three ways in which the media resist change, is exhibited when a responsible (i.e., relatively safe) element of the change-seeking movement "is given its own limited place...such as a reservation, a ghetto, or a kitchen." As a university professor geographically removed from the main population centers in Minnesota, perhaps Schleuning was seen as an isolated, and thus easy, target. The Fallon McElligott executives tried to further isolate her by symbolically banishing her to Africa—even offering to pay one-way, transportation costs. When a statewide feminist network came to Schleuning's aid, Patrick Fallon tried to force her back into what he perceived as a position of isolation by telephoning the Minnesota Women's Consortium office to assure the MWC that the conflict was between Fallon McElligott and Schleuning and did not involve the women's groups, thus attempting to render ineffective her network linkages.

Fallon did not offer Schleuning or the Women's Consortium what they really wanted: an apology. According to MWC staffer Grace Harkness, "a simple apology would have prevented all of this" (Fink, 1987, p. 1). She wrote to the *Minnesota Women's Press*:

People we have shown this (the letters and photo) to agree that the message is "go to hell" and "kiss my ass." There also is a universal astonishment at this rudeness. Most adults, even if they hated someone, would not do this, if only out of concern for their own good name.

So what makes the letter writer fair game for abuse? Is it because she's rural and educated? Is she old or young? Fat or thin? Or is it just because she's a woman? . . . The mind-set of these men bothers us. They earn their livings by words and ideas, so their weapons of abuse are words and ideas. Is this mind-set different from a man who's weapon is his fist or his gun? Or his position of authority as boss or husband? [sic]

The attitude seems to be that if a woman questions something you do, her suggestion is not to be seriously considered, but she is fair game for abuse. (Harkness, 1987, p. 5)

The response of the general public and the news media was equally negative. Schleuning said, "We know they must be getting tons of letters and telephone calls, because I'm getting copies of letters that have been sent to the ad agency." Schleuning also said she had telephone calls from newspapers and magazines such as *USA Today*, *The New York Times*, *The Wall Street Journal*, *Corporate Report*, *Advertising Age*, and *Advertising Week* (Menton, 1988, p. 9).

In addition to the letter-writing campaign by the women's groups, *Minneapolis/St. Paul Citybusiness* printed copies of the letters, angering the cities' business community. Twin Cities advertising executives expressed disappointment and outrage with Fallon and McElligott. Mary Gustafson, director of the Advertising Federation of Minnesota, said that the incident was unfortunate for the entire industry, but that it may heighten the ad community's sensitivity to minority groups and women ("Ad Agency Apologizes," 1988). Government officials became involved after the Minneapolis Civil Rights Commission invited principals of the ad agency to appear before the group to defend their letters, which Commissioners called both racist and sexist. Emma Hixson, Director of the Minneapolis Civil Rights Department, said that those who support civil rights were rightly angered by the letters. She said that the matter was discussed at a meeting of the local Intergovernmental Compliance Institute, a professional association for those who monitor affirmative action, and at a local National Association for the Advancement of Colored People (NAACP) executive meeting ("Fallon McElligott Controversy," 1988).

THE BOTTOM LINE

Money talks. Perhaps the most powerful response was the reaction of Fallon McElligott's clients to the unfolding scandal. The most widely publicized response was that of US West, the huge telecommunications company that runs telephone companies in eleven western states. US West was in the process of reviewing its corporate advertising plan and had already narrowed the competition to four ad agencies, including Fallon McElligott, which had served US West since the early 1980s. As news of the scandal spread, it was learned by the press that a group within US West called "US West Women" had been raising objections for about a year to Fallon McElligott's television ads for the company, which featured whooping cowboys on horseback, "hollering and kicking up dust against a backdrop of western scenery." Mary Beth Schurb, President of the Minnesota Chapter of US West Women, said that the campaign was based on a "macho theme" that did not convey the "pluralistic attitude" which her group, or her company, prefers (Wascoe, 1988, p. 3D). In an effort to head off further problems, Irv Fish, one of the ad agency's owners and its Chief Financial Officer, and Mary Weber, Fallon McElligott's US West Account Supervisor, met with the Minnesota Women's Consortium and asked the coordinator of the group to help spread the word that the agency is sensitive to women's concerns. Weber said that "it was never intended to be women versus men . . . but whoa! Clearly the rest of the world sees it as a feminist issue" ("Ad Agency Apologizes to Angry Women's Groups," 1987).

Eventually, Fallon McElligott was forced to retract. On December 30, Schleuning received a letter of apology from Fallon McElligott, which she described as "nice, very sincere, and long overdue." Schleuning stated that as a professional she could accept the apology, but "on a personal level, I can't imagine an apology will take away what those letters did." In addition to a letter of apology to Schleuning, the agency also sent a personal apology and a "courtesy note" to Gloria Griffin of the MWC, saying that the firm has always been sensitive to women's issues, but now is "a little more sensitive" to those issues (Smith, 1988, p. 1B).

In spite of the late apology, the boom was lowered when US West's Judi Servoss recommended that Fallon McElligott be dropped. She said her superiors concurred unanimously. On January 14, US West told Fallon McElligott that it no longer wanted the agency to handle its $10 million account (Gibson, 1988; Wascoe, 1988). Neala Schleuning told *Time* magazine: "This is Fallon McElligott's worst possible nightmare come true. I couldn't have set this one up if I had tried" ("Kiss That Job Goodbye," 1988). Patrick Fallon announced the withdrawal to his staff and apologized to them for the turn of events, saying that none of the agency's 124 employees would be laid off.

When agency officials appeared before the Minneapolis Civil Rights Commission later that month, Patrick Fallon apologized to the group for "insensitivity and arrogance," and told the Commission, "This has been a very, very painful, public lesson . . . We're a far more sensitive company than we were three or four weeks ago. I really believe if we can live through this period we'll be a better company . . .The world has given us a wake-up call" ("Ad Agency Apologizes," 1988, p. 5).

Whether or not the apology and "awakening" were sincere—or were just good business—is subject to speculation. Morgan addresses this point by stating that organizational behavior and our way of explaining behaviors allow no "official status" for such factors as aggression or hate. He states, however, that when such behaviors do break out into the open, "they are usually quickly banished through apologies, rationalizations, and punishments designed to restore a more neutered state of affairs . . . .Yet apologize, rationalize, punish, and control as we may, we do not rid organization [sic] of these repressed forces lurking in the shadow of rationality" (1986, p. 229).

DISCUSSION

There is no question that the Fallon McElligott case is a classic representation of sexism in the media. Here we see an ad agency, owned and run by males, producing ads that feature macho cowboy themes and representing women as "bitches." We see the agency giving public presentations which include references to "whores." I assert that of primary importance to researchers is that what emerged from the affair was a rare glimpse of organizational culture within an advertising agency, a culture in which men seemed to denigrate women, not only in the ads they produced, but in the way in which they communicated with a highly educated women who responded to their ads.

Since the 1970s, research on mass media, including the advertising industry, has been largely focused—to use systems terminology—on output. Content-and effects-oriented research methodologies have done a good job exploring how women are often negatively portrayed in television programs and advertising, in music videos and song lyrics, in newspaper and magazine articles, in children's cartoons, and in textbooks.[1] What has not been addressed as thoroughly is the question of *how*

[1]The prevalence of negative images of women and minorities in mass media programming and advertising is well documented and need not be reviewed further here.

these images of women are created and propagated by advertisers and programming producers–what organizational values, norms, cultures, and rituals allow these socially constructed negative images of women to be given further exposure and credence in the media? One conclusion I draw from this case study is to propose that media research must also be focused on the antecedents of what we see–again, to use systems terminology–on the input and throughput. In other words, now that we know what's coming out of the box, it's time to devote more of our energies on the questions that address how these images are getting *into* the box in the first place: How they are created by those within the system. This chapter has been attempt to conduct such an examination.

I also believe that this case study has demonstrated how structural sexism in a male-dominated media organization can be viewed as a psychic prison–a metaphor that has the interpretive power to go beyond the more simple image of organization as culture. This ad agency truly was a prison, albeit a mental prison, in which the domination by the male hierarchy is seen as a twisted extension of the dysfunctional patriarchal family. Yet, just as the family is changing in modern society, Fallon McElligott was changed, as exemplified by Fallon's admission that "this has been a very, very painful, public lesson . . . We're a far more sensitive company than we were three or four weeks ago. . . .The world has given us a wake-up call."

EPILOGUE

When surveying the changes at the agency in the wake of what came to be called "Fallongate," it seems likely that the uproar did, in fact, give Fallon McElligott a "wake-up call." The agency was beset by a number of setbacks between 1988 and 1990, losing a total of $25 million in billings–about 20 percent of its total business–in the first 8 months of 1988. In addition to the well-publicized US West response, Fallon McElligott lost such major accounts as Godfather's Pizza ($8 million) and *The Wall Street Journal* ($6 million). The agency also withdrew from consideration for the General Electric Company's consumer electronics account. Perhaps most ironic was the loss of the $2 million WFLD-TV account for which the *Dynasty* "Bitch, Bitch, Bitch" ads were originally produced (Geiger, 1988c). While it is difficult to ascertain what amount of the lost business was attributable to normal turnover and what amount was a result of the Dinka scandal, Patrick Fallon conceded to *Advertising Age* that the drain was "precipitated by a dumb move. There aren't many agencies that have gone through a Dinka crisis." *Advertising Age* also noted that after the controversy, the agency discontinued new business efforts for several months (Geiger, 1988b).

In late 1988, Fallon McElligott was further rocked when co-founder and creative director Tom McElligott revealed his alcoholism. In August he entered Minnesota's Hazelden Foundation treatment center, and by the end of the year McElligott resigned from the agency to join a competing ad agency. He moved to Chiat/Day/Mojo, a well-known Los Angeles agency in January 1990, but surprisingly, returned to the Twin Cities to form his own agency, McElligott Write Morrison White Advertising, in late 1990 (Geiger, 1988c; Keller, 1991). In addition to McElligott's departure, three additional "creatives" left the agency (Geiger, 1990, p. 44). In one further piece of irony, when Fallon McElligott's parent agency, Scali, McCabe, Sloves (SMS, a New York-based ad firm—part of the Ogilvy Group—which had owned 80% of Fallon McElligott since 1986), got into PR trouble over the Volvo "monster-truck" scandal, Patrick Fallon was brought in for damage control. Fallon was made vice chairman of SMS North America, while still remaining chairman of Fallon McElligott (Levin, 1990).

Patrick Fallon has been quoted more recently as saying that Fallon McElligott is "stronger now than at any time in its 10-year history" (Keller, 1991, p. 62). Even in late 1988, about $14 million of *new* business was acquired, which helped to offset the $25 million first-half exodus. Since 1989, Fallon McElligott has garnered contracts for about $39 million in new business, including Aveda Corporation, *The Minneapolis Star Tribune*, divisions of Amoco Oil Company and General Mills, and a $10 million deal with Ralston Purina. What could be the clearest evidence of Fallon McElligott having reacted positively to its "wake-up call" is that two women joined the creative team at Fallon McElligott in late 1990 (Keller, 1991, p. 62).

Perhaps the words of organizational theorist Gareth Morgan can best summarize the "Fallongate" case study:

> In viewing organizations as unconscious extensions of family relations we thus have a powerful means of understanding key features of the corporate world. We are also given a clue as to how organizations are likely to change along with contemporary changes in family structure and parenting relations. And we see the major role that women and gender-related values can play in transforming the corporate world. So long as organizations are dominated by patriarchal values and structures the roles of women in organizations will always be played out on "male" terms. Hence, the view of many feminist critics of the modern corporation: that the real challenge facing women who want to succeed in the organizational world is to change the organizational values in the most fundamental sense. (1986, p. 212)

REFERENCES

Ad agency apologizes. (1988, January 20). *Mankato Free Press*, p. 5.

Ad agency apologizes to angry women's groups. (1987, December 31). *USA Today*. Section B, p. 2 Col. 3.

Brittan, A. (1989). *Masculinity and power*. New York: Blackwell.

Brod, H. (1987). *The making of masculinities: The new men's studies*. Boston, MA: Allen and Unwin.

Butler, M., & Paisley, W. (1980). *Women and the mass media: Sourcebook for research and action*. New York: Human Sciences Press.

Coleman, B. (1987, December 21). Agency's reply to ad criticism dismays consortium. *Minnesota Women's Press*, p. 5.

Fallon McElligott controversy draws mixed responses. (1988, January 11). *Minneapolis/St. Paul CityBusiness*, p. 9.

Fink, L. (1987, December 28). Ad agency is target of angry women's groups: Fallon McElligott says it was only joking; others aren't so sure. *Minneapolis/St. Paul CityBusiness*, p. 1.

Geiger, B. (1988a, January 4). Fallon McElligott act 'shocks' city: Top execs involved. *Advertising Age*, p. 2.

Geiger, B. (1988b, August 15). Fallon falling from grace? *Advertising Age*, pp. 3, 8.

Geiger, B. (1988c, December 12). Fallon loses McElligott. *Advertising Age*, pp. 1, 67.

Geiger, B. (1990, January 22). Fallon fine, sans McElligott. *Advertising Age*, p. 44.

Gerbner, G. (1978). The dynamics of cultural resistance. In G. Tuchman, A.K. Daniels, & J. Benet (Eds.), *Hearth & home: Images of women in the mass media* (pp. 46-50). New York: Oxford University Press.

Gibson, R. (1988, January 14). Fallon McElligott loses a major client over 'stupid' reply to sexist ad charge. *Wall Street Journal*, p. 18.

Hampden-Turner, C. (1981). *Maps of the mind*. New York: Macmillan.

Harkness, G. (1987, December 21). Is it open season on women? *Minnesota Women's Press*, p. 5.

Hearn, J., & Parkin, W. (1987). *"Sex" at "work": The power and paradox of organisation sexuality*. Brighton, UK: Wheatsheaf.

Hewes, D.E., & Graham, M.L. (1989). Second-guessing theory: Review and extension. In J.A. Anderson (Ed.), *Communication yearbook* (pp. 213-248). Newbury Park, CA: Sage.

Janis, I. L. (1972). *Victims of groupthink*. Boston: Houghton Mifflin.

Keller, M. (1991, January). Fallon McElligott grows up. *Corporate Report Minnesota*, p. 62.

Kiss that job goodbye. (1988, January 25). *Time*, p. 53.

Klein, M. (1980). *Envy, gratitude and other works.* London: Hogarth Press.

Kohl, L. (1987, December 29). Ad annoys, agency offends this feminist. *St. Paul Pioneer Press Dispatch*, p. 10D.

Levin, G. (1990, December 24). Scali taps Fallon to bolster agency after Volvo fiasco. *Advertising Age*, p. 2.

Menton, S. (1988, January 4). Agency finally apologizes: But not before sending Mankato woman offensive letters. *Mankato Free Press*, p. 9.

Miller, A. (1988, January 18). A donnybrook in the ad world: Charges of sexism embroil a hot Minnesota firm. *Newsweek*, p. 55.

Morgan, G. (1986). *Images of organization.* Beverly Hills, CA: Sage.

Noddings, N. (1989). *Women and evil.* Berkeley, CA: University of California Press.

Plato. (1937). *The dialogues of Plato* (3rd ed.). (B. Jowett, Trans.). New York: Random House.

Smith, M.L. (1988, January 2). Woman offended by ad agency's presentation gets a belated apology. *Minneapolis Star Tribune*, p. 1B.

Spender, D. (1984). *Language and power.* Beverly Hills, CA: Sage.

Ugland, E. (1988, January 7). Ad agency taunts MSU feminist. Mankato State University *Reporter*, p. 1.

Wascoe, D., Jr. (1988, January 18). The woman who took on Fallon McElligott–and won. *Minneapolis Star Tribune*, p. 3D.

▼Chapter 6

Sexual Harassment in the Movies and Its Affect on the Audience

Jill Axelrod

American University
Washington, DC

- 1981 survey of female federal employees found that 43% had experienced sexual harassment
- 4 out of 10 women reported experiences of sexual harassment (New York Times/CBS News Poll, as cited in Wolf, 1991)

The law says sexual harassment is illegal, yet it persists in the workplace. Similarly, popular movies portray working women as victims of sexual harassment. While sexual harassment in the workplace is not encouraged, movies tend to endorse it. "Contemporary life is symbolized [sic] to a large degree by the way it is represented in the mass media" (Jamieson, 1985, p. 99). In particular, movies perpetuate the notion that in order for a business woman to be successful, sexual harassment is accepted as part of the job. If movies are truly a reflection of reality as Jamieson suggests, then sexual harassment of professional women in the movies is viewed simply as an act society deems appropriate.

Sexual harassment is the intentional use of words, gestures, and actions which annoy, alarm, or abuse another person in a sexual

I would like to thank Dr. Rhonda Zaharna, Assistant Professor of Communication and Dr. Jack Orwant, Director of the Master's Public Communication program, for their assistance and direction on this project.

way. The issue of sexual harassment is particularly significant today in light of the Thomas/Hill hearings in which allegations of sexual harassment were made against Judge Thomas by Professor Hill, a former employee of his. Professor Hill implied that she took no legal action against Judge Thomas because she was in a tenuous position. As a young, black, educated female, she was trying to establish herself as a professional and did not want to "burn her bridges." Women tend to view Judge Thomas' confirmation as a reaffirmation that the primarily male Senatorial staff who is "representative" of the public perceive charges of sexual harassment as irrelevant. The fact that Professor Hill remained silent for so long is not a unique situation.

Dr. Frances Conley, a Stanford neurosurgeon, left her job in June 1991, after publicly admitting 25 years after the fact, that she was being sexually harassed at work. It is a common trend for women to remain silent about such issues while trying to survive in the male-dominated workplace. When Dr. Conley was asked why she did not report her colleagues, she replied, "I thought I'd be a good neurosurgeon" (Wolf, 1991). In other words, furthering her career seemed more important at the time than risking all that she had worked for to defend herself from her harassers. As Emma Coleman Jordan, a Georgetown University Law professor said, "Keep silent, or risk destroying the hard-won gains of years of education and rigorous training" (Wolf, 1991, p. C2).

The mass media play an influential role in reinforcing sex-role stereotypes. "Sex-role stereotypes are set portrayals of sex-appropriate appearance, interests, skills, behaviors, and self-perceptions" (Benet, Daniels, & Tuchman, 1978, p. 5). This chapter focuses on the content of two movies, *Working Girl* and *Other People's Money*. It examines why sexual harassment shown in these movies is accepted by the masses through the media, as movies continue to portray women as victims, continually acquiescing to male dominance. The acceptance of sexual harassment by the audience is reinforced by several scholars who have examined the dominant male and submissive female stereotypes, as well as the media's effect on the audience and the audience's perception of the media.

WORKING GIRL – POWER AND SUBMISSION

Working Girl stars Tess, a young, attractive female secretary, striving to succeed in the male-dominated investment banking field. A tip from her male boss leads her to a gentleman in the arbitrage department who is looking for an assistant. An "interview" is arranged, and to Tess's surprise, it takes place in a limousine with champagne, drugs, and pornographic movies. Tess quickly discovers that the assistant he is looking for is not the professional assistant position she had in mind. She rebuffs his passes and storms out of the limousine. Angered that her boss set her up as if he were a pimp, Tess retaliates and loses her job. She begins her new job as an assistant to a female boss named Katherine. At a cocktail party, Tess watches as Katherine is sexually harassed by a male colleague. Katherine accepts the colleague's come-on as part of the job; she promises him drinks in return for a business deal. Afterwards, Tess approaches Katherine and states that she would have told the man to leave her alone. Katherine responds, "Never burn bridges, today's junior prick, tomorrow's senior partner."

This statement highlights the acceptance of sexual harassment in the workplace by implying that a successful woman doesn't fight back, but rather accepts such advances as part of her job. As Tess learned in her previous position, to fight back against the harasser is to lose the job. Sexual harassment is demonstrated in various other scenes throughout the movie. Men gawk at women on the street. A male colleague comments (with strong sexual overtones) on Tess's attire. Tess is persistently asked out to dinner by a colleague after she explicitly says no. The movie concludes when Tess finally proves herself to the men by conjuring up a creative and successful business deal. On one hand, Tess is portrayed as a strong woman who refuses her colleagues' sexual advances. On the other hand, her female role model and boss teaches her that sexual harassment can be used to the woman's advantage. A woman wanting to be successful in the male-dominated investment banking field can trade sex for "business deals."

OTHER PEOPLE'S MONEY – PLAYING THE GAME

Other People's Money stars Katie, a young lawyer trying to save her family's business from a takeover by a greedy New York City investor. When Katie first walks into the investor Larry's office, the camera, focusing from Larry's perspective, scans her body from head to toe. Immediately following Larry's "examination" of Katie begins the series of lewd comments and sexual propositions that occur throughout the movie (some of the language is as crude as that allegedly spoken by Judge Thomas to Professor Hill). Katie is not taken aback by Larry's behavior. Rather than drop the case or pass it on to another member in her firm, she sticks with her job and takes full advantage of Larry's advances. She uses her womanhood by teasing Larry with her sexuality. Not only is he interested in taking over her family's business, but he wants to get her into bed and propositions her at every encounter. At the shareholder's meeting where they come face to face over her family's business, Katie loses the battle to save the company, and Larry buys them out.

At this point, Larry thinks he's lost Katie for good. But days later, she calls him and suggests another business deal. Larry is excited about this invitation because he perceives it as another opportunity to get physically involved with Katie. This movie differs from *Working Girl* in that Katie plays the female victim who doesn't defend herself from the harassment. In fact, she's quite similar to Katherine, who accepts harassment as part of a woman's job in a man's world and uses it to what she thinks is her advantage. Ultimately, the audience does not know if Larry actually wins Katie. All that the audience does know is that Katie grants him another opportunity to try.

MALE/FEMALE STEREOTYPES AND
THE DOMINANT MALE/SUBMISSIVE FEMALE

Until recently, movies portrayed women in stereotypical female roles. Men are seen in positions of power, dominating the women. Women were and still are often portrayed in the subservient positions of house-wife, prostitute, "dumb blonde," and victim of sexual violence. More recent movies have taken the women's movement into account. Today's working women have a career and often a family. But as these working women attempt to survive as professionals in a "man's world," they fall prey to sexual harassment from their male counterparts.

Body language is often used to portray females as submissive to males. According to Professor Janet Mills (Mills as cited in Rubinstein, 1990), "men speak a body language that is high in status, power and dominance, while women speak a language of submission, affiliation, and passivity" (p. 93). Mills and Rubinstein suggest that professional women have a difficult role to fulfill. On the one hand, they are supposed to be powerful business people. On the other hand, they are expected to be feminine. Mills and Rubinstein go on to say that the two roles women are expected to play often have different, contradictory rules. Is it feasible for women to maintain their femininity and remain powerful forces in the workplace? As has been shown, Katie demonstrates in *Other People's Money* that a woman can be feminine and powerful, but is still cast as a victim of sexual harassment.

Not only does body language affect the stereotypical image of women, but their position of status is also relevant. Brown, Geis, Jennings, and Corrado-Taylor (1984) suggest that the unequal status relationships between men and women which people view daily in the mass media, at home, and at work perpetuate these stereotypical differences by associating stereotypes with a person's sex, rather than their social role status. Brown et al. discuss the fact that educated people support the equality of men and women on a conscious level, but in day-to-day living, unconscious attention takes over and supports the stereo-typical inequality between men and women.

Perceptions of men and women in positions of high status and low status appear to possess the same trait characteristics as those making up the male and female stereotypes. Men tend to be assigned roles in which they exhibit physical and intellectual power, thus reinforc-ing the stereotype that men are dominant. Women are usually portrayed in roles in which they are dependent on the man, which reinforces the female stereotype of submissiveness and dependency. Based on the male-female stereotypes, a person's status is, therefore, dictated by his or her gender. Furthermore, they suggest that placing women in low-sta-tus roles and men in high-status roles perpetuates the associated male-female stereotypes, thus continuing the cycle. Switching roles, thereby depicting the woman in a high-status role, and the man in the low-status position, alters the sex stereotypes.

A scene in which Larry calls Katie in the middle of the night demonstrates the movie's portrayal of male dominance and female sub-mission. In *Other People's Money*, Larry, in the powerful, dominant posi-tion, stands up while he sings to Katie over the phone. Katie, playing the passive, submissive female, is laying on her bed during this scene. Though Larry cannot see Katie, the audience can, and her posture is typical of the female seductress. While most women would be annoyed at receiving such a call, particularly from a rival business associate, Katie seems to enjoy it.

Mills and Rubinstein (in Rubinstein, 1990) suggest that a woman sitting between two men will constrict her body, giving more room to the men around her. This, too, is symbolic of male dominance and female submission. Such positioning is evident in *Working Girl*. At the critical business meeting where Tess is about to discuss her final business pro-posal, she is seated between two men. She sits with her hands folded in her lap, and her body is constricted. Meanwhile, the men are spread out with their arms on the table, sitting in more relaxed positions. This is rep-resentative of the powerful men and the submissive woman, regardless of the fact that this was Tess's big debut in the business world.

THE MEDIA'S INFLUENCE ON THE AUDIENCE VIA ALIGNMENT WITH SOCIAL GROUPS

Vincent Price (1989) suggests that when people do not have definitive opinions formed on a subject, that subject then becomes a public issue.

He believes that when there is conflict over this public issue, people will align themselves with their respective social groups. For example, on gender-related issues, men will align themselves with the male perspective and women with the female perspective. This alignment results in opposing or exaggerated views of group opinions which, in turn, leads to expressions of personal opinion consistent with these opposing or exaggerated views of group standards. He suggests that the media's role is to try and make sense of these issues by shaping perceptions and exerting influence.

Conflict arises over the issue of sexual harassment because the law says it is an illegal act, yet movies portray working women as recipients of sexual harassment, while the abusive men are never punished. Movies take it one step further when they portray women as using the harassment to their advantage; the advantage being advancement in a company, getting a business deal, or simply keeping the job in lieu of reporting the abuser. Basically, women who retaliate against their abusers are "punished," and women who accept the abuse progress. Surveys conducted during the Thomas/Hill hearings generally showed that professional women believed Professor Hill's allegations. Men tended to side with Judge Thomas, believing it was not in his character to commit such a crime. Moreover, as some people believe, if Judge Thomas did make such comments, why would Professor Hill continue working for him?

The issue is not whether sexual harassment is right or wrong because the law says it is illegal. The conflict arises when the law says such behavior is illegal, yet the movies accept and condone men sexually harassing working women.

According to Price's (1990) theory of alignment, it is the media's role to make sense of issues by shaping perceptions and influencing the viewer. In the case of sexual harassment, the media's influence is that of acceptance. Women viewing sexual harassment in *Working Girl* and *Other People's Money* will relate to Tess, Katherine, and Katie, and will align themselves with the women portrayed in the movies as witnessed by the toleration of sexual harassment as a means of professional survival. Men will align themselves with men in the movies and perceive women as willing participants. They are shown that sexual harassment is part of being a woman who's trying to make it in a man's world, reinforced by the fact that some women will take the abuse as did Katherine and Katie and even use it to their advantage. Neither woman took legal action to put an end to this type of behavior. When Katherine refused to "burn her bridges," she upheld a good working relationship with a male colleague. When Tess fought back, she lost her job. The audience is shown that those women who do retaliate will only hurt themselves.

MEDIA INFLUENCE THROUGH SYNTHETIC EXPERIENCES

"Ubiquitous electric (motion picture) and electronic (television and computers) media manipulate and rearrange not only the content but the processes of communicated experience, thereby shaping how the audience perceives and interprets the physical and social reality depicted" (Funkhouser & Shaw, 1990, p. 75). Through the media, it is possible for the public to be recipients of synthetic experiences. Synthetic experiences are those which a person hasn't personally experienced, but the action or situation is experienced indirectly through the media. Audiences encounter synthetic experiences through movies, TV sitcoms, advertisements, and other forms of mass media. The media take a situation or event and turn it into a "reality" for viewers who otherwise would not have experienced what is being depicted on screen.

Movies portray sexual harassment as acceptable for professional women in today's world, and this affects public opinion. Funkhouser and Shaw (1990) suggest several hypotheses that connect the increase in the depiction of synthetic experience with tendencies evident in our day-to-day life. Their first assertion deals with the fact that technology has led to an increase in audience expectations. Movie producers provide expertly edited scenes, background music, instant replay, slow motion, zoom shots, and various other techniques to provide the best possible final product. Producers use these "special effects" to exert some control over the audience's perception of what is occurring on the screen. Heightened expectations become a problem when, in reality, a situation doesn't occur as it did in the movies. Beer commercials tend to show bikini-clad women with perfect figures drinking their product. The average woman could have a hard time drinking beer and maintaining a perfect figure.

The same idea can be related to sexual harassment in the movies versus the reality of sexual harassment in the workplace. For example, Tess retaliated against her first boss because he sexually harassed her, and she was fired. She quickly finds a new job, and that is the end of the incident. In real life, Professor Hill spoke out against Judge Thomas, and she became a public spectacle. Every humiliating aspect of their conversations became front-page news, and she lost all privacy. The movies portray sexual harassment under the guise that the worst case scenario is that those who take action against their harassers may need to find new employment. But in reality, as evidenced in Professor Hill's case, the real price to pay is becoming headline news.

A viewer who is regularly exposed to a synthetic experience may become desensitized to the real-life incidents. They also suggest the viewer may perceive the experience at face value and assume that what they see is how the situation really exists. In other words, the events depicted in the movies are, to some people, reality. To relate this idea to sexual harassment, the desensitized viewer or the uncritical viewer may not see harassment as abnormal or wrong. In fact, sexual harassment may be perceived as a fact of life for professional women. Tess, Katherine, and Katie were sexually harassed, but were successful in their careers. The harassing behavior did not prevent them from climbing the corporate ladder because they accepted it and did not retaliate. Furthermore, their harassers suffered no ill consequences as a result of their illegal actions.

The women responded to their harassers with humor. Funkhouser and Shaw (1990) suggest that the media's depiction of synthetic events may not only have an effect on public opinion, but can potentially distort cultural views. They call this "societal contamination," which is an overdramatization of a situation or event, leading to distorted views.

Tess, Katherine, and Katie are successful career women, trying to work their way up the corporate ladder. Besides having to prove themselves as successful to their male colleagues, they also have to deal with sexual harassment from those very same colleagues. Danny DeVito, who plays the part of Larry, is a funny man in real life, and this humor is carried over to his movie character as well. He is constantly engaging in unprofessional behavior: groping at Katie, calling her at home in the middle of the night singing love songs, and inviting her to romantic meals. His actions, both verbal and nonverbal, are depicted in a comic manner, through snide remarks and absurd facial gestures. Katie's character is responsive to Larry's suggestive comments, but she never gives in to him. She combats his behavior in a laughable way, by telling him to behave and replying with witty responses. This, in turn, shows harassment as lighthearted and even humorous. If sexual harassment was meant to be taken lightly, it would not be illegal. But the manner in which these movies distort what should be a negative view toward sexual harassment conforms to Funkhouser and Shaw's (1990) idea of social contamination.

GRATIFICATIONS DERIVED FROM INFLUENTIAL MEDIA

Swanson (1987) suggests that "persons are described as motivated by psychological, social and sociocultural influences to use mass media to accomplish particular ends, conceived as 'gratifications'" (p. 238). Gratifications range from gaining knowledge to using the media as a form of relaxation. He further states that "people are thought to have some latitude in interpreting the meaning of messages in order to bend or shape media content in ways that serve their motivations or desires for particular kinds of gratification" (p. 242).

According to Swanson (1987), there is a relationship among the audience's motivation, message attributes, and the audience's interpretation of the content. Swanson suggests that popular media entertainment follows a particular format that is basic to the understanding of the uses and gratifications gained from this type of entertainment. The movie's plot centers around characters, conflict, and resolution. The characters tend to possess qualities either liked or disliked by the audience. The bulk of the plot, or conflict, is based on converging values, and the conclusion, or resolution, is when the "conventional view of virtue and manners usually are affirmed" (p. 247). The intent is for the audience to become a part of the story, and in a sense, "bond" with the characters. If the audience can relate to the movie on a personal level, the theme of the story will then possess real meaning for the audience. In essence, then, the "conventional view of virtue and manners" relayed in the outcome of the story attempts to clarify and reinforce what the audience already knows to be true.

If the media are attempting to influence the audience through alignment with social groups (Price, 1989) and synthetic experiences (Funkhouser & Shaw, 1990), it then follows that the media are able to control, to some degree, the types of uses and gratifications derived from watching particular movies. Following Swanson's (1987) format for popular media entertainment, the uses and gratifications gained by the audience becomes clearer. Women will "bond" with Katie, Tess, and Katherine. These characters represent career women, who possess enviable traits: They are successful, beautiful, and charming, which fulfills the conventional view and/or desire of today's woman. Though sexual harassment is not the focal point of the movies, it occurs throughout. The bond female members of the audience develop with the female movie characters opens the door to the acceptance of sexual harassment. For example, a woman may interpret the message as "if beautiful, successful Katie can endure such behavior from her male counterparts, I can too," or she may perceive sexual harassment as part of a working woman's territory. This may be reinforced by the fact that working women are portrayed as victims in many movies seen today.

Men, on the other hand, will "bond" with the male characters who are cast as handsome and successful in their careers. Sexual harassment of their female counterparts is part of the job. The message interpreted from the male perspective is that "if it is okay for the characters I can relate to in the movies, then it is okay for me."

The resolution of the conflict is the message that sexual harassment is acceptable. The law says it is illegal, yet women put up with it, men get away with it, and everybody wins in the business world. The message is molded to fulfill the viewers' motivations and/or desires, thus resulting in gratification. Gratification is achieved as a result of men and women forming bonds with their respective characters; the resolution is that everyone accomplishes their goals.

SUMMARY

In examining the content of *Working Girl* and *Other People's Money*, sexual harassment is prominent. The manner in which actors and actresses are cast, as the dominant male and submissive female, perpetuate the traditional sex-role stereotypes. Furthermore, these movies tend to endorse sexual harassment in the workplace. Through alignment with social groups and synthetic experiences, the media exert their influence on the subject of sexual harassment, that is, they give their approval. The audience, in turn, derives gratification at the conclusion of the movies when all the characters are winners. In effect, women and men align themselves with their respective gender groups, each viewing sexual harassment from a different perspective, but both groups accepting it. Women see sexual harassment from two angles: (a) speak out and then be fired or ostracized, or (b) accept it and then take advantage of it. If movies continue to portray women giving in to male dominance, thus reinforcing stereotypes, male dominance will continue to be a force in the real world, and sexual harassment will persist.

CONCLUSION

This chapter examined the possibility that sexual harassment, as seen in the movies, may consciously or unconsciously affect the audience's perception of sexual harassment in reality. Men and women who have never given a thought to sexual harassment may see *Working Girl* or *Other People's Money* and not notice that the female characters are being sexually harassed and/or "playing the game." In this case, audience perceptions are being affected on an unconscious level. Equally so, those who are sensitive to the issue of sexual harassment may also be affected by the stereotypical portrayal of women in these movies.

Subsequent to the Thomas/Hill hearings, the issue of sexual harassment has been brought to the public's attention. Perhaps the result will be a higher level of awareness regarding sexual harassment among women and men, both in the office and at the movie theater.

REFERENCES

Benet, J., Daniels, A.K., & Tuchman, G. (1978). *Hearth and home: Images of women in the mass media.* New York: Oxford University Press.

Brown, V., Geis, F., Jennings, J., & Corrado-Taylor, D. (1984). Sex vs. status in sex-associated stereotypes. *Sex Roles, 11,* 771-785.

Funkhouser, G.R., & Shaw, E. (1990). How synthetic experiences shapes social reality. *Journal of Communication, 40,* 75-87.

Jamieson, G.H. (1985). *Communication and persuasion.* London: Croom Helm.

Other people's money. (1991). Norman Jewison, [Producer] Warner Bros.

Price, V. (1989). Social identification and public opinion: Effects of communicating group conflict. *Public Opinion Quarterly, 53,* 197-224.

Rubinstein, G. (1990). Body politics In A. DeVito (Ed.), *Nonverbal communication: A reader,* (pp. 93-98), Prospect Heights, Il: Waveland.

Swanson, D. (1987). Gratification seeking, media exposure, and audience interpretations: some directions for research. *Journal of Broadcasting and Electronic Media, 31,* 237-251.

Wolf, N. (1991, October 13). Feminism and intimidation on the job: Have the hearings liberated the movement? *The Washington Post,* pp. C1 -C2.

Working Girl. (1989). Mike Nichols (Producer) Twentieth Century Fox.

Chapter 7

Sex and the Workplace: Watch Your Behind, or They'll Watch It For You

Mary Helen Brown

Auburn University

Auburn, AL

▼ Sexual harassment is one of the most talked about and least understood areas of organizational communication. Much controversy arises from a lack of understanding as to what exactly constitutes harassment (Gest, Saltzman, Carpenter, & Friedman, 1991; Saltzman & Gest, 1991). The narratives members use to relate organizational experiences may serve as an effective way to uncover and clarify perceptions and definitions of harassment on the job.

This chapter uses a creative narrative to express the experiences of women on the job. Specifically, the chapter: (a) underscores the role of stories as sense makers of organizational experience, (b) describes the utility of the creative narrative as a method of relating impressions of organizations, (c) presents a creative narrative developed from conversations with female professionals, and (d) discusses the conclusions that can be drawn from this narrative account.

STORIES AS SOURCES OF ORGANIZATIONAL INTELLIGENCE

Weick (1979) notes "there are no simple answers and there is no simple finite set of causes for anything that happens in an organization" (p. 246). Instead, members seek to balance or manage information equivocality through continual enactment, selection, and retention of information useful to organizational functioning. Information that has been used effectively is shaped retrospectively into sensible accounts of the activities that have occurred.

In several articles, Fisher (1984, 1985a, 1985b) argues that individuals structure the accounts of their experiences into narrative. Narrative is a key element in organizing and relating perceptions of life experiences. If a story "rings true" and is told competently, it is a persuasive, concrete form of communication considered familiar and credible by receivers.

In focusing specifically on organizations, Weick and Browning (1986) point out that stories are an effective way for members to organize and present complex information. This information then becomes the base of organizational intelligence guiding the course of future organizational events (Kreps, 1990).

Issues surrounding sexual harassment on the job are perceived as having a great deal of equivocality. In theory, sexual harassment exists if unwelcome sexual advances are made a part of employment or interferes with the work environment. In practice, however, sexual harassment is difficult to define, and the resultant definitions differ from worker to worker. Thus, sexual harassment like any other area of organizing is addressed continually and made sense of retrospectively through members' interactions. The accounts developed through this process form the basis of the definitions directing an organization's activities in this area.

Stories—the narratives members tell—have been found to be important sources of organizational information about equivocal events and definitions (Dandridge, Mitroff, & Joyce, 1980; Martin, 1982). Stories provide the reasons and evidence behind the definitions and interpretations at the root of organizational functioning (Brown, 1990). Hawes (1974) argues members use stories to place organizational events into an understandable context. Wilkins (1984) points out that stories make abstract concepts such as sexual harassment more concrete by providing specific, compelling versions of events that took place at some time in the past.

Stories also provide lessons about appropriate organizational conduct in the face of problematic situations (Kelly, 1985). These lessons would be encapsulated in a form that preserves the values of organizational members (Myrsiadis, 1987). For example, a person faced with a situation that could be construed as harassment could rely upon other members' narrative interpretations of similar episodes to: (a) determine whether the events should be considered harassment in the organizational context, and (b) provide guidelines regarding possible responses to the event and how those responses would be viewed in the organization's context.

In addition, stories about issues involving sexual harassment can provide members within organizations and among different organizations with points of bonding and shared experiences. Santino (1983), in a study conducted on the narratives of Pullman porters, found stories served as a common ground of experience. The Pullman porters expressed similar interpretations of events often involving overt or implied racism and/or harassment regardless of their time of employment or the geographic regions in which they served. Stories, then, reinforce an "us versus them" mentality separating "insiders from outsiders" (Harrison, 1987). For women in the workplace, stories may increase understanding of what constitutes sexual harassment by raising awareness of other women's conceptualizations of their experiences. Female members may sense they have experienced something similar to that expressed in the story.

Of course, stories do not exist as unitary entities in the organizational context (Shrivastava, Mitroff, & Alvesson, 1987). Competing, at times conflicting, stories can emerge about the same set of circumstances (Glaser, Zamanov, & Hacker, 1987). For example, an event might be considered harassment by one group, horseplay by another, a normal part of organizational life by a third group, and a misunderstanding by a fourth group. The set of circumstances surrounding the event would be shaped into separate narratives supporting each point of view.

The presence of conflicting narratives need not be viewed negatively or problematically by members. Instead, narratives could serve as organizational barometers of the membership's perceptions of experiences. By bringing together conflicting narratives, an organization's leadership could develop a platform of organizational intelligence from which to shape future policy and perhaps avoid similar issues (Kreps, 1990).

THE CREATIVE NARRATIVE AS A METHOD OF EXPRESSION

This chapter uses the creative narrative as a way to convey female professionals' perceptions of their organizational lives. Creative narratives employ the techniques of fiction writing—including setting, plot, and character development—to present factual content obtained through interviews (Brown & McMillan, 1991). The use of creative narratives has been called for and employed by several scholars to examine organizations through realistic fiction (for example, see Goodall, 1989; Pacanowsky, 1988; Van Maanen, 1988, 1990). The techniques of fiction writing can be used to create a story that "faithfully captures" the experiences of the subjects (Agar, 1990; Brown & McMillan, 1991).

The creative narrative that follows was developed from interviews with 62 members of a business and professional women's association attending their association's regional conference. Those interviewed had from 6 months to 45 years of professional experience. Most had been working for at least 15 years.

The author and a trained assistant conducted the interviews. The audio-taped interviews used open-ended questions focusing on recollections of their professional experiences, their perceptions of what life is like for women in organizations, and their recommendations for women entering their field. At no point did the interviewers mention harassment or request stories. As such, descriptions of harassment presented during the interviews emerged spontaneously.

Using the techniques described by Brown and McMillan (1991), themes were identified among the interview responses. These themes included: the isolation of women in the workplace, overt or subtle sexual advances, exclusion from career tracks, associating job behavior with gender stereotypes, developing different job classifications for men and women, and the notion that all negative job experiences do not necessarily rest in or result from sexual harassment.

The following story is created by using the words of the interviewees to serve as dialogue in a creative narrative communicating the themes above. The characters speak the words of the interviewees in a way that presents the themes covered in the interviews. The names of participants and characters, organizations and locations, have been changed.

WATCH YOUR BACKSIDE, OR THEY'LL DO IT FOR YOU

Jodie had agreed to meet them in the bar, actually the BARROOM, the sign said. She wasn't sure why she came to the conference. She should have been working instead of sitting through training and consciousness-raising groups. The women she'd met that afternoon assured her the meetings might be dull, but the place you really learned anything was over drinks after each day's last session and before the evening banquet.

Jodie was attending her first meeting of the Southeastern Region's Women of the Workplace (WOW) Association. So far in the meetings, she'd heard a lot of theories and advice about what she was supposed to be experiencing as a working woman, but not much of it seemed to apply. She hoped the bar would be different and scanned the room looking for a barely familiar face.

"There she is," a voice boomed through the dark. "Judy, we're back here."

Jodie peered through the dim lighting to a group in a corner amid the paneling and heavy oak furniture and spotted the three women she'd met earlier in the day and a woman who was completely unknown to her. A televised college football game was being waged silently over their heads.

"Introductions all around," said Chris, the most boisterous of the group. "Everybody, this is Judy."

"Jodie."

"Oops, sorry Jodie, I really haven't had that much to drink. Around the table we have Alice, Dorothy, Ellie, and I'm Chris."

"Jodie, we have one rule at this table. No twinkie drinks," Dorothy broke in.

"Pardon."

"It doesn't have to be alcohol; ice tea or Coke is fine, but we will have no pink drinks, no frothy drinks, no drinks named fuzzy anything, and, above all . . ." Chris waited for the others to join her.

"NO UMBRELLAS," they said in chorus.

"No problem, I'll have a draft," Judy said to the server who had wandered over to their table, "I get the feeling you've been coming to these for a while."

"Oh sakes yes," Chris explained, "I've been attending this conference for about 10 years; Ellie, didn't you and I start about the same time?"

"Right, but we're babes in the woods compared to these others."

"Alice and I have been attending these for at least . . . 15 or 20 years," Dorothy added, "And Alice, here, is a past president of this illustrious association."

"We have to work hard to get a word in edgewise with Alice in the group," Chris laughed.

The others joined in; Alice simply smiled.

"We decided we needed somebody new in this crew, and we liked what you had to say in that afternoon session, so welcome to the BARROOM Babes," Chris explained.

"I'm glad that trainer from Atlanta didn't hear that. We'd be lectured `til midnight. Lord, she's intense," Ellie broke in.

"I understand that language has power and that the way people are labeled can be hurtful, but that woman has some kind of a grudge or something," said Dorothy.

"Who hasn't been called honey, sweetie, or boom-chickie-boom-boom?" Ellie said, "Let's all raise our hands."

"My personal favorite is little lady. It's just part of it. I don't think they get it," Dorothy added.

"God, yes, but every now and then you can get even. Chris, tell Jodie about the Bubba who wanted the loan."

"You're going to love this. I'm a vice-president at the bank, and one of my responsibilities is approving high-risk loans. Anyway, my secretary had called in sick one day, and of course, all hell had broken loose, so I'm in the outer office digging through the files looking for who knows what, and in walks some big guy I now refer to as Bubba the Great. I've got one of those names so you don't know what I am, and Bubba the Great apparently didn't think a female human being would be handling money. All that math don't you know. So Bubba sees me behind the secretary's desk and says, `Darlin', me and old Chris need to tend to some bidness. So why don't you take your sweet self down the hall and bring us some coffee?'"

Gasps and laughs all around the table.

"I didn't say a word. I sent him in my office and asked him to wait. Then I went down the hall, put two cups of coffee and the fixings on a tray, and proceeded to take them in the office. I went around to my side of the desk and said, `Darlin', I'm Chris Bolton. So why don't you tell me why I should give your sweet self a loan.' You should have seen him shrink."

Everyone laughed, and Jodie asked, "Did he learn his lesson?"

"Bubbas are exempt from lessons."

Jodie responded, "What do you think about the conference?"

Alice answered, "Other than having presenters who watched too much of those Thomas/Hill congressional hearings, it's been pretty good."

"We are getting an awful lot about harassment this time around," Dorothy added. "I'm not saying it doesn't go on, but I'm not sure a bunch of women sitting around talking about it is going to help much. Seems to me that the men ought to be hearing about this. And things have improved so much. When I first started working at Williams Oil Company back in the 60s, I was sitting in a room with about seven or eight men. They were all bookkeepers; I was a secretary. And, they made about four times as much as I did for doing the same thing. Well, really they were doing less. I was busy typing well reports like they were supposed to be doing, and they would be sitting around talking about the ball game that weekend or throwing spit wads."

"Throwing spit wads? Full grown adult men?" Ellie asked.

"I'm not kidding. They had perfected the spit wad portion of their job description. I asked my boss about it, and he said he knew what was going on, but men couldn't be classified as secretaries, and women couldn't be classified as bookkeepers. And the salary scale for bookkeepers was higher than the salary scale for secretaries. I couldn't believe it. It's harder for them to get away with that now, but some of them come up with a way."

"I hear that."

"Amen."

Alice spoke up, "It seems to me that there are more women in management these days. When I first started at the textile plant, I remember feeling so isolated. The managerial offices were on the third floor of the plant. The work area was huge and took up the entire front two-thirds of the building. To get to the offices you had to go through the building, climb up some metal stairs at the back, and then go in the office area. Like I said, I was the first female manager to work there and hardly anyone would talk to me, but the worst part was that there was only one bathroom in the office area, and it was, guess what, a men's room. The women's room was in the plant area with the textile workers, halfway to the front. So every time I needed to go, I had to climb down the stairs, go halfway through the work area, tend to my business, go back through the work area, and climb back up the stairs. Talk about a long, lonely walk where everybody knows where you're going."

"God, how awful, but we're getting them back now," Chris responded, "We've taken over about 90% of the rest rooms in this hotel. I love those WO post-it notes stuck in front of the MEN."

"Talking about the bathroom reminds me of something that's going on at work," Ellie ventured.

"The conversation is deteriorating rapidly," Chris chuckled, "Ellie, I don't think Jodie knows your full name."

"Oh, goodness, Ellie, you must tell her," Dorothy noted.

"Eleanor Roosevelt Watson, thank you. My parents were proud Democrats. I'm lucky they didn't name me after their very favorite. I could as easily be Harriet Truman Watson."

The others laughed.

"Back to your story."

"Have I told you about the aphrodisiac copy machine?"

"No, and I think we'd remember it," Alice replied, chuckling.

"Now, wait. Don't get me wrong. I'm charmed and intrigued, but what does this have to do with bathrooms?" Chris sputtered.

"You know how they say women go to the bathroom in groups?"

"Yes," they responded.

"In our office we go to the copy room in a group. Golly, this is so nasty, but as long as we're talking about sex and all, you know in that movie with Lily Tomlin and Dolly Parton where the giant copier spits copies out all over Jane Fonda?"

Everyone nods or says "umm."

"Our company has one of those monstrosities and it's off in a room all to itself. I don't know how to put this, but whenever a woman goes in there by herself, the department head follows her, and . . . oh how should I put this? Becomes visibly . . . uh . . . aroused and . . . uh . . . er . . .

fondles himself."

"You're kidding."

"No, I'm not. He doesn't really do anything . . . other than to stand real close . . . and uh, well, you know."

"Oh, that's sick."

"Really, he doesn't do anything like that until the copier is running. And then it's well . . . I don't know . . . maybe it's the collating."

Everybody bursts out laughing.

"There isn't really anything we can do. Who do you tell when it's the boss? So we all go to the copier en masse. I don't care what's going on. If you need a copy, about six women will drop whatever they're doing and go with you. We look like the last episode of *Mary Tyler Moore* going through the hall to the room. Something about the numbers dampens his enthusiasm."

"Well that just beats all."

"Lesson Number One: You better watch your backside, or they'll do it for you."

"I don't think it would be any problem answering that one on that `Is This Harassment' quiz we took."

"My boss doesn't do anything like that," Jodie interjected, "but he does something that bothers the heck out of us."

"Do tell."

"He's this great big guy. I don't know. About six-five or so and pretty heavy. But when you disagree with him, which isn't hard because he's not real bright, he comes and stands over you real close and towers over you and speaks in this condescending voice and basically tries to intimidate you into agreeing with him or doing what he says. He only does this with women."

"Your basic bully. He's probably afraid a man would come back at him."

"Right. It makes you uncomfortable. But there's this one woman, Jennifer, who worked in the office and has more nerve than I would ever have, and one day he was pulling this stunt on her, and she said, `Frank, as close as you're standing to me all I have to do is raise my knee and you'll be looking up at me, and we'll see how you like it."

"Way to go Jennifer."

"What happened?"

"Before long he transferred her to headquarters. She got a raise and a promotion, but she had to move, and she wasn't happy about that. He did it because he was scared of her and wanted her out of his office. He couldn't find a reason to fire her, and he was probably too embarrassed to tell the boys about it."

"Male boss harassed by female employee. Details at 11:00," Chris chuckled, "I bet he didn't know what hit him."

"Have any of you worked for anyone who made sex a part of the job? Do it or else?" Alice asked.

"No, but I've heard enough about it."

"I haven't either, but one place I worked as a loan officer we had this one supervisor who blamed everything on out-of-control hormones. 'It must be that time of the month,' he'd say to almost everything. Oh, did that get old," Chris explained. "One Christmas, a lot of the female loan officers and almost all of the female tellers got together and bought him this really nice leather-bound appointment calendar. All through it we randomly circled days in red as period warnings and told him that was so he'd know when to avoid us."

"Oh my God, Chris, you didn't."

"Absolutely, and it shut him up pronto."

"Really, though, don't you think some of this harassment stuff gets out of hand," Dorothy said, "In our office we had a woman file a suit because she said she was being sexually harassed. Hell, she was being harassed because she was new."

"What do you mean?"

"Whenever there's a new person, whether it's male or female, red or yellow, black or white, we break them in with this little trick. One of the first staff meetings we have with the new person somebody says, 'did anyone bring the regmacarps we need to include with the proposal we're sending out?'"

"The what?"

"Regmacarps, they're dried fruit or something. The new person has no idea what they are, but you'd be amazed how they sit there like they do. So, the person running the meeting sends the new person to the supply room after the regmacarps."

"I love it. A company snipe hunt."

"Exactly. But this one woman went back to the supply closet. She was gone forever and finally came back with an antique box of carbon paper; it was so old the label was gone. I don't know how far down she had to dig, but she must have never seen any, and that was the only thing without a name, so regmacarps they were. When she came back wagging that ratty old box, everybody died laughing."

"I take it she was not amused."

"Amused . . . she filed a damn sex harassment complaint with the main office."

"You've got to be kidding."

"I'll admit she was being harassed, but it wasn't sex harassment. Some people can't take a joke. We all got called in and had to testify about the regmacarps and how just about everybody who came through that office went to look for the regmacarps. That it was a kind of an initiation ritual and all. Then we all had to sit through a lecture about how we should be more sensitive to the feelings of our co-workers and not send them to look for imaginary objects. Then we all had to write a formal apology to her—Dear Ms. So-and-so . . . Please accept my apology for my role in the unfortunate regmacarp incident."

"Unbelievable," Alice reflected, "There has to be a point where we're too sensitive."

"Or people need to grow up and get real," Chris added.

"And it's so hard to tell what's what these days with all this stuff going on," Alice added, "About the best I can do is tell my people if you wouldn't say or do it or wouldn't want it done to your wife, daughter, girl-friend, mamma, or grandmamma, it's probably harassment. But God only knows what some of them would do to their mammas."

"Isn't it so? But now it's time for me to go up and put on my power party clothes for the banquet," Ellie said, "Time flies when you're having drinks. Jodie, it's been a pleasure. I hope to see you later."

The group dispersed and the women went to their rooms to pre-pare for the next scheduled event. Jodie was finally glad she attended the conference, but wondered why more of it couldn't be this much fun.

CONCLUSIONS

The women in the BARROOM have much to say about sexual harass-ment. They point out harassment is indeed a problem and it exists in many forms. Some forms are overt—the manager in the copy room, the boss who blamed PMS for organizational problems, the different pay scale for bookkeepers and secretaries, and Bubba the Great. Other forms are more subtle—the manager who would physically attempt to intimidate female workers and the long walk to the women's room. No matter what form it takes, harassment is seen as harmful and as making the organization an unpleasant place to conduct business.

What's more, the women present coping strategies to handle these situations. For the most part, effective strategies are seen to employ ingenuity and some humor in turning the tables on the offender. The loan officer followed "Bubba's" lead and illustrated the folly of expecting a man to be doing a certain job. The bank workers presented their boss with a PMS schedule to alert him that his observation not only was not funny, but was, in fact, boring and offensive. Other solutions employ some form of power. Jennifer demonstrated she could retaliate physically if she chose. The women working for the Romeo of the copy room joined together to thwart his advances.

Further, the women in the story prefer these responses over the more officially sanctioned approaches, such as sensitivity training, consciousness-raising quizzes, and filing complaints, employed in the seminars they attended. Women, they report, should not be overly sensitive to language or actions in the workplace. The "get real" response to the complaint filed about the regmacarp hunt typifies the views of women who have faced harassment through their careers and have little regard for a co-worker who resorts inappropriately to formal channels to get revenge for her embarrassment. As noted, informal responses exhibiting creativity were more valued by this group.

However, the women acknowledge that while conditions may have improved and that ways exist to deal with harassment, problems remain. Jobs are still classified differently for men and women, often resulting in salary differences. Women must deal with demeaning language and unsavory characters. Also, while none interviewed reported personal experience with overt sexual advances, many implied it was a part of being a woman in an organization. Despite their boisterousness in relating some of their victories, the women's responses reflect a degree of resignation and concern that conditions persist despite training, news reports, legal advances, and the like. Further, the problems exist over a wide range of professions and organizations.

A creative narrative such as the one above may address these concerns. The story presents perceived problems and possible solutions in a way that is nonthreatening. Situations are familiar enough so that men and women may recognize similar situations in their workplace and begin to address them appropriately. Stories convey the information in a more vivid way than would be found in a training manual and thus may spur more conversation among organizational members about the presence and implications of harassing conditions in their workplace.

As noted, stories have power. Perhaps this story will have the power to begin addressing the problems associated with harassment in professional settings.

REFERENCES

Agar, M. (1990). Text and fieldwork: Exploring the excluded middle. *Journal of Contemporary Ethnography, 19,* 73-88.

Brown, M. H. (1990). Defining stories in organizations: Characteristics and functions. In J. A. Anderson (Ed.), *Communication yearbook 13* (pp. 162-190). Newbury Park, CA: Sage.

Brown, M. H., & McMillan, J. J. (1991). Culture as text: The development of an organizational narrative. *Southern Communication Journal, 57,* 49-60.

Dandridge, T. C., Mitroff, I. I., & Joyce, W. F. (1980). Organizational symbolism: A topic to expand organizational analysis. *Academy of Management Review, 5,* 77-82.

Fisher, W. R. (1984). Narration as human communication paradigm: The case of public moral argument. *Communication Monographs, 51,* 1-22.

Fisher, W. R. (1985a). The narrative paradigm: An elaboration. *Communication Monographs, 52,* 347-367.

Fisher, W. R. (1985b). The narrative paradigm: In the beginning. *Journal of Communication, 35,* 74-89.

Gest, T., Saltzman, A., Carpenter, B., & Friedman, D. (1991, October 21). Harassment: Men on trial. *U.S. News and World Report,* pp. 38-40.

Glaser, S. R., Zamanov, S., & Hacker, K. (1987). Measuring and interpreting organizational culture. *Management Communication Quarterly, 1,* 173-198.

Goodall, H. L. (1989). *Casing a promised land.* Carbondale: Southern Illinois Press.

Harrison, T. M. (1987). Frameworks for the study of writing in organizational contexts. *Written Communication, 4,* 3-23.

Hawes, L. C. (1974). Social collectives as communication: Perspective on organizational behavior. *Quarterly Journal of Speech, 60,* 497-502.

Kelly, J. W. (1985). Storytelling in high tech organizations: A medium for sharing culture. *Journal of Applied Communication Research, 13,* 45-58.

Kreps, G. L. (1990). Stories as repositories of organizational intelligence: Implications for organizational development. In J. A. Anderson (Ed.), *Communication yearbook 13* (pp. 191-202). Newbury Park, CA: Sage.

Martin, J. (1982). Stories and scripts in organizational settings. In H. A. Hasdorf & A. M. Isen (Eds.), *Cognitive social psychology* (pp. 255-305). New York: Elsevier-North Holland Press.

Myrsiadis, L. S. (1987). Corporate stories as cultural communications in the organizational setting. *Management of Communication Quarterly, 1,* 84-120.

Pacanowsky, M. E. (1988). Slouching towards Chicago. *Quarterly Journal of Speech, 74,* 453-467.

Saltzman, A., & Gest, T. (1991, November 18). Your new civil rights. *U.S. News & World Report,* pp. 93-95.

Santino, J. (1983). Miles of smiles, years of struggle: The negotiation of black occupational identity through personal experience narratives. *Journal of American Folklore, 96,* 393-412.

Shrivastava, P., Mitroff, I. I., & Alvesson, M. (1987). Nonrationality in organizational actions. *International Studies of Management and*

Organization, 17, 90-109.

Van Maanen, J. (1988). *Tales of the field: On writing ethnography.* Chicago: University of Chicago Press.

Van Maanen, J. (1990). Great moments in ethnography: An editor's introduction. *Journal of Contemporary Ethnography, 19,* 3-7.

Weick, K. E. (1979). *The social psychology of organizing.* Reading, MA: Addison-Wesley Publishing Company.

Weick, K. E., & Browning, L. D. (1986). Argument and narration in organizational communication. *Journal of Management, 12,* 243-259.

Wilkins, A. L. (1984). The creation of cultures: The role of stories and human resource systems. *Human Resource Management, 23,* 41-60.

Sexual Harassment on the College Campus

▼Chapter 8

The Power Game: Sexual Harassment on the College Campus

Kay E. Payne
Western Kentucky University
Bowling Green, KY

▼ Title VII of the Civil Rights Act of 1964 established that sex discrimination is illegal and that sexual harassment constituted sex
discrimination. Title IX of the Education Amendments of 1972
prohibits sex discrimination in educational institutions that receive federal funds. Yet, cases involving this type of discrimination have fallen
through the cracks. New legislation promoting anti-discrimination
statutes forces, even coerces, universities who receive any federal
money for any program to respond to all complaints of sexual harassment (Blum, 1988). This legislation represents a major victory for those
who have been struggling with matters of sexual harassment.

Singer (1989) reports that out of the many college students who
experience some form of sexual harassment every year, only 2% to 3%
of them report it. Students at one small university report that as high as
89% of women experienced sexual harassment at least once and that
many experienced it more than once (Mazur & Percival, 1989). (Men
also reported an 85% incidence of sexual harassment, but they perceive
and react to it differently than do women. Since men see sex as ego-
connected, and largely associated with the image of being macho, sexual harassment by a female professor assumes an enhancing rather than
destroying phenomenon. Because of the difference in response to sexual harassment, male professors as harassers and female students as
victims are the focus of this chapter.) The increasing problem ranges

from the use of sexual humor and innuendo, to comments about how a person dresses, to physical threats and sexual assaults. The effects of sexual harassment include emotional problems (Backhouse & Cohen, 1981; Gutek, 1985), physical problems (Hadjifotious, 1983), psychological problems (Crull, 1980; Tangri, Burt, & Johnson, 1982), and reduced performance (Crull, 1982).

Sexual harassment is not always recognizable because men's perceptions of what their behavior means are vastly different from women's (Fitzgerald, 1986). Involving complex two-way messages with intentions of accomplishing multiple and incompatible goals, sexual harassment is exacerbated by an imbalance of power (Bingham & Burleson, 1989). For example, the harasser may see himself as intending to exercise his power over women, protect his professional turf, enhance his macho self-image, and demonstrate his friendliness and helpfulness. The harassee may want to stop the harassment, deter future incidents, preserve her reputation, avoid retaliation, maintain rapport with her professor, and preserve self-respect, physical safety, and psychological well-being (Backhouse & Cohen, 1981; Bingham, 1988; Farley, 1978). While the harassee may want to stop it, she feels she cannot stop it because she does not understand the processes; therefore, she feels she has to go along with it. Sexual harassment involves unwelcome sexual advances, requests for sexual favors, and other verbal or physical conduct of a sexual nature (Johnson, 1983). Sexual harassment on the college campus by a professor implies an abuse of power. Even if the woman engages in sex willingly with her professor, does not report it to his supervisor, and does not lose any tangible benefit, the view by the American Association of University Professors is that, at best, he has breached his professional ethics.

This chapter argues that the formal structure of society reflects the myths of the environment rather than the demands of task activities. Since sexual harassment is a power issue rather than a sexual one (Mackinnon, 1979), power myths about men and women are described. This chapter examines the messages in four sexual harassment reports from women. Since the reports exhibit only a one-sided perception of the situation, only women's communication about the incident will be examined.

The power myths about men and women suggest that a sort of contest occurs during sexual harassment. Contests involve play, and play suggests that all those participating have a clear appreciation that play is occurring. Bateson (1955) describes the play of animals, indicating that they signal one another that play will begin, then playfully stalk, chase, and attack each other. On some other signal, the play stops. A well-known type of "guided doing" (Bateson, 1955, p.170) occurs. But, in the case of playing, if more than one participant is involved, then all must be freely willing to play. Everyone must understand the rules of play and have the power to refuse an invitation to play or to terminate the play once it has begun. In the case of sexual harassment, men appear to be playing a game in which women feel confused, feel unclear about the rules, and feel threatened by the more dominant participant. Women, however, who understand it as play and "roll with it" or harass right back are often described by men as fitting in better. But, in an unmatched contest, knowing when to quit remains the responsibility of the stronger player. The stronger player is the one who has the most power in the situation. The sexual harassment cases in this research indicate that the harassers "keyed" the women or signaled them that "play" was about to begin and that the women did not understand the rules of the game.

Willingness to play often determines who participates in a contest. Social judgment-involvement theory of persuasion (Sherif, Sherif, & Nebergall, 1965) has two key concepts, both of which are internally based in the receiver. The first of these concepts, anchor points or internal reference points, which each holds internally, are used when we make judgments about people or actions. We turn to our internal reference points and compare the information regarding the judgment with the relevant anchor points. You make your judgment only in reference to your anchors. The second part of the theory indicates that a concept may fall within a person's latitude of acceptance, of noncommitment or rejection. The theory predicts that receivers act extremely vulnerable to persuasion within their latitude of acceptance, are open to persuasion about concepts in their latitude of noncommitment, and are almost immune from persuasion in their latitude of rejection. The reports reveal at which latitude each woman reacted to the sexual harassment within the context of persuasion.

MYTHS ABOUT MEN AND WOMEN

Historically, humans have found life bewildering. To cope with confusion, uncertainty, and chaos, humans create a variety of symbols. To understand social problems, communication researchers have begun using symbolic artifacts, such as myths, to describe beliefs that bind people together and explain their worlds (Meyer & Rowan, 1978). Social structures cause rationalized rules which emerge from myths that may be irrational. Subsequently, myths become legitimized in the structure, and the rules and the structure perpetuate the myth. Once a myth becomes legitimized, humans accept it unquestioningly. Several myths about men, women, and power help to explain sexual harassment. After describing the power issue involved in sexual harassment, this chapter examines four myths associated with sexual harassment including: the looking-and-touching myth, the failure-to-report myth, the macho-man myth, and the consenting-adult myth.

Power

An ancient biblical myth describes the role of power in a sexual exchange. In Genesis 9:20-25 (Tyndale, 1971), an incident about Noah and his three sons sets up the power hierarchy in which Noah was seen naked by one of his sons. As a consequence, Noah cursed the son who saw him naked for the remainder of his life and for all the lives of that sons' descendants. The myth behind the power hierarchy, demonstrated in this episode, suggests that if someone saw you naked, you became vulnerable to them, perhaps because they "knew" you in a private way and consequently they gained power over you. In the Genesis episode, the strong belief in the myth threw the hierarchal power structure of the family out of balance. Sexual harassment can be viewed in this way, especially when it is seen as a power issue (MacKinnon, 1979) and understood in terms of this power hierarchy. If the path to power is through education, as our culture has for a long time claimed, then the established power hierarchy, held by males, is threatened because women have been admitted into the educational process.

The Looking-and-Touching Myth

When one person has access to another person's body, but the first person is not allowed the same privilege in return, touch becomes an indicator of status (Pearson, Turner, & Todd-Mancillas, 1991). Further, when a person's space is violated without permission, individuals frequently experience discomfort. Women tend to need smaller personal-space zones than do men (Hall & Sandler, 1984), so this may also be an indicator of status. When males and females view themselves with differing status, the rule which emanates from the looking and touching myth is that it is allowable for the person with higher status to touch and violate personal space, while the other does not feel free to reciprocate. Touching, therefore, may be viewed negatively by the individual who does not feel free to reciprocate. Looking, though much more subtle, extends the concept of touching, much like in the hierarchy episode of Genesis between Noah and his son. Looking and touching messages, then, subtly act as power plays; threatening sexual moves toward female students intensify the power message. Sexual harassment, therefore, acts in a gatekeeping role.

Failure to Report

Another myth suggests that if after an action occurs there is no punishment, then the action must have been acceptable behavior. Since women fail to report cases of sexual harassment, men deduce that nothing is wrong when, in fact, women may fail to report sexual harassment because they have been socialized to believe that their role acts as complementary (Watzlawick, Beavin, & Jackson, 1967) to the male harassers. In other words, women see themselves as of a different status, within the confines of male-female interactions. The socialization process suggests that women and men speak differently from each other (Lakoff, 1975), and among those differences females exhibit a more submissive, nurturing, unassertive style of communication. Also, the socialization process suggests that womens' communication lacks full confidence in the truth of their claims, consistent with the notion that their communication lacks power (Markel, Long & Saine, 1976; Shuy, 1969; Strainchamps, 1971). Dzeich and Weiner (1984) claim that they fail to report sexual harassment because they have feelings of powerlessness. Kramarae (1981) suggests that women believe certain kinds of communication, such as strong self-expression, exist outside of their role. She further says, that as women buy into that kind of socialization, they become members of a "muted group" (Kramarae, 1981, p. 1). So, when women do not speak up, or do not wish to stir up trouble, they demonstrate their membership in the "muted group." Additionally, women believe that no one would listen anyway. Or possibly, they may not know how to go about reporting such an incident. Male professors may believe, then, that since no one has complained, they must not be guilty.

Avoidance of reporting strategies simply indicate that students become sensitized to the power imbalance. Also, women predicted that if they reported the incident, the harasser would be less likely to stop the harassing behavior and more likely to retaliate against the victim (Bingham & Burleson, 1989). Most sexual harassment policies suggest that the first step in dealing with harassment is for the victim to confront the offender and simply ask him to stop. One woman reported that the process of confronting her harasser frightened her so much that she put her words in memo form because she could not speak them. When she confronted the harasser with the memo, she sat a moment, then ran to the restroom with a bloody nose. Her experience demonstrates how stressful it can be to confront the harasser. In fact, women often defend themselves against harassment with humor or by sidestepping the issue rather than confronting it head on.

138 Payne

The Macho-Man Myth

Men often perceive sexual moves toward a woman as just part of the macho self-image. The macho-man myth suggests that men must be involved with women sexually in order to think of themselves as "real men." Within this myth men also believe that they do not become real men until they have had their first sexual experience with a woman. Consistent with this myth is the notion that the male sex drive, once aroused, should not be denied. In fact, the myth holds that men are not capable of sexual restraint. Women in America have typically been assigned the responsibility of saying "no" or "stop" to men when they advance sexually (Rogers & Shoemaker, 1971), while that may not be true in other cultures. Men often excuse and defend one another when accused of wrongful sexual conduct by saying, "After all, they're only human." Dzeich and Weiner (1984) say that such an attitude suggests that man is at the mercy of his genitals.

Consenting Adult

Occasionally, women students find male faculty attractive. The professorial role holds attraction because it combines intellectual attainment and power (Dzeich & Weiner, 1984). The consenting-adult myth suggests that when one finds such a role/person attractive, sex follows. Since an unequal relationship exists, the power disparity creates a situation in which, even if the female student has sex with her male professor, she might not have done so were the person a peer. The consenting-adult myth seldom mentions "that true consent demands full equity and full disclosure" (Dzeich & Weiner, 1984, p. 75). Equity involves the option to leave (Kidder, Fagan, & Cohen, 1978), but, since female students need a grade, they see themselves as trapped. Full disclosure rarely occurs. Male professors seldom tell how many times it has happened before, or what their intentions are. They simply allow the naive student to believe she is special.

CASES

The following four stories appeared in *The Lecherous Professor* (Dzeich & Weiner, 1984)[1] and demonstrate the subtleties of sexual harassment. The stories incorporate concepts of "keying," suggest social rules devel-

[1]Reprinted from *The Lecherous Professor* by Billie Wright Dzeich. Copyright 1984 by Billie Wright Dzeich. Reprinted by permission of Beacon Press.

oped by myths, and reveal the levels of acceptance or rejection of the persuasion offered by the male professors. These four stories exhibit varying harassment behaviors and responses.

Case 1

I knew that this professor chased his students so when he started flirting with me in class, I just ignored it. I didn't want anything to do with all that, and it made me nervous. But, one day after class he sort of cornered me as I was leaving. He backed me up against the wall and was touching me and telling me that he wanted me. He was almost shaking and very intense. I was trying to figure out how to get out of there without an awful scene. He started telling me how his wife didn't like oral sex and he felt frustrated because he had so much to give and wanted to give it to me. He was sweating and shaking and said, "I have a magic tongue. That used to be my nickname." I couldn't believe it. I was frightened by him and wanted to laugh at the same time. I pulled away and ran out of the classroom. It still seems a little funny, but he stalks me in the halls and it's still scary to me. (p. 10)

Case 2

Dr. _____asked me to come to his office to help him rearrange his books. Maybe it was my fault for going in the first place. He has these high bookcases, and the only way you can reach them is to stand on this little stool. I remember I had on this blue tight skirt that made it hard for me to step off and on that stool, but the skirt was pretty long. After a while, he got up and walked over and started bumping the stool. At first I thought he was just kidding around, and I laughed. Then I got sort of scared because he almost knocked me over. I told him to be careful and that I didn't think he knew I was really scared. "I know you are, but the only way to keep from falling is for you to go about your business while I lay down on the floor here and watch you." I think that's exactly how he said it. I didn't know what else to do. I was afraid to leave, so I just kept on taking books down while he laid on the floor and looked up my dress at my underpants. Then I left, and he said thank you and never ever mentioned anything about it again. I guess I should have reported him to somebody, but I didn't know who. No one would have believed it anyway. (p. 10)

Case 3

I had a typing teacher who used to come up and sit by me when I was typing and touch the side of my breast. He'd make rude comments about my behind and he usually made it a point to pinch me. He'd keep me after class to discuss a paper or show me areas where I needed help. I was an A student, but he always wanted me to stay. If I said no, he'd get very defensive. I was afraid he might not give me the A I deserved. The final straw was when I had gotten ink on my sweater from the typing ribbon and he offered to help me get it off. Well, he put his hands up my shirt, feeling me up, and I pushed him away and yelled. I told my parents, and they said I should go to the Dean. I had my boyfriend come and wait for me after class. I didn't want to start trouble, so I didn't say anything. I decided to change my program and not to have him for a teacher anymore. Even though I wanted to tell the Dean, I was afraid it would just mean more trouble. (p. 9)

Case 4

Well, my freshman year I took a class. I didn't understand all of the readings, and by the time the final came around I found myself with an F. So I asked (my professor) him if I could talk to him about my grades, in his office. So I went to his office and he gave me a choice—either be with him or take the F. I was attracted to him a little, but there was no way I could take the F. So, I met him at his house, and I spent three hours with him in his bed. I had to close my eyes and pretend that I was with my boyfriend. I felt dirty, but I didn't get the F. He gave me a D. Was it worth it? Yes and no. I felt it was something I had to do to save myself. (p. 59-60)

UNDERSTANDING THE RULES OF PLAY

In attempting to understand sexual harassment as involving power not sex, we can begin to view it as play or a contest, and we transform what is serious into something playful. In so doing, we can establish certain rules for play, much like play in an arena rather than a street fight, where no rules operate. The following rules apply to play:

1. All those involved in play seem to have a clear appreciation that it is play that is going on.

2. The goal of play is not serious, there is no reward except that of winning.
3. The sequence of activity that serves as a pattern can be practiced, but unpredictable.
4. The stronger and more competent participant restrains him- or herself sufficiently to be a match for the weaker and less-competent player.
5. A great deal of repetitiveness occurs in play.
6. When more than one participant is involved, all must be freely willing to play.
7. Anyone has the power to refuse an invitation to play or to terminate the play once it has begun.
8. Frequent role switching occurs during play, resulting in a mix up of the dominance order.
9. All statements uttered during play are inherently untrue.
10. Signs are available to mark the beginning and termination of playfulness.

These rules of play have been adapted from Loizos rules of play in mammals (Jewell & Loizos, 1966). The important point for harassment participants is that both members understand the rules of play.

Keying

All of these cases have some elements in common. For example, in all four cases the women were "keyed" or signaled or invited to play, but they denied what was really happening. The women were "keyed" as follows: in the first case, "he flirted with me"; in the second, "he asked me to come to his office to rearrange his books" (not a normal request); in the third, when she was typing he touched the side of her breast; in the fourth, the "keying" is a blatant ultimatum "either be with him or take the F", but a mutual attraction suggests an earlier more subtle keying may have occurred.

The second part of game playing involves understanding the rules of the game. The cases indicate the women's varying levels of understanding. In the first case, the woman did not appear to understand the rules of the game as indicated by her comments: "I just ignored it"; "It made me nervous"; "I was frightened." The second case is similar to the first: "I thought he was just kidding around"; "I laughed"; "I got sort of scared"; "I didn't think he knew I was scared"; "I didn't know what else to do." In the third case, the woman seemed to play along with the professor: "I had a typing teacher who used to come up and sit by me when I was typing"; "He always wanted me to stay." When the intensity of the game escalated she caught on and refused to continue to play as indicated by her report: "The final straw." In the fourth case, the woman understood the rules of the game as indicated: "He gave me a choice"; "There was no way I could take the F"; "I met him at his house"; at which time she created a new game, "I had to close my eyes and pretend that I was with my boyfriend." The varying levels of understanding suggest differing knowledge of the rules of sexual game playing.

SOCIAL RULES DEVELOPED BY MYTHS

The looking-and-touching myth acts to extend the power disparity between men and women. Speaking words that shock and embarrass act to extend the myth. The cases indicate how the male professors shocked and embarrassed their victims as they wielded their power. For example, in the first case, "and was touching me"; "telling me he wanted me"; "his wife didn't like oral sex"; and "I have a magic tongue"; in the second case, "[he] looked up my dress at my underpants"; in the third case, "he'd make rude comments about my behind"; "pinch me"; "touch the side of my breast"; "put his hands up my shirt, feeling me up"; and in the fourth case, "be with him or take the F." Each example may be demonstrating the gatekeeping role played by the professor in an attempt to keep the power hierarchy in balance.

The failure to report suggests that nothing is wrong and extends the power imbalance. Male professors may believe, then, that since no one reported the incident, they got away with it. None of the stories in this research indicate that the women reported the professors to their superiors. The women communicate their nonreporting in these ways: in the first case, "he [still] stalks me in the halls"; in the second, "I guess I should have reported him to somebody"; in the third, "I wanted to tell the Dean, I was afraid it would just mean more trouble"; and in the fourth case, she simply made no report.

Some men still perpetuate a macho self-image by "scoring" with women. The implication of this myth involves a social rule which says that if the woman does not say no, then the man will advance until stopped. The myth acts to excuse men by suggesting that they cannot help themselves; it is beyond their control. The cases show examples of this: in the first case, "I ran out of the classroom"; in the second case, she did not stop the action; in the third case, "I pushed him away"; and in the fourth, she did not stop the action. The first case also suggests that this particular man was completely out of control, "he was sweating and shaking."

The consenting-adult myth suggests that when one feels attraction for a role or person, sex follows. When mixed with the game theory, as suggested by our discussion on keying, the power disparity creates a situation in which, even if the student has sex with the professor, she might not have done so were the person a peer. Since the women need a grade, the professors, in a sense, "trap their prey." Examples of the sense of being trapped are explained by the women: in the first case, "He sort of cornered me"; "He backed me up against the wall"; in the second case, "The only way to keep from falling is for you to go about your business while . . . "; in the third case, "he'd keep me after class"; "I was afraid he might not give me the A I deserved"; "I didn't want to start trouble"; in the fourth case, "I felt it was something I had to do to save myself." These examples suggest that the female students did not understand that their professors could receive punitive repercussions for such behavior. The system had not clarified to these women that such behavior was unacceptable to the governing body. Such information dissemination acts to clarify the "rules of the game," for both women and men.

SOCIAL JUDGMENT-INVOLVEMENT

As suggested by the social-judgment-involvement theory, one will make a judgment about a person or action after comparing it to internal reference points, which may fall within a person's latitude of rejection, noncommitment, or acceptance. In the reported cases cited in this research, the women were forced to accept or reject the professors and the suggested action, but they did have a choice in the matter, even if they could not see it clearly at the moment. In the first case, the suggested action was outside the woman's latitude of acceptance as characterized by her saying: "I didn't want anything to do with that"; "I couldn't believe it"; "I pulled away." The language entertains no acceptance of the idea. Because the professor acted in a way which was inside the victim's latitude of rejection, the action and the professor were both rejected.

In the second case, the report suggests that the action and the professor operated within the woman's latitude of noncommitment. Comments, such as, "I told him to be careful"; "I just kept on taking books down while he laid on the floor"; "I guess I should have reported him to somebody," suggest that she neither accepted/encouraged nor rejected/discouraged the action or the professor.

The third case suggests that the student had to decide between two incongruent sets of information. She wanted an A from the professor, and he was touching her and asking her to remain after class. Perhaps that was tolerable, until he put his hands up her shirt, at which time he clearly crossed over into her latitude of rejection. When he crossed the line she chose to reject the action, "I pushed him away and yelled" (she was now ready to risk losing the A, but by dropping out of the program, she expected retaliation in some form), and reject the professor, "I decided to change my program and not have him for a teacher anymore."

The fourth case suggests that the student had to decide between two sets of information—getting an F or going to bed with the professor. She initiated the conversation about her grades, and he offered the solution to the problem. Apparently, he and his suggestion fell within her latitude of acceptance, since she reported: "I asked him if I could talk to him about my grades, in his office" (depending on tone of voice); "I was attracted to him a little"; and "I spent three hours with him in his bed." It must have been well within her latitude of acceptance since she spent three hours with him. Her choice of action indicates that she accepted the action and the professor.

All of the students reacted to the behavior of the professors in differing ways. The important aspect which social judgment-involvement theory suggests to women is that even though they may not be able to change the behavior of someone else, they always have a choice as to how they will react to it. Women can create a situation which would make it uncomfortable for men to behave in sexually harassing ways, simply by their reaction to it. We do affect the behavior of children who experiment with behaviors that are socially unacceptable. The same principles can be applied to situations of harassment.

DISCUSSION

Male professors should not sexually harass female students. Dzeich and Weiner (1984) provide a list of warning behaviors which can signal colleagues and students that a situation is ripe for sexual harassment. First and foremost, the harasser appears always available, spending enormous amounts of time with female students in his office, during class breaks, or at the student union, and he uses these opportunities to gain private access to students. He engages in staring, leering, and ogling. He frequently comments on the personal appearance of students. He frequently touches female students. He uses excessive flattery and praise of students. His behavior in front of his colleagues changes by either deliberately avoiding or seeking encounters with his students. He frequently injects a "male versus female" tone into discussions, and, he persistently emphasizes sexuality in all contexts (Dzeich & Weiner, 1984, p 119). In the more advanced stages he will claim his "wife doesn't love him" or some variation of that theme. He also generally uses the same rhetorical "lines" on all his prey as he casts his "line" to see who will be reeled in.

While sexual harassment may be inappropriate behavior, male professors often do not recognize that they are behaving inappropriately. So, if women are hoping that they will change the behavior of harassers, those women may be in for a long wait. Psychologists have taught humans for a long time that we cannot change someone else, we can only hope to change ourselves. With this in mind, women need to take the initiative to change this action.

Female students need to have their consciousness raised about what constitutes sexual harassment. They need to recognize the warning behaviors of sexual harassers. They need to recognize that sexual harassment has become an issue which organizations now take seriously. So, when an individual experiences persistent sexual harassment, he or she does not have to put up with it. Ignoring the situation will not make it go away. Confronting it by legal means, if necessary, is a viable option. But, communicating the situation to someone else will immediately increase a victim's sense of confidence.

Feelings of powerlessness appear to be the single strongest element that continues to perpetuate sexual harassment. When women believe they are powerless or have no choice, they fail to act. Not understanding the "rules of the game" extends the problem. Failure to report harassment may indicate a problem within an institutional structure, such as no formal lines of communication for reporting such matters, no clear description of the rules of "the game," and no process by which women can claim their rights. Both sexes help create an environment ripe for sexual harassment. First, women try not to respond and hope it will go away; second, men attempt to impugn the reputations of the women attempting to change the system (Dzeich & Weiner, 1984); third, reputations of ritually active men are protected; and fourth, the issue of sexual harassment, until recently, has received little attention.

Recommendations

Most educational institutions sincerely want to improve the social and educational environment within which students, faculty, administrators, and support staff study and work. However, not addressing the problem of sexual harassment with information about specific conditions, policies, and practices may, inadvertently, increase unwanted sexual harassment. Information about such behavior can address and prevent the problem (Bogart & Stein, 1987). Implementing policies concerning sexual harassment and communicating these policies to everyone as part of orientation and training programs increases an understanding of the institutional expectations.

If an institution wants to avoid a law suit, an "open-door" policy should exist. This means that a student can approach a female administrator, who acts as a sexual harassment counselor, to discuss any problems he or she may be experiencing. The victim needs assurance that someone in authority will listen and has the power to stop the harassment without retaliation to the student. If an institution has no grievance procedure and does not concern itself with the welfare of its students on this issue, an institution's defense in a law suit about such matters would be seriously damaged.

Strayer and Rapoport (1986) say that after hearing a complaint, a specific time should be set to deal with the issue and to communicate to the complainant the results of the institution's investigation. Institutions also must be discreet when dealing with sexual harassment complaints because "the victim is usually embarrassed or humiliated enough without being put on display" (Caudillo & Donaldson, 1986, p. 14). Keeping such an allegation quiet, whether the complaint is legitimate or not, can also protect the institution's reputation.

The institution should also contact other members of the organization who would be concerned with the accusation. Specifically, the harasser's immediate supervisor should be notified that an investigation has begun. A review of institutional policy should be made, and recent laws should be studied. A review of the history of the department or area in which the sexual harassment has allegedly occurred should be conducted to become familiar with the complainant's and the accused's history. An institution then needs to conduct interviews, including past students of the alleged harasser, colleagues of the complainant, and, finally, the accused him- or herself. Once legitimacy has been established, the institution can take appropriate action.

The reasons for sexual harassment no longer matter. What does matter is what institutions do to protect themselves and others against harassers and how they respond to sexual harassment cases. No institution should take an accusation lightly. By following these suggestions, including the creation of policies and procedures, institutions lay a solid foundation for assisting those who find themselves having to cope with inappropriate behavior.

REFERENCES

Backhouse, C., & Cohen, L. (1981). *Sexual harassment on the job: How to avoid the working woman's nightmare.* Englewood Cliffs, NJ: Prentice Hall.

Bateson, G. (1955). This message is play. In B. Schaffner (Ed.), *Group processes* (pp. 124-242). New York: Josiah Macy, Jr. Foundation

Proceedings.

Bingham, S. (1988). *Interpersonal responses to sexual harassment.* Unpublished doctoral dissertation, Purdue University, West Lafayette, IN.

Bingham, S.G., & Burleson, B.R. (1989). Multiple effects of messages with multiple goals. *Human Communication, 16,* 184-216.

Blum, D. E. (1988). New civil-rights legislation seen forcing colleges to deal more directly with sexual harassment. *Chronicle of Higher Education, 34,* 22.

Bogart, K., & Stein, N. (1987). Breaking the silence: Sexual harassment in education. *Peabody Journal of Education, 64,* 146-63.

Caudillo, D.W., & Donaldson, R. M. (1986). Is your climate ripe for sexual harassment? *Management World,* July/August, p. 26.

Crull, P. (1980). The impact of sexual harassment on the job: A profile of the experiences of 92 women. In D.A. Neugarten & J.M. Shafritz (Eds.), *Sexuality in organizations: Romantic and coercive behaviors at work* (pp. 71-76). Oak Park, IL: Moore. 76-71.

Crull, P. (1982). Stress effects of sexual harassment on the job. Implications for counseling. *American Journal of Orthopsychiatry, 52,* 539-544.

Dziech, B.W., & Weiner, L. (1984). *The lecherous professor.* Boston: Beacon Press.

Farley, L. (1978). *Sexual shakedown: The sexual harassment of women on the job.* New York: McGraw-Hill.

Fitzgerald, K. (1986). Sexual blackmail: Schools get serious about harassment. *Ms. Magazine,* October, p. 24.

Gutek, B.A. (1985). *Sex and the workplace.* San Francisco: Jossey-Bass.

Hadjifotious, N. (1983). *Women and harassment at work.* London: Pluto Press.

Hall, R.M., & Sandler, B.R. (1984). *Out of the Classroom: A chilly campus climate for women?* Report for the Association of American Colleges, Washington, DC.

Jewell, P.A., & Loizos, C. (1966). *Play, exploration and territory in mammals.* London: Academic Rules-Press for the Zoological Society of London.

Johnson, J.M. (1983). Sexual harassment: A costly mistake. *Management World,* June, 14-16.

Kidder, L., Fagan, M., & Cohn, E. (1978). Giving and receiving: Social justice in close relationships. In M. Lerner & S. Lerner (Eds.), *The justice motive in social behavior: Adapting to times of scarcity and change* (pp. 235-259). New York: Plenum Press.

Kramarae, C. (1981). *Women and men speaking.* Towley, MA: Newbury House.

Lakoff, R. (1975). *Language and women's place.* New York: Harper and Row.

Mackinnon, C.A. (1979). *Sexual harassment of working women: A case of sex discrimination.* New Haven, CT: Yale University Press.

Markel, N.N., Long, J.F., & Saine, T.J. (1976). Sex effects in conversational interaction: Another look at male dominance. *Human Communication Research, 2,* 356-364.

Mazur, D.B., & Percival, E.F. (1989). Students' experiences of sexual harassment at a small university. *Sex Roles: A Journal of Research, 20,* 1-11.

Meyer, J., & Rowan, B. (1978). The structure of educational organizations. In M.W. Meyer & Associates (Eds.), *Environments and organizations: Theoretical and empirical perspectives* (pp. 78-109). San Francisco: Jossey-Bass.

Pearson, J.C., Turner, L.H., & Todd-Mancillas, W. (1991). *Gender and communication.* Dubuque, IA: William C. Brown.

Rogers, E.M., & Shoemaker, F.F. (1971). *Communication of innovations.* New York: The Free Press.

Sherif, M., Sherif, C., & Nebergall, R. (1965). *Attitude and attitude change: The social judgment-involvement approach.* Philadelphia: W.B. Saunders.

Shuy, R.W. (1969). *Sex as a factor in sociolinguistic research.* Paper presented at the Anthropological Society of Washington meeting, Washington, DC.

Singer, T.L. (1989). Sexual harassment in graduate schools of social work: Provocative dilemmas. *Journal of Social Work Education, 25,* 68-76.

Strainchamps, E. (1971). Our sexist language. In V. Gorneck & B.K. Moran (Eds.), *Women in sexist society.* New York: Basic Books.

Strayer, J.F., & Rapoport, S.E. (1986). Sexual harassment: Limiting corporate liability. *Personnel,* p. 26.

Tangri, S. S., Burt, M. R., & Johnson, L. B. (1982). Sexual harassment at work: Three explanatory models. *Journal of Social Issues, 38,* 33-54.

Tyndale, W. (1971). *The living Bible.* Wheaton, IL: Tyndale House.

Watzlawick, P., Beavin, J.J., & Jackson, D.D. (1967). *Pragmatics of human communication: A study of human interactional patterns, pathologies and paradoxes.* New York: W.W. Norton.

▼Chapter 9

Academic Sexual Harassment: Perceptions of Behaviors

Mary M. Gill
Buena Vista College
Storm Lake, IA

▼ Despite the fact that issues surrounding sexual harassment are receiving substantial media attention, we remain a society which is ineffective at identifying and eliminating harassing behaviors.since entering the workforce, women have experienced unwanted sexual attention (Berry, 1988). It wasn't until 1986 with the Supreme Court's decision in *Meritor Savings Bank v Vinson* that workers were granted legal protection against sexual harassment as a form of sexual discrimination. In short, the courts have recognized sexual harassment as an infringement of a person's protection within employment and educational settings.

Since the term "sexual harassment" was first used in 1974 (McCaghy, 1984), issues surrounding sexual harassment and discrimination have been filled with contradictions, conflicts, and ambiguity. Jaschik (1991) explains that "the gut issue is clear-cut. The nuances may not be" (p. 26). Although statistics vary, the consensus is that incidents of sexual harassment are substantially higher than the number of reported cases. One of the reasons for the prevalence of sexual harassment is that it is a complex problem and difficult to define. Often harassers are not aware that their behaviors are harassing.

This chapter addresses sexual harassment in higher educational environments. The primary focus is to report the findings of an exploratory study aimed at discovering what faculty and students know about the legal issues surrounding sexual harassment. Prior to discussing this study, profiles of sexual harassment, laws regarding harassment in higher education, and current approaches to studying harassment are considered.

PROFILING SEXUAL HARASSMENT

The Equal Employment Opportunity Commission (EEOC) defines sexual harassment in the workplace (e.g., Baker, Terpstra, & Cutler, 1990; Bingham, 1991; Bingham & Burleson, 1989; Clair, 1991) as "unwelcome sexual advances, requests for sexual favors, and other conduct . . . interfering with an individual's work performance, or creating an intimidating, hostile or offensive working environment" (Equal Employment Opportunity Commission, 1980).

The EEOC's definition is the framework for definitions of sexual harassment in academic environments. Although sexual harassment concerns are similar regardless of the environment, the academic environment is unique from the "traditional" organizational workplace (Brooks & Perot, 1991; Fitzgerald et al., 1988a; Fitzgerald, Weitzman, Gold & Ormerod, 1988b; Fitzgerald & Ormerod, 1991; Franklin, Moglen, Zatlin-Boring, & Angress, 1981; Maihoff & Forrest, 1983; Somers, 1982; Wood & Lenze, 1991). In essence, the law views students as "employees." As employees, students are afforded protections (similar to workers' protections) against factors that decrease their productivity, effectiveness, and opportunity.

The National Advisory Council on Women's Educational Programs is the leading source defining academic sexual harassment as "the use of authority to emphasize the sexuality or sexual identity of a student in a manner which prevents or impairs that student's full enjoyment of education benefits, climate or opportunities" (Underwood, 1987, p. 43). Till (1980) operationalizes this definition into five categories of behaviors:

1. generalized sexist remarks or behaviors;
2. inappropriate and offensive, but essentially sanction-free, sexual advances;
3. solicitation of sexual activity or other sex-linked behavior by promise of rewards;
4. coercion of sexual activity by threat of punishment; and
5. sexual assaults.

Fitzgerald et al. have recoined Till's categories to: (a) gender harassment, (b) seductive behavior, (c) sexual bribery, (d) sexual coercion, and (e) sexual assault, respectively (Fitzgerald et al., 1988a, 1988b;

Fitzgerald & Ormerod, 1991). Strauss (1988) is more specific in identifying 12 behaviors that constitute sexual harassment: touching, verbal comments, sexual name calling, spreading sexual rumors, gestures, jokes/cartoons/pictures, leers, too personal a conversation, cowering/blocking movements, pulling at clothes, students "making out" in public environments, and attempted rape or rape (p. 94). Regardless of the definition used, the work performance that is potentially affected is the student's learning or ability to complete assigned tasks.

None of the definitions imply that all sexual relationships within the educational setting constitute sexual harassment. For conduct to be considered harassing, it must be sufficiently severe or pervasive enough to alter the conditions of the alleged victim's opportunity for education or to create an abusive environment. Behavior, however, need not be blatant. Most cases involve subtle forms of harassment such as sexual joking and innuendo. As Strauss (1988) concludes, sexual harassment is in the eye of the beholder. What may be harassment to one person may be flirtation to another, with the line between these two concepts vague at best. According to Underwood (1987), the crux of any sexual harassment claim is that the alleged sexual advance is unwanted or unwelcome.

Part of the problem of effectively identifying and dealing with sexual harassment stems from males and females viewing it differently. Petersen and Massengill (1982) report that two-thirds of male executives compared to fewer than one-third of female executives believe that the amount of sexual harassment is greatly exaggerated. Males respond favorably to sexual attention from females, generally feeling flattered rather than angry or confused. Sexual harassment also occurs less often to males than to females, seems to be less severe, and does not appear to have such a negative impact. Women are three times more likely to be harassed than men (Strauss, 1988).

Sexual harassment occurs frequently in academic settings. Most studies report 30% to 50% of students and 15% to 30% of faculty (largely female) members experience some form of harassment (Blum, 1991; Jaschik & Frentz, 1991; McKinney, 1990; McMillen, 1991; Rubin & Borgers, 1990; Strauss, 1988; Winks, 1982). Grauerholz (1989) estimates that as many as 60% of students experience harassment in the form of jokes or off-the-cuff remarks. Fitzgerald et al. (1988a, 1988b) report that 37% of faculty members engage in harassing behaviors. Winks (1982) reported that 1 in 5 female students had been subjected to sexual attention from male teachers, with one-fourth of the females responding to an American Psychological Association questionnaire having had sexual contact with an educator.

Many of the harassment cases involve teacher/student or student/student interactions. Strauss (1988) reported that an average of

50% of female students reported having been victims, with 30% of the harassment done by teachers. The harassment occurred anywhere from occasionally to several times a day and took place in the classroom during class or in the hall between classes. In most cases, harassers have a history of harassing behavior. Evidence suggests that a teacher who has taken advantage of a student will try it again if his or her behavior has been ignored and unpunished (Winks, 1982).

Although the number of reported cases is staggering, actual cases are suspected of being higher than the number of reported cases. Incidents involving student-to-student harassment were reported 75% of the time, while staff-to-student harassment was reported 50% of the time. Students not reporting staff-to-student harassment generally felt that the authorities would believe the staff member over the student (Strauss, 1988).

Although women tend to be victims more often than men, any person can be a victim of sexual harassment. Research shows that women between the ages of 24 and 34 are the most likely victims, while the harasser tends to be male, older than the victim, of the same ethnic and cultural background as the victim, and in a position of higher authority than the victim (Fitzgerald et al., 1988a, 1988b; Hazzard, 1988; Peterson & Massengill, 1982; Strauss, 1988; Winks, 1982).

Despite these profiles of the victim and harasser, we should not assume that male superiors are the harassers and female subordinates are the victims. The EEOC indicates that:

1. A man as well as a woman may be the victim of sexual harassment and a woman as well as a man may be the harasser;
2. The harasser does not have to be the victim's supervisor; and
3. The victim does not have to be the opposite sex of the harasser.

In short, the crucial inquiry is whether the harasser treats members of one sex differently from members of the other sex (Hazzard, 1988).

Regardless of the definition used, sexual harassment creates a negative educational environment. A report by the American Council on Education concluded that the "entire collegiate community suffers when sexual harassment is allowed to pervade the academic atmosphere" (McMillen, 1986b, p. 16). Sexual harassment disrupts the right to an equal education by interfering with the student's psychological, social, and physical well-being. In addition, the student's attendance, learning, course choices, grades, and ultimately his or her economic potential are adversely impacted (Strauss, 1988).

Whether the harassment is subtle or blatant, the effect of harassment cannot be understated. Bingham and Burleson (1989) report that sexual harassment has been linked to (a) emotional problems such as increased stress; (b) physical manifestations such as headaches, high blood pressure, and heart disease; (c) psychological complications such as decreased levels of confidence and lowered self-esteem, as well as relationship difficulties; and (d) reduced efficiency in task performance. Although this research focused on job situations, there is little reason to expect that the effects in the educational arena are different. Victims of harassment report feelings similar to those identified by rape victims. Anger was the most common response offered by 75% of the women, with the combination of anger and confusion also mentioned by 30% of the women (Strauss, 1988).

SEXUAL HARASSMENT LAW

The American Association of University Professors (AAUP) traditionally opposes any practice that interferes with academic freedom. With the increased attention on sexual harassment, however, there has come a growing concern for striking a balance between faculty freedoms and broader ethical standards. The AAUP's *Statement on Professional Ethics* highlights the responsibility faculty members have to avoid any exploitation of students and establishes that harassment or intimidation is inconsistent with academic freedom ("*Sexual harassment,*" 1983).

In addition to the AAUP's guidelines, litigation has prompted changes in students' rights. A key case introducing new protections for students was *Dixon v Alabama Board of Education* (294 F.2d 150 (5th Cir. 1961)). In this case, the court rejected the idea that education in state schools is a "privilege" to be dispensed according to whatever conditions the state deems appropriate. This case became part of the U.S. Supreme Court jurisprudence with cases such as *Tinker v Des Moines School District* (393 U. S. 503 (1969)) and *Healy v James* (408 U. S. 169 (1971)) when the Supreme Court established that students are contracting parties having rights under expressed and implied relationships with the institution (Kaplan, 1985). In short, students were granted expressed rights as citizens which could not be abridged.

Although many of the cases concerned with student rights originated in public education, cases such as *Healy v James* have occurred through the postsecondary arena. Postsecondary institutions, however, continue to have considerable latitude in selecting, interpreting, and changing the contract terms to which students are subjected. According to Kaplan (1985), despite the weak view taken by postsecondary institutions, contract theory creates a two-way street which becomes a source of meaningful rights for students and the institutions they attend.

Despite the advances originating in the 1960s, it was not until

1986 with the Supreme Court's decision in *Meritor Savings Bank v Vinson* (106 S. Ct. 2399 (1986)) that sexual harassment was defined as a form of sexual discrimination. As discrimination, harassment is in violation of Title VII of the Civil Rights Act of 1964 and Title IX of the Education Act of 1972. Although Title VII makes it unlawful to discriminate against an individual based on several features, only one of which is gender, Title IX is the primary legal source governing sex discrimination in academic policies (Kaplan, 1985; Underwood, 1987).

Although there are exceptions to those institutions covered under the anti-discriminatory practices of Title IX (e.g., private undergraduate institutions, undergraduate institutions that have always been single-sex institutions, and religious institutions), most public-supported undergraduate, professional, vocational, and graduate schools are governed by Title IX. Sexual discrimination is defined in Section 106.21(b) which states that an institution shall not:

> (i) Give preference to one person over another on the basis of sex, by ranking applicants separately on such basis or otherwise; (ii) Apply numerical limitations upon the number or proportion of persons of either sex who may be admitted; or (iii) Otherwise treat one individual differently from another on the basis of sex. (Kaplan, 1985, p. 239)

Even though this section refers largely to admission standards, the courts have interpreted and extended its scope to include discrimination that would hinder students' opportunities to enter and continue academic pursuits.

Once harassing behavior has been alleged, several individuals may be named in the legal action. In addition to the individual charged with performing the harassing behavior, the institution or administrative body that employs the individual can be found liable when the institution fails to take action on the harassment allegation or if the institution has not adopted specific procedures to deal with sexual harassment. Although frequently named in legal proceedings, institutions are often excluded from litigation when clear statements opposing sexual harassment and policies for handling harassment charges are on public record at the institution. In other words, the presence of carefully worded and adhered to sexual harassment policies help institutions from being found liable for an employee's harassing behavior (Gill & Wardrope, 1991).

Sexual harassment also may be viewed as a criminal offense. Anytime there is unwanted sexual touching, the incident is considered sexual assault as well as sexual harassment (Strauss, 1988). Thus, harassment charges may be supplemented with criminal assault charges when sexual touching has occurred.

APPROACHES TO STUDYING HARASSMENT

Sexual harassment research has focused on power relationships and gender issues as well as analyzed environmental, organizational, and individual factors. This research has relied on two sociological theories for its conceptual framework: conflict theory (e.g., Fitzgerald et al., 1988a, 1988b; Fitzgerald & Ormerod, 1991; Hoffman, 1986; McKinney, 1990) and role theory (e.g., Dziech & Weiner, 1984; Fitzgerald et al., 1988a, 1988b; Fitzgerald & Ormerod, 1991; Terpstra & Baker, 1986; Valentine-French & Radtke, 1989).

Conflict theory emphasizes power differences and competition between different groups. Much of the concern in applying conflict theory rests with examining the effects that differences have on definitions of behaviors, involvement in behaviors, and reactions to behaviors. In studying sexual harassment in higher education, conflict theory focuses on differences in achieved power (e.g., academic rank or position) and ascribed status (e.g., gender). Power differences combined with competition for resources or prestige influence definitions of, frequency of, and responses to sexual harassment. Thus, sexual harassment as a form of intimidation is one way for higher-status and power individuals to maintain power and control over lower-status persons.

From a conflict theory perspective, we would expect that males would most often be the harassers and possess higher academic ranks and that women would be the harassed and those in lower ranks. In addition, those in power positions have influence over what behaviors are identified as harassing. As a result, males and those in higher-ranking positions will tend to be more tolerant of sexual harassment and to see it as a less serious problem than females and those in lower-status positions. Regardless of sex, students represent a lower status position than any faculty member.

Role theory looks at how the positions held by individuals and the responsibilities and privileges associated with the positions or roles affect views of harassment. For example, career roles, sex roles, and victim or harasser roles are important factors in determining what behaviors are sexually harassing. Relevant questions from a role theory perspective consider how faculty/faculty harassment is viewed as compared to faculty/student or student/faculty harassment. With role theory, it is argued that certain behaviors are not considered as sexual harassment in certain positions and contexts. For example, some individuals may see behaviors as expectations of the male role or faculty role. This may be especially likely in predominantly male environments. Furthermore, victims of harassment, fulfilling the role of victim (and likely being female), would be hesitant to formally report sexual harassment, but would rather deal with it informally or attempt to ignore it (McKinney, 1990).

In applying conflict and role theory, researchers have largely concentrated on experiences dealing with harassment. Subjects are asked to identify their experiences with harassment. In a few cases, subjects have been asked to read scenarios and to indicate whether harassment is occurring. Research has looked at differences among student levels by considering how undergraduate students view harassment compared to graduate students (e.g., Fitzgerald et al., 1988a, 1988b; Fitzgerald & Ormerod, 1991; McKinney, 1990; Schneider, 1987). Gender differences have been considered by looking at the experiences men and women have with harassment (e.g., Baker et al., 1990; Benson & Thomson, 1982; Fitzgerald & Ormerod, 1991; Grauerholz, 1989; Mazer & Percival, 1989a; McKinney, 1990). Other researchers have concerned themselves with attitudes and responses to harassment or the feelings associated with harassment (e.g., Hunter & McClelland, 1991; Mazer & Percival, 1989b; Valentine-French & Radtke, 1989). A relatively recent concern has been over contrapower issues in which persons holding a position of lesser power harass those with greater power (e.g., Fitzgerald et al., 1988b; Fitzgerald & Ormerod, 1991; Grauerholz, 1989; McKinney, 1990). Similarly, these researchers also have considered peer harassment—harassment occurring between people in the same power level.

Regardless of the approach taken, much of the research suggests that an examination of behavior not specifically tied to personal examples is needed. Virtually all of the research, however, asks subjects about their involvement with harassment—not what they know about harassment. Several scholars suggest that the latter approach would be more revealing because they would learn more about whether individuals know what sexual harassment is and what can be done about it (e.g., Brooks & Perot, 1991; Fitzgerald et al., 1988a; Fitzgerald & Ormerod, 1991; Jaschik & Frentz, 1991; Rubin & Borgers, 1990). Even with the research asking subjects to consider specific scenarios, subjects are asked whether harassment is occurring from the same experiential focus. Rather than a concentration on what constitutes harassment and what specific features are present, subjects are asked to react to these situations.

Current Study

The present study takes an approach based on what specific behaviors constitute sexual harassment. The objective is to test subjects' knowledge about the legal dimensions of harassment, rather than being primarily concerned about their experiences or personal involvement with harassment. Despite several researchers suggesting that specific behaviors should be probed, little study of this type has been done, particularly as is relevant to academic harassment. This study concentrates on subjects' assessments of behaviors and legal issues, not on their personal involvement and feelings associated with harassment. Also of importance is that subjects are asked about key legal issues. While a few earlier studies provided scenarios and asked subjects to provide reactions, these studies did not specifically probe subjects' understanding of what constitutes sexual harassment. Earlier work has indicated that the prevention of harassing situations is the most effective manner of addressing academic harassment (e.g., Gill & Wardrope, 1991, 1992).

Because much of the existing literature suggests (e.g., Fitzgerald et al., 1988a) that subjects are unwilling to identify behavior as sexual harassment unless it is severe and overt behavior (e.g., forced sexual relations), it was hypothesized that subjects would identify overt behavior as sexual harassment more readily than subtle sexual harassment.

Hypothesis 1: Severity of behavior will influence perceptions of sexually harassing behaviors.

Second, because the literature suggests that men and women view harassment differently, it was hypothesized that gender differences would emerge.

Hypothesis 2: Gender of subject will affect perceptions of sexually harassing behaviors.

Finally, experience with harassment was not a critical feature for this study. Because the primary focus was on what subjects knew about legal issues surrounding sexual harassment, a research question investigated whether position or role differences (differences among professors, graduate student assistants, and undergraduate class members) affected perceptions of harassing behaviors.

Research Question: Does position in the educational structure affect perceptions of harassing behaviors?

METHODOLOGY

Participants

Surveys were distributed to faculty and students in three departments at a large midwestern university. The departments were selected because of the number of faculty and graduate students as well as the similarity in class size (fewer than 40 students) and class interaction patterns (students interacted with one another and the instructors).

Of the total usable surveys (n = 128), 54 surveys were completed by males and 74 by females. Approximately equal numbers of professors, graduate assistants, seniors/juniors, and sophomores/freshmen were represented. This information was treated in two ways. One level of analysis used the six positions and were referred to as positions. Another analysis created three class categories: *Instructors* constituted professors through graduate teaching assistants; *Upper Class* constituted senior and junior class-standing individuals; and *Under Class* constituted sophomore and freshmen class-standing persons. Each analysis is explained later.

Participants were asked whether they had been involved in sexual harassment cases in academic settings. Of the 128 asked, 110 had no involvement with sexual harassment charges in academic settings. Participants who responded that they had involvement with harassment cases were also asked if they were harassed or charged with harassment. Of the 18 involved with harassment cases, 15 felt they had been harassed. Of these 15, 13 were females harassed by males holding superior positions (most of whom were graduate students; n = 8). The remaining three participants involved with harassment cases were full-time male professors who had been charged with harassment by students.

Materials

The surveys first asked subjects to provide their definition of sexual harassment. After providing this definition, subjects responded to 30 items using a 5-point scale ranging from strongly disagree to strongly agree. The items identified behaviors constituting sexual harassment (e.g., "A teacher saying to his or her class 'women should not serve in combat duties' constitutes sexual harassment") or probed specific legal issues related to harassment (e.g., "A teacher may be sexually harassed by a student"). Subjects also responded to items assessing their involvement with harassment. If involved, they were asked to provide an account of what happened.

RESULTS

Scale Assessments

The specific scale items made up seven factors for which Cronbach's alpha were calculated. One scale representing male/female relationships achieved a very low reliability coefficient (α =.37). The remaining scales representing female/female relationships (α =.53), male/male relationships (α =.57), physical behavior (α =.62), opinions or joking (α =.65), power relationships (α =.69), and verbal interaction patterns (α =.87) were deemed sufficient for further study. Because this study is exploratory, scales which are .60 or higher are generally considered acceptable. The two scales near .60 were included because they were near the cutoff and represented same gender compositions (male/male and female/female) which no previous study considered.

Perceptions of Behaviors

Subjects were asked to provide their "definition of sexual harassment in the classroom." These data were coded using a coding scheme based on Till's and Fitzgerald's definitions. The coding scheme included nine categories corresponding to key components of sexual harassment such as (a) overt behavior can be harassing, (b) the attention must be unwanted, (c) subtle behavior can be harassing, (d) the harasser is in a position of authority, (e) harassment occurs regardless of position of harasser, (f) harassment occurs even if harasser indicates he or she is joking, (g) harassment can involve either sex, (h) harassment can be physical, and (i) harassment can be verbal.

Two independent research assistants coded the definitions. A Cohen's Kappa was calculated revealing a reliability coefficient of .76, which is considered excellent (Landis & Koch, 1977). Disagreements were resolved through discussion. The results of the coding were submitted to a chi-square analysis and are reported in Table 1. Overall, the data demonstrate that subjects recognized blatant behaviors, that harassment can involve either sex, and that verbal comments can constitute harassment most readily. The results indicate support for Hypothesis 1 in that blatant behaviors were viewed as harassment substantially more often than subtle behaviors. Despite subjects not indicating that subtle behaviors constitute harassment, substantial numbers did recognize that verbal behaviors may be harassing. It is important to distinguish between verbal and subtle forms of harassment. Although

Table 1. Coded Analysis of Supplied Definitions

Coding Category	No. of Subjects Responding
Overt behavior can be harassing (a)*	123 bcdef
The attention must be unwanted (b)	28 acdefghi
Subtle behavior can be harassing (c)	52 abdefghi
Harasser is in a position of authority (d)	24 abceghi
Harassment occurs regardless of the position of harasser (e)	90 abcdf
Harassment occurs even if harasser indicates he/she is joking (f)	13 abcdeghi
Harassment can involve either sex (g)	108 bcdf
Harassment can be physical (h)	99 bcdf
Harassment can be verbal (i)	107 bcdf

Note. Total number of possible subjects responding was 128.
*Each subscript after the number indicates statistical significance with that item at $p < .05$.

harassment may be verbal and subtle, verbal harassment may also be blatant. Thus, even though subjects recognize verbal remarks as potentially harassing, it does not mean that they similarly understand that the behavior or remark need not be blatant for harassment to have occurred.

A primary purpose of this study was to investigate what subjects knew about specific legal issues regarding sexual harassment. Several statements tested subjects' knowledge about key legal issues. Table 2 demonstrates response differences among men and women for these statements, while Table 3 presents differences among positions. Sex and position differences are discussed later. Items 5 and 6 probe blatant behaviors. These results suggest that Hypothesis 1 was not confirmed. When specifically probed about blatant behavior, subjects disagreed or strongly disagreed that behavior had to be blatant or that physical contact had to occur for harassment to occur. Although subjects were not explicit about whether distinctions needed to be made between subtle

Table 2. Perceptions of Key Legal Issues According to Gender

Response	1	2	3	4	5*
1. Sexual harassment may occur between male instructors and female students.					
male	9	7	11	18	6
female	5	11	17	29	12
total	14	18	28	47	18
2. Sexual harassment may occur between female instructors and male students.					
male	3	3	13	29	6
female	1	0	14	48	11
total	4	3	27	77	17
3. Sexual harassment may occur between male instructors and male students.					
male	4	1	23	17	9
female	1	8	27	24	14
total	5	9	50	41	23
4. Sexual harassment may occur between female instructors and female students.					
male	2	2	18	24	8
female	3	5	23	37	6
total	5	7	41	61	14
5. Physical contact must occur for sexual harassment to take place.					
male	33	14	3	2	2
female	49	17	5	1	2
total	82	31	8	2	3
6. Behavior must be blatant for harassment to occur.					
male	13	26	8	4	3
female	34	27	8	4	1
total	47	53	16	8	4
7. Clear legal guidelines exist for harassment.					
male	13	24	10	6	1
female	31	26	10	5	2
total	44	50	20	11	3
8. Campuses have offices which handle sexual harassment complaints.					
male	4	10	23	12	5
female	9	11	37	12	5
total	13	21	60	24	10

*Subjects responded to statements using a 5-point scale ranging from strongly disagree to strongly agree. A "1" represented strongly disagree.

Table 3. Perceptions of Key Legal Issues According to Position

Response	1	2	3	4	5*
1. Sexual harassment may occur between male instructors and female students.					
Instructor**	4	3	9	18	9
Upper Class**	5	7	11	13	6
Under Class**	5	8	11	16	3
total	14	18	31	47	18
2. Sexual harassment may occur between female instructors and male students.					
Instructor	0	2	6	24	11
Upper Class	1	0	4	14	21
Under Class	0	3	5	17	18
total	1	5	15	55	50
3. Sexual harassment may occur between male instructors and male students.					
Instructor	0	0	12	20	11
Upper Class	1	5	16	10	10
Under Class	4	4	22	11	2
total	5	9	50	41	23
4. Sexual harassment may occur between female instructors and female students.					
Instructor	0	0	8	23	12
Upper Class	2	2	12	24	2
Under Class	3	5	21	14	0
total	5	7	41	61	14
5. Physical contact must occur for sexual harassment to take place.					
Instructor	33	7	1	1	1
Upper Class	30	7	2	1	2
Under Class	19	17	5	1	1
total	82	31	8	3	4
6. Behavior must be blatant for harassment to occur.					
Instructor	18	18	3	3	1
Upper Class	20	13	7	1	1
Under Class	9	22	6	4	2
total	47	53	16	8	4
7. Clear legal guidelines exist for harassment.					
Instructor	2	7	8	16	10
Upper Class	2	5	4	15	16
Under Class	2	4	5	17	15
total	6	16	17	48	41
8. Campuses have offices which handle sexual harassment complaints.					
Instructor	5	11	9	12	6
Upper Class	5	7	8	14	8
Under Class	4	10	9	12	8
total	14	28	26	38	22

*Subjects responded to statements using a 5-point scale ranging from strongly disagree to strongly agree. A "1" represented strongly disagree.

**Instructor constitutes full professors through graduate teaching assistants; Upper Class constitutes senior and junior class standing; Under Class constitutes sophomore and freshman class standing.

and overt behaviors in providing their definitions, they apparently recognized that behavior does not have to be blatant or that touching does not have to occur for harassment to exist.

Gender Assessment

Subjects' responses to each of the scaled factors were submitted to a 2 (gender) x 6 (position—professor, graduate student, senior, junior, sophomore, freshman) ANOVA. Two factors emerged for gender confirming Hypothesis 2. The factors that identified overt behavior (F [3,114] = 8.66, p = .004, eta^2 = .19) and intention of humor (F [3,114] = 5.49, p = .021, eta^2 = .13) were significant. These results suggest that men and women evaluated the necessity of behavior being blatant and whether humor or joking altered the assessment of harassment differently. Although both men and women tended to believe that behavior did not have to be blatant for harassment to occur, men (M = 2.13) felt more strongly than women (M = 1.72) that behavior did have to be blatant for harassment to occur. The opposite trend was observed for evaluating the presence of joking. Women (M = 2.56) viewed the presence of joking or opinion statements as harassment more strongly than did men (M = 2.15). Apparently, women were more willing to recognize subtle forms of harassment.

Results of the coding procedure of the open-ended definitions were submitted to a chi-square analysis to determine whether sex differences occurred. This procedure revealed no significant differences (χ^2 [df=8, c.v. 15.51] = 4.72, n.s.).

Position Differences

Subjects' responses to each of the scaled factors were submitted to a 2 (gender) x 6 (position—professor, graduate student, senior, junior, sophomore, freshman) ANOVA. No interaction effects or effects due to position were significant. Thus, the Research Question was answered by no differences due to position emerging. Apparently, whether professors or freshmen students, similar assessments of harassing behaviors were made.

Results of the coding procedure of the open-ended definitions were submitted to a chi-square analysis to determine if class (instructor, upper class, under class) differences occurred. Because no differences due to position were observed, and means were virtually identical for professors and graduate assistants, seniors and juniors, and sophomore and freshmen, broader data categories were used by using three levels of class which grouped instructors, upper-class students, and underclass students into classes. This procedure revealed no significant differences (χ^2 [df=16, c.v. = 26.30] = 25.52, n.s.).

DISCUSSION

This study sought to test subjects' knowledge of legal issues surrounding sexual harassment behaviors. While much previous work has focused on subjects' experiences with harassment, this research concentrated on perceptions of behaviors rather than experiences with harassment.

Overall, the hypotheses were confirmed. Hypothesis 1 stated that overt behavior would be recognized as harassment more than subtle types of harassment. This hypothesis was partially confirmed by overt behavior accounting for the most variance and by the frequencies of responses as displayed in Table 1. Consistent with other work, subjects appeared more certain of overt behavior being defined as harassment, but were less willing to identify subtle forms as harassment (Baker et al., 1990; Fitzgerald, & Ormerod, 1991; Hunter & McClelland, 1991).

Consistent with the existing literature, Hypothesis 2 was confirmed as demonstrated by men and women viewing harassment differently. Consistent with the current literature (Peterson & Massengill, 1982; Strauss, 1988; Winks, 1982), women were more willing to identify subtle forms of harassment. Despite the recent uncertainty that has occurred, in part because of the Thomas hearing (McMillen, 1991), overall perceptual patterns among women and men have changed very little.

On the one hand, it is encouraging that position differences did not occur. Apparently, whether professors or freshmen, similar understanding of sexual harassment occurs. On the other hand, figures from the cross-tabulations reported in Tables 2 and 3 demonstrate that, overall, people need to know more about the specifics of the legal circumstances of sexual harassment.

Interesting results occur when considering the specific legal statements identified in Tables 2 and 3. The first four address gender combinations of harassment. With these, we would expect that the knowledgeable response would be a "4" or "5." Yet, with the exception of male teachers/female students (Item 1) and female teachers/female students (Item 4), the preponderance of responses indicated a neutral position of agreement rather than strongly agreeing. By nature of the scales, subjects responding with a "3" indicate a neutral stance. While it is somewhat comforting to know that the majority of subjects identified that any gender combination may be involved in harassment, the numbers identifying uncertainty or incorrect assessments should cause concern. Clearly, more open discussions should be conducted on college campuses identifying specific issues of sexual harassment to help heighten awareness and hopefully prevent future occurrences.

Items 5 and 6 address blatant behavior issues. The correct responses would be a "1" or "2" indicating disagreement with the written statement. As predicted, the blatant forms of harassment seem to be better understood by subjects. The preponderance of responses indicate that subjects were willing to say that behavior does not have to be blatant or involve contact for harassment to take place. It is interesting that subjects are willing to say that behavior does not have to be blatant, yet in providing their definitions, subjects were not explicit about subtle issues. Thus, although they seemingly understood that subtle forms of harassment exist, they were less willing to identify specific subtle forms of harassment.

Responses to Item 6 are alarming. While it may be expected that individuals do not know the specific guidelines, it is alarming that the majority of responses indicate that clear guidelines do not exist for determining harassment. With the recent advances of the Vinson decision, and with most institutions adopting the recommended AAUP guidelines, it would be expected that more subjects would be familiar with existing procedures, even if they are unfamiliar with the specific details of those procedures. While clear guidelines exist, there seems to be a feeling of mistrust in how the guidelines are applied. Clearly, more open discussion and training in legal issues would aid in reducing this secrecy effect. A possible explanation may rest with the media attention surrounding the Thomas hearings. With strong opinion and sentiment supporting both Hill and Thomas, subjects may have been more confused by what really constitutes harassment and how harassment is viewed. Thus, subjects operationalized this uncertainty as the procedures were not clearly delineated.

The last item asks about specific campus offices which address or handle harassment complaints. Similar to the guidelines issue, subjects seem uncertain about the existence of these offices. This finding suggests that college campuses need to concentrate greater attention on identifying who the administrative agency is that is responsible for setting harassment policy and detailing what the specific procedures include.

From the results and patterns which emerge, it seems evident that greater treatment of sexual harassment issues on college campuses should occur. Workshops or training sessions that identify specific behaviors (subtle and blatant) and how these issues may be addressed seems warranted (e.g., Gill & Wardrope, 1992, have proposed a step process which can be used by individual departments to enlighten their students and faculty members).

While few would argue that sexual harassment should be ignored, one of the leading fears in increasing discussion is associated with "false claims." Winks (1982) found that several administrators feared that bringing the issue into the open would increase the number of cases, when, in fact, ignoring the incidents may escalate the problem (Strauss, 1988). Given that sexual harassment causes psychological and social damage to the victim should be impetus enough to override our fear of increased investigation. McMillen (1986a) suggests that we have a moral and ethical obligation to develop clear policies that protect students from sexual harassment. In addition to helping the students receive the best education, these policies can help shield higher education institutions from potential liabilities. In addition, evidence suggests that the teacher (or person) who has taken advantage of a single student will try it again if his or her behavior has been ignored and unpunished (Winks, 1982). We do not help the situation by hoping that the cases that occur are isolated examples.

While several educational issues may be dealt with most effectively by having a carefully prepared procedure for when they occur, sexual harassment issues are best treated with prevention. Failure to adequately prepare instructors about sexual harassment issues can result in hazards, not only for the teacher, but for students, administrators, the department, and the institution. Because intention is not an issue in determining whether litigation is justified, instructors must be aware of how their behavior is being perceived by students. The crucial inquiry is whether the alleged harasser treated a member or members of one sex differently from the other sex (Hazzard, 1988). As Strauss (1988) has explained, the major difficulty with harassment cases is that sexual harassment is in the eye of the beholder. What may be harassment to one may be flirtation or conversation to another.

This study offers a unique look at sexual harassment in the academy. While most previous work has concentrated on individuals' experiences with harassment, this study sought to test people's understanding of harassment and the legal issues involved. The responses from this study are particularly rich given that the majority of respondents had no personal involvement with harassment. Although we might expect that people who have been involved with harassment cases have a good understanding of harassment issues, the vast majority of respondents had no personal involvement with harassment and yet seemed to have a minimal understanding of harassment issues.

REFERENCES

Baker, D. D., Terpstra, D. E., & Cutler, B. D. (1990). Perceptions of sexual harassment: A re-examination of gender differences. *The Journal of Psychology, 124,* 409-416.

Benson, D. J., & Thomson, G. E. (1982). Sexual harassment on a university campus: The confluence of authority relations, sexual interest, and gender stratification. *Social Problems, 29,* 236-251.

Berry, M. F. (1988). How to teach controversial constitutional issues facing women. *Magazine of History, 3,* 30-32.

Bingham, S. G. (1991). Communication strategies for managing sexual harassment in organizations: Understanding message options and their effects. *Journal of Applied Communication, 19,* 88-115.

Bingham, S. G., & Burleson, B. R. (1989). Multiple effects of messages with multiple goals: Some perceived outcomes of responses to sexual harassment. *Human Communication Research, 16,* 184-216.

Blum, D. E. (1991, October 9). Environment still hostile to women in academe, new evidence indicates. *Chronicle of Higher Education, 38,* 1, 20.

Brooks, L., & Perot, A. R. (1991). Reporting sexual harassment: Exploring a predictive model. *Psychology of Women Quarterly, 15,* 31-47.

Clair, R. P. (1991, October). *A study of strategic responses to sexual harassment: An analysis of women's narratives.* Paper presented at the annual convention of the Speech Communication Association, Atlanta, GA.

Dixon v Alabama Board of Education, 294 F.2d 150 (5th Cir. 1961)

Dziech, B. W., & Weiner, L. (1984). *The lecherous professor: Sexual harassment on campus.* Boston, MA: Beacon Press.

Equal Employment Opportunity Commission. (1980, November 10). *Guidelines on discrimination because of sex* (29cfr Part 1604. Federal register 45 (210)). Washington, DC: U.S. Government Printing Office.

Fitzgerald, L. F., & Ormerod, A. J. (1991). Perceptions of sexual harassment: The influence of gender and academic context. *Psychology of Women Quarterly, 15,* 281-294.

Fitzgerald, L. F., Shullman, S. L., Bailey, N., Richards, M., Swecker, J., Gold, Y., Ormerod, M., & Weitzman, L. (1988a). The incidence and dimensions of sexual harassment in academia and the workplace. *Journal of Vocational Behavior, 32,* 152-175.

Fitzgerald, L. F., Weitzman, L. M., Gold, Y., & Ormerod, M. (1988b). Academic harassment: Sex and denial in scholarly garb. *Psychology of Women Quarterly, 12,* 329-340.

Franklin, P., Moglen, H., Zatlin-Boring, P., & Angress, R. (1981). *Sexual and gender harassment in the academy: A guide for faculty, students and administrators.* New York: Modern Language Association of America.

Gill, M. M., & Wardrope, W. J. (1991, April). *"I wish I hadn't said (or done) that": Sexual harassment and the basic course instructor.*

Paper presented at the Central States Communication Association Annual Convention, Chicago, IL.

Gill, M. M., & Wardrope, W. J. (1992). To say or not; to do or not—those are the questions: Sexual harassment and the basic course director. *Basic Communication Course Annual, 4,* 94-114.

Grauerholz, E. (1989). Sexual harassment of women professors by students: Exploring the dynamics of power, authority, and gender in a university setting. *Sex Roles, 21,* 789-801.

Hazzard, T. (1988). *Affirmative action and women in higher education.* Tallahassee, FL: Florida State University, Department of Educational Leadership. (ERIC Document Reproduction Service No. ED 303 416)

Healy v James, 408 U.S. 169 (1971).

Hoffman, F. L. (1986). Sexual harassment in academia: Feminist theory and institutional practice. *Harvard Educational Review, 56,* 105-121.

Hunter, C., & McClelland, K. (1991). Honoring accounts for sexual harassment: A factorial survey analysis. *Sex Roles, 24,* 725-752.

Jaschik, M. L., & Frentz, B. R. (1991). Women's perceptions and labeling of sexual harassment. *Sex Roles, 25,* 19-23.

Jaschik, S. (1991). U. S. plans policies to fight harassment and bias at colleges. *Chronicle of Higher Education, 37,* 1, 26.

Kaplan, W. A. (1985). *The law of higher education.* San Francisco, CA: Jossey-Bass, Inc.

Landis, J. R., & Koch, G. G. (1977). Measurement of observer agreement for categorical data. *Biometrica, 33,* 159-174.

Maihoff, N., & Forrest, L. (1983). Sexual harassment in higher education: An assessment study. *Journal of the National Association for Women Deans, Administrators, and Counselors, 46,* 3-8.

Mazer, D. B., & Percival, E. F. (1989a). Ideology or experience? The relationships among perceptions, attitudes, and experiences of sexual harassment in university students. *Sex Roles, 20,* 135-147.

Mazur, D. B., & Percival, E. F. (1989b). Students' experiences of sexual harassment at a small university. *Sex Roles, 20,* 1-22.

McCaghy, M. D. (1984). *Sexual harassment: A guide to resources.* Boston, MA: G. K. Hall and Company.

McKinney, K. (1990). Sexual harassment of university faculty by colleagues and students. *Sex Roles, 23,* 421-438.

McMillen, L. (1986a). Council offers sexual harassment policy guidelines. *Chronicle of Higher Education, 33,* 16.

McMillen, L. (1986b). Many colleges taking a new look at policies on sexual harassment. *Chronicle of Higher Education, 33,* 1.

McMillen, L. (1991). A mixed message for campuses seen in Thomas hearings. *Chronicle of Higher Education, 38,* 1,14.

Meritor Savings Bank v Vinson 106 S.Ct. 2399 (1986).

Petersen, D. J., & Massengill, D. (1982). Sexual harassment—a growing problem in the workplace. *Personnel Administrator, 27*, 79-89.

Rubin, L. J., & Borgers, S. B. (1990). Sexual harassment in universities during the 1980s. *Sex Roles, 23*, 397-411.

Schneider, B. E. (1987). Graduate women, sexual harassment and university policy. *Journal of Higher Education, 58*, 46-65.

Sexual harassment: Suggested policy and procedures for handling complaints. (1983). *Academe, 69*, 15a-16a.

Somers, A. (1982). Sexual harassment in academe: Legal issues and definitions. *Journal of Social Issues, 38*, 23-32.

Strauss, S. (1988). Sexual harassment in the school: Legal implications for principals. *NAASP Bulletin, 72*, 93-97.

Terpstra, D. E., & Baker, D. D. (1986). A framework for the study of sexual harassment. *Basic and Applied Social Psychology, 7*, 17-34.

Till, F. J. (1980). *Sexual harassment: A report on the sexual harassment of students*. Washington, DC.: National Advisory Council on Women's Educational Programs.

Tinker v Des Moines School District, 393 U.S. 503 (1969).

Underwood, J. (1987). End sexual harassment of employees, or your board could be held liable. *American School Board Journal, 174*, 43-44.

Valentine-French, S., & Radtke, H. L. (1989). Attributions of responsibility for an incident of sexual harassment in a university setting. *Sex Roles, 21*, 545-555.

Winks, P. L. (1982). Legal implications of sexual contact between teacher and student. *Journal of Law and Education, 11*, 437-478.

Wood, J. T., & Lenze, L. F. (1991). Strategies to enhance gender sensitivity in communication education. *Communication Education, 40*, 16-21.

▼Chapter 10

Sexual Harassment at North Carolina State University

Rebecca Leonard
Laura Carroll Ling
Gail A. Hankins
Carolyn H. Maidon
Paul F. Potorti
Janet M. Rogers
North Carolina State University
Raleigh, NC

INTRODUCTION AND REVIEW OF LITERATURE

In the late 1970s, when a Yale University undergraduate woman sued a male professor for offering her a higher grade in exchange for sexual favors, the problem of sexual harassment on campus earned national attention. Only recently in the history of higher education has the sexual harassment of women students by their male professors, and also junior faculty by senior professors and staff by supervisors, been identified and responded to in a serious fashion. Sexual harassment on campus has been largely a "hidden problem" until the last few years (Project on the Status and Education of Women, 1978).

Early surveys attempting to document the scope and incidence of sexual harassment focused on women in the workplace and found

170

anywhere from 50% to 92% of the respondents had experienced some form of sexual harassment (Sandler & Associates, 1981). These early surveys, however, were largely informal and exploratory, and the results were not generalizable to larger populations because the researchers used nonrandom, self-selection sampling (Maihoff & Forrest, 1983; Whitmore, 1983). These surveys were useful because they did provide valuable descriptive information on the nature, incidence, and effects of sexual harassment at a time when very little was known about the problem. They also served as a foundation for later research.

Within the last decade, a considerable amount of research on sexual harassment in higher education has been pursued at individual institutions. Since 1980, at least a dozen campus surveys have been conducted (Adams, Kottke, & Padgitt, 1983; Allen & Okawa, 1987; Benson & Thomson, 1982; Brown & Maestro-Scherer, 1986; Fitzgerald et al., 1988; Johnson & Shuman, 1983; Maihoff & Forrest, 1983; Metha & Nigg, 1983; Oshinsky, 1981; Scott, 1984; Whitmore, 1983; Wilson & Kraus, 1983). The results of these surveys are somewhat difficult to compare because the definitions of sexual harassment, sampling procedures, populations studied, and research methodologies often vary from one study to another. Taken as a whole, however, these studies clearly indicate that sexual harassment is a serious and widespread problem for students, faculty, and staff at colleges and universities today.

Most of the campus studies define sexual harassment behaviors in terms of one or both of two major categories: gender harassment (sexist remarks and behaviors) and variously defined levels of sexual advances, bribery, and coercion (see, for example, Allen & Okawa, 1987, and Fitzgerald et al., 1988). Incidence of sexual harassment is typically reported in terms of the percentage of respondents who have experienced one or more of the sexual harassment behaviors being investigated.

All of the studies include undergraduate women students in their research samples; a few include both men and women undergraduate students (Adams et al., 1983; Fitzgerald et al., 1988; McCormack, 1985; Sigal, Gibbs, Belford, Ronan, & Gervasio, 1987). In general, women students are shown to be harassed significantly more than men, with men experiencing one or more forms of sexual harassment 5% or less of the time, and incidence among women averaging approximately 30% of the time (Dziech & Weiner, 1984).

The sexual harassment of staff and faculty has been investigated in only two institutional studies (Fitzgerald et al., 1988, and Metha & Nigg, 1983). Extrapolating from the current body of research conducted in the university setting, however, it seems reasonable to conclude that the longer a woman pursues her education and professional career, the more likely it is that she will experience one or more forms of sexual harassment. For example, graduate women can experience more harassment than undergraduate women and professional staff and faculty more than students. Moreover, research at two major universities in the Fitzgerald et al. study (1988), found that among female faculty members, administrators, and staff, women administrators reported more experiences of sexual harassment than either faculty or staff women.

An area of further research yet to be fully explored is the sexual harassment of faculty and staff on campus. Comparisons within and across the three major campus groups—students, faculty, and staff—can and should be made in order to better understand the pattern of sexual harassment in the university setting. Most surveys have focused on students, while only the two cited above have looked at patterns among faculty and staff. As in the case of research among student populations, there is a problem comparing data across samples due to the use of different instruments, samples, and subsamples. Nonetheless, for individual institutions to obtain a full and accurate assessment of the incidence of sexual harassment on campus, survey research must include faculty and staff as well as students in the research sample. Critical insights about the nature and extent of sexual harassment in higher education, which are inclusive of faculty and staff, ideally will result in the further development and refinement of institutional policy on sexual harassment, the removal of barriers to the career development of women in higher education, and the reduction and prevention of sexual harassment on campus.

In Spring 1989, an interdisciplinary team of researchers at North Carolina State University initiated a research project to determine the scope and incidence of various types of sexual harassment behaviors experienced by four groups of women on campus: undergraduate women, graduate women, technical and clerical women staff (hereafter referred to as staff), and teaching and nonteaching professional women (hereafter referred to as faculty). The purpose of the research was to discover types of sexual harassment behaviors experienced by women in each group; the occurrence of each type of behavior; the profile of harassers; the responses of the victims to the harassment; factors which would make victims more likely to report incidents of sexual harassment; and victims' knowledge of the university policy on sexual harassment.

METHOD

Sample

A computer-generated random sample was chosen from four groups of females on campus: undergraduate women students, graduate women students, women staff, and women faculty. Men were not included in any sample because sexual harassment of male students has been found to occur in 5% or fewer of male subjects (Fitzgerald et al., 1988).

The total sample size was 1,364. This total sample included 10% of the available undergraduate women students (574 undergraduates), 10% of the available graduate women students (115 graduate students), 25% of the available staff women (500 staff), and 25% of the available faculty women (175 faculty).

A total of 527 responses of the 1,364 surveys sent were received (38.63%: 30.31% of undergraduates, 40.86% of graduates, 40.60% of staff, and 58.85% of faculty returned the survey).

Procedure

Surveys were mailed to the 1,364 subjects utilizing campus mail whenever possible. Included with the survey was a cover letter describing the research and assuring confidentiality and instructions for completing the questionnaire, including definitions of five different types of sexual harassment. Each survey was color coded and numbered to aid in identification of the respondent sample group.

Survey Instrument

The survey used for this research was adapted from that used at the University of Illinois at Urbana-Champaign, a campus similar in size and mission to North Carolina State University (Allen & Okawa, 1987). Four general types of sexual harassment were identified by Allen and Okawa: unwanted sexual statements, unwanted personal attention, unwanted sexual propositions, and unwanted physical or sexual advances. A fifth type of sexual harassment (unwanted sexist statements) was added to the survey for this present research. Additional changes from the original Allen and Okawa survey were made for this present research to account for the inclusion of female employees among the subjects surveyed.

The survey was constructed to answer seven research questions:

1. What are the types of sexual harassment behaviors experienced by women at North Carolina State University?
2. What is the incidence of occurrence of each type of behavior?
3. What differences are there in the type and incidence of sexual harassment across the four sample populations?

4. What is the profile of perpetrators of sexual harassment?
5. How do victims respond emotionally and behaviorally to sexual harassment?
6. What do women at North Carolina State University know about the campus policy on sexual harassment and about campus grievance procedures?
7. What factors would make it more likely that victims would report sexual harassment?

Analysis of Data

For each question, frequencies and percentages were tabulated, except for eight questions, in which respondents were asked to write free responses. For these questions, a content analysis was conducted.

RESULTS

Type and Incidence of Sexual Harassment

Unwanted sexist comments were defined as "jokes or remarks that are stereotypical or derogatory to members of one sex." The majority of respondents (60.12%) reported that they never experienced unwanted sexist comments. But 39.88% did report experiencing unwanted sexist comments one or more times in the previous five years. Almost 7% of the respondents reported that such an incident happened to them at least once, 21.77% said that it occurred several times (2-5 times), and 11.18% reported that it occurred many times (more than 5 times). In Table 1 the percentage of respondents reporting incidents of unwanted sexist com-

TABLE 1. Percentage of Respondents Reporting Incidence of Unwanted Sexist Comments

Group	Never (%)	Once (%)	2-5 (%)	5+ (%)
Graduate Students	6.74	0.58	0.77	0.96
Undergrad. Students	20.81	3.66	7.13	1.73
Faculty	7.90	0.96	6.94	3.85
Staff	24.66	1.73	6.94	4.62
TOTAL	60.12	6.94	21.77	11.18

ments are shown by number of incidents and category of respondent.

Of those respondents who reported one or more unwanted sexist comments, 32.85% said that there was only one perpetrator, 57.97% said that several (2-5) faculty or staff members made unwanted sexist comments, and 9.18% of the respondents said that many (more than 5) faculty or staff members made unwanted sexist comments (58.33% of the graduate students, 43.08% of undergraduates, 68.85% of the faculty, and 62.32% of the staff respondents who experienced this form of sexual harassment reported that several faculty and staff members made unwanted sexist comments). Slightly over half (52.31%) of the undergraduate students said that only one faculty or staff member made unwanted sexist comments to them.

Most of the respondents (77.78%) said that the perpetrator of unwanted sexist comments was male, and 22.22% of the respondents said that sexist remarks were made by both males and females. No respondents reported that unwanted sexist remarks were made by females only.

Of those respondents reporting that they had experienced unwanted sexist comments made by faculty or staff members, the majority (77.29%) said that the remarks were made by a white harasser. No graduate students or faculty respondents reported that unwanted sexist comments were made by an African-American, while 6.15% of undergraduates (4 respondents) and 5.80% of staff (4 respondents) said the comments were made by an African-American. Only one undergraduate student (1.54%) said that the individual who made the unwanted sexist comment was an Asian.

The second category of sexual harassment was *unwanted sexual statements*, which were defined as "unwanted jokes, remarks, or questions directed to you which have sexual implications or sexual content." Again, a large percentage of the respondents (82.85%) said that they never experienced a faculty or staff member making unwanted sexual statements to them personally, but 6.43% of the respondents reported that unwanted sexual statements were made to them personally at least once, 8.97% reported several (2-5) incidents, and 1.75% of the respondents reported hearing unwanted sexual statements many (more than 5) times in the previous five years. However, neither graduate students nor undergraduate students reported that unwanted sexual statements were made to them more than 5 times. Table 2 shows the percentage of respondents reporting unwanted sexual statements by category of respondent and number of incidents.

Of those respondents reporting one or more incidents of unwanted sexist statements, 55.68% said that only one individual was responsible for the statements, 43.18% said that several (2-5) individuals made the comments, while only one respondent (a staff member) said that sexual

TABLE 2. Percentage of Respondents Reporting Incidence of
Unwanted Sexual Statements

Group	Never (%)	Once (%)	2-5 (%)	5+ (%)
Graduate Students	8.38	0.39	0.39	0.00
Undergrad. Students	30.80	1.56	1.17	0.00
Faculty	13.26	2.53	3.12	1.17
Staff	30.41	1.95	4.29	0.58
TOTAL	82.85	6.43	8.97	1.75

statements were made to her by more than 5 faculty or staff members.

The majority (92.05%) of the respondents who experienced this form of sexual harassment reported that the unwanted sexual statements were made by male faculty or staff members, while one staff respondent (1.14%) said the statement was made by a female perpetrator, and 3 faculty and 3 staff (6.82%) reported unwanted sexual statements were made to them by both males and females.

The majority of respondents (79.55%) who reported one or more incidents of unwanted sexual statements said the statements were made by a white perpetrator. Four staff respondents (4.55%) said that the perpetrator was an African-American, while one graduate student and one staff respondent said the individual making the comment was an Asian (2.27%). Also, one staff member said that the perpetrator was an American Indian (1.14%).

Unwanted personal attention, the third type of sexual harassment, was defined as "unwanted letters, calls, visits, pressure for meetings, dates, etc., where personal or romantic interest in you was implied, but no sexual expectations were stated." The majority of the respondents (89.96%) reported that they never experienced unwanted personal attention from a faculty or staff member, but almost 5% (4.83%) said that they experienced unwanted personal attention one time, while 4.44% said that they had experienced unwanted personal attention several times (2-5 times). One undergraduate and 3 staff respondents (0.77%) reported that they experienced unwanted personal attention many times (more than 5 times). Table 3 shows the percentage of respondents reporting unwanted personal attention by category and number of incidents.

Of the respondents reporting one or more incidents of unwanted personal attention, the majority (73.08%) said that only one perpetrator was involved. Twenty-five percent reported that several individuals (2-5) gave them unwanted personal attention (2 undergraduates, 4 faculty, and 7 staff), while 1 staff respondent (1.92%) reported that many (more than 5) individuals were responsible for the unwanted personal attention.

All respondents who reported one or more occurrences of unwanted personal attention reported that males were the perpetrators. Most (82.69%) of the respondents (1 graduate student, 9 undergraduate students, 16 faculty, and 17 staff) reported that the attention was from a white perpetrator, while 13.46% of the respondents (2 faculty and 5 staff) reported that the perpetrator was African-American.

Unwanted sexual propositions were defined as "unwanted demands or invitations for sexual favors." Most (96.48%) of the respondents said that they had never experienced unwanted sexual propositions. In fact, no graduate students reported any such incidents. But 2.34% of the respondents (1 undergraduate, 7 faculty, and 4 staff) reported that they had experienced unwanted sexual propositions one time, and 1.17% of the respondents (1 faculty and 5 staff) said that unwanted sexual propositions were directed to them many (more than 5) times. Table 4 shows the percentage of respondents reporting unwanted sexual propositions by category and number of incidents.

Of the respondents reporting incidents of unwanted sexual propositions, 77.78% (1 undergraduate, 8 faculty, and 5 staff) reported

TABLE 3. Percentage of Respondents Reporting Incidence of Unwanted Personal Attention

Group	Never (%)	Once (%)	2-5 (%)	5+ (%)
Graduate Students	8.88	0.19	0.00	0.00
Undergrad. Students	31.47	1.35	0.19	0.19
Faculty	16.22	1.74	1.93	0.00
Staff	33.40	1.54	2.32	0.58
TOTAL	89.96	4.83	4.44	0.77

TABLE 4. Percentage of Respondents Reporting Incidence of Unwanted Sexual Propositions

Group	Never (%)	Once (%)	2-5 (%)	5+ (%)
Graduate Students	8.98	0.00	0.00	0.00
Undergrad. Students	33.40	0.20	0.00	0.00
Faculty	18.55	1.37	0.20	0.00
Staff	35.55	0.78	0.98	0.00
TOTAL	96.48	2.34	1.17	0.00

that only one individual was responsible for making the sexual proposi-
tion. Four staff respondents (22.22%) said that several (2-5) individuals
were responsible for making the unwanted sexual propositions. All of the
respondents reported that the perpetrators were male. The majority
(77.22%) of the respondents reported that the perpetrators were white (1
undergraduate, 7 faculty, and 5 staff), and one faculty and 4 staff
(27.78%) said that the perpetrator was an African-American.

Unwanted physical or sexual advances, the fifth type of sexual
harassment, was defined as "unwanted touching, hugging, kissing,
fondling, sexual intercourse, or other sexual activity." The majority
(91.78%) of the respondents reported that unwanted physical or sexual
advances were never made to them, but 3.72% of the respondents (1
graduate student, 5 undergraduate students, 6 faculty, and 7 staff) said
that unwanted physical or sexual advances were made to them at least
once, while 3.91% of the respondents (1 graduate student, 7 faculty, and
12 staff) said that advances were made toward them several times (2-5
times). One faculty member and 2 staff members (0.59%) reported that
advances were made to them many times (more than 5 times). Table 5
shows the percentage of respondents reporting unwanted physical or
sexual advances by category and number of incidents.

TABLE 5. Percentage of Respondents Reporting Incidence of Unwanted Physical or Sexual Advances

Group	Never (%)	Once (%)	2-5 (%)	5+ (%)
Graduate Students	8.81	0.20	0.20	0.00
Undergrad. Students	32.68	0.98	0.00	0.00
Faculty	17.22	1.17	1.37	0.20
Staff	33.07	1.37	2.35	0.39
TOTAL	91.78	3.72	3.91	0.50

Of those respondents who reported one or more incidents of
unwanted physical or sexual advances, 73.81% (2 graduate students, 5
undergraduate students, 11 faculty, and 13 staff) said that only one individual was responsible for the advances. Three faculty and 8 staff
(26.19%) reported that several faculty or staff members (2-5) were
responsible for the advances. The majority (97.62%) of the respondents
reported that the perpetrator or perpetrators were male, while one staff
member (2.38%) said that the perpetrator was a female.

The majority of the respondents (78.57%) who reported one or
more incidents of unwanted physical or sexual advances reported that
the perpetrator or perpetrators were white (2 graduate students, 4 under-

graduates students, 14 staff, and 14 faculty). One faculty member and 5 staff members (14.29%) reported that the perpetrator or perpetrators were African-American, while 1 undergraduate (2.38%) said that the perpetrator was an Asian.

When asked, "Have you ever avoided taking a class from or working with an NCSU faculty or staff member because of the person's reputation for engaging in any of the previously mentioned behaviors?", 6 graduate students, 14 undergraduates, 15 faculty, and 17 staff (11.93%) reported that they had, while the majority of the respondents (88.07%) said that they had not avoided a faculty or staff member because of their reputation.

One Incident in Detail

Respondents who reported having experienced sexual harassment of any kind were asked to describe one incident in detail. Instructions stated: "We want to learn from your experiences so we would like to ask you to give us some detailed information about one specific incident. For questions 7-18, please think about the *one incident* that was most personally distressing to you." Approximately 29% of the respondents provided detailed information about one incident of sexual harassment.

The first of these questions addressed the sex of the faculty or staff member involved in the incident. Nearly all faculty and staff members reported as perpetrators in the incidents were male (98.03%). Three respondents (1 faculty and 2 staff) said the perpetrator in their incident was another woman.

The next question concerned the primary relationship of the perpetrator to the respondent at the time of the incident. Of respondents reporting a specific primary relationship with the faculty or staff member involved in the incident, professor/teacher was the relationship mentioned most often (27.81%), followed by supervisor of university employment (7.95%), graduate teaching or research assistant (6.62%), academic advisor (3.31%), and department head or dean (2.65%). Over half (51.66%) of those reporting a primary relationship to the perpetrator reported some relationship other than those mentioned above and specified the perpetrator to be, for example, a stranger encountered walking across campus or someone working in the same department. Of the four groups of subjects, graduate students were most likely to report professor/instructor in describing the primary relationship of perpetrator to respondent. Respondents in the faculty/staff groups were the most likely to report some relationship other than those specified on the survey, such as a stranger encountered walking across campus or someone working in the same department.

The behaviors reported by respondents discussing a specific incident in detail in descending order were *unwanted sexist comments* (57.89%), *unwanted personal attention* (16.54%), *unwanted physical or sexual advances* (12.03%), and *unwanted sexual statements* (11.27%). Two percent of respondents reporting a specific incident in detail said the perpetrator had made *unwanted sexual propositions.* Faculty and staff were the only respondents reporting sexual propositions in this section of the survey.

The largest number of respondents reporting an incident in detail said that it occurred in a classroom or lab (32.45%) or place of campus employment (29.14%). Also mentioned was a faculty or staff office (19.21%), during a trip off-campus or in some other off-campus setting (9.27%), during a meeting on campus or in some other on-campus setting (7.95%), and during a phone conversation or through the mail (1.99%).

Undergraduate students reporting an incident in detail were most likely to say it occurred in a classroom or lab (77.08% of the responses by undergraduates), while graduate students reporting an incident in detail were equally likely to say it occurred in a classroom or lab (45.45% of grads) or in a faculty or staff member office (45.45% of graduate students). Members of the staff reporting an incident were most likely to say that the incident occurred in their place of campus employment (60.86% of the staff respondents). Members of the faculty were slightly more likely to say the incident occurred in their place of campus employment (32.61% of faculty said this) than in the office of a faculty or staff member (30.43% of the faculty said office).

The next question asked respondents about the effects of their experience with sexual harassment. The effects reported most frequently were avoidance of the perpetrator or situations involving the perpetrator (65.75%) and strong emotions such as anger, anxiety, or depression (65.52%). Several respondents reporting specific effects also reported impaired work performance (15.38%) and negative feelings about self (14.62%). Of the four groups, staff and faculty were the most likely to say that they experienced strong emotions. Faculty and staff were also the most likely to say they avoided the perpetrator or situations involving the perpetrator.

The next two questions were open-ended, allowing for more detailed and specific remarks and comments. Only those respondents who reported an incident of sexual harassment were asked to complete these questions. Upon receiving the surveys, the comments were compiled anonymously to avoid any chance that the respondent could be identified.

The first of these questions asked: "In order to help us better understand sexual harassment, we would like to know more about the incident you experienced. Please write as much or as little as you feel comfortable with in order to describe the incident." Respondent descriptions varied from incidents of *sexual comments* to *sexual advances*. One graduate student wrote: "(The perpetrator) mentioned reluctance to take me on as a graduate student because I was female, and 'might get married.'" Another graduate student wrote:

I'm tired of women being abused, even verbally, to make a joke or prove a point. The reported 'incident' was merely a joke with women as the butt of it, but it really wasn't funny. It's just like a joke about 'niggers' or 'pollocks' [sic]—it's not funny. I lost all respect for the professor for having to stoop so low to attempt humor and fit in, even though he jokingly apologized to the women present. He made me uneasy.

Remarks from faculty and staff often involved cases in which the perpetrators were members of the respondents' departments. For example, a faculty member wrote: "This person approached me, inebriated, with a couple of friends at a reception at a professional meeting. He leered, made personal comments, and tried to persuade me to go to dinner with him. This was not the first time I had encountered this type of behavior from this individual."

Another faculty member wrote: "(Harassment) started out as just compliments. Then to innuendos, jokes in private, the jokes in public about our having 'something going on.' Then asking personal questions in private—such as was I sexually active, have I ever been unfaithful to spouse, etc."

The next question sought to discover the effects of sexual harassment and read: "Please describe the *effects of this one incident* on your life, your work, and/or your school work, in your own words."

Answers ranged from respondents commenting that the incident had "no effect" upon them, to "anger," or to "taking actions to avoid the perpetrator." One graduate student wrote: "I would like to have a baby while...in graduate school but I don't think I could...because I believe he would hold a grudge and ruin my career." An undergraduate wrote, "I lost respect for the instructor and dropped the class." Another undergraduate commented: "This incident made me feel very uncomfortable about my overall safety on and around campus. I'm afraid of being alone on campus at any time of day or night. I now make sure that someone is with me all times."

A member of the faculty wrote: "I feel I am locked in a dead-end job because my ideas and concerns are not taken seriously. I get little respect for the professional position I have in the department." Another faculty member wrote: "Although I knew it was irrational to think these advances were my fault, I could not help but wonder what the other individuals present must think of a woman who elicited this kind of behavior."

A staff member wrote: "(The incident) made me worry if I had in some way led him on, or was there something (in the) way I dressed, acted, etc. It made me self-conscious, nervous, angry. It made it difficult to interact with co-workers."

Respondents who had reported an incident of sexual harassment were asked if they expressed objections about the behavior to the person involved in the incident, and, if so, whether or not the behavior stopped following their objections. Nearly half (43.84%) of the respondents said they expressed objections about the behavior to the person involved. Of the four groups, members of the staff reporting a specific incident were the most likely to say they expressed objections to the perpetrator (43.75% who expressed objections were staff), and faculty members were the second most likely to express objections (31.25% of the respondents were faculty).

Nearly half of the respondents reporting a specific incident who also reported expressing their objections to the perpetrator said the behavior did not stop after they expressed their objections (45.31%), while 50% reported the behavior did stop.

Respondents were asked about the people with whom they discussed the harassing incident, such as friends, parents or other family members, resident advisor or other residence hall staff, faculty member, counselor, sexual harassment liaison, supervisor, or co-worker. Respondents reporting a specific incident who said that they did talk with someone about it were most likely to say they discussed it with friends (71.22%), co-workers (35.16%), and parents or other family members (31.09%). Among the four groups, undergraduate students were the most likely to say they discussed the incident with friends (about half of the respondents who said they would talk with friends were undergraduates), but in all groups the percentage who listed friends as someone with whom they would discuss the sexual harassment was high (90.91% of graduate students, 76.60% of undergraduate students, 69.23% of faculty, and 61.90% of staff). Undergraduate students were also the most likely to talk with parents or other family members, and faculty were most likely to say they discussed the incident with co-workers, although staff also seemed likely to talk with co-workers about the incident.

A large percentage of respondents said they did *not* talk with any of the people in the university who are designated to receive complaints (sexual harassment liaisons). Only one of the 111 respondents answering this question said that she had talked with a sexual harassment liaison. Nor did the respondents report talking with their supervisor (only 17 said they did; 97 did not), a counselor (4 did; 109 did not), a resident advisor or other residence hall staff (2 undergraduates did, but 42 undergraduates and 9 graduates did not), or a faculty member (21 did; 98 did not).

Respondents were asked if they complained to a university official or office about the incident, and if so, to whom was the complaint made, any action resulting from the complaint, and their satisfaction with the outcome. Only 4.79% of the respondents reporting a specific incident said they made a complaint to a university official or office, and only undergraduate students, faculty, and staff respondents reported making these complaints (a total of only 7 respondents complained, and 139 did not complain). These seven respondents reporting a specific incident who said they made a complaint to a university official or office listed senior faculty member (1 respondent), campus security (1 respondent), dean (2 respondents), and department head (3 respondents) as those to whom the complaint was made.

Of the seven respondents making a specific complaint to a university official or office, four reported that action was taken after the complaint was made. The outcomes reported were: one respondent reported an apology was made to her by the offender; one respondent reported that she had a discussion with her supervisor; one respondent said the offender was removed from his or her position; and one respondent said the offender's behavior changed in a positive direction. Of these four respondents, two reported that they were satisfied with the outcome.

If the respondent did *not* report making a complaint, she was asked to indicate the reasons for her decision not to complain. The leading factor was the feeling by the respondent that she handled the situation adequately (98 respondents). Other leading factors in the decision not to complain by those reporting this behavior were not perceiving the problem as one the university could or would help with (79), concern that no action would be taken (47), concern about retaliation (46), concern about personal responsibility for the incident (46), and embarrassment at being involved in the incident (40). Lack of knowledge about where to complain (33), concern about actions that would be taken (35), concern about anonymity (30), and concern about not being believed (20) also figured prominently in the reported reasons to not complain.

Visibility of Campus Policy

All survey respondents were asked about their awareness of campus policy on sexual harassment, federal law prohibiting sexual harassment, and their knowledge of campus resources for help with sexual harassment cases. Most (82.51%) of the respondents said that prior to the survey they *were* aware that campus policy prohibits sexual harassment. Respondents in the faculty and staff groups were more likely to report awareness of the campus policy than were respondents in the two student groups, although 70% or more of those in the two student groups reported awareness of the policy.

All graduate students who responded to the question concerning awareness of the federal law prohibiting sexual harassment said they were aware that it is prohibited by federal law. Undergraduate students, faculty, and staff respondents answering this question were somewhat less likely to say that they were aware that it is prohibited by federal law, but the percentage of respondents in each group was high (87.36% of the undergraduate respondents; 89% of faculty, and 92.55% of staff).

Respondents were asked to list any university office that they thought was officially designated to answer questions about sexual harassment, take reports, or give advice on informal and formal complaints. Human Resources, the Counseling Center, Campus Security, and the Affirmative Action Office received the highest number of mentions among those responding to the question. Sexual Harassment Liaison was mentioned by only 3% of the respondents. Nine percent of those answering this question said they did not know of a university office designated to respond to issues of sexual harassment.

Respondent Suggestions

The next question sought to discover the factors that would make respondents more likely to report an incident of sexual harassment. A very high percentage of the respondents (96.35%) said that assurance of protection from retaliation would increase the likelihood that they would report an incident of sexual harassment. Similarly, 96.08% reported that they would be more likely to report incidents of sexual harassment if they thought the complaint would be taken seriously, while 94.43% said that they would be more likely to report if they knew that confidentiality would be assured. Other important issues to the respondents concerned the importance of the person to whom they report having authority to take action (90.25%), having an investigation team that is independent of the department of the perpetrator (90.14%), clear and uniform consequences for specific behaviors with severity of the punishment increasing with the severity of the incident (89.94%), having a certain person designated by the campus to handle initial complaints (81.42%), and having the person responsible for hearing the complaint be a member of their own sex (73.85%).

DISCUSSION

Types and Incidence of Sexual Harassment

The survey instrument utilized in this study identified five types of sexual harassment behaviors: unwanted sexist comments, unwanted sexual statements, unwanted personal attention, unwanted sexual propositions, and unwanted physical or sexual advances. Almost 40% of the respondents reported experiencing *unwanted sexist comments* one or more times within the last five years, and slightly more than half of them said they had experienced *unwanted sexist comments* several times. Seventeen percent of the respondents experienced *unwanted sexual statements*, and almost 11% reported several incidents. Slightly over 10% were victims of *unwanted personal attention;* almost 5% had experienced it once and 5% several times. Almost 4% reported that *unwanted sexual propositions* were directed toward them. Eight percent of the respondents were victims of *unwanted physical or sexual advances*; almost 4% only one time and over 4% several times. Overall, 29% of the respondents said that they had experienced one or more forms of sexual harassment and went on to complete the section of the survey asking them to discuss one incident in detail. Eight percent of those who completed that section were graduate students, 32% were undergraduates, 30% were faculty, and 31% were staff.

Other campus studies report that 9% to 37% of the students sampled experience one or more forms of sexual harassment (Allen & Okawa, 1987; Benson & Thomson, 1982; Maihoff & Forrest, 1983; Markunas & Joyce-Brady, 1987; McCormack, 1985; Metha & Nigg, 1983; Wilson & Kraus, 1983). Some institutional surveys document that 50% to 76% of women students have experienced sexual harassment (Adams et al., 1983; Fitzgerald et al., 1988). Twenty-seven percent of the combined student samples in this research reported experiencing sexual harassment.

Overall, 30% of the combined faculty and staff samples in this study (working women) reported one or more forms of sexual harassment. This is consistent with the Fitzgerald et. al. study (1988), which reported 34% of the workers experienced gender harassment. But it is considerably higher than the percentage of faculty and staff reporting sexual harassment in the study conducted at Arizona State University (Metha & Nigg, 1983). Metha and Nigg found 13.7% of their faculty sample experienced sexual harassment; 43.7% of the faculty sample in this study reported sexual harassment. Metha and Nigg (1983) found 11.2% of the staff sample in their study had experienced sexual harassment; 23.2% of the staff sample in this study said they had experienced sexual harassment.

The type of sexual harassment behavior most often reported by respondents in this study was *unwanted sexist comments*. This was the most commonly reported sexual harassment behavior by all four groups of respondents. Thirty-eight percent of the undergraduate students said they had experienced unwanted sexist comments, while 26% of the graduate students, 60% of the faculty respondents, and 35% of the staff respondents reported incidence of unwanted sexist comments.

When all four groups of respondents are combined, the incidence rate decreases as the level of seriousness of the harassment increases (with the exception of the most serious type of harassment, *physical or sexual advances*). Table 6 shows the relationship of the types of sexual harassment (least to most serious) to the percentage of respondents reporting one or more incidents of harassment.

While this pattern of decreasing incidence and increasing seriousness holds true for each group of respondents, the faculty and staff

TABLE 6. Relationship Between Incidence Rate and Level of Seriousness of Sexual Harassment

	Level of Seriousness	Incidence Rate
Least	Sexist Comments	40%
	Sexual Statements	17%
	Personal Attention	10%
	Sexual Propositions	4%
Most	Physical/Sexual Advances	8%

groups accounted for 63% of the responses in the *sexist comments* category, 80% of the responses in the *sexual statements* category, 81% of the *personal attention* category, 95% of the *sexual propositions* category, and 83% of the *physical or sexual advances* category of behavior. It seems that undergraduate and graduate students, while experiencing some of the more serious forms of sexual harassment, are primarily victims of *unwanted sexist comments*. But women in the work force at

NCSU are much more likely than students to experience all forms of sexual harassment and especially the more serious forms. The faculty and staff respondents were also more likely than students to report multiple incidents of harassment, either by the same perpetrator or by different perpetrators, although all groups of respondents reported multiple incidents at a fairly high rate. Fifty-eight percent of the undergraduates, 63% of the graduates, 71% of the faculty, and 76% of the staff respondents said that more than one faculty or staff member perpetrated the sexual harassment incident. Apparently, the longer a woman pursues her professional career at NCSU, the greater are her chances of becoming a victim of sexual harassment.

It is unclear why the pattern of decreasing incidence with increasing seriousness does not hold true for the most serious category of sexual harassment, *physical or sexual advances.* Twice the number of respondents reported physical or sexual advances (8%) than reported sexual propositions (4%). It may be that the broad definition of physical or sexual advances used in the survey was too inclusive. The definition included a wide range of behaviors, from unwanted touching, hugging and kissing, to fondling, sexual intercourse, or other sexual activity. It is not possible to determine which of those behaviors respondents had experienced. It may be, for example, that most, or all, of the respondents reporting incidence of physical or sexual advances had experienced unwanted touching or hugging and not fondling or sexual intercourse. Yet, the category did not allow the respondents to identify which behavior they experienced. Had the survey separated into different categories the various behaviors, the rate of decreasing incidence with increasing seriousness of offense may have continued to hold through all of the categories of sexual harassment behavior.

An examination of answers to the free response question, in which respondents were asked to describe in their own words the one incident that was most personally distressing to them, shows that all of the behaviors specified in the definition of unwanted physical and sexual advances were experienced by respondents (except for sexual intercourse). If *physical advances* (unwanted touching, hugging, and kissing) had been separated from *sexual advances* (unwanted fondling, sexual intercourse, or other sexual activity), free responses indicate that about 60% of those reporting this type of sexual harassment experienced physical advances and 40% experienced sexual advances. We might assume, then, that if the category had been separated into two categories, about 5% of the respondents (overall) would have reported incidence of physical advances and 3% (overall) would have reported sexual advances. Though that would still not clearly show a descending incidence with increasing seriousness of the categories of behavior, the difference would not be as dramatic as the data presently indicate.

In both the Fitzgerald et al. (1988) and Allen and Okawa (1987) studies, incidence of sexual harassment increased each year a woman student attended the University. Sophomores experienced more than freshmen, juniors more than sophomores, and so forth. Graduate students were sexually harassed at the highest rate among all students. At NCSU, the highest percentage of students reporting sexual harassment in every category were juniors, although graduate students were the second highest, except for the category of unwanted sexist statements, in which seniors were slightly higher than graduate students. It may be that the trend shown on other campuses of graduate students having higher incidences of sexual harassment than other classifications of students does not emerge here because the sample of graduate students in this study was rather small. Only 47 graduate student responses were received. But the sample (10%) was the same as that for undergraduate students, and the return rate among graduate students was almost 41%, as opposed to a 30% return rate among undergraduate students. It may be that by the time a student reaches her senior year, she has either learned how to discourage potential perpetrators, or she has become so conditioned to the harassment that when asked she is unable even to identify it and report it. As one woman student told us, "My parents told me I'd better get used to it, because that's the way it was in the real world."

Profile of Sexual Harassers

The overall percentage of respondents identifying males as perpetrators in the five categories of behavior ranged from 78% to 100%. Both males and females were identified as perpetrators in the categories of *sexist comments* (22% of the respondents said perpetrators of sexist comments were both male and female) and *sexual statements* (8% of the respondents identified the perpetrators as both male and female). But no females were identified as perpetrators in the categories of *personal attention* or *sexual propositions*, and only one person reported that *physical or sexual advances* had been made to her by both male and female perpetrators. At NCSU, 56% of the faculty and staff population is male (75.8% of faculty are male; 40.9% of staff are male). Sandler and Associates (1981, p. 52) found "male harassment of female students and employees is the most common kind of sexual harassment because in most work and academic settings, the majority of supervisors or professors are men." Adams et al. (1983) found that only male perpetrators were identified by all of the women students, and one-half of the male students who were victims of sexual harassment. Allen and Okawa (1987) discovered that women who had experienced sexual harassment identified 99% of the perpetrators as male.

The majority of the respondents who reported they had experienced some form of sexual harassment identified the perpetrator as white. Seventy-eight percent of the perpetrators in the *sexist comments* category were white, as were 80% of the perpetrators of *unwanted sexual statements*, 83% of the perpetrators of *unwanted personal attention*, 72% of those stating *unwanted sexual propositions*, and 79% of the perpetrators of *unwanted physical or sexual advances*. At NCSU, 81% of the male faculty and staff population is white (68.6% of faculty males are white; 67.7% of staff males are white).

African-Americans were the next most frequently reported perpetrator of sexual harassment, but there were considerably fewer African-American perpetrators than white. African-Americans were said to be perpetrators by 4% of the victims of *unwanted sexist comments*, 4-1/2% of those making *unwanted sexual statements*, 13% of those giving *unwanted personal attention*, 28% of the perpetrators of *unwanted sexual propositions*, and 14% of those making *physical or sexual advances*. Staff respondents were the most likely of any group to report the perpetrator as an African-American. At NCSU, 14.9% of the male faculty and staff population is African-American (2.6% of faculty males are African-American; 31.1% of staff males are African-American).

Of the respondents who completed the part of the survey asking them to discuss one sexual harassment incident in detail, undergraduate students were the most likely to report that the perpetrator was their professor or instructor (70% reported this finding). The next most common perpetrator of sexual harassment for undergraduate students was a teaching or research assistant (17% reported teaching or research assistant as perpetrator). Forty-six percent of the graduate students who suffered sexual harassment said that the perpetrator was their professor or instructor, and 18% said it was their academic advisor. Faculty and staff respondents were more likely to report the perpetrator as an administrator, another academic professional, a university employee, or a colleague sharing their work space (78% of the faculty listed one or more of these as perpetrators, as did 72% of the staff respondents). Seven percent of the faculty said the perpetrator was their department head or dean. Nineteen percent of the staff respondents said the perpetrator was the supervisor of their university employment. Apparently, those people with whom a student or professional woman spent the bulk of her on-campus time were the most likely to be perpetrators of sexual harassment.

Respondents describing one incident in detail were also asked to identify where the incident occurred. The undergraduate students identified their classroom or lab as the place where the majority of the harassing behaviors took place (77%). This is not surprising, since undergraduates come in contact with their most common perpetrator (professor or instructor and graduate teaching or research assistant) in classrooms and labs, where the most commonly reported type of harassment for undergraduates (unwanted sexist statements) is most likely to occur.

Classroom or lab (listed by 46% of graduate student respondents) and faculty or staff member's office (also listed by 46% of graduate student respondents) were the most common sites of sexual harassment of graduate students. Since the most commonly reported perpetrators of sexual harassment by graduate students were professors or instructors and academic advisors, classroom and office would be the likely locations for their behaviors.

Thirty-three percent of the faculty respondents and 61% of the staff respondents said that their place of campus employment was the most likely site of harassment. Next most likely for both faculty and staff was the perpetrator's office (30% of faculty and 15% of staff said their perpetrator's office). This is consistent with the types of harassment commonly experienced by faculty and staff respondents and with their relationship to the perpetrator (administrator, colleague sharing work place, supervisor, etc.). More than 26% of the faculty said that the harassing behaviors occurred during a road trip off-campus and/or at a meeting on-campus. Apparently, the least serious types of harassment (sexist comments and sexual statements) occur in public settings (classes, labs, meetings), and the more serious types of sexual harassment (personal attention, sexual propositions and physical or sexual advances) take place behind closed doors (offices).

Effects and Responses to Sexual Harassment

All four groups of respondents reporting incidents of sexual harassment identified the most common effect of harassment was strong emotions (such as anger, anxiety, and depression). Sixty-six percent of the respondents said that they had experienced strong emotions as a result of the sexual harassment. Avoidance of the person or situations involving the person was also mentioned by 66% of the victims as a response to the harassment. All groups except the graduate students also reported experiencing negative feelings about themselves (15%) and impaired work performance (15%). Six percent of the respondents reported impaired academic performance and 4% identified physical problems, altered academic or career plans, or altered employment or career plans. Other research has found the effects of sexual harassment to include avoiding classes and work settings, physical symptoms, interference with performance in class or at work, disillusionment, lowered self-esteem, strong emotions, altered career plans, depression, and an inability to sleep (Adams et al., 1983; Allen & Okawa, 1987; Benson &

Thomson, 1982; Fitzgerald et al., 1988; Markunas & Joyce-Brady, 1987; Sandler & Associates, 1981).

Fifty-six percent of the victims of harassment said that they did not express their objections about the behavior to the perpetrator. Of the 44% who did express their objections to the behavior, only half said that the behavior stopped as a result of their objections. A majority of the victims of sexual harassment are apparently not translating their strong emotions into appropriately assertive behaviors in response to the harassment. Avoiding the harasser or situations involving the harasser seems to be the method of choice by victims of sexual harassment. Adams et al. (1983) found that for both female and male student victims, the most common response to sexual harassment was to ignore the behavior and avoid the perpetrator.

When respondents were asked if they talked to anyone about the incident, undergraduates were most likely to say they talked with friends and family members. Graduate students listed their friends and family, but also said they talked with co-workers about the harassment. Faculty and staff also identified friends, co-workers, and family members, and faculty added they talked with other faculty as well. Overall, friends (71% of the respondents) and co-workers (35% of the respondents) were those most often chosen as confidants.

Only 29% of the faculty and 23% of the staff reported that they talked with a supervisor about the incident of sexual harassment. A few undergraduate students and faculty said they talked with a counselor, and only one person reported talking with a sexual harassment liaison, who was officially designated as a resource person within the various colleges and schools on campus. Victims of sexual harassment at NCSU are talking with people they know well about the incidents, but are largely withholding information about their experience from people who might officially take action against the perpetrator.

Visibility of Campus Policy and Reporting Procedures

All respondents were asked if they were aware that sexual harassment is prohibited by campus policy and by federal law. Eighty-two percent of the respondents did know that campus policy prohibits sexual harassment, and 91% knew that sexual harassment is illegal under federal law. Undergraduate students were the most likely to report that they were not aware of the policy or the law, but even so, the majority of undergraduates did know of both (70% said they knew about campus policy, and 87% said they knew about the federal law). However, when respondents were asked to identify any university office that is officially designated to answer their questions about sexual harassment, give them advice, and take their reports, only 30% of all respondents could identify these offices as Human Resources (19%), the Affirmative Action Office (8%), the College or School Sexual Harassment Liaisons (3%), and the Office for Women Student Concerns (2%). Respondents say they know that NCSU prohibits sexual harassment, but they apparently have little knowledge of what office or person(s) are designated to help them if they become victims.

When respondents were asked to identify factors that would make them more likely to report an incident of sexual harassment to a university office or official, all four groups listed protection from retaliation as the most important factor (96% of all respondents listed protection from retaliation). Ninety-four percent said they would be more likely to report incidents if they had assurance of confidentiality. Other factors that were identified as important were having an investigation team that is independent of the department of the person involved (90%), knowing the person they report to has the authority to take some action (90%), having clear and uniform consequences for specific behaviors (90%), having certain persons designated by the campus to handle initial complaints (81%), and having the person responsible for hearing the complaint be of the same sex as the victim (74%).

Almost 30% of the respondents sampled in this survey said they had been a victim of sexual harassment in the last 5 years, and a large percentage of those have knowledge of campus policy and federal law. Yet, they apparently have little knowledge of the campus procedures set up to protect them and little faith that they will be protected if they report the incident. Only 5% of the respondents who reported that they were sexually harassed within the last 5 years at NCSU (7 out of 139 victims) made a complaint to any university official or office. Action was reportedly taken in 4 of those 7 reports, but only 2 victims said that they were satisfied with the outcome.

In an attempt to determine why victims of sexual harassment do not choose to report the incident(s), the same group of respondents were asked to identify factors that led them to their decision not to complain. The most common factor (71% of the respondents) was that the victim felt she had handled the situation adequately, even though only 7 reported the incident, and the second most common response to the incident was avoiding the perpetrator. However, 61% of the victims reported that they did not report the incident because they did not think it was a problem with which the university could or would help them. Apparently, victims have little faith that the institution will help them and that the risk of further exposure outweighs the potential gain in stopping the harassing behavior. These results are again quite consistent with those found by Allen and Okawa (1987).

CONCLUSIONS

Sexual harassment is a significant problem for women students, faculty, and staff at North Carolina State University. A high percentage of respondents experienced one or more forms of sexual harassment, and many of those experienced repeated incidents. Faculty and staff women experienced sexual harassment at a higher rate than women students. Sexual harassment interferes with the educational and professional climate for female students, faculty, and staff at North Carolina State University.

Perpetrators of sexual harassment are almost exclusively male and are mostly white. They are faculty, teaching and research assistants, academic advisors, supervisors, administrators, and colleagues of NCSU women. Sexual harassment is not limited to a few work units, but exists throughout the entire university.

Although women at NCSU are aware that the university has a policy prohibiting sexual harassment, a large percentage of respondents said that they did not believe the university would or could do anything to stop sexual harassment. Only a small percentage of respondents could identify any office or person designated to give information about sexual harassment reporting procedures or take reports. The most common response to sexual harassment is avoidance. Few respondents confronted the harasser or reported the incident to the proper authorities.[1]

REFERENCES

Adams, J.W., Kottke, J.L., & Padgitt, J.S. (1983). Sexual harassment of university students. *Journal of College Student Personnel, 24*, 484-90.

Allen, D., & Okawa, J.B. (1987). A counseling center looks at harassment. *Journal of NAWDAC, 51*, 9-16.

Benson, D. J., & Thomson, G.E. (1982). Sexual harassment on a university campus: The confluence of authority relations, sexual interest and gender stratification. *Social Problems, 29*, 236-51.

---

[1]The authors forwarded five recommendations to the university administration along with this study, all of which were accepted. The recommendations were that the university should: renew efforts to educate victims about reporting and grievance procedures; assure victims of confidentiality, protection from retaliation, and that action will be taken against perpetrators; staff an anonymous hotline to offer victims information about their rights; renew efforts to educate all faculty and staff about sexual harassment and the consequences of harassing behaviors; and conduct this survey every five years.

Brown, W.A., & Maestro-Scherer, J. (1986). *Assessing sexual harassment and public safety—a survey of Cornell women.* Ithaca, NY: Cornell University, Office of Equal Opportunity.

Dziech, B. W., & Weiner, L. (1984). *The lecherous professor: Sexual harassment on campus.* Boston: Beacon Press.

Fitzgerald, L.F., Shullman, S.L., Bailey, N., Richards, M., Swecker, J., Gold, Y., Ormerod, M., & Weitzman, L. (1988). The incidence and dimensions of sexual harassment in academia and the work place. *Journal of Vocational Behavior, 32,* 152-175.

Johnson, M.P., & Shuman, S. (1983). *Sexual harassment of students at the Pennsylvania State University.* University Park, PA: Pennsylvania State University. (ERIC Document Reproduction Service No. ED 250 984)

Maihoff, N., & Forrest, L. (1983). Sexual harassment in higher education: An assessment study. *Journal of NAWDAC, 46,* 3-8.

Markunas, P., & Joyce-Brady, J. (1987). Underutilization of sexual harassment grievance procedures. *Journal of NAWDAC, 50,* 27-32.

McCormack, A. (1985). The sexual harassment of students by teachers: The case of students in science. *Sex Roles, 13,* 21-32.

Metha, A., & Nigg, J. (1983). Sexual harassment on campus: An institutional response. *Journal of NAWDAC, 46,* 9-15.

Oshinsky, J. (1981). *Sexual harassment of women students in higher education.* Dissertation Abstracts International, 42 (2-A), 555.

Project on the Status and Education of Women. (1978, June). *Sexual harassment: A hidden issue.* Washington, DC: Association of American Colleges.

Sandler, B.R., & Associates. (1981). Sexual harassment: A hidden problem. *Educational Record, 62,* 52-57.

Scott, J. (1984). *Sexual harassment behaviors, management strategies, and power-dependence relationships among a female graduate student population.* Dissertation Abstracts International, 44 (10-A), 2983-4.

Sigal, J., Gibbs, M., Belford, S., Ronan, G., & Gervasio, A. (1987, April). *Sexual harassment on three college campuses.* Paper presented at the Annual Convention of The American Psychological Association, NY. (ERIC Document Reproduction Service No. ED 289 091).

Whitmore, R.L. (1983). *Sexual harassment at UC Davis.* Davis, CA: University of California-Davis. (ERIC Document Reproduction Service No.ED 248 824).

Wilson, K.R., & Kraus, L.A. (1983). Sexual harassment in the university. *Journal of College Student Personnel, 24,* 219-224.

▼Chapter 11

Reporting Sexual Harassment: Reconciling Power, Knowledge, and Perspective

Judith K. Bowker
Oregon State University
Corvallis, OR

▼ Women who must decide whether or not to report sexual harassment face several predicaments. Extending far beyond questions of immediate strategy, some of these predicaments are rooted in the nature of the fundamental faculties of rhetoric. Historically, these faculties have emanated from public, legal and political events; the faculties are defined and named—indeed, invented—by scholars, mostly males. Since decisions whether to report sexual harassment are made mostly by women, ontological and epistemological questions arise, questions that cast doubt on how or if fundamental faculties of rhetoric remain useful and catalytic in nature within this specific human context.

Reporting sexual harassment entails argument and persuasion, two central concerns of rhetorical study. Many scholars contemplate argument and persuasion as having objective existence apart from the contexts in which they occur. These scholars acknowledge the need to modify argument and persuasion to accommodate certain immediate contexts; audience analysis is an example of such an accommodation. However, in these acts of contextualizing, the fundamental presumptions scholars make regarding the essence of the nature of argument and persuasion—in other words, the ontological stance from which the epistemological foundations are shaped—remain fundamentally unchanged. As a result, the means by which argument and persuasion are fit into the context may change; the central presumptions of what constitutes argument and persuasion do not.

Those traditional perspectives were invented and developed largely by a homogeneous, dominant group. Their design of these rhetorical interventions is used to guide and evaluate human acts; such guidance and evaluation attempt to set parameters for social interaction. Legal decisions about sexual harassment are such a set of parameters. To define policy in regard to sexual harassment, legal rhetoric will bring together standard presumptions about what constitutes argument and persuasion with that group's perceptions of people's reports of the event; this combination fashions what has been called contextualization.

We have made some basic epistemological and ontological presumptions to arrive at this conceptualization of rhetoric. We believe that contextualization accomplishes accommodation to all human circumstances. I suggest that because of those basic presumptions, contextualization is incapable of transforming our conceptualization of rhetoric to make it constructively functional for women reporting sexual harassment.

I suggest that in the case of sexual harassment, victims (largely women) face an unprecedented dilemma; they are forced to use a rhetorical process (of which the legal procedure is a metaphor) that by its very nature omits their own ontological integrity, as they are members of a group that is not the dominant power in the culture. Harassment is a private, usually unobserved behavioral manifestation of power and dominance. The existence of harassment is accorded by the hierarchical character of a culture; consequently, a double bind is created when sexual harassment is managed by using standards of persuasion and decision making derived from the dominant group of that hierarchy.

What is acclaimed as contextualization of argument and persuasion is contextualization only insofar as those rhetorical devices fit within the ontological framework from which they emerged. What has been termed "contextualization" does not attempt to accommodate differing epistemologies or ontologies. By its very nature, then, rhetoric used to institute forms for social evaluation privileges the dominant cultural group while disenfranchising all others. Thus, women making decisions about whether to report sexual harassment face complex conundrums of personal and intellectual integrity.

The construction of a more inclusive conceptualization of rhetoric can result in the renovation of our communication practices in this regard. Such a construction looms as a momentous task, one not to be achieved in a few years and perhaps not even in a lifetime. Indeed, learning how to recognize and accord credibility to other ontologies, long suppressed and ignored by our dominant epistemological practices, appears impossible. Nevertheless, the attempt must begin.

Collaboration of perceptions, experiences, and thoughts is one way to discover and explore such an unknown ontology. Temporarily noncritical scrutiny of contributions from those in the disenfranchised groups might allow the necessary time for a now invisible ontology to develop. I propose we collaborate by conversing about unique or significant aspects of the phenomenon of men and women confronting one another about sexual harassment. We can disclose to each other our various perspectives; the collection we amass will provide us with a multitude of ideas and useful compounds between and among which to construct a more ontologically sensitive rhetoric.

Toward that end, I contribute these thoughts about how the relationship between epistemology and ontology might affect our conceptualizations of rhetoric regarding sexual harassment. I confess I make little distinction between what scholars symbolize as "rhetoric" and what they term "communication." Further, I perceive concepts such as rhetoric and communication not only as scholars choose to describe them, but also as they are used and experienced by people other than scholars. Sometimes the two appear congruent; other times they do not. Making the two uses—academic and public—distinct seems momentarily inconsequential and perhaps even adverse during this process of brainstorming.

The thoughts that follow, therefore, may breach academic convention; nonetheless, I believe they can be evidenced by human experience. Deriving from those thoughts are six areas of inquiry I consider critical for framing an ontologically sensitive rhetoric that could represent referents perceived by all parties within the experience of sexual harassment. Questions raised by deliberating these issues are not readily answered; I leave them at the conclusion of this work as possible catalysts for the next reflection by myself or others.

EPISTEMOLOGICAL BARRIERS

What we believe about the nature of knowledge predisposes us with inclinations about whether genuinely to engage assorted epistemologies. If we believe knowledge is attainable and knowable, we cannot also believe it is not. Historically, the general, Western, rhetorical perspective has derived from an epistemology that has at its nucleus duality, such as truth and nontruth. That duality defines what can be known and how it can be known. Although some contemporary rhetorical positions have been more inclusive, the heritage of dualistic thinking is evident in social interactions such as political parties, competitive ideologies, and the design of the mechanism we call the legal system. Since the basis of duality is either/or, inherently, this dualistic epistemology omits and ignores other epistemologies.

To discern truth from nontruth, traditional Western thinkers have developed specific criteria, for example, evidence. Using those criteria in various combinations, Western thinkers decide what is convincing proof and what is not. The formula for the appropriate combination of criteria is dictated by the variables of a given situation. Once people commit their thinking to that plateau of duality, the rhetoric of separation and distinction—that is, discerning truth from nontruth or proof from nonproof—encompasses no other epistemologies.

This Western rhetorical perspective, following a separatist epistemology, pervades the thinking and teaching of those in dominant power in this Western culture. Consideration of the epistemological preferences of the dominant power in a culture sheds light on how people in that culture are socialized to interpret the existence of and the value of other perspectives. What we believe those perspectives to be, the value we assign to perspective taking, and the value we assign to interplay among perspectives are socially constructed and instructed in relation to that dominant epistemological position. Understanding that position helps clarify how or if other ontologies—those shaping how that dominant influence will be received by members of the nondominant groups in a culture—survive, are coopted, or are replaced.

In an effort to discover how the epistemologies or ontologies differ between people of different power classes, one approach is to describe discrepancies between the circumstances of experience of the two groups represented in sexual harassment: the harasser and the one harassed. Those differences constitute the needs to be met by a more inclusive epistemology.

Outlining a concrete shape of a new model of epistemology is premature. These present ruminations are meant to envision pertinent components, however disparate, to be included. If the new model is to embrace multiplicity and diversity (and ambiguity), the process of creating that model also needs to embody multiplicity to coordinate means and end. Simultaneously embracing diverse perspectives may facilitate affecting multiple perspectives.

A first step is to seek out heretofore unbidden perspectives. Trading among perspectives requires temporary suspension of familiar delineations, delineations so familiar that we may no longer be aware of their existence. Our socialization teaches us to act in exactly an opposite manner; a plan to include, integrate, and relate in an effort to achieve simplicity is an opposite concept than we are expecting. However, this temporary complexity encountered by the accommodation of multiple perspectives may be a necessary step toward making visible an inclusive epistemology.

Relocation from that which we have collectively—though perhaps implicitly—agreed exists to that which we may now or at some future time agree exists can generate ambiguity and uncertainty. From our present epistemological basis, we perceive ambiguity and uncertainty as process; we interpret their characters as exigence; for the most part, we do not perceive exigence acceptable as an end.

Our common response, then, is to search for the end by imploding into the mass of previously verified "knowledge" or perspective to find the demarcations of the edges of the duality. Within this mass, we find comfort in rules and limits that have been socially and historically authenticated or validated. We know the precise locations of the basic tenets of our ideology.

However, implosive reactions cannot embrace "knowledge" outside of those preestablished parameters. Such is the case with scholars who apply standard rhetorical perspectives to the situation of sexual harassment. If a pervasively dominant group exists in a culture, the epistemology and the ontology of that group cannot be the epistemology and ontology of any lower power class group of a culture. Inherently, the lower power class group experiences the world from a different perspective than does the dominant group; how they know who they are and how they determine the substance of knowledge is calibrated in some measure by their relationship to the dominant group. The dominant group creates their own perspective without that component; ironically, if the perspective of the dominant group were truly an inclusive one, dominance would not exist and all groups would have the opportunity to interchange epistemologies and ontologies.

In the case of sexual harassment, then, those women who do not share the views of the dominant culture and who have been sexually harassed by men who do share that view, must mismatch their own ontology with another group's epistemology. Similarly, at the moment of the harassing event, men would have to accommodate that same mismatch to have all knowledge of the perspectives of their actions. Scholars who press standard rhetorical perspectives onto sexual harassment experiences are applying dissimilar ontological and epistemological frames.

One way to ameliorate this dilemma is to derive an epistemology that serves many ontologies. Such an epistemology might better accommodate our struggle to define sexual harassment and create policies about discerning who has and who has not sexually harassed another person. The need for means of settling claims of sexual harassment offers a window of opportunity to begin work toward developing an epistemology that can be ontologically sensitive.

One approach to creating this new knowledge is to contrast the traditional rhetorical framework with the experiences as they are expressed by those involved. The private and secretive nature of sexual harassment may dramatically alter the function, the character, and the essence of rhetoric. If rhetoric is epistemological, then studying incongruencies between the framework and the expressed experience may indicate possibilities for new exploration. In regard to the human experience of sexual harassment and the reporting thereof, examining the specific and unique epistemological and ontological considerations may help define the nature, mark the limits, and discern the power of rhetorical intervention, intervention such as traditional argument and persuasion.

SIX AREAS TO EXAMINE

To begin this collaborative effort, I collected thoughts about epistemological and ontological elements undergirding the cultural phenomenon of sexual harassment. I began with those elements that most directly interfered with the viability of women reporting incidents of sexual harassment. Meant to be neither exclusive nor inclusive, these six areas of inquiry represent those thoughts.

1. Persuading the More Powerful

One useful area of inquiry is the exploration of the nature of the persuasion of a more powerful human culture by a less powerful one. The essences of persuasion are isolated from issues of power except in analogical terms. Is persuasion as manifested by two people of relatively equal economic and political positions different than the phenomenon used by dyads of dramatically unequal power? Does contextualization have the capacity to level the difference? Does the basic, dualistic presumption of the rhetorical strategy of persuasion preclude it from being serviceable in power mismatches of certain magnitudes?

Do presumptions about the catalytic character of rhetoric mislead us to conclusions about its usefulness? Implications about power held by one faction of a culture or subculture may change dramatically the functions of persuasion and the capacity of rhetoric to have an impact on the relationship between itself (rhetoric) and action. Since rhetoric has been developed by the dominant cultural group, perhaps its ability to serve the lower power-class groups should be examined.

Fundamental to the problems of power and persuasion is the symbolic nature of sexual harassment. In other forms of "proof," we direct inquires toward the referent, using such devices as evidence to check perceptions. Our intention is to verify the referent and discover "proof," which, for some, leads to truth.

Sexual harassment creates a dilemma because it is not sexual harassment until it is so interpreted. Sexual harassment is not the physical act; it is the interpretation of that physical act. We never leave the symbolic framework. A person can deny harassment is working because he or she can rhetorically define that harassment was not present; therefore, following standard principles to debate either the "truth" or "proof" of the event is ineffective.

The private and interpretative nature of sexual harassment are the unique qualities that directly connect this human experience to epistemological and ontological questions. Even within that private setting, acts of sexual harassment can be strategically planned to accomplish duplicity; care is often taken to ensure that the acts can be interpreted in different ways. The public scrutiny endemic to traditional rhetorical forms of argument and persuasion is thus co-opted. For example, in argumentation, evidence is defined as something potentially verifiable; sexual harassment occurs in private. Each of the persons involved interprets the act individually; no traditional means of validation exist.

Only if the harasser violates others—who then contribute individual episodes—can traditional means of validation be used, and then only to a limited extent. How many testimonies of citizens in a lower power class equal the testimony of one citizen from a higher power class? The nature of sexual harassment creates a "truth" for a victim who is a member of the lower power class; that victim's "truth"—experienced individually in a moment unobserved by any corroborating person—cannot be validated within a system constructed to serve the epistemology of the higher power class.

Other cases may share the private and interpretative nature of sexual harassment; however, sexual harassment is defined by these characteristics. What is left of our rhetorical means for decision, then, is the characters of the individuals. Our culture affords more power and arguably more value to men than to women; politically, economically, relationally, and domestically, our tradition favors male over female. In the case of sexual harassment, then, decisions are made based on character rather than other commonly used means of perception checking; moreover, argument and persuasibility are defined by social order rather than by individual character. The system becomes a closed circle.

Investigations into the relationship between culturally based power and functions of argumentation and persuasion may help clarify the components necessary for the design of an ontologically sensitive epistemology.

2. Persuasion and a Closed System

Another area to explore is the nature of persuasion when the content of the persuasion pertains to constructs inside a closed system, and the source of persuasion is outside that system. In particular, what is the character and internal congruency (of conceptualization, strategy, and effect) of persuasion used by a source outside a closed system when the purpose of the persuasion is to reconfigure reality as it is perceived by participants inside such a system?

Using a biological metaphor, the function of this persuasive action is to inject into a closed system antibodies from other epistemological and ontological perspectives, perspectives which exist only outside that closed system. In the case of sexual harassment, the question is important: Does an outside rhetorical perspective (in the case of sexual harassment, a perspective held by a group with less social power) inherently possess the capacity to be transferred through the protective membrane of a closed system? Without public verification—the source of authenticity for lower power-class groups—can rhetorical means derived from within that closed system confer on those outside the system a means powerful enough or pervasive enough for their purposes? In addition, can that "outsider" abate the rapid societal reproduction of historically closed-system components?

3. Physical Difference as a Component

Closely aligned with issues of power and accessibility are issues of physicality. Although the nature of sexual harassment is symbolic, an analysis of the phenomenon must include reflections about the role of physical size and strength in creating meaning for this event. Unequivocally, we validate that physical dominance of one group over another creates an imbalance of physical strength. In general, we invoke rhetorical means in those instances to achieve equal status. If the rhetorical means has been constructed from an ontology emanating from the physically more powerful group, and if the epistemology has then derived from that ontology, then resistance to using those rhetorical means by the less powerful group seems necessary. Not only would the rhetorical means handicap the lower power-class group, but it even may be advantageous to the higher power-class group.

As a result, given the private and isolated nature of this human interaction, that physical imbalance may be the basis for the existence of unique fields through which individuals involved in cases of sexual harassment interpret truth and the reality of the moment. That private nature may elevate issues of physicality and power; arguing and persuading about matters of sexual harassment may be fundamentally different than argument and persuasion in regard to other topics that concern the sexes, for example, abortion. Rooted in controversies contrasting biology with socialization, questions are germane about how comparative physical strength—not between individuals but between groups—affects ways of knowing.

4. Physicality and Symbolization

In a more abstract sense, examining our system of assigning symbols to human experiences creates questions about the inherent power of the human invention of communication in contrast to the inherent power of the human experience of fear. At that abstract level, we can envision sexual harassment as the symbol (in terms of human action) for which the physical imbalance between the sexes is the referent.

The question to ponder is whether within the nature of argumentation and persuasion exists the power to disengage the socially constructed link (symbols and predisposition to belief that "truth" will resolve dissonance) between sexual harassment and physical dominance; further, and perhaps more important, is the power to disengage the two equal to the primal force that engages that linkage? Does the nature of this kind of persuasion that disengages such a linking differ from another kind of persuasion, the nature of which is to disengage mental symbols from mental referents or mental symbols from referents that are not life-threatening?

Derivative from this issue are questions about the essential power of rhetoric. Does that power derive from an epistemology or does it derive from its creator? Does rhetoric in Western culture enjoy a socialized power, one afforded to rhetoric (and the law) because it has been designed, revised, and touted by those who have been accorded power by the culture? Does rhetoric possess an order of power that can competently interact with power ontologically accessed?

Perhaps the fundamental capabilities of rhetoric, of human communication as we know it, are too limited to engage the central problems of sexual harassment; perhaps the precepts of physical dominance in this particular, isolated human interaction supersede rhetorical means. This open-ended thought provides an opportunity for exploration in dramatic divergence from accepted socialized practices.

5. Empowerment for Ontological Visibility

Notions of empowerment seem to suggest that lower power-class groups—and others—can invent power sources and resources through rhetorical means. The goal of empowerment is to manifest an ontology not otherwise apparent. These endorsements of empowerment would seem to respond to the questions and issues raised in the preceding sections.

However, the feasibility, the plausibility, and the viability of the empowerment ideology are all called into question by examination of the fit between the empowerment ideology and the power resources used for rhetorical constructs. Perhaps the paradox that rhetorical strategies evolve from a higher power-class epistemology must be explored more carefully. Can an empowerment strategy created from within the confines of such an epistemology appropriately and efficaciously produce a means by which a separate ontology might become visible? From within that closed system, might there be bases of privileged power that would always be left unanswered and unaffected?

With regard to sexual harassment, can empowerment strategy accomplish its ends without the cooperation of the higher power class? Can women's experiences be verified by means consistent with their ontology, and men's with theirs, without the agreement of the dominant power in the culture? If not, does the acknowledgment of empowerment strategy simply assuage the dissimilarities between the experiences of men and women, absorbing them into the dominant ontology?

6. Abdication of Power

Following questions about securing acquiescence from the dominant power in a society, my final thoughts revolve around the nature of the abdication of power by that group. To understand the incidence of experiencing and reporting sexual harassment, we must explore the nature of persuading a high power class to abdicate power in light of the prospect that this dominant group may never again regain that power without violating its own, newly instituted ethical standards.

To set policies that encompass the ontological perspectives of all parties involved in sexual harassment, one approach would be to replace canons of verification with ones more inclusive of the means by which all participants in the action make that verification. Should the dominant group choose to accept the new means, it would abdicate all power with no recourse for regaining it. To date, most sexual harassment policies still accord the responsibility for verification to the person being harassed; in the isolated, private context, that person is made responsible to name the act in an unambiguous manner. Such policies retain for the dominant the resident power. They preserve the ontology of one group while denying that of the other.

Can diverse ontologies be represented with a single perspective? Can an epistemology serve multiple ontologies? Is persuading a dominant group to abdicate power in this way—thus changing its basic presumptions about its relationship to others in the world—essentially as violent an act as denying or interfering with social access by lower power-class people to their own ontologies? This aspect of persuasion is given little account in most recommendations for immediate strategies and policies about sexual harassment.

CONCLUSION

A framework of complex and perhaps—in some cases—unpalatable questions emerge from a contemplation of these quandaries. Can the epistemology of the dominant cultural power embrace the ontological issues manifested by the victims' needs to "prove" acts of sexual harassment? Given the nature of the presumptions and conceptualizations of rhetoric, can persuasion and argument respond to sexual harassment issues in ways that appropriately serve both harasser and victim?

Is change in the structure of social conditions and relationships of physicality possible only when cataclysmic internal innovation spontaneously occurs within the closed system? What are the dimensions of such an event? In terms of sexual harassment, might the hearings involving Clarence Thomas and Anita Hill be named as such a cataclysmic event? Did that event break the existing circle of presumption and supposition?

If we presume it did, we observe that in the aftermath of those hearings, a new order has begun to emerge that redefines argument and persuasibility; a new circle is formed. However, that circle seems to have retained the same shape as that which it is replacing. In reference to sexual harassment, perhaps the case needs to define argument and persuasibility to a greater extent than argument and persuasibility need to define the particular case.

To accomplish a different reality in regard to sexual harassment, is internal instigation of change necessary from within a closed system if that system is the dominant cultural power? To actuate the change, must that internal instigation be accompanied by persuasion from those with perspectives from outside the system? In either case, does the closed, dominant system not retain the principle resources of power and central authority to delegate identity and knowledge? In so doing, does it not also retain reproductive rights and privileges?

What means reduce the rate of reproduction of rote, deleterious standards of behavior, standards that have in the past nurtured sexual harassment? Does this particular closed system nurture within its boundaries the strategies for such a reduction?

These questions do not have answers for the present. Perhaps we will discover them to be rhetorical questions. Nevertheless, these questions are useful as perspective-giving backdrops for strategies planned and policies devised in regard to the reporting and the incidence of sexual harassment. As victims of sexual harassment struggle in an irrational climate—made so by the incoherent juxtaposition of their own ontology and of the epistemology within which they must act—they continue to make decisions about whether or not to report sexual harassment. Perhaps the collaboration begun with this work might better align power, perspective, knowledge, and the means by which we know. In the end, such a constellation might illuminate a new justice.

Responding to Harassment

▼Chapter 12

Sexual Harassment Responses of Working Women: An Assessment of Current Communication-Oriented Typologies and Perceived Effectiveness of the Response

Robin P. Clair   Michael J. McGoun
Purdue University   Cleveland State University
West Lafayette, IN   Cleveland, OH

Melissa M. Spirek
Bowling Green State University
Bowling Green, OH

▼ The term *sexual harassment* was catapulted into public view when Anita Hill appeared before Congressional members and charged Clarence Thomas, then Supreme Court nominee, with badgering her for dates, discussing pornography, and making bawdy

The first author is grateful to Cleveland State University for providing a research challenge grant which funded this project. The first author also acknowledges Betsy Campbell, Katie Namen, Cindy Rauser, Annie Streepy, and Kelly Thompson for their outstanding work on this project. Furthermore, Ed Schiappa, Cynthia Stohl, and Ruth Smith offered helpful advice and criticism along the way. Finally, Timothy Hack and Jill Rudd offered their support while I struggled with the sensitive issue of sexual harassment. Thank you.

210 Clair, McGoun, & Spirek

comments. Hill's testimony suggested that these actions continued even after Thomas was named director of the Equal Employment Opportunity Commission (EEOC). The apparent irony of this particular situation is that Thomas was director of the institution responsible for dealing with sexual harassment (Equal Employment Opportunity Commission, 1980). This would, for all practical purposes, eliminate the recourse of taking action through formal organizational channels. Even though the Hill-Thomas hearings brought the topic of sexual harassment to the forefront of public concern, our study, which preceded the congressional hearings, found that Hill's reported experiences were not unique.

A study of 20,000 government employees conducted by the U.S. Merit Systems Protection Board (U.S. MSPB) in 1981 indicated that 42% of women and 15% of men reported encountering sexual harassment within the previous two years (Fairhurst, 1986). Although men may be harassed by women or other men, the majority of sexual harassment is projected toward women by men (Fain & Anderton, 1987). Furthermore, like Anita Hill, most women do not report sexual harassment through formal organizational channels (Collins & Blodgett, 1981; Tangri, Burt, & Johnson, 1982).

If 17% of harassed women report quitting their job due to the experience (Loy & Stewart, 1984), and less than 5% use formal channels to defray harassment (Tangri et al., 1982), then the other 78% of harassed employees are "putting up with it," as described by a current educational video ("Sexual harassment", 1991). It might be more accurate to say that approximately 78% of harassed female employees respond to sexual harassment at an informal level.

Bingham (1991) recognizes and reminds us that not all harassment is the same, nor can all harassment be dealt with at an interpersonal level. Yet, "many sexual harassment situations may be managed successfully through face-to-face communication," and "successful management of sexual harassment by individuals is likely to be enhanced when appropriate and easily accessed support from the organization is in place" (p. 110). The study of interpersonal responses to sexual harassment is not intended to usurp sociopolitical studies nor to discourage justifiable legal action or dismiss the accountability of organizations; rather, the purpose is to assess one of the possible recourses to sexual harassment. Furthermore, the pervasiveness of informal interpersonal responses to sexual harassment is well documented and justifies an in-depth analysis of responses in order to evaluate their effectiveness (see Bingham, 1991).

A vast majority of researchers who study responses to sexual harassment devote their efforts to typologizing the responses according to the communicative effectiveness of the message. Communication effectiveness equates with assertiveness (Gruber, 1989), transcendence

(Wood & Conrad, 1983), or rhetorical message design logic (Bingham & Burleson, 1989). While each of these three typological treatments are valuable, pragmatic, and heuristic, they are also constraining due to the nature of typologies. Consequently, each of the typologies may lead researchers to frame responses to sexual harassment in a limited way. The purpose of this empirical analysis is to review and compare women's responses to sexual harassment according to three communication-oriented typologies: (a) the assertiveness typology (Cammaert, 1985; Gruber, 1989; Maypole, 1986), (b) the design-logic and goal-structure typology (Bingham & Burleson, 1989), and (c) the responding-to-paradox typology (Wood & Conrad, 1983).

TAXONOMIES/TYPOLOGIES

Typologies are inherently limiting. The very function of a typology is to take rather complex issues, concepts, or items and offer a system for classification or categorization. A typology is "a powerful analytic tool that affects even our most basic understandings of the world" (Gathercoal, 1991, p. 4). Taxonomies are too easily dismissed as being atheoretical, when in fact they "silently shape the process of inquiry and influence a priori the nature of the resulting theories and observations" (p. 5). Typologies often result in a virtually preanalyzed assessment of the subject under investigation by limiting "the conditions under which it is possible to know them" (Foucault, 1973, p. 70). In terms of sexual harassment, taxonomies may reflect a patriarchal bias in the ordering or classification of responses to sexual harassment. Thus, taxonomies may be ideological and hegemonic. Consequently, to accept typological treatments of sexual harassment responses uncritically may unwittingly support a dominant world view.

Obversely, typologies can guide research toward elegant and useful theories which may illuminate the sources of and solutions to a problem. Therefore, it is paramount that we review the current sexual harassment typologies in order to assess their ability to exhaustively classify the response strategies to sexual harassment and discuss the resulting implications. Although Gutek (1989) wisely suggests that we should extend beyond the framework of typologies in order to understand the complexity of sexuality in organizations, it is equally critical that we assess the heuristic value of current typologies, since they contribute to theory and guide future research.

SEXUAL HARASSMENT RESPONSE TYPOLOGIES

As noted earlier, the U.S. MSPB undertook a massive data collection to investigate sexual harassment among government employees. Based upon the results of that study, social scientists launched research programs in several directions, one of which was to investigate sexual harassment responses in terms of an assertiveness typology (Cammaert, 1985; Gruber, 1989; Maypole, 1986). In addition, Bingham and Burleson (1989) offer a typology of sexual harassment responses that are concerned with both the goals of the victim and the communication strategy used to convey the message (also see Bingham, 1991). Finally, Wood and Conrad (1983) describe what can be considered a typology of responses to the professional woman's paradox. We believe this typology can be applied to the more specific paradox encountered in sexual harassment. Each of these three typologies will be briefly reviewed.

Passiveness/Assertiveness Typology

Maypole's (1986) assertiveness typology places sexual harassment responses into four categories along a continuum of assertiveness: avoidance, diffusion, negotiation, and confrontation. Using Maypole's typology and continuum as a reference point, Gruber (1989) argues that the four-part typology is too simple and that the nuances of different responses should be categorized into several subtypes.

Avoidance. Avoidance responses, the least assertive strategy, emotionally or psychologically keep the victim from encountering the discomfort of harassment (e.g., ignoring, quitting). Tangri et al., (1982) suggest that the majority of respondents used avoidance, ignored the situation, or did nothing in response to sexual harassment. Gruber (1989) suggests that few studies report quitting as a strategy, but this may be due to the fact that most studies ask the respondents about sexual harassment at their present place of employment. Loy and Stewart (1984) reported that approximately 17% of the respondents used transferring or quitting as an option when questioning included previous places of employment. Women who used legal recourse or transfer/quitting as options suffered the most emotional and physical symptoms of stress; while women who ignored the harasser experienced the least stress-related problems (Loy & Stewart, 1984). Gruber (1989) comments that nonrecognition or masking (i.e., doing nothing or going along with it), and quitting or asking for a transfer, suggest very different ways to avoid harassment, some of which may be better categorized under the rubric of diffusion.

Diffusion. Diffusion is considered slightly more assertive than avoidance and includes such tactics as trivializing the encounter or making a joke of the matter. Reframing the event so that it is trivialized or joked about is a means of "pretense," which results in a "working consensus" (Goffman, 1959, pp. 9-10). Specifically, the event is framed to minimize its impact so that working people can maintain their present role. Gruber (1989) adds that telling co-workers or seeking social support as a form of diffusion allows the individual to minimize the emotional impact when negotiation seems too risky.

Negotiation. Negotiation is even more assertive than diffusion. "It involves reactions that are more symmetrical to the actions of the harasser and more attuned to the recipient's perception of the interaction" (Gruber, 1989, p. 3). Negotiation can be a direct request for the harasser to stop or a bargaining tool with some leverage such as threatening to tell a superior. Gruber (1989) considers indirect threats of exposure, which could result in embarrassment or a form of sanctioning, as types of negotiation. Gruber (1989) suggests that "seeking outside help," or more specifically, seeking legal or informational advice (Cammaert, 1985) should be considered a form of negotiation because it is less often used as a direct confrontation and is more often used as a bargaining tool.

Confrontation. Finally, the most assertive response is direct confrontation, in which harassed people respond in a direct and forceful manner or take their complaint to organizational officials. Confrontation is "telling" not "asking" (Gruber, 1989). Confrontation is often selected in organizations where sexual harassment charges are legitimated through organizational policy, turned to as a last resort, or chosen because the intensity of the harassment is so extreme that the victim needs to respond either verbally or physically at the immediate time of the attack (Gruber, 1989). In addition, the victim may report it to administrative or police authorities (Cammaert, 1985).

Design Logic and Goal Structure Typology

A second communication-oriented typology of responses to sexual harassment was provided by Bingham and Burleson (1989). The authors designed their typology based upon the work of O'Keefe (1988), which elaborates on the complexity of messages in two ways: (a) the goal structure may be complex (e.g., a woman wishes to stop the harassment and maintain a healthy working relationship with the harasser), and (b) the design logic or communication strategy may vary in its complexity. Three basic communication strategies are discussed and explained by

Bingham and Burleson (1989). First, a woman could respond spontaneously and emotionally using an *expressive* strategy (e.g. "You make me sick," p. 192). Second, a harassed employee might respond in a straightforward and functional way by identifying the speech act and providing a *conventional* response (e.g., "No, I certainly will not cooperate with you—not in the way you mean," p. 192). Third, the harassed worker might respond in a *rhetorical* manner by recognizing that rhetorical situations are constructed symbolically and can be reconstructed through redefining or reframing (e.g., "I realize you're just joking about this, but I don't find it especially funny," p. 193).

Bingham and Burleson (1989) presented 577 undergraduate students with two hypothetical scenarios of working women encountering sexual harassment. The scenarios supplied different response choices in terms of their design logic and goal structure. The results of the study indicate that the use of messages containing sophisticated design logics and multifunctional goal orientations were perceived by the students as "maintaining relational rapport with the harasser" (p. 208). However, this finding may have been an artifact of the study because the authors only provided multifunctional messages that combined stopping harassment with a positive-oriented goal (i.e., maintaining the working relationship through some form of face saving).

"Significantly, however, messages reflecting more sophisticated design logics or goal structures were not perceived as more effective at stopping the harasser from engaging in objectionable behavior" (Bingham & Burleson, 1989, p. 209). Again, this conclusion may be due to the choice of examples provided by the authors for the students to judge (i.e., multiple goals were limited to two in number when it is possible for women to have many goals). Furthermore, the use of prosocial goals (i.e., saving the harasser from facing a negative identity) may have been perceived by the students as weak or ineffectual for its inherent condoning of the behavior. When the behavior is condoned through face saving and deflected as being wrong, the mixed message may seem to negate itself. Finally, the design logics do not include transcendence.

Responding to Paradox Typology

Wood and Conrad (1983) suggest that when women are placed in situations that are double binding they feel trapped. They explain that the concept of "professional woman" is in itself a paradox propagated in organizations. The term "professional" has long been equated with male stereotypical behaviors, which means that when a woman is attacked for using stereotypically female patterns of managerial communication, she is faced with defending her "professionalism." Obversely, if she is attacked for using a masculine style, she is faced with defending her "womanness" (Conrad, 1990). Wood and Conrad suggest that several response choices exist with respect to dealing with the paradox. Women can perpetuate the paradox, redefine the situation, or transcend the paradox. These response styles can also be applied to sexual harassment.

Perpetuating the paradox. When people communicate in ways that maintain patterns of communication that are psychologically unhealthy or double binding, they are perpetuating a paradox. Watzlawick, Beavin, and Jackson (1967) argue that people often fall into this trap because they are mystified by a behavior that sends contradictory messages. Communication that contributes to this pattern includes: acceptance, counter-disqualification, and withdrawal. Acceptance of sexually harassing remarks or behavior may be exemplified when women allow the harassment to continue because they believe the acts are justifiable based upon their gender or job type. Counter-disqualification is an offensive rather than defensive pattern of launching attacks at the other individual or at one's self (Wood & Conrad, 1983). Withdrawal may include such extremes as quitting.

Redefining the situation. Based on the work of anthropologist, Gregory Bateson (1972), Watzlawick et al. (1967) suggest that communication behavior that reframes the situation may help to break the double bind, but will not completely transcend the situation. Redefining or reframing refers to viewing the situation in terms other than harassment and then dealing with the situation accordingly. For example, a woman could reframe the sexual harassment as a joke and then suggest that she does not care for that type of humor (e.g., "I know you meant that as a joke, but it's really not funny to me").

Transcending the paradox. According to Wood and Conrad (1983), transcending the paradox may be the only viable means of breaking the double bind. Transcending a paradox requires that harassed workers recognize the situation as harassment by viewing the situation from a larger framework. Thus, if a male co-worker or superior continually comments on the alluring qualities of a woman's figure, clothing, perfume, or hair style, stands "too" close or hugs or kisses her, she must recognize that these are not compliments, but forms of sexual harassment. If the same woman reframed the situation, she might say, "I know you're trying to be complimentary, but I'm not looking for compliments of that kind." If, on the other hand, the woman transcended the situation, she might say, "These are not compliments. They are sexually harassing remarks and behaviors." She transcended the situation by commenting on the communication event.

PERCEPTION OF EFFECTIVENESS

Wood and Conrad (1983) did not empirically test their typology or their assumption that transcendence would be the most effective means of curtailing paradox. Bingham and Burleson (1989) tested their typology using factor analytic techniques: however, they did not test actual case studies. The Bingham and Burleson results indicate that some responses may be better at maintaining interpersonal relationships, but none are perceived as more advantageous in stopping harassment. It is important to note that both the Bingham and Burleson model, as well as the Wood and Conrad model, limit their focus of attention to verbal informal/interpersonal replies.

Livingston (1982) utilized the data collected by the U.S. MSPB to investigate the relationship between type of response and the successfulness of the resolution as perceived by the victim. The author reported that 47% of the women who took formal action thought the situation improved due to their response; however, 33% of the women who took formal action thought the situation became worse due to their response. Livingston (1982) explains that although objecting to the harasser was an increasingly assertive response strategy, the satisfaction with its results was questionable. Sixty-five percent of the women who used an assertive objection felt the response had helped to improve the situation, while 59% of the women who avoided the harasser thought the situation improved. Furthermore, 43% of the women thought "their most assertive response made no difference," while 54% of the women said "their most assertive response made things better" (p. 15). The mixed results might be explained more by the content of the message than the fact that the victim responded forcefully instead of politely or formally as compared to informally.

Based upon the above literature review of sexual harassment, the following research questions will be explored. First, how do women respond to sexual harassment based upon the proposed typologies? Second, how useful and valuable are these three particular typologies for the study of sexual harassment? Finally, the question of whether certain responses are perceived to be more effective than others will be addressed.

METHOD

Sampling Procedures

Fifty women were selected on the basis of a quota sample which matched U.S. Census data in the areas of race, marital status, job occupations, and whether the woman worked part time or full time. The sampling strategy included collecting the U.S. Census figures for working women in the categories listed in Table 1. The first author calculated the ratios for a sample of 50 employed women and then worked with 5 undergraduate students who devised a grid on paper, representative of the categories. The students then used a networking system to fill the quotas. Specifically, the students began with relatives, friends, acquaintances, and moved to friends-of-friends, coworkers, and acquaintances, and finally to strangers until they had met the quota requirements. All 50 women were selected from a large midwestern metropolis. The undergraduate students then requested an interview with these working women.

The 50 women were individually interviewed in person by volunteer undergraduate female students. The undergraduate students were trained in interviewing techniques at three meetings which the five interviewers attended. The undergraduate volunteers helped to write the questions and design the questionnaires in terms of ordering the questions. All questions were placed on an interview form which the interviewer used to jot down notes while the respondent was talking. In addition, all of the interviews were tape-recorded with the permission of the respondents. Although probing questions varied from interview to interview, this variation was more a function of dealing with different respondents than different interviewers.

Gruber (1989) claims that the majority of studies asked women about sexual harassment that occurred at their present position. The advantage of this procedure is that women address their most current experiences. The two disadvantages are: (a) it eliminates the extreme response of quitting; and (b) it affects the amount of confrontation a woman reports. In order to overcome this methodological caveat, the interviewers asked respondents to discuss current or past situations of sexual harassment.

Specifically, the interviewers asked respondents several general questions about their jobs. They focused their questions on what the women liked and disliked about their jobs. After hearing about both the positive and negative aspects of the individual's job, the interviewers asked about the most frustrating aspects of the job and how the interviewees coped with these frustrations. Respondents were then asked if they had ever encountered sexual harassment on the job. The unstructured probing questions that followed were left to the discretion of the interviewer to determine if the subject should be further pursued. Finally, the respondents were asked if they had ever encountered job discrimination.

The first author and second author each independently placed the interviewees' responses into one of the categories as described by Maypole. Responses that crossed categories were labeled as such and reported as combinations of different style responses. Interrater reliability was acceptable (K = .88). Discrepancies occurred with two responses. Resolution was achieved when the coders agreed that one response should be described as confrontational and the other as an example of negotiation. Furthermore, chi-squares were computed to address whether statistically significant relationships among the categorical responses and between the categorical responses and occupation, marital status, race, and part/full-time status existed.

The first author and third author each independently placed the interviewees' verbal responses into one of the categories described by Bingham and Burleson. A Cohen's kappa statistic was computed to assess interrater reliability (K = 1.0). Once again, chi-squares were computed to address the relationship between the goal-structures and design-logics categories and between the goals/logics strategies and occupation, marital status, race, and part/full-time status.

RESULTS

Several minor discrepancies occurred between the expected and the achieved ratios for the sample population, which indicated primarily a difference in perception on the part of the interviewer and the interviewee. These discrepancies included job occupation and difficulty filling quotas across all four categories with respect to part/full-time or marital status.

The resulting sample of women that reported encountering sexual harassment on the job numbered 24 in all (48%). With regard to marital status, 8 women were single, 11 married, and 5 divorced or widowed. Twenty-one of the respondents were white; three were black. Seventeen respondents were full-time employees and seven were part-time. Generally, the results indicated that a lower number of Hispanic women reported sexual harassment than would be expected by comparable percentages within the United States census (0% of Hispanics and others reported experiencing sexual harassment). The sample of women who reported harassment also shows slightly higher percentages of single and divorced women reporting harassment, with fewer married women reporting harassment (married 11/27—41%, single 8/16—50%, divorced/widowed 5/7—70%). Race and part- or full-time status did not demonstrate any major differences from expected ratios (see Tables 1-4).

Exploratory chi-squares were computed to test for significant relationships between the strategies themselves and the strategies within the sociodemographic variables. None of the chi-squares were significant. This indicates that the strategy the women selected based either on the passive/assertive continuum (Typology I) or the goals or design logics (Typology II) had little, if anything, to do with their occupation, race, marital status, or employment status (see Tables 1-4).

PASSIVENESS/ASSERTIVENESS TYPOLOGY

Among the women in this study who reported that they had encountered sexual harassment, their various responses ranged from "walking away" or "making a joke of it" to confronting the harasser, seeking outside support, or considering legal action. With respect to the general response categories established by Maypole (1986), 11 women used avoidance, 3 women used diffusion, 7 women used negotiation, and 3 women used confrontation. However, these numbers require qualification due to responses crossing categories. Many women responded by avoiding the issue and rationalizing it through diffusion, others combined techniques of negotiation and confrontation. Finally, some women offered different response styles contingent upon the type of harassment or the status of the harasser. The subtypes are explained within the general categories and presented below.

Avoidance

Of the 11 women using avoidance techniques such as ignoring it, walking away, or doing nothing, 3 women took the most extreme form of avoidance and responded by quitting their job. One woman suggested that at her previous place of employment, the sexual harassment started off as joking, but persisted and eventually became more serious. She said, "I felt that I was jeopardizing my job, and that individual's job. And I saw that there was no reason for that, so I had to leave."

One worker reported that at her job the men at work made jokes that were in poor taste and would give her unwanted hugs. She simply reported quitting, but added that if it were to happen today, she would

Table 1. Census and Sexual Harassment Frequencies According to Occupation

	Managerial Professional	Technical Sales	Service	Production	Laborers	Farming
Census Number	12,289	22,803	9,182	1,153	4,372	561
Census Percentage	24.4%	45.3%	16.2%	2.0%	8.0%	1.0%
Sample Expected	12	23	9	2	4	1
Sample Achieved	12	21	9	3	4	1
Sexually Harassed Ratio	5/24	7/24	8/24	3/24	1/24	0/24
Sexually Harassed Percentage	20.8%	29.2%	33.3%	12.5%	4.2%	0.0%
Typology I						
Avoid	6	1	4	0	0	0
Diffuse	1	1	1	0	0	0
Negotiate	1	3	2	1	0	0
Confront	0	1	0	1	1	0
Typology II						
Conventional Unifunctional	1	0	0	0	1	0
Rhetorical Multifunctional	0	3	0	1	0	0

Note. Census Figures are based upon the U.S. Bureau of Labor Statistics, Employment and Earnings, January 1988, for Employed Civilians during 1987.

immediately retain a lawyer. The third respondent acknowledged that the sexual harassment she encountered was not "blatant," but she could tell it was harassment and she simply quit her job.

The majority of women whose responses were placed into the avoidance category did not report how they handled the situation, but implied that they did nothing and were left with an uneasy feeling. Several women offered rationalizations for having done nothing, such as "I was too young to handle it," "There's a lot of it out there," and suggested that to confront all of the sexual harassers that they encountered would be an overwhelming task.

Avoidance/Diffusion

Other workers' responses that primarily fell into an avoidance category also used diffusion when explaining sexual harassment. For example, one woman reported that her manager would try to kiss her. She responded with: "I just sorta got up and walked away and made a joke of it." An employee in a similar situation said that when the man at work would "come up behind me and rub against me . . . I just kept avoiding him . . . It got to be kind of a joke." Thus, these women were both ignoring and diffusing it at the same time. Another respondent explained that she handled it differently when it was a superior as opposed to someone more similar in organizational status. She would just "blow 'em off" and not take it seriously if it was management, but if the harasser was one of the cooks in the restaurant, she would "blow 'em off and tell them to keep away from you." This woman avoided and diffused management, but she avoided and confronted co-workers of equal status. Another woman combined avoidance and diffusion by saying she would "just blow it off and smile at them," so they knew their advances were not getting her upset.

Six of the 14 women who used avoidance or diffusion reported that they would use different methods in the future, suggesting that the previous method of response was not the most successful. Some of the approaches that women said they might use in the future included: "threatening," "prosecuting," "I wouldn't let him get away with it," "I would have found a lawyer immediately, "I would call someone," and "handle it better." One woman suggested that the response needed to be in line with the harassment and that she would take more drastic action if the harassment was more serious.

Table 2. Census and Sexual Harassment Frequencies According to Race

	White	Black	Hispanic & Others
Census Number	43,634	6,730	4,296
Census Percentage	82.0%	11.0%	7.0%
Sample Expected	41	6	3
Sample Achieved	41	6	3
Sexually Harassed Ratio	21/24	3/24	0/24
Sexually Harassed Percentage	87.5%	12.5%	0.0%
Typology I			
Avoid	10	1	0
Diffuse	2	1	0
Negotiate	7	0	0
Confront	2	1	0
Typology II			
Conventional Unifunctional	2	0	0
Rhetorical Multifunctional	3	1	0

Note. Census Figures are based upon the U.S. Bureau of Labor Statistics, Employment and Earnings, January 1988, for Employed Civilians during 1987.

PARADOX TYPOLOGY AND GOAL STRUCTURE AND DESIGN LOGIC TYPOLOGY

Although the results continue with the passive/assertive categories of "negotiation" and "confrontation," the previous passive/assertive categories did not lend themselves as readily to the more verbally oriented categories of reframing or transcending paradox and goal-structure/design-logic typologies. Thus, at this point more so than in the previous sections the analysis allows for an overlapping of the typological categories.

**Table 3. Census and Sexual Harassment Frequencies
According to Marital Status**

	Married	Single	Divorced or Widowed
Census Number	32,000	13,617	8,424
Census Ratio	59.2%	25.0%	15.6%
Sample Expected	29	13	8
Sample Achieved	27	16	7
Sexually Harassed Ratio	11/24	8/24	5/24
Sexually Harassed Percentage	45.8%	33.3%	20.8%
Typology I			
Avoid	4	3	4
Diffuse	3	0	0
Negotiate	2	4	1
Confront	2	1	0
Typology II			
Conventional Unifunctional	0	1	1
Rhetorical Multifunctional	1	3	0

Note. Census Figures are based upon the U.S. Bureau of Labor Statistics, Employment and Earnings, January 1988, for Employed Civilians during 1987.

Negotiation, Reframing, and Transcending

Gruber (1989) regards the choice of seeking outside help as a means of negotiation usually selected by a victim who finds avoidance and diffusion inadequate. One woman reported, "I contacted an organization that dealt with women being sexually harassed on the job. I didn't really follow through because I would really need a lot of support from other people that had been harassed and nobody was willing to do anything about

Table 4. Census and Sexual Harassment Frequencies According to Part and Full Time Employment

	Part Time	Full Time
Census Number	12,587	34,672
Census Ratio	23%	63%
Sample Expected	14	36
Sample Achieved	17	33
Sexually Harassed Ratio	7/24	17/24
Sexually Harassed Percentage	29.2%	70.8%
Typology I		
Avoid	3	8
Diffuse	1	2
Negotiate	2	5
Confront	1	2
Typology II		
Conventional Unifunctional	0	2
Rhetorical Multifunctional	1	3

Note. Census Figures are based upon the U.S. Bureau of Labor Statistics, Employment and Earnings, January 1988, for Employed Civilians during 1987.

it. It was shortly after that I quit." This employee found seeking outside support just as inadequate as avoidance or diffusion and thus turned to a less assertive strategy of quitting. She reported that in future incidents she would take "the same steps, but . . . would probably be a lot more direct. I would be more confronting now than I was then."

An additional six women, who responded to sexual harassment by way of negotiation, used reframing. Reframing is one form of negotiation that fits well into Goffman's (1959, 1963, 1974) concept of framing experiences. It allows each individual to maintain their current work-related role primarily through face saving. Negotiated reframing is slightly different from reframing in order to diffuse or mask the incident entirely. Diffusion is a pretense that the harassment is not really harassment or that it did not really bother the victim when in fact it did. Negotiated reframing may allow the harasser to save face and allow the victim to acknowledge her discomfort with the male's behavior. Two women specifically used this form of negotiation.

One woman reported that men at the workplace harass her in varying ways from critiquing her clothing and shoes in an inappropriate way to rubbing her knee. Although she said, "You almost want to dish it back, really bad," she controlled that urge and instead used face-saving techniques or diplomatic negotiation by saying, "I know it's joking. [She clearly explained in the interview that she knows it is not joking.] And I know you're just kidding around, but there's a limit . . . Look, it makes me look bad." This employee allowed the harasser to save face by suggesting that his intentions were not harmful, but that he had clearly crossed the line in terms of the "limit." The respondent reported that this technique worked well for her so far, but that she recognized that she might need to change her tactics if the harassment was more serious.

This passage reflects the respondent's use of diplomacy by relieving the offender of responsibility for his actions and limits any serious intentions by framing the incident as "kidding around." Bingham and Burleson (1989) would describe this response as a rhetorical multifunctional message; it redefines the situation, persuades the harasser to stop, and maintains the work relationship. Wood and Conrad's typology (1983) would also place this response in the category of redefining/reframing. This response has not yet transcended the paradox.

A second respondent used a face-saving technique by saying to her manager, "Listen, Pat you know I really like you and I'm very fond of you, but I'm not fond of you in that way." This respondent used diplomacy by complimenting the manager before telling him indirectly that his advances were not welcomed. The respondent reframed what she considered mild harassment into a display of fondness by the harasser. Like the previous message, this particular response typifies what Bingham and Burleson (1989) refer to as a rhetorical multifunction message (i.e., rhetorically, it redefines the situation, and displays the two goals of persuading the harasser to stop and deflecting a negative identity away from the harasser). The respondent continued to tell the interviewer that when the harassment was not too intense, like in the case of her manager, she felt she handled it quite effectively. The former harasser has since become one of her "strongest supporters" in the organization.

Another form of negotiation is to threaten indirectly to expose the individual so as to cause him embarrassment or more serious sanctions. One woman reported that when a married man asked her out she responded by saying, "I'll meet you there with your wife and we can all have dinner." A second respondent said, "I just told him, individually, that it was pretty rude considering that he was married. And it really was an injustice to his wife." These statements are similar to what Bingham and Burleson (1989) refer to as a conventional unifunctional message: "It issues a directive for the harasser to stop" and supplies a reason for the harasser to comply (p. 192). The directive to stop is not clearly stated, but rather implied. A threat to expose the man as married or expose him to his wife is also implied. It would seem that both the directive and the threat are covert. Wood and Conrad (1983) would probably describe these statements as reframing the situation because the women take the harassment out of the work arena and into the private domain.

An additional negotiation technique is to speak to the harasser about his actions in a direct, but not a forceful or confrontive, manner. One woman said that when she and her boss debated issues, if she was right, then he would say, "Go take your nice ass and get out of here." Her response to this treatment was to take it seriously and say, "You know, you don't have to say that." This response does not fit neatly into Bingham and Burleson's typology, however an agreed upon best fit is the rhetorical multifunctional category. The message suggests that sexual harassment is problematic and that the harasser may transcend the behavior if he so desires. The message is unique in that the woman seems to have transcended the harassment as Wood and Conrad (1983) describe transcendence, but she takes it a step further by offering pedagogical assistance to the harasser so that he can transcend sexist behavior as well.

Confrontation, Reframing, and Transcendence

Although confrontation is generally one of the least employed strategies, three respondents in the present study confronted their harassers, one indirectly and two directly. The indirect confrontation is described below:

> Yes, I had this operator, my first year, who would constantly ask me for sex. Every morning he be waiting to ask me for sex. And he would always tell me he'd pay me, that he'd give me his check whatever it took for me to have sex with him. I brought my boyfriend on the job and he stopped [laughing].

The respondent was quite satisfied with the results of this strategy, which circumvents formal channels. The message sent by the victim in this case might be considered an actualized threat. That is, she skips over the verbal threat (e.g., "If you don't leave me alone, I'll tell my boyfriend and he'll take care of you") and enacts what would have been threatened. The woman's response is a nonverbal rhetorical message. Although the message is apparently unifunctional, the woman could have several other goals, including retribution or retaliation. The design logic goes well beyond a spontaneous emotional response; it could be considered a reframing technique, since it moves the work relationship out of the public domain and into the private domain of interpersonal relationships. However, this type of nonverbal response is not a representative choice in the Bingham and Burleson typology.

A direct confrontation was reported by another respondent who said, "I set him straight. He wasn't my type." This particular message redefines the harassment into the harasser's request for sexual companionship and then insults the harasser by suggesting that he is inferior (i.e., not her type). This response could be classified as a rhetorical multifunctional message because it rhetorically redefines the situation and functionally attempts to stop the harassment and denigrate the harasser.

In a second example of a direct approach, one woman said, "You better not do that because it is sexual harassment." Bingham and Burleson (1989) offer similar responses, but none capture the strength of this message or its obvious use of metacommunication. The woman does not deflect the harasser by redefining or even directly (i.e., conventionally) responding to the harassment, rather, she makes a statement about his communication, "it is sexual harassment," thereby employing metacommunication or transcendence.

The respondent was satisfied with this approach. She even offered advice to other women who might find themselves in the same situation. She said you have to "nip it in the bud." Further, she said that harassment is "just a bunch of baloney" and at times it can be "scary," but if a person is strong she can handle it.

CONTINGENCIES AND OVERLAP IN STRATEGIC RESPONSES

Sexual harassment against women in the workforce may range from innuendos to physical attacks and may be instigated by co-workers, customers, superiors, or subordinates. Different responses are occasionally employed depending on the status of the harasser and the type of sexual harassment. One woman explained that "if I picked up every innuendo and made a battle of it, I'd be worn out." She continued to say that when "guys are telling real sexist jokes, I just leave," but "one guy propositioned me and I just talked to him. Another guy blew kisses and smacked his lips at me. I never figured out what to do with him, and then he quit." This individual had a repertoire of responses dependent upon the type of harassment encountered. Several other women agreed that more intense harassment may call for more serious recourse.

DISCUSSION OF TYPOLOGIES

Specifically focusing on the value of the typologies, it is important to reiterate that each of the three typologies offers a valuable framework for studying sexual harassment, yet each inherently possesses limitations and biases as well. In addition to supporting Gruber's point that the assertiveness typology lacks refinement, the results of the present study indicate several other areas of concern. First, the bipolar continuum of assertiveness leaves one wondering if assertiveness is the only attribute worthy of study. Second, the typology may evidence a male bias toward responses with its focus on the stereotypical male trait of assertiveness (e.g., women who use ignoring the harasser as a strategy are implementing a statement of negation, and depending upon the relationship between harassed and harasser, the negation might be quite powerful). Finally, the assertiveness typology promotes dualism (i.e., passive/assertive responses), which tends to frame the responses in an overly simple and artificial way. Glennon (1983) suggests that this artificiality or duality might be overcome by combining instrumentalism and expressivism into one framework.

Bingham and Burleson's (1989) typology attempts to synthesize instrumentalism (e.g., goal function) with expressivism (e.g., design logic). The typology suggests that women are not limited to a single dimension. However, the authors only offer two goals (i.e., face saving and stopping the harasser) and three "design logics." The emphasis placed upon face saving needs to be supplemented with additional interpersonal goals, since only 2 of the 10 women employing negotiation strategies in this study used face-saving techniques. Seeking retribution, stress reduction, communication control, or systemic goals such as offering role models to other working women or building coalitions against sexual harassers could also be goal options. The "design logics" also offer evidence of limitations with respect to the types of rhetorical strategies available (e.g., sarcasm, humor, and creativity are not discussed). Finally, this typology limits the communication situation to functional goals and rhetorical devices to determine efficacy, which neglects historical ramifications, power contingencies, and constraints due to the prevailing ideology.

Wood and Conrad's typology extends beyond passive/assertive communication and the rhetorical designs of reframing, but does not offer multiple goal functions. While their rhetorical designs move beyond reframing to include transcendence, they do not offer a description of one response encountered in the present study. One woman transcended the situation and even pointed out to the offender that he too can transcend the situation. This behavior might be called "alter-naturing." She provided an alternative for the harasser that could free him from what seems natural (i.e., assuming the harasser believes that it is natural for men to degrade women).

Despite the restrictions found for each of the typologies in this study, women do seem to exhibit a range of responses that could be explained in terms of assertiveness. However, to limit interpretations just to assertiveness seems overly restrictive and may be a deterrent to more sophisticated frameworks. Similarly, support has also been found for Bingham and Burleson's design-logic and goal-function typology. However, as the authors have noted, the typology does not address nonverbal exchanges or more complex concerns about sexual harassment at the organizational or societal level. Finally, some support has been found for Wood and Conrad's typology, especially with respect to the use of transcendence. Furthermore, this typology may be extended to include a form of transcendence, which is accompanied by statements that attempt to alter the nature of the paradox. These typologies offer valuable frameworks to guide the categorization of sexual harassment responses, but researchers must be aware of the inherent limitations of each of the typologies. Future research on sexual harassment should give serious attention to typological treatment of the issue.

BEYOND THE CURRENT TYPOLOGIES

The current study gathered responses from women who actually had encountered sexual harassment. While the sample size is small and the participants' responses were based upon recall, their messages may reflect the more natural qualities of the situation, and more specifically, the wording of their responses. The messages tended to be brief, which seemed to be a function of the message and not the individual's propensity to be more or less verbal.

Although the responses were succinct, they packed powerful messages that often lent themselves to multiple interpretations. For example, the woman who suggested that the man bring his wife along sent out a variety of messages at both the content and relational levels through the use of sarcasm. The statement could be interpreted to mean that sexual harassment is obnoxious, or that sexual harassment might be condoned, but certainly not from a married man, or it could imply fooling around is all right as long as the married man is honest with his wife, or as long as he lets her participate. Of course, the most obvious interpretation is that the victim does not condone sexual harassment and reminds the man that he has a wife at home who probably would not condone it either. Her use of sarcasm allows humor to reduce tension, diffuse possible retaliation from the harasser while insulting him, as well as offer multiple meanings that confuse the harasser to some degree. This technique maintains the interpersonal relationship, deflects harassment, offers retribution, reduces stress, and allows the woman to regain control of the communication situation.

Multiple interpretations, as well as multiple goals, are evident in other responses such as "You're not my type." Once again, the remark lends itself to multiple interpretations. For example, sexual harassment is not condoned, or I condone this behavior, but not from someone like you. The sarcastic message allows the woman to insult the man and feel that she has achieved a sense of retribution. The woman who said to the man quite succinctly, "You know, you don't have to say that," is addressing several issues in one sentence: (a) he should take notice of his behavior; (b) he has the freedom to decide whether to act this way or not; and (c) she does not condone this behavior. It is interesting to note that of the two respondents who employed transcendence, only one demonstrated multiple message use (i.e., "You know, you don't have to say that") and neither seemed to incorporate sarcasm or humor as did the reframers (i.e., "It is sexual harassment").

Another communication commonality among the responses was the use of covert threats embedded within the messages. While the two women who mention that the man is married do not explicitly threaten to tell the wife, the man knows that the possibility exists. The covert threat allows the woman to strategically position herself in the sense that the harasser has no idea what her next move will be. Another example of the use of covert threats with strategic positioning is when the woman says, "You better not do that because it is sexual harassment." The man does not know how the woman will handle the situation if he persists in his actions.

IMPLICATIONS FOR FUTURE RESEARCH

Future studies should focus on synthesizing the passive-assertive typology, uncovering additional goals as well as rhetorical strategies, investigating how "alter-naturing" moves beyond transcending the paradox, and exploring the creation and use of multiple-meaning messages or strategically ambiguous messages as strategic positioning (see Eisenburg, 1984, for a discussion of strategic ambiguity). In addition, what role the messages play as part of the "deep structure games" (Frost, 1987) found in organizations needs to be investigated. If researchers argue to maintain the use of typologies, then future studies may ask why so much attention focuses on categorizing the victims responses much to the neglect of categorizing the assailant's actions. For example, Daly (1984) suggested that harassers often frame their actions in terms of "harmless entertainment," which provides further criticism of the woman if she challenges their behavior: "Can't she take a jock/joke?" (p. 209). By categorizing these different types of harassment (e.g., jock/joke), women may be provided with names for behavior they were previously at a loss to describe and a means for assessing the paradoxical frame.

Based upon the results of this study, one could advise women to use messages with multiple meanings, face saving with covert threats, strategic positioning, or transcendence coupled with or without alternaturing in response to sexual harassment. However, several areas should be further investigated before advice is systematically provided. For example, some women were quite happy with ignoring or negating the harasser, while others were dissatisfied with this approach. In addition, researchers should continue to investigate the relationship between severity of the harassment and power or status differentials with relation to sexual harassment responses. Furthermore, and more critical to the problem of sexual harassment in the workplace, scholars should investigate the causal factors. Future studies should continue to address the psychological profile of the harasser (Booth-Butterfield, 1989; Livingston, 1982), the role-related aspects (Gutek & Morasch, 1982), the structure of the organization (Kanter, 1976, 1977), and most important, the formation of society (Daly, 1975).

REFERENCES

Bateson, G. (1972). *Steps to an ecology of mind.* New York: Random House.
Bingham, S. G. (1991). Communication strategies for managing sexual harassment in organizations: Understanding message options and their effects. *Journal of Applied Communication, 19,* 88-115.
Bingham, S.G., & Burleson, B.R. (1989). Multiple effects of messages with multiple goals: Some perceived outcomes of responses to sexual harassment. *Human Communication Research, 16,* 184-215.
Booth-Butterfield, M. (1989). Perception of harassing communication as a function of locus of control, work force participation, and gender. *Communication Quarterly, 37,* 262-275.

Cammaert, L. (1985). How wide spread is sexual harassment on campus? *International Journal of Women's Studies, 8* (4), 388-397.

Collins, E. G. C., & Blodgett, T. B. (1981). Sexual harassment: Some see it, some won't. *Harvard Business Review, 59* (2), 77-95.

Conrad, C. (1990). *Strategic organizational communication: An integrated perspective* (2nd ed.). Fort Worth, TX: Holt, Rinehart, and Winston.

Daly, M. (1975). The qualitative leap beyond patriarchal religion. *Quest, 1,* 20-40.

Daly, M. (1984). *Pure lust: Elemental feminist philosophy.* Boston: Beacon Press.

Eisenburg, E.M. (1984). Ambiguity as strategy in organizational communication. *Communication Monographs, 51,* 227-242.

Equal Employment Opportunity Commission. (1980). Title 29—Labor, Chapter XIV—Part 1604—*Guidelines on discrimination because of sex under Title VII of the Civil Rights Act of 1964, as amended adoption of interim interpretive guidelines.* Washington, DC.

Fain, T.C., & Anderton, D.L. (1987). Sexual harassment: Organizational context and diffuse status. *Sex Roles, 5/6,* 291-311.

Fairhurst, G. T. (1986). Male-female communication on the job: Literature review and commentary. In M.L. McLaughlin (Ed.), *Communication yearbook 9* (pp. 83-116). Beverly Hills, CA: Sage.

Foucault, M. (1973). *The order of things.* New York: Vintage.

Frost, P. J. (1987). Power, politics, and influence. In F.M. Jablin, L. L. Putnam, K. H. Roberts, & L. W. Porter (Eds.), *Handbook of organizational communication* (pp. 503-548). Newbury Park, CA: Sage.

Gathercoal, R. (1991). *Toward taxonomic reflexivity in organizational communication.* Unpublished paper, Purdue University, West Lafayette, IN.

Glennon, L. M. (1983). Synthesism: A case of feminist methodology. In G. Morgan (Ed.), *Beyond method* (pp. 260-271). Newbury Park, CA: Sage.

Goffman, E. (1959). *Presentation of self in every day life.* New York: Doubleday Anchor Books.

Goffman, E. (1963). *Behavior in public places: Notes on the social organization of gatherings.* Glencoe, IL: The Free Press of Glencoe.

Goffman, E. (1974). *Frame analysis: An essay on the organization of experience.* Cambridge, MA: Harvard University Press.

Gruber, J. E. (1989). How women handle sexual harassment: A literature review. *Sociology and Social Research, 74,* 3-7.

Gutek, B. A. (1989). Sexuality in the workplace: Key issues in social research and organizational practice. In J. Hearn, D.L. Sheppard, P. Tancred-Sheriff, & G. Burrell (Eds.), *The sexuality of organization* (pp. 56-70). London: Sage.

Gutek, B.A., & Morasch, B. (1982). Sex-ratios, sex-role spillover, and sexual harassment of women at work. *Journal of Social Issues, 38* (4), 55-74.

Kanter, R. M. (1976). The policy issues. *Signs: Journal of Women in Culture and Society, 1* (3), 282-291.

Kanter, R.M. (1977). *Men and women of the corporation.* New York: Basic Books.

Livingston, J. A. (1982). Responses to sexual harassment on the job: Legal, organizational and individual actions. *Journal of Social Issues, 38* (4), 5-22.

Loy, P., & Stewart, L. (1984). The extent and effects of the sexual harassment of working women. *Sociological Focus, 17,* 31-43.

Maypole, D. (1986). Sexual harassment of social workers at work: Injustice within? *Social Work, 31* (1), 29-34.

O'Keefe, B.J. (1988). The logic of message design: Individual differences in reasoning about communication. *Communication Monographs, 55,* 80-103.

Sexual harassment: Walking the corporate line [video]. (1991). Santa Monica, CA: Salinger Films.

Tangri, S.S., Burt, M.R., & Johnson, L.B. (1982). Sexual harassment at work: Three explanatory models. *Journal of Social Issues, 38* (4), 33-54.

Watzlawick, P., Beavin, J., & Jackson, D.D. (1967). *Pragmatics of human communication.* New York: W.W. Norton.

Wood, J. T., & Conrad, C. (1983). Paradox in the experiences of professional women. *Western Journal of Speech Communication, 47,* 305-322.

▼Chapter 13

Managing Gender Conflicts in the Supervisory Relationship: Relationship-Definition Tactics Used By Women and Men

Vincent R. Waldron
Arizona State University West
Phoenix, AZ

Chris Foreman
Robert Miller
University of Kentucky
Lexington, KY

Senator Heflin:	Now, Ms. Berry, have you made any statements that suggested that the allegations of Anita Hill were the result of Ms. Hill's disappointment and frustration that, Mr. Thomas didn't show any sexual interest in her? . . .
Ms. Berry-Meyers:	That's what I said . . .
Senator Heflin:	You said that to a newspaper?
Ms. Berry-Meyers:	Yes, I did.
Senator Heflin:	What were the facts pertaining to that?
Ms. Berry-Meyers:	Just my observations of Anita . . . um . . . wishing to have greater attention from the Chairman. I think she was used to that at the Department of Education. Um . . . wanting to have direct access to his office,

	speaking in just highly, highly admirable terms toward the Chairman in a way, sometimes, that didn't indicate, um . . . just, um . . . professional interest. Those were my impressions.
Senator Heflin:	. . . What you just related, are you saying that those set of circumstances made you believe she had a sexual interest?
Ms. Berry-Meyers:	That she had a crush on the Chairman? Yes.
Senator Heflin:	. . . And will you recite those statements and things that you observed again?
Ms. Berry-Meyers:	It's in my written testimony, sir . . .
Senator Heflin:	Well, I'm asking you now if you would recite them again . . . I didn't understand that anything you said had any effect relative to sexual relations. They appear to be more professional and an attempt to have greater access to him from a professional viewpoint . . .
Ms. Berry-Meyers:	That's *your* impression. My impression was that Anita wished to have a greater relationship with the Chairman than just a professional one.
Senator Heflin:	So you say the fact that she didn't have as much access and other things, that they indicate . . . uh . . . sexual interest as opposed to a professional or work interest?
Ms. Berry-Meyers:	Exactly.
Senator Heflin:	How do you distinguish between the two? . . .
Ms. Berry-Meyers:	In a work environment, in a busy office . . . to think that you should any hour of the day, anytime that you want, to be able to walk in, have time with him . . . um . . . indicated to me more of a proprietary interest than a professional interest.

—Senator Howell Heflin questioning Phyllis Berry-Meyers, former Special Assistant at the Equal Employment Opportunity Commission, during Judiciary Committee confirmation hearings for Supreme Court nominee Clarence Thomas (10/13/91).

Much of the extensive questioning during the congressional hearing investigating Anita Hill's charges of sexual harassment against her former supervisor, Supreme Court nominee Clarence Thomas, attempted to reconstruct the routine communication patterns that characterized their relationship before, during, and after the alleged sexual harassment incidents. The testimony raised several issues addressed in this chapter. What is the nature of the behavior female subordinates (like Ms. Hill) use to define and maintain their relationships with male supervisors? How could such behavior serve to prevent or promote real or perceived sexual harassment and gender bias? How are male and female subordinates different and similar in their use of such relational behavior? How might third parties (exemplified by Senator Heflin and Ms. Berry-Meyers) perceive and misperceive such behaviors?

The confirmation hearings dramatically illustrated a series of communication dilemmas and paradoxes experienced routinely and most acutely by many female workers with male supervisors (MacKinnon, 1979; Wood & Conrad, 1983). Advancement in most organizations is facilitated by frequent, informal communication with one's supervisor (Waldron, 1991). However, when a female subordinate establishes this type of communication relationship with the boss, third parties may misinterpret her relational intentions (one possible explanation for Ms. Berry-Meyer's "impression"). Worse, female subordinates sometimes find that their friendly behavior is misinterpreted by powerful males who view it as an invitation to redefine the relationship from professional to intimate (Benson & Thomson, 1982). In addition, more so than males, female workers who engage in informal interaction about family or personal issues risk being viewed as "unprofessional" by male supervisors. Finally, when females avoid these unwelcome perceptions by engaging in more impersonal, assertive, and direct relational behavior, they risk being perceived as unfriendly or aloof (Bingham, 1991; Epstein, 1980), another charge directed at Hill by witnesses supporting Thomas.

Controlling gender-based bias and avoiding sexual harassment are part of the everyday work experience of many women. Many of the communication choices made by women working with male supervisors and co-workers, even in the course of routine work interactions, must take into account the potentially negative consequences associated with being female in a work environment in which males hold the most powerful positions. Mixed-sex supervisory relationships present communicative challenges to males as well. But, as the Anita Hill-Clarence Thomas hearings illustrated, the relational behavior of females who bring charges of sexual harassment against male supervisors can be subjected to extraordinary scrutiny and speculation. In most organizations, it is women who are subjected to harassment and negative bias, and therefore it is most likely women who have developed relational communication strategies to prevent, or at least manage, these problems.

In this chapter we are primarily interested in the role of routine relational communication in preventing incidents involving sexual harassment and in managing gender bias. We present survey and interview data that document the tactics used by female and male subordinates to define and maintain their relationships with supervisors. We argue that women, more than men, are required to use relationship-maintenance tactics that actively discourage gender-biased perceptions and, in some cases, sexual harassment. We demonstrate that communication research on these issues has considerable applied value, both in enlightening public discussion of sexual harassment in the workplace and in providing guidance to supervisors and subordinates in preventing gender-based work problems.

THE ROLE OF SUBORDINATES IN DEFINING SUPERVISORY RELATIONSHIPS

Attempts by subordinates to control gender bias and sexual harassment in the workplace can be understood in terms of a broader view of subordinate-initiated communication. Subordinates typically are disadvantaged by the power inequities that define formal supervisory relationships. Not surprisingly, many organizations experience a dearth of meaningful subordinate-initiated communication and, intentionally or not, suppress subordinate communication that might question the status quo. The symptoms of this problem are familiar: subordinate ideas remain untapped, supervisors complain that they learn about problems only after they become serious, and inequities and injustices are rarely openly discussed. One negative consequence is that female subordinates, those most likely to experience harassment and gender-based discrimination, often choose not to voice their concerns to management, particularly when their supervisor is the source of the problem.

Upward communication about sexual harassment and related problems may be increased by the creation of formal organizational policies and grievance procedures and through education programs (Livingston, 1982; Meyers, Berchtold, Oestrich, & Collins, 1981). However, women typically experience sexual harassment in face-to-face interpersonal settings, seek to remedy harassment by interpersonal interaction with the harasser, and sometimes report sexual harassment in face-to-face encounters with supervisors or others. Accordingly, the interpersonal communication used by women to manage harassment should be of interest to researchers and to organizational practitioners seeking to assist women in responding to sexual harassment (Bingham, 1991).

Communication can be viewed as a strategic process through which messages facilitate the achievement of interpersonal goals

(Brown & Levinson, 1978; Clark & Delia, 1979). Bingham (1991) has described sexual harassment in terms of three widely used types of interpersonal goals. *Task* goals are typically described as the defining purpose for which communication is used. A female subordinate faced with sexual harassment probably has a task goal of stopping the harassing behavior. Other types of task objectives may also apply in a given work situation (e.g., achieving promotion, accomplishing a work assignment). Subordinates also have *identity* objectives; they communicate in a manner that preserves their reputations, self-respect, and general well-being. Finally, subordinates communicate in a manner consistent with *relational* objectives: seeking to establish and maintain acceptable levels of communication contact, professional respect, formality, and affiliation.

While it is typical to view task objectives as primary and relational and identity goals as secondary (e.g., Dillard, Segrin, & Harden, 1989), the importance of the supervisory relationship to subordinate advancement makes relational goals a particularly important consideration when employees consider whether to discuss difficult or sensitive topics with a supervisor. Achievement of an acceptably defined relationship may be a prerequisite to the achievement of such long-term task goals as career advancement, or even short-term task goals, such as enlisting the supervisor's assistance in combating sexual harassment by a co-worker. Our research starts with the assumption that some, if not most, female employees with male supervisors intentionally use communication that defines the relationship in a manner that prevents or inhibits harassing behavior and discourages gender bias.

Subordinates use two broad classes of behavior to define supervisory relationships. Type 1 behaviors comprise the routine, enduring patterns of daily communication that gradually shape and define the relationship. Type 2 behavior, deployed during critical relational episodes, is direct and potentially risky communication, with the force to threaten or dramatically change the nature of the relationship. Tactics used by subordinates to initiate and manage conflicts with the supervisor, to gain the supervisor's compliance with a proposal, or to lodge a complaint might be of this type. Sexual overtures and resistance to sexual harassment are also Type 2 relationship definition behaviors.

Arguably, subordinates who are aware of, and skilled at, Type 1 behavior may reduce the frequency of Type 2 occurrences or may minimize the personal and relational risk associated with such occurrences (Waldron, Hunt, & Dsilva, 1991). Type 1 behavior creates a relational framework that determines the subordinate's subsequent choice of Type 2 behaviors (when they are necessary), and just as important, influences how the supervisor and others interpret Type 2 behavior. A subordinate who has established a history of conforming with reasonable supervisor expectations and rules may appear less threatening to that supervisor when protesting rules that are unfair or inappropriate (Waldron, 1991). Similarly, a subordinate who maintains the supervisory relationship by frequently engaging in friendly and informal talk may find it easier to initiate discussion about potentially controversial matters such as harassment by a co-worker or gender-related biases. The Type 2 behavioral options available to women who choose to resist sexual harassment face to face have received some attention in the literature (e.g., Bingham, 1991; Bingham & Burleson, 1989; Booth-Butterfield, 1989). Type 1 behavior, which has received less research attention, is the focus of the remainder of this chapter.

RELATIONSHIP MAINTENANCE TACTICS

The Type 1 relationship definition tactics used by women and men, and the effects of these tactics in creating and maintaining acceptably defined supervisory relationships, have only recently received research attention. A series of studies using focus group and survey techniques identified relationship-maintenance tactics reportedly used by women and men with opposite-sex and same-sex supervisors (Waldron, 1991; Waldron & Hunt, 1992; Waldron, et al., 1991). Initially, a list of 51 unique relationship maintenance behaviors was derived from focus group discussions with working adults in a variety of professions and organizations. These behaviors were described in a survey that asked employees to indicate the extent to which they used each behavior to maintain their supervisory relationship. A subsequent factor-analytic study of survey responses provided by 518 full-time employees revealed four primary tactic types. The behaviors associated with each type are summarized in Table 1 and explained below.

Personal-informal tactics. Personal-informal tactics emphasize frequent interaction and personal content rather than task-related content. They include: frequent small talk, informal discussion of nonwork concerns, the sharing of jokes and compliments, and related behaviors. Subordinates who use these relationship-definition tactics apparently use informal interaction to build and maintain friendship ties with the boss.

Contractual-conforming tactics. These tactics appear to demonstrate the subordinate's willingness to conform to or exceed organizational and supervisory expectations, organizational procedures, and general communication conventions (e.g., politeness norms). Rule following, deference to the supervisor, and respect for relational, organizational, and

TABLE 1. Subordinate Tactics for Maintaining Relationship with Supervisor

Personal Tactics

Ask about her/his personal life
Share jokes or amusing stories with him/her
Talk with him/her frequently even when I have nothing important to discuss
Frequently engage her/him in small talk
Compliment her/him frequently
Talk about past experiences we have shared
Encourage him/her to discuss problems of being a supervisor
Share my future career plans with him/her

Contractual Tactics

Am sure to follow the rules she/he has established
Remain polite toward him/her
Respond with a positive attitude when she/he asks me to do something
Make sure I have a clear understanding of what my supervisor thinks my responsibilities are
Accept criticism from her/him
Ask her/his advice on work-related matters
Keep his/her secrets confidential
Always stick by agreements we have made
Carefully follow her/his suggestions for doing the work

Regulative Tactics

Avoid delivering bad news to her/him
Sometimes stretch the truth to avoid problems with her/him
Make sure supervisor is in a good mood before discussing important work-related matters
Talk only superficially with him/her
Avoid asking her/him for direction
Appear enthusiastic even when I am not
Share my frustrations with co-workers, not her/him
Avoid the expression of extreme positive emotion in his/her presence

Direct Tactics

Speak up when I feel he/she has treated me unjustly
Explicitly tell her/him how I expect to be treated at work
Make it known when I am unhappy about something at work
Discuss openly any problems in my relationship with her/him
Frequently offer my opinions
Make sure she/he knows when I have been successful

societal requirements are central themes. Individuals favoring these tactics appear to view the relationships with the supervisor and the organization as a kind of contract and use communication to reduce ambiguities about terms of the contract and their compliance (cf. Graen & Schiemann, 1978).

Regulative-defensive tactics. Some subordinates carefully control contacts with the supervisor to prevent further damage to a poor relationship or to avoid making relational mistakes through careful control of contacts with the supervisor. These regulative or defensive tactics involve calculated management of impressions and emotions, editing or distortion of messages constructed for the supervisor, and avoidance of meaningful or potentially negative interaction.

Direct tactics. Direct relationship maintenance tactics explicitly define relational expectations, protest relational injustices, and voice subordinate opinions. Subordinates describing this approach view themselves as exhibiting these behaviors in their regular contacts with the supervisor, not just in isolated episodes (as in the Type 2 relationship definition described above).

DIFFERENCES AND SIMILARITIES IN TACTICS USED BY WOMEN AND MEN

Some researchers and theorists detect differences in the communication preferences or behaviors of female and male employees (Baker, 1991; Infante & Gorden, 1989; Kipnis & Schmidt, 1988; Lituchy & Wiswall, 1991; Mainiero, 1986; Penley, Alexander, Jernigan, & Henwood, 1991; Rafaeli & Sutton, 1989; Schlueter, Barge, & Blankenship, 1990), while others do not (Brown, 1979; Fairhurst, 1986; Gayle, 1991; Hirokawa, Kodama, & Harper, 1990; Kipnis, Schmidt, & Wilkinson, 1980; Schilit & Locke, 1982; Wilkins & Anderson, 1991). Little of this research has addressed subordinate communication, and very few researchers have addressed relationship maintenance communication. Shea and Pearson (1986) found that females used more direct relationship maintenance strategies with male co-workers who sought to escalate the relationship (i.e., make it more intimate). They did not examine supervisory relationships. In a footnote, Waldron (1991) reported small gender effects on maintenance strategies, noting that females appeared to use more conforming tactics in their supervisory relationships, while males used more direct tactics.

Our intention was to expand the small base of data pertaining to gender differences in maintenance communication through a survey study and through interviews with employed women. We started with no well-formed hypotheses, but we expected supervisory relationship maintenance to be a different and potentially more demanding task for female subordinates with male supervisors. Women might be expected to manage their relational communication in work settings more carefully then men, simply because female behavior is more often the object of misperception and unfavorable sex-role stereotypes (for a review see Fairhurst, 1986). In contrast to the more prevalent male-male relationship, members of mixed-sex superior-subordinate relationships might have to regulate their communication to avoid third-party perceptions of romantic involvement (Quinn, 1977) and to minimize relational risks (Cody, McLaughlin, & Schneider, 1981). In addition, females must maintain close working relationships, often with male supervisors, in a communication climate that sometimes includes sexually ambiguous and/or sexually harassing communication (Gutek & Morasch, 1982), and females are more likely than males to be the target of such harassment (U.S. Merit Service Protection Board, 1981).

SURVEY STUDY

Data were collected using a multipart survey that included 29 Likert-type items describing relationship-maintenance tactics and demographic items. These 29 tactic items are those that best defined the four maintenance styles in the factor analyses reported by Waldron (1991).

Respondents

Subjects were 202 working adults. The responses of eight individuals were eliminated due to missing data. The sample was 42.4% male and 57.6% female. The median age was 29 years ($r = $ 19-62). The median tenure in the current organization was 2.7 years ($r = $ 1-42). Median value for tenure in the current job was 1.9 years ($r = $ 1-37 years). The large majority of respondents (88%) worked full time (more than 32 hours per week), while the remainder worked part time. Approximately one-third of respondents (31.4%) described themselves as supervisors. A majority of respondents (67.4%) reported that their supervisors were male. In response to open-ended questions about the nature of their jobs and organizations, respondents described a wide variety of occupations and work settings. No one occupation or industry was disproportionately represented in the sample.

Respondents were recruited over a 4-month period using net-work sampling. Students enrolled in undergraduate organizational communication classes distributed surveys to nonstudent friends, family members, co-workers, and other adult (aged 18 or older) contacts working in local organizations. Students received a small amount of course credit for their efforts. They were instructed not to recruit fellow students. Respondents either mailed the survey to the researchers or returned it in a sealed envelope via their student contact. Respondents were informed that the data they provided would be used for research purposes and asked to provide an address where a summary of the results could be mailed. Confidentiality of individual responses was guaranteed. Approximately 76% of the surveys distributed in this manner were returned.

Results

Principle Components Analysis was used to determine if the factor structure of the 29 relationship-maintenance items was similar to that reported previously (Waldron, 1991). Consistent with this previous work, a scree test suggested that a 4-factor solution was acceptable. After Varimax rotation, the pattern of loadings was also consistent with previous work, although 4 of the 29 items failed to load at above .40 on any factor. Cronbach's Alpha was computed for those items loading at above .50 on a given factor (see items in Table 1). This procedure yielded values of .79 for the Personal factor, .70 for the Contractual-Conforming factor, and .75 for the Direct factor. The Regulative factor had a relatively low Alpha (.62). Composite measures were formed by summing scores for individual items.

A 2 (subordinate sex) x 2 (supervisor sex) ANOVA was used to examine mean differences on each of the four composite maintenance measures. (Average correlation among the dependent variables was .15, suggesting MANOVA was inappropriate.) Table 2 presents the means for the composite measures. For personal tactics, ANOVA revealed a significant interaction effect (F (1,199)=3.9, p <.05.) With male supervisors, the mean levels of personal tactics were similar for male (23.4) and female (23.5) subordinates. With female supervisors, female subordinates reported more personal tactic use (25.1) than their male counterparts (20.5).

A main effect for subordinate sex was found for contractual maintenance tactics, F(1,199)=5.36, p < .02, eta-square = .027), with females (χ = 30.0) scoring higher than males (χ = 28.7). No significant main effects were found for supervisor sex.

**TABLE 2. Relationship Maintenance Tactic Use as a
Function of Gender**

Tactic	Subordinate Gender	
	Male	Female
Personal*	23.0	24.2
Contractual**	28.7	30.0
Regulative	14.3	15.0
Direct	22.6	23.1
	Supervisor Gender	
	Male	Female
Personal	23.4	24.9
Contractual	29.4	29.7
Regulative	14.5	15.1
Direct	23.6	22.0

*this variable influenced by interaction effect, $p < .05$
**significant main effect, $p < .05$
Note: With the exception of the regulative measure, the tactic measures are composites derived from the sum of five 7-point Likert-type items, derived from the behavioral descriptions in Table 1. The regulative measure is derived from four items.

INTERVIEW STUDY

To collect qualitative data regarding the relational communication used by women to control sexual harassment, we conducted in-depth interviews with female employees. A semi-structured interviewing procedure was used. The women were first asked to discuss sexual harassment in general (e.g., what it is or is not, whether they believed it to be an issue or not, any personal experiences they had encountered, etc.). Other questions asked specifically about relationships they have had (past and present) with immediate supervisors and the ways in which they maintained these relationships through their communicative behaviors (e.g., any differences between having a male supervisor and a female supervisor). Data from interviews with four women are incorporated into the discussion below. The women were:

• *Diane*–age 40; currently director of emergency services in a hospital; has been at this position for about two years. She has an MBA with an emphasis in health services. Most of her 20+ years in the workforce have been in the health care industry.

• *Linda*–age 33; currently staff assistant in a department of a mid-size university with 12 full-time faculty members; has been at this position for two years. She has worked for the university for five years and is pursuing her B.A. on a part-time basis.

• *Sally*–age 54; currently manager of operations at corporate headquarters for an electrical manufacturing organization; has been at this position for about five years. She has been employed by the same organization for 33 years, having advanced from a secretarial position.

• *Susan*–age 45; currently a price negotiator for a manufacturing company; has been at this position for about two years. In the previous 18 years she worked on the shop floor, then in the clerical pool, and from there worked her way through the ranks to her current position.

Summary of Gender Differences and Similarities

The results of the two studies support several conclusions about differences in relationship definition activities of male and female subordinates.

1. *Female subordinates invest more communicative effort in maintaining acceptably defined supervisory relationships.* The evidence for this conclusion is found in the higher mean scores for females on all four relationship-maintenance measures (as shown in Table 2). Perhaps because they are more likely to be the target of sexual harassment, females may think more about the relational implications of their communication. As Diane noted in her interview:

I've always felt more responsibility . . . to guard against perceptions of the relationship being more than it is . . . I probably feel more of an accountability with my own actions, thinking, gosh, What did I do? What did I say? How would it be perceived?

When asked if women take more of the responsibility for defining relationships in a way that prevents sexual harassment, Linda responded:

Yeah, because I think men are just too stupid to realize it. I really do. Maybe stupid is too strong of a word. I think they're just uneducated, and a lot of the ones I work with are in the age, time period, that they just weren't brought up to think about those things . . . Women have always been looked at as pretty much as the caretaker, of children,

and now, she gets to take care of herself . . . and I think teaching
men is part of taking care of everything . . . I just think it is a matter
of constantly, every single day, educating them.

Sally had the strongest views about the extent to which sexual
harassment could be controlled by women:

Now, there's all sorts of sexual harassment. I think 97% of it, I think
the female has the opportunity to stop it. [But] there is that point
where they have somebody who won't take no for an answer... and
to me that's *really* sexual harassment.

*2. Female subordinates use more conforming-contractual commu-
nication in maintaining their supervisory relationships.* The survey
results indicated that female subordinates were more likely to use this
type of relationship-maintenance behavior, a finding consistent with at
least one previous study (Waldron, 1991). Recognizing that gender bias
works against them, female subordinates may be extraconforming to
eliminate any ambiguities regarding the role appropriateness of their
relational behavior. Rule following, demonstrating a positive attitude, and
strict conformity to supervisor expectations may serve as "debiasing"
strategies for females. Sally reported, " I probably had to prove myself a
little bit more and work a little bit harder than males in similar positions."
The other females we interviewed felt they had to be particularly careful
around male co-workers and supervisors to be perceived as "professionals." Linda reported:

I know with some people I stop myself before I get any more personal with them because they would look at me in a nonprofessional
way. And it might be taken in the wrong way. Not necessarily that
they would act on it but just their perception of me would be dim and
I don't really want that.

Susan described how conforming to the formal definition of her
job helped her fight gender bias.

The thing that offends me most (I came out of the clerical pool
myself, I'm a negotiator) is combating the stereotype that women
have the typing to do, the filing to do. I will say this, I never carried
coffee unless it was written in my contract, which it never was.

The interviewees generally agreed that they felt less pressure to manage such perceptions with female supervisors. Diane noted that she had an excellent professional relationship with her male supervisor:

> . . . but just given the fact that it is a male-female relationship, I believe that I'm always aware of the potential for [sexual harassment]. And indeed there are things that I say or don't say because he is a male boss, that would not be considered if he were a female boss.

3. *Female and male subordinates use equal amounts of personal-informal communication to maintain relationships with male supervisors, but with female supervisors, women use more personal-informal communication and men use less.* Females we interviewed reported using the casual talk and friendly joking associated with personal-informal relationship maintenance tactics. Linda used this approach with some male supervisors, but not others.

> Some of them you feel like you can be more causal in your conversation and even make funny jokes or something like that, and it will be taken for nothing more than it's given as. Some of them, well, you know, "I just better not do that with them."

This kind of informal talk is commonplace in the manufacturing environment where Susan works:

> I want to explain something . . . we joke a lot, and maybe if someone stood on the side and heard us talk to men maybe they would say there was all sorts of stuff going on . . . That's just shop talk.

Sally seemed to view things similarly:

> Again, a younger person coming into the workforce would . . . be sensitive to some things. But, since we've been around and grew up in a manufacturing atmosphere, people [will say] "what are ya doin' tonight" and that stuff and you just laugh it off.

The survey data suggest that males and females seem to be most different in their use of personal relationship-maintenance communication with female supervisors. Males were less personal and females more personal in these cases. The females we interviewed confirmed that relationships are maintained differently with same-sex supervisors. Diane supervises both male and female employees:

> I think that my current [female] employees . . . say things to me, in front of me, that I know they would not say in front of a male boss. There's just no doubt. I think there is a certain freedom in a same-sex environment to discuss these things that you would not do in the mixed-sex environment.

4. *Males and females use roughly similar amounts of regulative and direct relationship maintenance communication.* Diane and Linda, who work in white-collar settings, described a kind of interpersonal vigilance that permeates their relationships with male supervisors. Consistent with the regulative approach to relationship maintenance, they depersonalize their conversations with some males and "remain on their toes" to guard against perceptions of impropriety. Diane described a past incident in which she was sexually harassed that led her to regulate her relational behavior more carefully.

> I was young, and very naive, and I think that I might have engaged in behaviors that would be construed as flirtatious or sexual bantering, or just picking up on something that was said and going with it. Where, indeed now I would not have let it; it would be dropped like a lead balloon and left right there.

Sally and Susan both work in manufacturing environments, and both described direct rather than regulative-defensive maintenance tactics. Susan uses directness routinely, "If I have anything to say to any of my bosses, I just say it. I ask them to appreciate me . . . and I go and bitch just to get them off my back." She thinks a defensive approach can be counterproductive in her work environment.

> Sometimes it kind of depressing to see women come in who are on the defensive and shouldn't be. Because a lot of times you use joking around to lighten up the atmosphere or whatever. Here, everybody's worked together so long it's more like a family and nobody takes it serious.

However, Sally thinks that to prosper in her predominately male workplace, females should use the kind of emotional control associated with regulative-type maintenance tactics:

> If you take a very naive person, even in this day and time, and they wore their feelings on their sleeves, then they could be intimidated [by male talk]. You know, you got to be a big girl.

Susan believes that to manage sexual harassment, "all you have to do is say 'no' and be very blunt about it." She described her aggressive response upon hearing a male attribute her success to "sleeping around" with the boss.

> I took my fist and cold-cocked that little sucker, and said [to him] "file a grievance." And I've never had a problem. I have never had another comment, to my face, about anything I have done.

Linda also felt that a direct, if less confrontational, approach to defining relationships was required with males who had initiated inappropriate behavior.

> It's a matter of . . . holding your ground. You know, once you've come out and said, "I don't want you talking like this to me anymore. I don't want you doing this to me anymore." And you've made complaints. To not be...to be really careful to not fall back into it. Because then you're going to lose credibility and they're not going to believe a thing you've said.

5. *The mix of relationship maintenance tactics may be more important than the use of any single tactic.* Both the survey and the interview data provide indications that women use not just one relationship-maintenance tactic with male supervisors, but rather a mix of tactics that allows them to define the relationship as simultaneously friendly and professional. In particular, women appear to use contractual tactics, and in some cases direct tactics, to ensure that personal-informal communication is not misinterpreted. It can be concluded from the discourse quoted above that Sally and Susan both routinely engage in informal bantering with male co-workers and subordinates, but also use direct tactics to retain professional respect and to fight potential gender bias.

6. *The relationship maintenance tactics used by female subordi-*

nates are adapted to their unique organizational and relational circumstances. Although the survey data suggest that females report more use of at least one tactic type (contractual-conforming), it is clear that both genders use all four tactic types to some extent. From our interviews, it appears that the ability to adapt tactics to the current state of the relationship and to prevailing norms in the work environment is critical to these women. For example, both Diane and Linda adjusted their relationship maintenance tactics based on the age of the males with which they interacted. Diane believed that males who were substantially younger than she were less likely to misinterpret her informal, friendly banter.

> I relate to younger males differently than males of the same age or males that are older than I am. I don't ever perceive there ever being a sexual relationship . . . That has led me to discuss things with younger males, or to bring up things, or to be casually flirtatious, or to say things I would indeed never say to a male who was my age, or older, or a boss, or whatever.

Linda felt that older males required more education (from her) about sexual harassment. Sally and Susan indicated that the nature of the manufacturing environment allowed them to be more informal in their interactions with males, but also required them to be more direct in combating bias. Linda's observation seemed to capture the obligation felt by these women (apparently not shared by the males they worked with and for) to monitor their relationships and adapt their behavior to male co-workers and supervisors.

> I think you constantly have to be on your toes when you're working with this many professional people. There's a lot of different kinds of personalities here and some of them . . . when they talk to you will stay far away and some of them will get right next to you. And you know who those people are.

7. *Female subordinates are keenly aware of the potential relational perceptions and misperceptions of third parties.* The more frequent use of contractual tactics by females may reflect an intuitive awareness of the damage to career and reputation that might be done by third-party perceptions of their relationship with a male supervisor or co-worker (as in the Anita Hill-Clarence Thomas case). In referring to her informal bantering with male co-workers, Diane noted:

I thoroughly believe that the male in these instances would not perceive it as being sexually, you know, sexual harassment . . . on my
part. But I have thought, 'God! What do the other people that have
seen me think, when I say these things around these guys?'

Applications of Relationship Maintenance Research

The data have some obvious implications for practitioners whose role it
is to educate workers about sexual harassment and related issues, to
conduct training on the relational behaviors that help women manage
harassment and gender bias at work, or to investigate charges of sexual
harassment. The following principles seem most useful.

1. *Draw on the relational experiences of women working in the
organization.* The data indicate that women monitor work relationships
closely and are probably more attuned than most males to the relational
behaviors and conditions that lead to harassment. If male supervisors
and co-workers are in fact less aware of such problems, trainers should
document the problem in their organization through a survey of females.
A database that documents the extent of the problem and the kinds of
relational behaviors that females view as problematic should be compiled and used as part of education efforts. In other words, training
should provide for some of the education of men that women (like Linda)
feel obligated to do through their interactions with male co-workers. The
data suggest that the behaviors that women consider harassment and
the behaviors they use to manage harassment depend on the nature of
the work environment. Accordingly, the women who work in a given
environment, and their accumulated experiences, should be considered
the most credible sources for training materials.

2. *Emphasize early intervention.* Training that emphasizes Type
1 relational behavior by definition teaches men and women how to manage relationships in a manner that decreases the occurrence of harassment incidents or gender-based misunderstandings. The females in this
study appear to use a variety of relationship-maintenance tactics that
closely monitor relationships and anticipate potential problems. Several
specific early intervention techniques could be used.
    First, the use of informal feedback-seeking behavior would permit
members of mixed-sex dyads to identify behaviors that are perceived as
potentially inappropriate. For example, male supervisors might be encouraged to consult with other supervisors (male and female) about their relational behavior to gain alternate interpretations and identify potential problem areas. Alternately, trainers might (through role-play sessions) provide

supervisors with practice in seeking feedback from female subordinates about the extent to which the supervisors' behavior is threatening. In addition, male and female supervisors can be taught to encourage their female subordinates to use direct relationship-maintenance tactics. The establishment of routine directness creates a framework for open and early discussion of harassment by a female subordinate who perceives harassment or gender-based bias in her work environment.

3. *Recognize multiple goals.* Those who investigate claims of sexual harassment should be aware of the task, relational, and identity goals of female subordinates. Women who are harassed must consider not only their near-term task goals (prevent or stop the harassment), but also their long-term task goals (career advancement), their identities (many women feel it is their obligation to deal with harassment interpersonally), and the value of maintaining a working relationship with the harasser. As Anita Hill apparently did, many females will seek to maintain at least a functional relationship with a harassing supervisor because the career consequences of a severed relationship are perceived to be too negative. Females are caught in a double bind. If they stay in such a relationship, their harassment charges may be disbelieved. If they leave, their career prospects are diminished. Males rarely face this dilemma. Highly direct or avoidant relationship-definition tactics may prevent harassment, but when employed individually, these tactics may sacrifice relational or identity objectives or long-term task (career) objectives. Training should sensitize both men and women to the communication dilemmas faced by women and should help women identify preventive tactics which meet multiple communication objectives (Bingham, 1991).

4. *Emphasize behavior.* Training of both males and females should emphasize that relationships are defined by specific communication behaviors, not simply attitudes or good intentions. The quality of the relationship and the extent to which negatively gender-biased impressions influence it are partially a function of recurrent behavior patterns. The behaviors listed in Table 1 are a starting point for individuals who wish to examine their own relationship-maintenance preferences. Role-play exercises can be used to help supervisors and subordinates modify or supplement their relational behavioral repertories. It is clear from the data that females use varied combinations of relational behaviors (e.g., both personal and direct tactics) to manage their work relationships. The women interviewed advocated direct relational behavior with potential harassers, a recommendation echoed in some of the sexual harassment literature (e.g., Booth-Butterfield, 1989). However, not all women will be comfortable with such behavior, and some women may conclude that

the relational costs of directness may not justify is use, particularly in less acute harassment situations (Bingham, 1991). Experienced females may be enlisted as trainers to help less experienced females develop the relational behaviors that are effective in meeting their communication goals and well suited to their individual communication abilities and personalities.

5. *Reduce ambiguity.* The women in this study appear to use contractual-conforming tactics as a hedge against gender bias and potential harassment. Supervisors who are clear about the rules and expectations that govern the workplace can help in this effort. When ambiguity exists, female employees are more likely to experience gender bias. To use a mundane but appropriate example, a supervisor of a predominantly male work group, who makes clear that notetaking at meetings would be a rotated duty, eliminated the possibility that this traditionally clerical job be foisted upon female subordinates. Clarity on this relatively minor issue may make it unnecessary for the female to protest to her male colleagues about the matter. Too often, women who protest these injustices are viewed as unnecessarily argumentative by male co-workers and supervisors (Farley, 1978; MacKinnon, 1979). Training programs that expose males to this type of dilemma could encourage supervisors to eliminate unnecessary ambiguities.

6. *Account for third-party bias.* Training programs should demonstrate how co-workers might perceive and misperceive relational behaviors. The potential for third parties to apply different standards when evaluating male and female relational behavior should be emphasized. The potential uses of contractual, regulative, and direct maintenance tactics by members of mixed-sex supervisory dyads to counter relational misperceptions could be stressed in training programs.

7. *Examine relational history.* The women in this study appeared to use considerable communicative effort to prevent or counter harassment and related problems. Those who investigate harassment charges should examine the relational history that preceded the incident. In some cases, the harassing behavior may persist over long periods, despite the female's interpersonal attempts to control the problem. To the uninitiated investigator, the lack of a prior formal complaint may make the charges appear less serious. However, the use of relationship-definition tactics to control harassment is often the only viable response available to women. A history of such efforts would argue that a sexual harassment charge is not the result of a simple misunderstanding, but instead the manifestation of repeated inappropriate relational behavior.

REFERENCES

Baker, M.A. (1991). Gender and verbal communication in professional settings. *Management Communication Quarterly, 5*, 36-63.

Benson, D.J., & Thomson, G.E. (1982). Sexual harassment on a university campus: The confluence of authority relations, sexual interest and gender stratification. *Social Problems, 29*, 236-251.

Bingham, S.G. (1991). Communication strategies for managing sexual harassment in organizations: Understanding message options and their effects. *Journal of Applied Communication Research, 19*, 88-115.

Bingham, S.G., & Burleson,B.R. (1989). Multiple effects of messages with multiple goals: Some perceived outcomes of responses to sexual harassment. *Human Communication Research, 16*, 184-216.

Booth-Butterfield, M. (1989). Perception of harassing communication as a function of locus of control, work force participation, and gender. *Communication Quarterly, 37*, 262-275.

Brown, P. & Levinson, S. (1978). Universals in language: Politeness phenomena. In E.N. Goody (Ed.), *Questions and politeness: Strategies in social interaction* (pp. 56-289). Cambridge: Cambridge University.

Brown, S.M. (1979). Male versus female leaders: A comparison of critical studies. *Sex Roles, 5*, 595-611.

Clark, R.A., & Delia, J.G. (1979). Topoi and rhetorical competence. The *Quarterly Journal of Speech, 65*, 187-206.

Cody, M.J., McLaughlin, M.L., & Schneider, M.J. (1981). The impact of relational consequences and intimacy on the selection of interpersonal persuasion tactics: A reanalysis. *Communication Quarterly, 29*, 91-106.

Dillard, J.P., Segrin, C., & Harden, J. (1989). Primary and secondary goals in the production of interpersonal influence messages. *Communication Monographs, 56*, 19-38.

Epstein, N. (1980). Social consequences of assertion, aggression, passive aggression, and submission: Situational and dispositional determinants. *Behavior Therapy, 11*, 662-669.

Fairhurst, G.T. (1986). Male-female communication on the job: Literature review and commentary. In M.McLaughlin (Ed.), *Communication yearbook 9* (pp. 83-116). Beverly Hills: Sage.

Farley, L. (1978). *Sexual shakedown.* New York: McGraw-Hill.

Gayle, B.M. (1991). Sex equity in workplace conflict management. *Journal of Applied Communication Research, 20*, 152-169.

Graen, G., & Schiemann, W. (1978). Leader-member agreement: A vertical dyad linkage approach. *Journal of Applied Psychology, 63*, 206-212.

Gutek, B.A., & Morasch, B. (1982). Sex ratios, sex role spillover and sexual harassment of women at work. *Journal of Social Issues, 38*, 55-74.

Hirokawa, R.Y., Kodama, R.A., & Harper, N.L. (1990). Impact of managerial power on persuasive strategy selection by female and male managers. *Management Communication Quarterly, 4*, 30-50.

Infante, D.A., & Gorden, W.I. (1989). Argumentativeness and affirming communicator style as predictors of satisfaction/dissatisfaction with subordinates. *Communication Quarterly, 37*, 81-90.

Kipnis, D., & Schmidt, S.M. (1988). Upward-influence styles: Relationship with performance evaluations, salary, and stress. *Administrative Science Quarterly, 33*, 528-542.

Kipnis, D., Schmidt, S.M., & Wilkinson, I. (1980). Intraorganizational influence tactics: Explorations in getting one's way. *Journal of Applied Psychology, 65*, 440-452.

Lituchy, T.R., & Wiswall, W.J. (1991). The role of masculine and feminine speech patterns in proposal acceptance. *Management Communication Quarterly, 4*, 450-465.

Livingston, J.A. (1982). Responses to sexual harassment on the job: Legal, organizational, and individual actions. *Journal of Social Issues, 38*, 5-22.

MacKinnon, C.A. (1979). *Sexual harassment of working women: A case of sex discrimination*. London: Yale University Press.

Mainiero, L.A. (1986). Coping with powerlessness: The relationship of gender and job dependency to empowerment-strategy usage. *Administrative Science Quarterly, 31*, 633-653.

Meyers, M.C., Berchtold, J.M., Oestrich, J.L., & Collins, F.J. (1981). *Sexual harassment*. New York: Petrocelli Books.

Penley, L.E., Alexander, E.R., Jernigan, I.E., & Henwood, C.I. (1991). Communication abilities of managers: The relationship to performance. *Journal of Management, 17*, 57-76.

Quinn, R.E. (1977). Coping with cupid: The formation, impact of romantic relationships in organizations. *Administrative Science Quarterly, 22*, 30-45.

Rafaeli, A., & Sutton, R. (1989). The expression of emotion in organizational life. *Research in Organizational Behavior, 11*, 1-42.

Schilit, W., & Locke, E. (1982). A study of upward influence in organizations. *Administrative Science Quarterly, 27*, 304-316.

Schlueter, D., Barge, J.K., & Blankenship, D. (1990). A comparative analysis of influence strategies used by upper and lower level male and female managers. *Western Journal of Speech Communication, 54*, 42-65.

Shea, B.C., & Pearson, J.C. (1986). The effects of relationship type, partner intent, and gender on the selection of relationship maintenance strategies. *Communication Monographs, 53*, 352-364.

U.S. Merit Systems Protection Board. (1981). *Sexual harassment in the federal workplace: Is it a problem*. Washington, DC: Government Printing Office.

Waldron, V.R. (1991). Achieving communication goals in superior-subordinate relationships: The multi-functionality of upward maintenance tactics. *Communication Monographs, 58*, 289-306.

Waldron, V.R., & Hunt, M.H. (1992). Hierarchical level, length, and quality of supervisory relationship as predictors of subordinates' use of maintenance tactics. *Communication Reports, 5*, 82-89.

Waldron, V.R., Hunt, M.H., & Dsilva, M. (1991, October). *Communicative bases of leader-member exchange: Subordinate upward influence and relationship maintenance tactics.* Paper presented to at the annual conference of the Speech Communication Association, Atlanta.

Wilkins, B.M., & Anderson, P.A. (1991). Gender differences and similarities in management communication: A meta-analysis. *Management Communication Quarterly, 5*, 6-35.

Wood, J.T. & Conrad, C. (1983). Paradox in the experience of professional women. *Western Journal of Speech Communication, 47*, 305-322.

▼Chapter 14

Preventing the Problem: Preparing Faculty Members for the Issues of Sexual Harassment

Kathleen M. Galvin
Northwestern University
Evanston, IL

▼ Professors in certain areas of the communication arts and sciences are at increased risk for allegations of sexual harassment due to the unique nature of their curricular and co-curricular contacts with students. At special risk are those senior faculty members who refuse to acknowledge the change in campus climate, clinging to pedagogical approaches that may be considered discriminatory in the current educational context, and those faculty members who espouse certain methods that may be compatible with professional behavior in the arts or therapy arenas, but that are inappropriate for a general college classroom. Administrators have a responsibility to provide students with a learning climate in which no group experiences a chilly climate or hostility in the learning process. At the same time, administrators need to prepare faculty for a world in which the old pedagogical approaches, or certain activities found in a particular professional milieu, leave them open to charges of sexual harassment, a term which encompasses gender harassment as well.

Persons in the communication, media, and arts areas may mindlessly engage in pedagogical behavior within curricular and co-curricular contexts which students or colleagues could construe as sexual or gender harassment. When discussing this topic, many males and females report viewing much of the so-called sexual harassment behavior as normal, natural, and unconscious (Stokes, 1983). To claim naiveté about

257

the sexual or gender implications of methodological approaches or cur-
ricular/co-curricular situations is not an excuse that serves the faculty
members or their students effectively. Faculty members must be educated, *within their academic context*, to consider their content-related contacts with students in light of a broadly conceived interpretation of sexu-
al/gender harassment. The intent of this approach is to increase the general level of faculty awareness on this topic, to explore a range of pedagogical issues or approaches and their possible interpretations, including
potential cultural implications, and to prevent the unaware faculty member from encountering charges of sexual and gender harassment.

An exploration of this approach must include: (a) a brief review
of definitions of sexual harassment/gender harassment and the traditional university procedural approaches to dealing with this issue; (b) a
description of certain circumstances in which curricular and co-curricular
instruction in communication, media, and performance may present
unique concerns; and (c) a description of prevention strategies designed
for faculty in our field.

THE CURRENT APPROACHES

Definitional Issues

On a college campus the term sexual harassment implies "misuse of
power and role by a faculty member" (Dzeich & Weiner, 1990, p. 21).
Specific attempts to operationalize the concept have led to multiple, similar definitions and lists of potentially problematic behaviors (Fitzgerald,
1990). For example, The National Advisory Council on Women's
Educational Programs suggests that sexual harassment may be
described as:

1. generalized sexist remarks or behavior;
2. inappropriate and offensive, but essentially sanction-free, sexual advances;
3. solicitation of sexual activity or other sex-linked behavior by
   promise of rewards;
4. coercion of sexual activity by threat of punishment; and
5. assaults (Till, 1980).

In 1978, the Association of American Colleges' "Project on the
Status and Education of Women" provided a descriptive list of specific
actions that might constitute sexual harassment including:

- verbal harassment or abuse
- subtle pressure for sexual activity
- sexist remarks about a woman's clothing, body, or sexual activities
- unnecessary touching, patting, or pinching, leering or
- ogling at a woman's body
- constant brushing against a woman's body
- demanding sexual favors accompanied by implied or overt threats concerning one's job, grades, letters of recommendation, and so forth
- physical assault.

The following description demonstrates how one university (Northwestern University, 1991) portrays the problem of sexual/gender harassment for an audience of administrators, faculty, staff, and students:

Sexual harassment is unsolicited and unwanted verbal or physical conduct of a sexual nature that offends a person and interferes with that person's academic or employment activities and opportunities at the University. Such conduct creates an environment that may be intimidating, hostile, or offensive. Sexual harassment may range from unwelcome advances and requests for sexual favors to other verbal or physical conduct of sexual nature. Sexual harassment introduces a personal element into what should be a sex-neutral situation.

The University material concludes with a list of examples of sexual harassment as follows:

- Pressure for sexual activity
- Unnecessary touching, patting, or hugging
- Offensive sexual graffiti
- Disparaging remarks to a person about his or her gender
- Inappropriate sexual innuendos
- Verbal sexual abuse
- Obscene gestures
- Gratuitous references to various parts of body
- Coerced sexual intercourse.

This material demonstrates the current broad conception of sexual harassment, which includes a subset that some refer to as gender harassment. The Modern Language Association's Commission on the

Status of Women in the Profession distinguished gender harassment as a specific type of sexual harassment saying:

> It consists of discriminatory behavior directed against individuals who belong to a gender group that the aggressor considers inferior . . . The forms are often verbal—statements and jokes that reveal stereo-typical discriminatory attitudes. (Dziech & Weiner, 1990, p. 22)

These examples should demonstrate the broad-based conceptualizations of sexual harassment, conceptualizations that remain foreign to many faculty members. Therefore, when Metha and Nigg (1983) include circumstances such as exposure to sexual jokes in class, exposure to labels for pursuing a male-dominated profession, or avoidance of mentoring relationships to avoid sexual pressure as evidence of sexual harassment, the concept widens beyond the scope understood by many faculty members.

The current definitions of sexual and gender harassment remain fluid and varied, but they contain enough similarity to provide a workable template for the development of effective prevention strategies and investigation procedures.

Procedural Responses

Responding to the general change in campus climate and strong legalistic language depicting institutional responsibility, most institutions have mounted a series of initiatives to address this issue. These institutions are becoming increasingly aware of the EEOC Title VII guidelines, which suggest an employer is responsible for acts of sexual harassment when the employer or its agents or supervisory employees know or should have known of the conduct, unless immediate corrective action was taken.

A literature search of current writings reveals significant attention to two areas: (a) assessing the scope of sexual harassment on campus (Maihof & Forrest, 1983; Mazer & Percival, 1989; Popovich, Licata, Nokovich, Martelli, & Zoloty, 1986; Reilly, Lott & Gallogly, 1986), and (b) investigating and managing such cases (Robertson, Dyer, & Campbell, 1988; Simon & Forrest, 1983). For university personnel, the latter approach focuses almost exclusively on policy development, policy dissemination, and the conduct of investigations. In most cases, educational programs are designed for potential victims, but there appears to be few preventive efforts aimed at faculty. Faculty encounter little beyond printed literature and dire warnings, evidence of an incomplete prevention approach. The presumption seems to be that faculty should know the boundaries for interaction between themselves and students. Yet, issues of ambiguity raised by many current cases make it clear that many faculty remain uninformed about the range of actions, which puts them at risk of sexual harassment charges.

CURRICULAR/CO-CURRICULAR CONCERNS

A walk through the campus buildings that house departments dedicated to communication media or the arts would provide administrators with glimpses of academic life, which include the following:

- a directing instructor remarking on the sexuality exuded by a theater student in an acting scene
- a voice instructor holding a student's rib cage while demonstrating diaphragmatic breathing
- the communication instructor leading an interpersonal exercise involving personal self-disclosure
- a television production teacher hanging over a camera operator's shoulder while checking camera angles
- an acting instructor writing responses to a very personal student journal
- a design instructor driving off-campus with a student to find costumes and props
- a film instructor discussing the portrayals of sexuality in the films of Truffaut and Bergman
- the basic-speech course instructor discussing attributes of male and female communicators
- a journalism teacher supervising interns at off-campus sites.

None of these circumstances may involve overt sexual pressure, yet each of these circumstances has the potential to raise issues of sanction-free sexual harassment or generalized sexist behavior or remarks.

Although there are numerous documented cases in which faculty make explicit and blatant attempts to exercise power and involve students in sexual bargaining circumstances, a high percentage of problematic cases involve the following: inappropriate humor; unnecessary touching; remarks about women's bodies, clothing or sexual activities; and gender preference in classroom interaction. Often these circumstances arise when there are opportunities for informal or personal student-instructor contact. Dzeich and Weiner (1990) describe the roles in which educators who are engaged in sexual harassment commonly are found as the counselor-helper, the confidante, the intellectual seducer, the opportunist, and the power broker (pp. 122-124). Most of these categories reflect a behavior that has "gone over the line" in terms of degree and that involves a rather personal involvement with a student. Dzeich and Weiner provide a related list of warning signs which they suggest may be "misinterpreted as sinister when they are simply examples of clumsy professional or social style" (p. 119). Their tentative list of warning signs includes:

- Staring, leering, ogling
- Frequently commenting on the personal appearance of the student
- Touching out of context
- Excessive flattery and praise of the student
- Deliberately avoiding or seeking encounters with a student in front of colleagues
- Injecting a "male versus female" tone into discussions with students or colleagues.

It appears obvious that professors in particular instructional settings and disciplines are at greater risk than those in others. The professor who lectures to 300 and has graduate assistants running the discussion sections or labs would seldom find himself or herself in danger of crossing a line in individual student contact. The instructor of smaller classes, particularly those that involve material which may be considered to fall within the affective domain of knowledge, or the professor who encounters students in small groups, one-on-one sessions, and co-curricular activities, is at greater risk for crossing the line simply out of mindlessness. Therefore, it appears that (a) theater faculty, particularly those involved with performance, directing, and production; (b) media faculty, particularly those involved with production, internships, and gender perspectives; and (c) communication faculty, particularly those involved with interpersonal/relational communication are at higher risk and more in need of preventive information than faculty in other disciplines. For example, in describing the "intellectual seducer," Dzeich and Weiner explicitly suggest this kind of "seduction" is evident when a professor uses class content to gain access to personal information about the student. They cite as problematic, courses in psychology, sociology, and literature in which the student is invited to engage in self-disclosure. For many persons teaching in the field of communication, such behavior is expected and valued as congruent with the goals of the course content.

In describing the "opportunist," these authors describe the person who takes advantage of the physical setting or of occasional circumstances to gain intimacy with students, often using equipment or subject matter to gain physical access to students, and hence, to "cheap feels" (1990, p. 123) The music professor teaching diaphragmatic breathing is cited frequently as an example. Given these descriptions it is clear that, without directed education, certain faculty members may put themselves at risk of sexual harassment charges due to the nature of their relationships with students within a curricular or co-curricular context.

PREVENTION

Administrators should support the development of prevention programs that relate to both general and discipline-specific issues, in addition to providing the obvious and necessary plethora of printed descriptions of examples of sexual harassment and showing the few general commercial videotapes available (usually shown to TA's). Although there have been recent attempts by scholars to contextualize sexual harassment within a communication frame (Bingham, 1991; Hickson, Grierson, & Linder, 1991), the focus is not placed on teaching the discipline. Therefore, by using a communication perspective, chairpersons and key faculty in communication, media, and theater can and should develop prevention approaches for instructors who may unwittingly cross the line. As part of this strategy, administrators should:

1. Communicate that all charges of sexual harassment will be taken seriously and investigated fully.
2. Communicate that rumors of sexual harassment will be directly addressed. Faculty need to be made aware of the existence of rumors about their behavior, and administrators must be prepared for conversations that describe the rumor and describe the institutional stand. If appropriate, the faculty member may articulate ways to dispel or defuse the rumor.
3. Develop workshops designed to identify specific strategies for creating a classroom climate that is hospitable across differences of gender and culture.
4. Develop workshops to encourage faculty awareness of discipline-specific areas of risk and to aid faculty to develop preventive approaches to be used in classes or co-curricular contexts.

A pilot program at Northwestern's School of Speech is attempting to reflect a preventive approach adapted to curricular and co-curricular areas. For example, a meeting with the acting faculty in the theater department was arranged during which time the following occurred:
The general University Guidelines on sexual harassment were

reviewed and an explanation of the School's administrative commitment to a supportive climate for all students was addressed. Participants were informed of the current school policy to alert faculty to rumors about them. The major portion of the meeting was devoted to a discussion of pedagogical approaches and academic content in theater which, improperly handled, could place an acting instructor at risk for a charge of sexual harassment.

The premise of the session was that acting teachers faced unique pedagogical circumstances in terms of possible student misunderstandings, and hence, their risk of charges of sexual harassment increase. These charges may arise from a student who believes a teacher has acted inappropriately toward him or her, or the charges may arise from other students who believe favoritism or excessive attention to one student of a sexual nature creates a hostile climate for other class members. Topics for discussion included the following:

- Discussing dramatic literature. Faculty explored the sensitive issues of discussing a wide range of sexual preferences and sexual practices inherent in dramatic literature.
- Providing oral feedback to scenes. Faculty discussed sensitivity to the use of language while critiquing a scene or side-coaching a scene, particularly scenes with strong sexual overtones.
- Using touch and body work. Faculty examined ways to display sensitivity to various levels of student comfort with touch, an issue with strong gender and cultural implications.
- Responding to student acting journals. Faculty discussed possible misunderstandings that could arise through these privately written messages.
- Commenting on student appearance. Faculty discussed the need to frame such comments within an instructional context.
- Holding student conferences. Faculty discussed the ambiguous messages which could be sent to a student or classmates by certain types of private conferences.
- Working on productions. Faculty discussed the possible difficulties that arise when faculty and students work together on shows, particularly since such activity often involves a shifting in role boundaries.

At the close of the session faculty raised related issues such as handling students who report having been sexually abused in childhood or dealing with students who resist all physical contact in acting classes.

The sexual harassment literature indicates that faculty in communication, media, and theater may mindlessly engage in pedagogical behavior within curricular or co-curricular contexts, which students or colleagues could construe as sexual harassment. There is a need for discipline-based prevention programs as a way to educate faculty and to reduce the incidence of such charges. This position is consistent with a current call for communication-based training programs to contribute to the institutional management of such problems (Bingham, 1991; Stokes, 1983). Using communication as the content and the method for conducting discipline-specific sexual harassment education programs for faculty has the potential to serve as a strong preventive measure.

REFERENCES

Bingham, S. G. (1991, June). Communication strategies for managing sexual harassment in organizations: Understanding message options and their effects. *Journal of Applied Communication Research, 19*(2), 88-115.

Dzeich, B., & Weiner, L. (1990). *The lecherous professor* (2nd ed.). Boston: Beacon Press.

Fitzgerald, L. F. (1990). Sexual harassment: The definition and measurement of a construct. In M. A. Paludi (Ed.), *Ivory power: Sexual harassment on campus* (2nd ed., pp. 21-44). Albany: State University of New York Press.

Hickson, M., III, Grierson, R. D., & Linder, B. C. (1991). A communication perspective on sexual harassment: Affiliative nonverbal behaviors in a synchronous relationships. *Communication Quarterly, 39*(2), 111-118.

Maihoff, N., & Forrest, L. (1983). Sexual harassment in higher education: An assessment study. *Journal of NAWDAC, 46*(2), 3-8.

Mazer, D. B., & Percival, E. F. (1989). Ideology or experience? The relationship among perceptions, attitudes, and experiences of sexual harassment in university statements. *Sex Roles, 20*(3-4), 135-147.

Metha, A., & Nigg, J. (1983). Sexual harassment on campus: An institutional response. *Journal of the National Association for Women Deans, Administrators, & Counselors, 46*(2), 9-15.

Popovich, P. M., Licata, B. J., Nokovich, D., Martelli, T., & Zoloty, S. (1986). Assessing the incidence and perceptions of sexual harassment behaviors among American undergraduates. *The Journal of Psychology, 120*(4), 387-396.

Project on the Status and Education of Women (1978). *Sexual harassment: A hidden issue* (Report No. 20). Washington, DC: Association of American Colleges.

Reilly, M. E., Lott, B., & Gallogly, S. M. (1986). Sexual harassment of university students. *Sex Roles, 15*(7-8), 333-358.

Robertson, C., Dyer, C. E., & Campbell, D. (1988). Campus harassment: Sexual harassment policies and procedures at institutions of higher learning. *Signs, 13*(4), 792-812.

Sexual harassment policy statement. (1991). Evanston, IL: Northwestern University.

Simon, A., & Forrest, L. (1983). Implementing a sexual harassment program at a large university. *Journal of NAWDAC, 46*(2), 23-29.

Stokes, J. (1983). Effective training programs: One institutional response to sexual harassment. *Journal of NAWDAC, 46*(2), 34-38.

Till, F. J. (1980). *Sexual harassment: A report on the sexual harassment of students.* Washington, DC.: National Advisory Council on Women's Educational Programs.

Chapter 15

Preventing Sexual Harassment Through Male-Female Communication Training[1]

Cynthia Berryman-Fink
University of Cincinnati
Cincinnati, OH

▼ Since the EEOC published its Guidelines on Sexual Harassment in November 1980, a plethora of articles have offered information and advice to help organizations understand the problem, prevent instances of its occurrence, and reduce organizational liability regarding sexual harassment. The literature provides definitions and criteria for sexual harassment determinations (Bryson, 1990; Caudill & Donaldson, 1986; Deane, 1986; Howard, 1991; Hoyman & Robinson, 1980; Lewis & Johnson, 1991; Popovich, 1988; York, 1989), data on the prevalence of harassment in organizations (Biles, 1981; Gutek, 1985; York, 1989), sample company policy statements for prohibiting sexual harassment (Biles, 1981; Deane, 1986; Driscoll, 1981; Kronenberger & Bourke, 1981), general advice to organizations dealing with sexual harassment (Caudill & Donaldson, 1986; Driscoll, 1981), and recommended procedures for investigating complaints (Jossem, 1991; York, 1989).

One theme which clearly emerges from the vast literature is a call for organizations to conduct workshops or training programs on sexual harassment. For over a decade, the human resources literature has urged organizations to include training, along with policy statements,

[1]While it is clear that sexual harassment is not exclusively a cross-gender phenomenon, the vast majority of instances of sexual harassment occur between men and women. Therefore, this chapter focuses exclusively on male-female issues in sexual harassment.

complaint procedures, and progressive disciplinary measures for offenders, as the components of an effective and thorough organizational response to sexual harassment. A variety of specific training recommendations has been proposed. Hoyman and Robinson (1980) call for personnel specialists to receive sensitivity training so that they can develop rapport with employees and handle the confidentiality of sexual harassment complaints. Others claim that it is necessary to teach supervisors to recognize sexual harassment (Deane, 1986; Hoyman & Robinson, 1980; Koen, 1989; Spann, 1990), to improve supervisors' competencies in listening to subordinates' complaints (Renick, 1980), or to inform supervisors of the procedures for handling claims (Kronenberger & Bourke, 1981). Waxman (1990) proposes training to help managers define their responsibility regarding sexual harassment, while Lewis and Johnson (1991) call for training to develop managers' interpersonal problem-solving skills so that they can balance the rights of both the complainant and the alleged harasser. Others recommend workshops to help victims understand their rights and cope with incidents of sexual harassment (Howard, 1991; Popovich, 1988).

While there does seem to be merit in training human resources specialists, supervisors, managers, and victims in how to recognize and deal with sexual harassment, none of these recommendations are proactive in preventing or reducing the incidence of harassment in workplace organizations. In addition to teaching supervisors how to recognize, detect, and deal with sexual harassment, organizations need to educate employees about professional behavior that is neither sexually intimidating nor sexually inviting. To be permanently effective, rather than merely reactive, training programs should include nonsupervisory employees in the collective creation of a workplace climate free of sexually harassing behavior.

There have been calls for training to help employees redefine appropriate work behavior between men and women. Spann (1990) articulates the need for employees to move beyond policy statements and complaint procedures to problem prevention through work-climate alteration. Driscoll (1981) recommends that sexuality be included in affirmative action programs and employee team-building sessions. Popovich (1988) calls for role playing and discussions among nonsupervisory employees to clarify perceptions of sexual harassment. Through training, organizations can articulate expected behaviors and suggest rules for the new roles created when women enter a predominantly male department, organization, or occupation (Stringer, Remick, Salisbury, & Ginorio, 1990). Lewis and Johnson (1991) posit that sexual harassment based on a hostile work environment will not be eliminated without a change in the organization's culture. They recommend, as part of an effective training program, an analysis of how the current workplace culture assigns roles, status, and rewards to male and female employees. Some training programs call for organizations to change the dynamics of interaction between men and women in the workplace (Biles, 1981), to help men and women employees understand each others' interpretations of behavior (Booth-Butterfield, 1989), or to help the sexes discuss and confront issues of sexuality on the job (Waxman, 1990).

Personnel administrators, managers, and supervisors alone cannot be expected to significantly reduce the amount of sexually harassing behavior in contemporary organizations. While those in leadership positions must be trained to communicate and enforce a company's policies and procedures on sexual harassment, interventions with employees at all levels also must occur in order to create a workplace culture in which self-monitoring and coworkers' sanctions prevent episodes of harassment from occurring or escalating.

The literature on sexual harassment consistently points to power differences between women and men resulting from society's traditional sex-role socialization as a major cause of sexual harassment. Stringer et al. (1990) assert that power is a primary component of sexual harassment, and that a culture which attributes more power to men than to women provides males with the natural gender power to harass and deprives females of the power to resist or report harassment. Popovich (1988) attributes the higher incidence rates of sexual harassment of females rather than of males to women's less powerful job positions and to the unequal distribution of power between the sexes in society. Gutek (1985) explains that whether sexual harassment is viewed from an organizational, legal, or feminist perspective, unequal power relationships between women and men rooted in cultural expectations "spill over" to work contexts and provide a foundation by which sexual harassment is legitimized in the workplace. Renick (1980) and Biles (1981) cite cultural conditioning as a factor encouraging the practice of sexual harassment. Expectations that women are passive and submissive and that men are aggressive and dominant create an environment conducive to harassment. Case (1991) attributes a sexually harassing and hostile workplace culture to gender-specific patterns of language and nonverbal messages which create asymmetrical power relationships between men and women in society and in organizations. Attributing sexual harassment to power differences between men and women is a common explanation throughout the sexual harassment literature (Betz & Fitzgerald, 1987; Collins & Blodgett, 1981; Tangri, Burt, & Johnson, 1982).

Thus, it can be argued that if power differences between the sexes contribute to sexual harassment, then equalizing power between male and female employees should reduce the incidence of sexual harassment. There are various sources of organizational power which can be altered to create more symmetrical power distributions between male and female employees. Power equalization may be achieved through the equitable distribution of formal roles and salaries (Stringer et al., 1990), through balanced ratios in the numbers of male and female employees (Kanter, 1979), and through structural changes that replace hierarchies with decentralized structures to spread power (Kanter, 1983). Another mechanism to alter power dynamics in organizations is to change the culture of communication—to replace interaction rules that linguistically position men as more powerful and women as less powerful in organizational interactions. Gender-communication training, which changes the power imbalances inherent in male-female interaction, can be an effective way to prevent sexual harassment in organizations. Such an approach is consistent with numerous recommendations urging organizations to include male-female communication as a necessary component in sexual harassment training programs (Biles, 1981; Booth-Butterfield, 1989; Driscoll, 1981; Gutek, 1985; Kronenberger & Bourke, 1981; Lewis & Johnson, 1991; Rowe, 1981; Spann, 1990). What follows is a description of a training program for sexual harassment prevention. First, it describes male-female communication patterns which can perpetuate power differences and contribute to a sexually harassing environment. Then it presents techniques for developing an organizational culture based on balanced communicative power leading to a professional, nonsexualized work environment.

MALE-FEMALE COMMUNICATION STYLES

Research has shown that men and women communicate differently on a number of dimensions. Six communication differences, three verbal and three nonverbal, which reflect power discrepancies and have implications for sexual harassment, are discussed. After a profile of male-female communication styles is provided, training recommendations are made for redirecting employees' communication and eliminating the communicative power basis of sexual harassment.

Verbal Communication

Self-Disclosure. A number of studies have found that women are more likely than men to reveal personal information, reactions, and feelings to others (DeForest & Stone, 1980; Dindia & Allen, 1990; Greenblatt, Hasenauer, & Freimuth, 1980; Jourard, 1961; LeVine & Franco, 1981; & Morton, 1978). If women in the workplace typically reveal more personal information than men do, a clear power differential is created. Information is a source of power. Revealing information is tantamount to giving up power. Disclosing feelings, in particular, puts one in a position of vulnerability. Withholding information is a power-based strategy in many business situations. Thus, the preferred female behavior of self-disclosing puts women in a less powerful position, while the preferred male behavior of withholding disclosure gives men a power advantage.

Sex differences in self-disclosure also can contribute to misunderstandings which serve as an impetus to sexual harassment. Women, who talk about personal feelings and information with male colleagues, may do so because it is a comfortable and habitual style of communicating and because it is a way to develop workplace friendships. Males, however, often misinterpret friendliness from females as sexual interest. A study by Abbey (1982) showed that men perceive friendliness from women as seduction. Thus, we see sex-based differences in self-disclosure contributing to sexual harassment. In allegations of sexual harassment, men often say they were merely responding to sexual interest shown by women, while the women often deny manifesting sexual cues.

Assertiveness. Studies have consistently shown men to be more aggressive than women (Doyle & Paludi, 1991; Hoppe, 1979; Jacklin, 1989; & Maccoby & Jacklin, 1974). Women are more likely to be verbally nonassertive, while men are more verbally assertive and verbally aggressive (Hess, Bridgewater, Bornstein, & Sweeney, 1980; & Pearson, Turner, & Todd-Mancillas, 1991). This sex difference is tied to organizational power. To communicate assertively shows power and control. An aggressive style of behavior could be considered an inappropriate or intimidating display of power. Nonassertive behavior puts women in a powerless or one-down position in which their rights can be violated by others. Aggression by males and nonassertive responses by females contribute to the asymmetrical power exchanges which serve as a springboard to sexual harassment. Traditional sex-role conditioning expects men to be the sexual aggressors, pressuring and persisting in their overtures to women. Society expects women, on the other hand, to be tactful, not forceful, in rejecting unwanted attention from men. This cycle of male aggressiveness and female nonassertiveness inherent in sex-role expectations contributes to the creation and perpetuation of sexual harassment in the workplace.

Interruption. Research has demonstrated that men interrupt women more than women interrupt men (Baird, 1976; Thorne & Henley, 1977; Zimmerman & West, 1977). Interruption is a mechanism for conversational dominance. It is a way to control the conversational topic and speaking time. Interrupting others asserts power. Tolerating interruptions puts one in a submissive or less powerful position. Interrupting, used more frequently by males, and tolerating interruptions, a typically female response, serves to further create and reinforce unequal power balances between men and women. While it is difficult to directly connect conversational interruptions to sexual harassment, there is a relationship between topic control and harassment. In their allegations of sexual harassment, many women have described males repeatedly changing conversational topics away from work-related issues and redirecting them to sexual references. Men's perceived right to introduce such topics, coupled with women's inability to disallow such topic shifts, can perpetuate a harassing work environment.

Nonverbal Communication

Personal Space. Research has shown that women have smaller personal space zones and that men are more likely to intrude on women's personal space than vice versa (Bate, 1988; Evans & Howard, 1973; Frieze, 1974; Henley, 1977; & Leventhal & Matturro, 1980). Henley (1977) explains how personal space usage is tied to power. More powerful individuals are allowed to command more space and to invade the space of others. Less powerful individuals are expected to tolerate invasions of their personal space. Case (1991) shows how men's prerogatives to enter the personal space of women maintain power relationships and contribute to a sexually harassing work environment. Thus, sex-role expectations regarding personal space allow men to move closer to women than is professionally appropriate and deprive women of the power to resist invasions of their space. Such sex differences in space norms can contribute to a frequently reported type of sexually harassing behavior—male employees leaning over, cornering, standing too close to, or physically intimidating female employees.

Touching. Research findings indicate that men touch women more than women touch men (Bate, 1988; Deaux, 1976; Henley, 1973; Leathers, 1986; & Major, 1981). Men are expected to initiate touch with women, while women are expected to be the recipients of male touch. Sex differences in touch contribute to both power asymmetries and sexual harassment in the workplace. When males are allowed to touch females, who are not granted the same privilege in return, touch becomes a symbol of power and status. Even in nonhuman behavior, unilateral touch between dominant and submissive animals reveals which animal has more power (Lawick-Goodall, 1971). In addition to revealing interactional power dynamics, unilateral touch manifested by male employees brushing against, hugging, pinching, grabbing, fondling, patting or kissing female employees is a frequently cited type of sexually harassing behavior in the workplace.

Smiling. Research shows that women smile more often than men do (Argyle, 1975; Bate, 1988; Frances, 1979; Hall, 1984; Mayo & Henley, 1981; & Parlee, 1979). While smiling is usually associated with happiness, frequent smiling can be interpreted as appeasement or approval-seeking cues. Pearson et al. (1991) explain that women lose power when they overuse smiles because they appear less genuine and increase their vulnerability. Smiling by women can make them seem emotional and vulnerable, while men's tendency to avoid smiling makes them appear strong and stoic (Arliss, 1991). In addition to sex differences in smiling frequency, there are indications that men and women use smiles for different reasons. When men smile, it is to represent some pleasant inner state. But women smile to promote pleasantness in their communication with others (Arliss, 1991). Male-female differences in smiling not only reinforce power inequities, but they also can lead to misunderstandings relevant to sexual harassment. Women's smiles in response to males' sexual behavior in the workplace may be interpreted by men as signaling interest, whereas women's use of such smiles may be a habitual way to appear polite and pleasant, even in response to harassing behaviors. This explanation is consistent with research suggesting that men impute more sexual meaning into male-female interactions than do women (Abbey, 1982; Major & Heslin, 1982; & Zellman & Goodchilds, 1983). Because women smile so much, their smiles are difficult to read. Men will naturally read those smiles according to the way they have been conditioned to interpret most interactions with women–sexually.

To summarize, male and female communication styles differ in a number of ways. Those differences create and reinforce power imbalances which provide the foundation for sexual harassment in the workplace. Women's tendencies to self-disclose to their male colleagues may be interpreted by the men as flirtatious, intimacy seeking, or signaling sexual interest. Men, who are expected to be verbally and sexually aggressive in society, may carry that behavior to their workplace interactions with women. Women, who have been conditioned to be nonassertive, may not possess the skills to forcefully tell men when overtures are unwanted, intimidating, and interfering with job performance. Men, comfortable with interrupting and changing conversational topics, may redirect workplace communication to inappropriate sexual topics and women, by virtue of their typical conversational roles, may not know how to disallow sexual topics at work. Women in the workplace may allow men to invade their personal space and to touch them. Men may believe that women find close interaction distances and touch comfortable and welcome in the workplace. Women, conditioned to smile in a variety of circumstances, even uncomfortable ones, may find that men in the workplace are attributing sexual motives to their smiles. Communication styles, then, can provide the impetus for a chronically sexually harassing environment to emerge in an organization. The sex-role conditioned behavior typically manifested by men and women can predispose men to engage in harassing behaviors and deprive women of the strategies for assertively reacting to and preventing the escalation of harassment. Because men and women communicate in different cultural arenas, their interactions take on a cross-cultural quality (Tannen, 1990). It is not surprising, then, that the same behavior can result in discrepant interpretations by women and men. Research shows that men and women differ significantly in their perceptions of whether a particular behavior constitutes sexual harassment (Beauvais, 1986; Booth-Butterfield, 1989; Coles, 1986; Collins & Blodgett, 1981; Konrad & Gutek, 1986; Padgitt & Padgitt, 1986; Popovich, Licata, Nokovich, Martelli, & Zoloty, 1986; Powell, 1983; & Reilly, Lott, & Gallogly, 1986).

If male and female employees bring different communication behaviors to the workplace, and if those styles contribute to both power imbalances and sexual harassment, then sexual harassment prevention training must include interventions for male-female communication styles as well as descriptions of policy statements, complaint procedures, and supervisory responsibilities. Training, the purpose of which is to bring about a convergence of behaviors and perceptions between male and female employees, will alter the organizational culture in such a way so as to make sexual harassment unlikely. The following training recommendations are proposed to bring about the empowerment of all employees, to free both sexes from rigid, outdated sex-role expectations, and to develop greater communication flexibility for employees.

TRAINING PROGRAM

Berryman-Fink and Fink (1985) proposed a training program to bring about gender-flexible or androgynous management behavior in organizations. While their program was designed for managers, many of the same recommendations would apply to a sexual harassment prevention program for employees. A training program at management or employee levels, the objective of which is to replace sex-role restricted communication with gender-flexible communication, should follow the four steps of needs assessment, delineation of objectives, workshop facilitation, and evaluation outlined by Berryman-Fink and Fink (1985). Here we provide some activities trainers can use to help participants replace gender

stereotypical communication with gender-flexible communication.
First, trainees must be made aware of their sex-stereotypical communication behaviors and the limitations of those behaviors before they can begin to expand their styles. Trainers can distribute surveys on self-disclosure or assertiveness to provide participants with profiles of their typical behaviors. A breakdown of scores for female and male participants likely will reveal women scoring higher on self-disclosure and lower on assertiveness, with the scores reversed for men. Trainees might also recall or keep a diary of examples of their disclosing or assertive behaviors. Male participants likely will recall or record a greater number and variety of instances of their assertiveness, while the females likely will provide more instances of their disclosures. Role-play practice in which the men experiment with self-disclosure and the women experiment with assertiveness will help participants expand their communication flexibility. Participants can help create the role-play scenarios by suggesting actual work situations related to disclosure or assertiveness. Female trainees should practice handling persistent sexual overtures with assertiveness rather than politeness, and the males should practice replacing sexually oriented behavior with professional workplace behavior. Participants should discuss the misunderstandings which occur when women do not assertively confront initial instances of sexual harassment or when self-disclosure intended to show friendliness is interpreted as flirtatiousness.

While there is not a standard test to measure one's interruptions, audio-tape recordings of workplace conversations or meetings likely will reveal sex differences on this dimension. Trainees can practice behavior reversal in workshop sessions–women should force themselves to interrupt men, and men should allow themselves to be interrupted by women. This will allow participants to feel the power or powerlessness accompanying each style. Women should practice disallowing unwanted sexual topics, and men should practice monitoring tendencies to introduce sexually oriented topics into workplace conversations.

Similar techniques of behavior identification and modification can be used to create flexibility in the three areas of nonverbal communication. Trainers could ask participants to provide workplace examples of gender-typical use of personal space, touch, and smiles. Women employees often can recall many instances when their space was violated or they were touched against their will. The trainer should probe the feelings of intimidation, helplessness, or lack of power resulting from such episodes. Men often report that such behaviors were meant to be friendly, not threatening. The trainer should probe the men's feelings of confusion, resentment, or anger when women interpret physical closeness or touch differently from the way the men intended them. Role plays can equip men with the ability to monitor when they are moving into a woman's personal space and to adjust their distance to an appropriate professional norm. Women can practice clearly communicating to men when close positioning and touch is inappropriate and unwelcome.

An effective way for women to become aware of their tendency to overuse smiles is to watch themselves on video-tape. A video-taped sample of any portion of a training program or a workplace meeting likely will show women smiling more frequently in relation to more topics than men. Outside of training, women can remind each other when they are smiling in a situation that would not call for a smile. The goal is not to eliminate women's smiles, but to display them only when they are situationally appropriate. Male participants should be encouraged to discuss how they interpret women's smiles and to use the techniques of perception checking—questioning a woman's affective state when unsure of her feelings or reactions.

As we have seen, male-female communication differences have implications for sexual harassment. Male-female communication training as part of a sexual harassment prevention program can provide employees with an awareness of their stereotypical behaviors and can help them develop gender-flexible communication skills. This does not mean that males should communicate in a feminine style, or that females should adopt masculine behaviors. Rather, both sexes must be equipped with the skills of behavioral flexibility. Training in male-female interaction dynamics is not meant to replace company policy statements, complaint procedures, and disciplinary measures regarding harassment. Rather, it is a way to complement standard human resources practices by teaching employees to communicate in such a way so as to prevent the occurrence of sexual harassment. Male-female training should not put responsibility on one sex for modifying its behavior, while the behavior of the other sex remains unchanged. A key to the effectiveness of such training is that both males and females have responsibility for adjusting their behavior. Since men and women are constrained by sex-role socialization, both sexes must work together to break free of conditioning, to overcome misunderstandings, to eliminate interactional power differences, and to create a workplace culture that is equitable, professional, and free of sexual harassment.

REFERENCES

Abbey, A. (1982). Sex differences in attributions for friendly behavior: Do males misperceive females' friendliness? *Journal of Personality and Social Psychology, 42*, 830-838.

Argyle, M. (1975). *Body communication.* New York: International

Universities Press.

Arliss, L. P. (1991). *Gender communication*. Englewood Cliffs, NJ: Prentice-Hall.

Baird, J. E. (1976). Sex differences in group communication: A review of relevant research. *Quarterly Journal of Speech, 62*, 179-192.

Bate, B. (1988). *Communication and the sexes*. New York: Harper and Row.

Beauvais, K. (1986). Workshops to combat sexual harassment: A case study of changing attitudes. *Signs, 12*, 130-145.

Berryman-Fink, C., & Fink, C. B. (1985). Optimal training for opposite-sex managers. *Training and Development Journal, 39*, 27-29.

Betz, N. E., & Fitzgerald, L. F. (1987). *The career psychology of women*. Orlando, FL: Academic Press.

Biles, G. E. (1981). A program guide for preventing sexual harassment in the workplace. *Personnel Administrator, 26*, 49-56.

Booth-Butterfield, M. (1989). Perceptions of harassing communication as a function of locus of control, work force participation, and gender. *Communication Quarterly, 37*, 262-275.

Bryson, C. B. (1990). The internal sexual harassment investigation: Self-evaluation without self-incrimination. *Employee Relations Law Journal, 15*, 551-559.

Case, S. S. (1991, October). *Courtroom use of linguistic analysis to demonstrate a hostile work environment for women*. Paper presented at the 14th annual conference of the Organization for the Study of Communication, Language and Gender, Milwaukee, WI.

Caudill, D. W., & Donaldson, R. (1986). Is your climate ripe for sexual harassment? *Management World, 15*, 26-27.

Coles, F. (1986). Forced to quit: Sexual harassment complaints and agency response. *Sex Roles, 14*, 81-95.

Collins, E. G. C., & Blodgett, T. B. (1981). Sexual harassment: Some see it and some won't. *Harvard Business Review, 59*, 76-95.

Deane, R. H. (1986). Sexual harassment: Is your company protected? *Business, 36*, 42-45.

Deaux, K. (1976). *The behavior of men and women*. Monterey, CA: Brooks/Cole.

DeForest, C., & Stone, G. L. (1980). Effects of sex intimacy level on self-disclosure. *Journal of Counseling Psychology, 27*, 93-96.

Dindia, K., & Allen, M. (1990, November). *Sex differences in self-disclosure: A meta-analysis*. Paper presented at the annual convention of the Speech Communication Association, Chicago.

Doyle, J., & Paludi, M. A. (1991). *Sex and gender*. Dubuque, IA: W. C. Brown.

Driscoll, J. B. (1981). Sexual attraction and harassment: Management's new problems. *Personnel Journal, 60*, 33-36, 56.

Evans, G. W., & Howard, R. B. (1973). Personal space. *Psychological Bulletin, 80*, 334-344.

Frances, S. J. (1979). Sex differences in nonverbal behavior. *Sex Roles*,

5, 519-535.

Frieze, I. H. (1974). *Nonverbal aspects of femininity and masculinity which perpetuate sex-role stereotypes.* Paper presented at the annual meeting of the Eastern Psychological Association.

Greenblatt, L., Hasenauer, J. E., & Freimuth, V. S. (1980). Psychological sex type and androgyny in the study of communication variables: Self-disclosure and communication apprehension. *Human Communication Research, 6,* 117-129.

Gutek, B. (1985). *Sex and the workplace.* San Francisco: Jossey-Bass Publishers.

Hall, J. A. (1984). *Nonverbal sex differences: Communication accuracy and expressive style.* Baltimore, MD: Johns Hopkins University Press.

Henley, N. M. (1973). The politics of touch. In P. Brown (Ed.); *Radical psychology* (pp. 421-443). New York: Harper & Row.

Henley, N. M. (1977). *Body politics: Power, sex and nonverbal communication.* Englewood Cliffs, NJ: Prentice-Hall.

Hess, E. P., Bridgewater, C. A., Bornstein, P. H., & Sweeney, T. M. (1980). Situational determinants in the perception of assertiveness: Gender-related influences. *Behavior Therapy, 11,* 49-57.

Hoppe, C. M. (1979). Interpersonal aggression as a function of subject's sex, subject's sex-role identification, opponent's sex and degree of provocation. *Journal of Personality, 47,* 315-329.

Howard, S. (1991). Organizational resources for addressing sexual harassment. *Journal of Counseling and Development, 69,* 507-511.

Hoyman, M., & Robinson, R. (1980). Interpreting the new sexual harassment guidelines. *Personnel Journal, 59,* 996-1000.

Jacklin, C. N. (1989). Femininity and masculinity: Issues of gender. *American Psychologist, 44,* 127-133.

Jossem, J. H. (1991). Investigating sexual harassment complaints. *Personnel, 68,* 9-10.

Jourard, S. M. (1961). Age trends in self-disclosure. *Merrill Palmer Quarterly, 1,* 191-197.

Kanter, R. M. (1979). *Men and women of the corporation.* New York: Basic Books.

Kanter, R. M. (1983). *The change masters.* New York: Simon & Shuster.

Koen, C. M., Jr. (1989). Sexual harassment: Criteria for defining hostile environment. *Employee Responsibilities and Rights Journal, 2,* 289-301.

Konrad, A., & Gutek, B. (1986). Impact of work experiences on attitudes toward sexual harassment. *Administrative Science Quarterly, 31,* 422-438.

Kronenberger, G. K., & Bourke, D. L. (1981). Effective training and the elimination of sexual harassment. *Personnel Journal, 60,* 879-883.

Lawick-Goodall, J. (1971). *In the shadow of men.* Boston: Houghton-Mifflin.

Leathers, D. G. (1986). *Successful nonverbal communication: Principles and applications.* New York: Macmillan.

Leventhal, G., & Matturro, M. (1980). Differential effects of spacial crowding and sex on behavior. *Perceptual and Motor Skills, 51,* 111-119.

LeVine, E., & Franco, J. M. (1981). A reassessment of self-disclosure patterns among Anglo-Americans and Hispanics. *Journal of Counseling Psychology, 28,* 522-524.

Lewis, K. E., & Johnson, P. R. (1991). Preventing sexual harassment complaints based on hostile work environments. *SAM Advanced Management Journal, 56,* 21-36.

Maccoby, E. E., & Jacklin, C. N. (1974). *The psychology of sex differences.* Stanford: Stanford University Press.

Major, B. (1981). Gender patterns in touching behavior. In C. Mayo & N. M. Henley, (Eds.); *Gender and nonverbal behavior.* New York: Springer-Verlag, 3-37.

Major, B., & Heslin, R. (1982). Perceptions of cross-sex and same-sex nonreciprocal touch: It is better to give than to receive. *Journal of Nonverbal Behavior, 6,* 148-162.

Mayo, C., & Henley, N, M. (Eds.). (1981). *Gender and nonverbal behavior.* New York: Springer-Verlag.

Morton, T. L. (1978). Intimacy and reciprocity of exchange: A comparison of spouses and strangers. *Journal of Personality and Social Psychology, 36,* 72-81.

Padgitt, S., & Padgitt, J. (1986). Cognitive structures of sexual harassment. *Journal of College Student Personnel, 27,* 34-39.

Parlee, M. B. (1979). Women smile less for success. *Psychology Today, 12,* 16.

Pearson, J. C., Turner, L., & Todd-Mancillas, W. (1991). *Gender and communication.* Dubuque, IA: W. C. Brown.

Popovich, P. M. (1988). Sexual harassment in organizations. *Employee Responsibilities and Rights Journal, 1,* 273-282.

Popovich, P. M., Licata, B. J., Nokovich, D., Martelli, T., & Zoloty, S. (1986). Assessing the incidence and perceptions of sexual harassment behaviors among American undergraduates. *The Journal of Psychology, 120,* 387-396.

Powell, G. N. (1983). Definition of sexual harassment and sexual attention experienced. *The Journal of Psychology, 113,* 113-117.

Reilly, M., Lott, B., & Gallogly, S. (1986). Sexual harassment of university students. *Sex Roles, 15,* 333-358.

Renick, J. C. (1980). Sexual harassment at work: Why it happens, what to do about it. *Personnel Journal, 59,* 658-662.

Rowe, M. P. (1981). Dealing with sexual harassment. *Harvard Business Review, 59,* 42-46.

Spann, J. (1990). Dealing effectively with sexual harassment: Some practical lessons from one city's experience. *Public Personnel Management, 19,* 53-69.

Stringer, D. M., Remick, H., Salisbury, J., & Ginorio, A. B. (1990). The power and reasons behind sexual harassment: An employer's guide to solutions. *Public Personnel Management, 19,* 43-52.

Tangri, S. S., Burt, M. R., & Johnson, L. B. (1982). Sexual harassment at work: Three explanatory models. *Journal of Social Issues, 38,* 33-54.

Tannen, D. (1990). *You just don't understand.* New York: William Morrow.

Thorne, B., & Henley, N. (1977). Sex and language: Difference and dominance. *Language in Society, 6,* 110-113.

Waxman, M. (1990). Institutional strategies for dealing with sexual harassment. *Employee Responsibilities and Rights Journal, 3,* 73-75.

York, K. M. (1989). Defining sexual harassment in workplaces: A policy capturing approach. *Academy of Management Journal, 32,* 830-850.

Zellman, G. L., & Goodchilds, J. D. (1983). Becoming sexual in adolescence. In E. A. Allgeier & N. B. McCormick (Eds.). *Changing boundaries: Gender roles and sexual behavior* (pp. 49-63). Palo Alto, CA: Mayfield.

Zimmerman, D. H., & West, C. (1975). Sex roles, interruptions, and silences in conversation. In B. Thorne & N. Henley (Eds.). *Language and sex: Difference and dominance* (pp. 105-129). Rowley, MA: Newbury House Publishers.

▼Chapter 16

Sycophancy and Servitude: Harassment and Rebellion

Gerald M. Phillips
Susan Jarboe

The Pennsylvania State University
University Park, PA

INTRODUCTION

This chapter presents an alternative to the popular wisdom about sexual harassment. The optimism with which social scientists view the natural law is a bezoar in the brain. It results in a consensus that Freud was wrong; thus, somehow, people can be trained to overcome their primal sexual drives. Corollary is the consensus that there are "men's" and "women's" rules, one of which must be ascendant.

This chapter presumes that male-female relationships conform to a hierarchical scheme in which power is the central issue. Gender interacts with social custom and history to constrain the way men and women act to achieve the prime directive: preservation of the species through sexual consummation (Ardrey, 1966; Wilson, 1978). We live in a society in which technology has outraced evolution; thus interpersonal relations have not progressed much past Neanderthal rules. Furthermore, we acknowledge Ernest Becker's (1968) notion of anthropodicy; we believe humans are as likely to be evil as good. We have no illusions about the felicity of the connubial relationship. Men may procreate recreationally and women because they feel their biological clocks ticking. Sexuality is natural to humans. Some religions abjure intercourse and acknowledge celibacy as a sacrifice, an unnatural state. Thus, when we deal with sexual harassment, we work around a fine line between protecting people who do not want to indulge in sexual activity without reversing the natural law.

Our commentary, while not entirely serious, is not facetious. We seek both seminal and generic ideas (sic) harmonious with reality. We obviated the slimmest possibility of sexual tension, interfering with it by working via email. Thus, gender, often the basis of harassment, was not an impediment. At any event, harassment is defined by a person who feels harassed. There is no formal taxonomy, and it is not a legal condition. The harasser may believe his actions to be legitimate. It may seem normal to the person being harassed, as well. The sine qua non of harassment is that someone with power uses it to humiliate someone who has none. People with power know they have it. The powerless know who has power over them. Any given male may concede power to a female and thus permit himself to be harassed. But a voluntary relationship with a dominatrix is paradoxical, as when a husband says to his wife, "Take charge," and she does. The husband assumed the natural law gave him the power to give up the power. The illusion is created that the female has power. She does not. She only has a valuable service commodity, to wit, sexual access with which to bargain. The male uses physical power, money, or seduction to gain access; a combination of artistic and inartistic proofs. Harassment could be distinguished from seduction by the use of inartistic proofs to gain nonconsensual sexual access. This is based on the civilized notion that the woman has control over access to her sexual parts.

INTRODUCTION TO THE METAPHOR

The authors draw their metaphor for harassment from medieval feudalism when male privilege was clearly defined by both law and custom. For example, the Lord of the manor was owed certain dues from the peasant to wit: a portion of the crops, service in the ranks, and a goose at "Micklemas." Often the lord had droit de seigneur, that is, the right to first intercourse–defloration–with any peasant bride. The distribution of power at the medieval court was entirely inartistic. Trials were by combat. Kings bought loyalty with money or enforced it by force of arms. Courtiers took oaths. There was no appellate jurisdiction.

The same is true of corporate organizations today. Whoever has the power to withhold funds has the power to control behavior. There are elaborate shams maintained to provide the illusion of democratic control and employee participation, but the primary force is the power structure; make no mistake about it. Those who like to eat and depend on their paychecks for sustenance are obliged to get along by going along. Though many corporations provide a veneer of democratic management, the power lies with the person who authorizes the paychecks, and there is no appellate jurisdiction.

Harassment, as practiced in medieval society, is a proper analogy for contemporary social relationships. The basic model of sexual harassment harkens back to the expulsion from Eden, adapted in each generation to social exigencies. Adam's first love was a female demon named Lilith, who taught the stupid aborigine how to get in out of the rain. God could not tolerate the thought of marrying his creation to a creature like that (although it is not clear who created Lilith), and so he provided Eve as an alternative, a sexual vessel with which Adam could be "fruitful and multiply." There are alternative stories (see Robert Graves's *The White Goddess* [1948], for explanations of the origin of the world from a female perspective). The sense of this ancient legend was that woman was naturally the male's intellectual superior, and, in fact, it was Eve who discovered the truth, that she was being exploited, and was responsible for the expulsion from Eden. Getting evicted by the Big Boss because of her gender may have been the first cited case of sexual harassment.

In medieval times, power over serfs, vassals, peasants, and other hoi polloi was a perquisite of nobility. In the medieval court, the prince controlled the duke; the duke had suzerainty over the earls and counts, who in turn had their subordinates neatly arranged and assigned to specific tasks, as ladies in waiting, knights, squires, yeomen, vassals, and drudges. It was a virtual organization chart. This system of organization is referred to as a "pecking order" or in India as a "caste system." We preserve it in the form of military ranks, organization charts, and through references to economic classes.

Power is customarily maintained by control over resources backed up with physical force. Some also ascribe it to charisma, but charisma is merely a resource of physical appeal. Resources include money, sexual access, hedonistic pleasure, physical or financial security, and authority to delegate power–not necessarily in that order. Power is backed up by law-enforced agencies capable of exerting physical force. Without force, the law of the jungle prevails (what Clarence Thomas calls "the natural law"). That means without legal protection, men, because they are physically stronger, can bash women. (Nietzsche pointed out that laws were the refuge of the weak.)

There is another paradox, however. People are protected from the inartistic proof of harassment by the inartistic proofs of the law. No one ever persuaded a mugger and rapist to quit. It takes brute force, including incarceration. The salient feature of this system, in its contemporary isomorphism, is that it is tacit and enforced by social norms, local customs, and the Common Law. Constitutions and statutes are enacted by the magnanimous strong to protect the weak, although it is "unnatural" to do so. It is irrelevant whether participants in the social system acknowledge their power or even use it. It is conferred by the system. Many men, in fact, may not be aware of the power they hold over women; many women, naive as they may be, do not recognize their social vulnerability. Formal law only works to prevent violations that jeopardize the majority. It may be natural to steal and murder, but it is also dangerous. Sexual harassment does not create public jeopardy.

The street gang is an example of what we are talking about. It is natural for boys to gather in groups (e.g., teams or fraternities) and be bound by codes of behavior. A member must not betray his fellow members. When someone blows the whistle, he is known as a "rat" or "squealer," and is socially shunned. The extreme penalty may be loss of membership in the gang (and sometimes loss of life). The law can do nothing about shunning; it works in cases of blatant legal violation. Women, when empowered, act out the male systems in sodalities, sororities, and coffee klatsches.

People are initiated into organizations, although now it is called acculturation. It happens differently for men and women. For men, it involves a ritual like those of the medieval military orders. These organizations persist today, mostly without female members, in the form of Elks, Masons, and Kiwanians. These organizations are hierarchical with perks associated with rank; such as the right to pick on those below them in rank or to harass available females.

A CASE IN POINT: THE HILL-THOMAS AFFAIR

The current evidence that the feudal system still prevails was the Hill-Thomas encounter. Although the facts of the case may be in dispute, it is a perfect example of the labyrinthine issues of the contemporary court (pun intended). Thomas, a member of the petty nobility elevated by the largesse of a bountiful lord (President Bush), was served by Hill, who performed various menial functions in a servile rank. Thomas, in a contemporary version of droit de seigneur, allegedly made sexual demands on Hill. At one time this might have been taken as "it goes without saying" by both parties. It seemed that Mr. Thomas was so steeped in his understanding of the white hierarchy that patronizingly granted his position, that he was not even aware he was demeaning his underling whose rights had also been patronizingly granted. He saw it as his right to be rude and crude (like his patrons and models), and it was her (traditional) obligation to put up with it. In fact, it is not unusual for petty nobles (and some not so petty; harassment regulations do not apply to members of Congress) to make overt sexual demands on female underlings. Often, the females comply in the expectation of privilege and reward. They accept the role of courtesan. Ms. Hill, however, had second thoughts. She took the lip service of the "powers that be" seriously. This was a dangerous error on her part, and she had to be put in her place lest her model stir dissension in the ranks. This was done most incisively by the overwhelming confirmation of Thomas and his elevation to the true nobility.

The Hill-Thomas case makes it clear that confrontation is ineffective. For one thing, we do not know exactly what Thomas did. He probably made some tasteless remarks, some lewd suggestions. Well, good grief, what red-blooded man hasn't when confronted with a "sexy looking chick" like Anita (who would probably be referred to diminuitively as "Teenie" in our corporation). We do not know what kind of a person Hill was. Was she "asking for it?" You can't replay history. Testimony conflicted. But it was clear that the person with power had the support network to produce testimony that favored him. Hill was hiding out in Oklahoma moderately successful, but in so doing, she had surrendered her access to power. Consider the ignominy of someone who had washed the feet of the mighty to be a laborer in the vineyard of the Oral Roberts Law School. Ms. Hill took her shot at fame and glory. She lost. Perhaps there will be a contract for a TV movie forthcoming; perhaps a denial of tenure. Her other alternative is to hide. The natural law became very important. Mr. Thomas believed in the natural law which, to some, means that men are *entitled* to sexual access when they want it and that women are vessels (as one male psychiatrist insensitively put it, "seminal spittoons"). The testimony in the Hill-Thomas affair leaves little doubt that Thomas was aware of the privilege conferred upon him by his white masters and was quite insensitive to the discomfort it caused others. Hill, on the other hand, had obviously bought into the fiction that prevails among upper middle-class educated women, that they are "equal." In fact, affirmative action, from which both benefited, conveys an illusion of equality which spares one from conceding the receipt of undeserved privilege. The comments of both genders during the Hill-Thomas hearings were quite instructive. A great many women called Ms. Hill "pushy" and accused her of being a woman spurned. A great many men rallied to Thomas's defense who would have otherwise rejected him because of his race, since his vindication meant their exoneration, as well.

Alan Dershowitz in *Chutzpah* (1991) notes the difference between the effects of upward mobility naturally earned and that conferred by government fiat. More sophisticated interpretations of the natural law, however, point to animal species in the wild, where the females have considerable choice in the matter of intercourse. The imperative, of course, is to get the best together so they can breed a better species.

This can be done simply by putting a birth control chemical in all water supplies, spraying it in the air, or licensing couples deemed fit to bear children. Then couples could indulge in rampant and uncontrolled sex to their hearts' content without overpopulating the world. Simple religious mandates for birth control do not work: poping with overcopulation is not the same as coping with overpopulation.

YESTERDAY'S LEGENDS, TODAY'S REALITIES

Admission to membership in a corporation through employment empowers the supervisor to take control and obligates the employee to comply. An employee may complain through channels and gripe to peers. The organizational system is perpetuated through organization charts that empower, job descriptions that specify, and an exchange of gossip, myths, stories, legends, and other folklore about the nature of control and the obligations of the underlings. This is often referred to as "climate." Sometimes it is referred to as "culture," but it is not clear whether that refers to literacy or pearls. There are at present, however, no methods of calculating harassment isotherms.

The gang and the corporation are similar in fundamental structure to the feudal system. The feudal system assigned powers, privileges, perquisites, and duties to people of various rank. These were spelled out in detail through oaths and rituals. People rose in rank by learning to play their roles properly (as in the Templars, Knights of Malta, Masons, etc.). The hierarchical distribution is also quite clear in the street gang. It is done by specialized role: leader, war leader, and so on. In the fraternity, pledges occupy the lowest rung, senior jocks, the highest.

The corporation gives the appearance of rationality via job descriptions; those for the lower levels are explicit and refer to number of keystrokes demanded or widgets to be burnished. They also provide machine safety regulations, not out of consideration for the employee, but in fear of OSHA and insurance retribution. There are no interpersonal details other than general rules which prevent employees from interfering with others in the performance of tasks. This kind of job description sustains ranks and keeps men and women on relative parity. Especially in unionized plants, men and women are required to do the same work and receive the same pay. Their sexual interaction is a matter of personal business. Thus, women may be insulted by comments, but they cannot be intimidated into granting sexual favors (except by their foremen).

Job descriptions for supervisory positions are written more loosely. They provide information about goals and objectives and the range of authority and over whom it may be exercised in their quest. There is little consideration given to the means by which authority can be exercised, although there is often instruction provided in methods of displaying authority (or leadership) in general. Authority can be shown by the command "act or report immediately" to "I am saving up your violations for later retribution." Persons over whom authority is exercised often remain in suspense about what they have done that is meritorious and reprehensible, and the outcome usually comes on an annual basis in the form of a salary adjustment or promotion. This is often preceded by some sort of quality assessment interview in which the authority figure displays his feathers and the employee cringes appropriately. In any case, subordinates have good reason to be sycophants. One never offends the duke, the chieftain, the general, the gang leader, or the supervisor. In fact, one seeks active means to secure their goodwill.

Everyone in an organization is beaten on by someone else and, in turn, has someone to beat on. The top dog lives in fear, always the victim of an ambiguous power structure, at war with other top dogs, jockeying for position, negotiating. What lurks in the mind of every leader is the possibility that the underlings may be revolting. (Often, they are.)

Peers haze newcomers into the prevailing culture. This is referred to as acculturation, a term used to delude sociologists into believing some sort of equity operates in the organization. Everyone must know where he or she fits and how to stay there or to move to a higher position. (In medieval times, this was often done by jousting. The winner advanced, the loser was buried.)

There is both sense and sensibility (with apologies to Jane Austen) in this. Resources must be allocated and power distributed. Authorities must sustain their position. That means some people must control others. Part of this has stemmed from cultural axioms: whites outrank blacks, men are "superior" to women, Gentiles are more acceptable than Jews, and so on. The Japanese argue their economic advantage comes from homogeneity. All of this is Darwinian. The African kob is a case in point. Males stake out "stamping grounds" and fight for them. The winners have access to the choice females; the losers slink away celibate. This ensures that the strongest males mate with the strongest females and the species endures.

THE CHAIN: SUPERORDINATE AND SUBORDINATE

The people in charge retain their power only if their subordinates perform. Thus, they must either please or overpower those over whom they have authority. But, if they fail to please their own supervisors, they can assign blame to their subordinates and punish them—if they don't get punished by those who have authority over them. There is always someone one rung above. Each superordinate has power to compel others to comply, but in turn faces the paradox of owing their power to that compliance.

Obligations can be spoken and unspoken. Position descriptions are really not a protection. Supervisors can make requests not included in the job description or organization chart, as long as they can get away with it. In fact, many position descriptions conclude with, "perform other duties as requested." Nothing irritates a supervisor more than to hear the subordinate say, "That's not in my job description." Harassment lies in the domain of the unwritten obligations, and subordinates must comply with requests to sustain the goodwill of the supervisor. Technically, there are limits to what can be demanded and remedies against unreasonable requests. The covert way in which harassment is conducted, however, prevents the victim from speaking out or seeking remedies. Onus probandi is on the victim.

In *Tom Brown's School Days* (Hughes, 1911), for example, Tom is roasted on an open fire by upper classmen because of his refusal to render service to Flashman, for whom he was "fag." No one could report, for fear of suffering the same fate. This conspiracy of silence holds so long as employment is maintained. The code remains in force as a means of mutual protection. Whistle blowers do so at their own risk.

We can clarify our definition: *Harassment is any unauthorized act directed by a superordinate at a subordinate.* It may include, but is not confined to, requests for personal favors and privileges (including sexual access), extortion, demanding bribes, threats of retribution (firing, exile to North Dakota), ragging and teasing, blaming, insulting, and orders to perform personal tasks. When a subordinate objects or attempts to defend him- or herself, the presumption (the power) is with the superordinate. Subordinates rarely win. Guerrilla warfare or sabotage may be cathartic, but they rarely change anything. Complaints usually bring retribution. The law imposes an overwhelming burden of proof on the complainer, so amelioration of harassment is entirely dependent on the goodwill of the superordinate. The subordinate may choose to take it, or leave it, literally.

PRINCIPLES OF SURVIVAL

Our question now is *how does one survive harassment* or avoid it altogether? In the Middle Ages, survival was a very literal concept. Failure to please the person in power could mean literal death; now it is more likely to mean loss of economic viability. Machiavelli, Castiglione, and Debrett provide the texts for the following discussion.

In medieval society it was the obligation of the noble lower on the hierarchy to perform acts of obeisance and obsequiousness. This included cringing, bringing "tribute," and combat. It also included euphuism (á la Lyly, 1902) and sycophancy. Machiavelli (1897) provided a guide to the forms of those acts, all apparently Aristotelian "inartistic proofs." The person at the top also had inartistic proofs such as brute force and the denial of goods and privileges at his disposal, so long as he had loyal underlings to exert force on command. Females were not particularly effective in the Middle Ages. Those who won did so by the grace of the males they chose to serve (or by lineage). Those who deviated were raped, imprisoned, tortured, and often killed.

Castiglione (1900) provides operating rules for fulfilling the job description of "courtier." They are quite the same as the social rules that prevail in corporate America. There was a chain of persecution which stopped with the serfs on the bottom of the pyramid, who could beat on each other in sheer frustration. (Occasionally Jews were provided for this purpose. If Jews were unavailable, Armenians, homosexuals, slaves, and women would do.) Those on top assumed the serfs would exhaust themselves beating on each other, thus guaranteeing that they would not organize and revolt.

Men of humble birth had the choice between lackey and warrior. Warriors were expected to lay down their lives for their noble. They spent their days practicing their art of chivalric killing. They also could make certain demands on females. In case of trouble, however, they were required to make blood sacrifice or engage in self-immolation (sometimes like beta baboons in a pack) in order to save the life of their noble. Take note of how closely this pattern followed the animal prime directive in re: the deployment of alphas and others in the pack. It is primal.

Lackeys were required to cringe and bow and perform whatever menial tasks were required. Male warriors could aspire to rise through the ranks to knight (if they killed enough of the enemy and earned the gratitude of their noble). Older males (who survived) were usually given organizational and logistical tasks or made drudges who were required to clean the chamberpots, much as the lower classes tend to the elderly in nursing homes today.

At the very bottom of the heap were drudges, usually female, and slaves, assigned to clean the privies and tend the children. Contemporary females keep things in order in nursing homes and day care centers. These people are generally exempt from sexual harassment. They are harassed enough economically.

Order was kept by professional enforcers or knights. They were rewarded by regular food and the spoils of war, including women. Raping, looting, pillaging and the spoils of war sustained their loyalty to their masters. So, they risked their lives for a "roll in the hay" and a patent of land. They could aspire to exceptional reward by doing something distinctive like killing a dragon, finding the Holy Grail, or preventing an assassination.

Harassment can be found on all levels of the system. Where groups were relatively equivalent in strength, scapegoats were readily available. There were village idiots to torment and minority groups to exclude (depending on your era). In the final crunch, however, no one really objected to harassment for to do so would be to bring down the system. The imperative was to sustain the system, for without it, people would have no one to harass. It was also important for each layer to have someone *below* it so they would have someone to harass.

The whole process was and is very complex. Fundamental to it, however, is gender differentiation. By force of arms (men often held clubs while women used theirs to hold babies), men subjugated women relatively early in human history. Today, that same biological imperative drives the relationship between men and women. The more they are brought together in the workplace, the more it is necessary for men to find ways to keep women in their place. In the medieval court, some semblance of order could be kept by keeping men and women apart and providing chaperonage. Of course, the flip side was that women were legitimate spoils of war–and still are, in some places.

Some groups managed to exist independent of "the system." Various military orders like the Knights of Malta or the Templars took on an identity of their own which was respected by the nobles because of their association with the religious quest. The pope held power by association with the supernatural, although without troops, he had mostly the trappings of office and public respect (somewhat like most chairmen of the board).

There were other notable exceptions to this process. Some males and females had the ability to entertain, and if they performed that function well, they were exempted from other tasks. Gladiators, for example, were required to do nothing but compete. Actors were to act, and jesters to amuse. The jester held a very special role, perhaps the only member of the hierarchy permitted to speak his mind, so long as it amused the noble. Comedy has been a traditional minority occupation, a popular profession for upwardly mobile members of harassed minority groups, one in which they can retain their integrity. Bill Cosby, for example, notes that being a comic was a way to avoid physical threat on the streets. Today, women are moving into comedy and Rita Rudner, Jennie Jones, Paula Poundstone, "The Love Goddess," Judy Tenuta, and literally hundreds of others nightly do their own harassing of male "oppressors."

Also exempt from the harassment chain were "specialists." Scribes, for example, were particularly important. The ability to read and write was so rare and valuable that those who could do it were a special class. The Catholic Church retained much of its power through its control of literacy (cf. Umberto Eco, *The Name of the Rose*, 1983). Privilege also accrued to valued practitioners, hence, the guild system, which restricted the number of trained technicians, which, in turn, enhanced their value and made them objects of protection.

A few members of the nobility also became patrons of the arts and sustained the work of painters, sculptors, and musicians. The protection given medieval artists may be the source of the contemporary institution of scholarly grants. (Check the activity of Mobil Corporation on public television.) Artists with patrons were free to create as they were moved. Today high-tech specialists of both genders possess special immunity from economic fluctuations. Artists (and writers), unfortunately, have lost a good deal of their funding and concomitantly, a good deal of their protection. Some now must work for a living.

Courtiers and employees must choose exceptional service, sycophancy, or servility as their means of survival. The difference in today's corporation is the lack of naked force and the removal of the privileges of raping, looting, and privilege. Persecution becomes merely harassment. The pretense of democracy, however, removes the element of chivalry, the protection of virginity, and all of the professed respect for woman as mother and madonna. The situation remains much like medieval times. Women, in order to show obeisance and allegiance, had to perform both their required and implied tasks. Young ladies in waiting had to wait to perform required service for the female royalty they served. They were trained to bow and genuflect, bring food, swing fans, and stand by for other requests, somewhat like contemporary secretaries serving their male masters by bringing coffee and wearing tight sweaters. They were also expected to function as courtesans, which included flirting with male nobility; sometimes they were selected as concubines. It is this latter process that represents the threat to contemporary women.

SOME CONTEMPORARY EXAMPLES OF
THIS SYSTEM IN OPERATION

On the morning of December 24, 1991, Helen Gurley Brown (1963) told of how, when she was young, she and her colleagues "sported" on the job with the males with whom she was employed, by removing each other's underwear in rollicking sessions of chase and capture. She acknowledged she did not want to remove the "joy" of males and females working with each other. She then conceded she had not believed "date rape" existed either, until she got hundreds of letters from readers. She talked of the synergy of males and females working together, but did not take note of the conventional wisdom, summed up below in the humorous listing of differential degradation, to wit:

- He is aggressive; she is pushy.
- He is firm; she is stubborn.
- He is angry; she has PMS.
- He is discreet; she is secretive.
- He complains; she whines.
- He exposes fraud and corruption; she gossips.

If he has pictures of his wife and family on the desk, he is a good family man. The same pictures on her desk show her "real" priorities.

In medieval times, men and women were clearly in different categories. Women were allowed no aspirations. The few with powers had it by inheritance. Those who were safe, like nuns, had chastity as their defense, but they were not safe from predatory armies of another faith. Chastity belts protected some women from involuntary intercourse, but made them slaves in other respects. Harems were common in the east. The rest of the women, the old and the homely, played their assigned roles, however demeaning they were. Today, because of economic exigencies (to put it bluntly, we need women because they work for less), women are given the tacit promise that they can aspire to the same rewards as men. Women buy into this because couples want a standard of living that cannot be attained by one income anymore. This implies that they have both sexual privilege and protection. Presumably, the sexual revolution gave women the right to initiate sexual contact or refuse it, as they chose. Men, on the other hand, were admonished to respect women's space and not impose themselves.

African Americans and others are also ineligible for some competitions by an unspoken contract, though not by law. African American males have some extraordinary economic capabilities. They have the power to dominate sports, a recreational commodity highly valued by the economically powerful white male majority. So, African Americans get some respect, and, as the record of Wilt Chamberlin demonstrates, they are not sexually harassed. Quite the contrary! Women, too, may aspire to careers in entertainment. Madonna and her ilk are living icons of the route to power for women: entertainment and a sound investment portfolio (or, as Ivana Trump illustrated, a favorable divorce settlement). Part of their success, however, depends on sexual advertisement.

Life in the contemporary corporation differs only slightly from that at the medieval court, mainly because the "powers that be," in our case, the Congress of the United States, have given lip service to certain entitlements. Via the shibboleths of equal opportunity and affirmative action, they have arranged the system so that tokens are offered. For example, in an erudite and entirely humorless article in the October 1990 issue of the *ACA Bulletin*, (Hickson, Grierson, & Linder, 1990) three scholars talk of harassment as if 1) they know what it is, and 2) they know what to do about it. They talk of "lechers," "mental groping" (mental undressing is a more common phrase), "victims," "social touching," "foreplay harassment," and so on. The experts close with a one page prescription of remedies, such as "acknowledge the problem," "keep matters confidential," "don't ignore the problem," and "bring a case in federal court." The application of these formulas might well entirely separate men and women in the workplace or make them antagonists in expensive court cases.

The piece is typical of those currently disseminated. They do not impress the victims. Women know slogans do not solve the problem. Blacks also know that protestations of equal opportunity are meaningless and, as a result, they have sought their own isolation and political activity. Both females and blacks demand that their voices be heard, as though adding a book or two to required reading in the schools would change things. They won't. They are placebos and lull the victims into a false sense of security.

White males learn two things. The first is to act as if they understand the problems. If they do this effectively, they keep blacks in "their place" and may con women into sexual access. Second, they learn that they retain final authority in much the same fashion as they had it in the 1400s. They adjudicate the complaints that are made against them. Consequently, they cannot lose. Unfortunately, there is no biologically neutral third sex to mediate disputes.

Despite the artistic rhetoric, women who are not mainly wives and mothers are regarded as courtesans and drudges. The few privileged females (by the grace of affirmative action or consummate performance skill) are permitted the privilege of flirtation, an activity which had become a high art in medieval times when virginity was both a virtue and a protected commodity. The boys still nudge and wink and refer to women by their body parts or with pejorative nouns.

The media provide a number of graphic examples of the operation of the system. Dan Fielding on *Night Court* is a perfect example of the cringing courtier. Even Judge Harry Stone, comic figure though he is, demands Dan's cringing and crawling. Dan, in turn, has his lackey, the millionaire bum (later killed by a falling piano making Dan a rich man), who must, nevertheless, cringe to keep his job. Christine wishes to maintain her independence, but her job demands that she flirt with Harry and even get involved in an affair. She may fend off Dan, however. They are equals. Harry is gallant enough to let her off the hook, but there is no doubt he has droit de seigneur. Her position is underlined by her quick seduction and impregnation by a member of the minor constabulary, her instant divorce, and the reinstitution of her dependence on her patron, the judge. Bull is the physical defender, Roz, the jester (a female jester is becoming more and more de rigueur these days, another lip service to political correctness). There is also a court clerk, generally exempted from the carrying on. He is a black scribe, consequently treated with civility.

LA Law provides a more complex example. There is ambiguity, as in the case of Roxanne, scribe to Brackman, but courtesan to Becker. All appear to be Jewish and are rendered savory only by the comic aspects of their roles. Note that the Jewish stereotypes are flawed comically, while the gentiles are flawed tragically, another sign of hierarchy. The other Jewish female (Bloom) is also fat. McKenzie (Protestant) is in charge. His subordinate partner, the Jewish Brackman, handles the money. Kuzak and Sifuentes (Catholic) now have their own firm. All of the female members of the organization end up in bed, some in seriatim, with the partners. Grace van Owen, the ineluctable blonde, is made a tragic figure. The older competent "shikse" is granted a Jewish husband, but is tempted by a young male babysitter. Rollins, the one black character, is given special recognition (affirmative action) via sexual access to a blonde white woman.

Commercial advertising confirms the popular wisdom about the role of women. They are to conform to a particular body size and shape much like medieval women were forced to conform to confining and artificial dress styles. Men in a certain station in life have access (droit de seigneur again) to unlimited beer and women, associated, of course, for commercial purposes. The cultivated art of courtesanship of medieval times has been democratized and made available. All women have equal opportunity in the profession of prostitution. They may sell their body, in reality, in exchange for privilege, the image of their body for media recognition. If they allege their "virtue" has been taken, onus probandi is on them to prove the rape. There is no democracy in sex, and there never has been.

Men expect sexual submission as a right of position; women go through the routines as a rite of position (pun intended). This model is harmonious with what prevails in the rest of the animal kingdom. There is, however, in humans, the ephemerals of courtesy, chivalry, and law. The continuing confrontation about date rape is nothing more than publication of what was once private business. The fact that people actually believe something can be done about it is an indication of how powerful the promise is. Women are trained to believe that men can and will respect their rights, which, of course, makes them easier victims for rape, seduction, and/or harassment.

The prime directive of medieval chivalry was sexual access. The knight had the privilege of sexual access to the woman he saved from the dragon. (Some virgins would have preferred the dragon.) The rules of being a gentleman applied only to the lists and the battlefield. Contact between males and females was publicly discreet and chaperoned, but in private, there was a massive tradition of sado-masochism testified to by a pervasive literature of pornographic control of women by their male masters. This genre reached its peak in Victorian times, when the notorious *Man With a Maid* (Anonymous, 1968) was in vogue, and more recently, when *Story of "O"* (Reage, 1965) made the international best-seller list. Companies do a thriving business in films illustrating techniques of bondage and domination, a recurrent underground theme shared throughout the male culture. The media have even become so bold, recently, as to suggest sado-masochism is normal and often elected by the women.

Women who bought the promise and attempted to achieve parity in the workplace forfeited what few claims they had on protection. On the whole, Thomas's treatment of Hill was trivial harassment; she was the courtesan, but she was not assaulted. Women who are raped and brutalized when they attempt to exercise their rights pay the full contemporary price for violation of the code. "They asked for it!" is the excuse.

Americans have never bought into the chivalric code formally, but their vestigial remnants, the eating clubs and fraternities, plus the networks of clubs and organizations that exclude women, demonstrate that a conception of hierarchy exists. On campuses, we presently have guidebooks to political correctness which espouse fair play for women; in essence, they set goals with no means of implementation and call them "solutions."

A COMPENDIUM OF MOSTLY INEFFECTIVE RESPONSES

Documentation. However innocent day-to-day "joking" and "getting coffee" may look, they could be construed by males as a willingness to provide sex. Women cannot keep records and prosecute every suspicious glance. Women must be exceedingly perceptive to discover precisely when a remedy can be sought and from whom. However, it is hard for women to know whom to trust. People may be untrustworthy, but legal documents are sometimes worth the paper they are printed on.

An ounce of prevention is not necessarily a cure, but it helps. A tight job description can fix the range of allowable activity and restrain supervisors from infringement. When the contract is written out, both parties know their rights and privileges. Such arrangements may often be one-sided, but at least they are specific and someone wronged knows it and knows what to do about it.

Mentoring. In medieval times, women, despite pledges by men to honor and protect them, had no genuine protection for person or property except through patronage, or in special cases, by of inheritance of position. Contemporary women refer to the present-day equivalent of patronage as "mentoring" without understanding the term. Few know that Mentor was the name of a human, the teacher of Ulysses's son, Telemachus. Mentor taught him to draw the bow, so that when his father came home from the war, they could recognize each other. The contemporary metaphor suggests that some newcomers to the organization get "mentored" by some older and wiser member who teaches him (pronoun consciously selected) the ropes. The mentor teaches whom to trust, whom to fear, and with whom to curry favor. Women complain they are barred by gender from obtaining mentors. Furthermore, they are suspicious that when they are approached, confidentially by men, it is more for purposes of seduction than support.

They confuse the role of mentor. What they say they want is accurate advice, but what they want is someone to tell them how to live their organizational lives, protect them from harm, and push them ahead in the hierarchy, that is, patrons. Most understand that their position in the organization is precarious unless they have the favor of some powerful male. Having that favor does not guarantee that the protector will not, himself, make sexual demands (cf. Billy Wilder's *The Apartment*).

Take note that power is attractive! Some women are drawn to it like moths to a flame, and its attraction can destroy them. Women fail to believe the worst about men. One of the interesting "findings" by counselors of beaten women is their illusion that the battering is "natural behavior" or that they "brought it on themselves."

Sexual overtures in the corporate suite are frequent, and sexual innuendos are incessant. Female knights-in-the-making are often surprised to discover that their advanced degrees, scholarly achievements, and technical skills often provide little protection. Their qualifications may sustain their pay level or support continued employment. When it comes to harassment, however, attractiveness is not a relevant criterion. We must keep in mind that the principle of "women's liberation" supposedly gives them sexual parity. To the average male, that is a license to larceny—"they were asking for it!"

Etiquette. Potential sexual jeopardy depends mainly on the custom of the court (currently referred to by social scientists as "norms" or "climate"). An earlier generation had ostensible protection via etiquette, a vestige of medieval courtesy. It was valid, however, only so long as women stayed out of the workplace. Emily Post (1975) died before acquaintance rape became public. Etiquette is now a way to make the best-seller list and it protects no one.

Conformance. Employees are expected to dress properly. (The dress code in the medieval court was very rigid.) Teresa Fischette was fired by Continental Airlines for refusing to wear makeup, and Ann Hopkins alleged she was denied a partnership at Price Waterhouse for being "unfeminine." The dress code, unwritten of course, is fluid enough so that women can be forced to dress as courtesans even if they reject the role. The power suits, now the uniform of aspiring female executives, are carefully tailored to expose sufficient leg and most have slits to use strategically. A woman may be a knight from the forehead up, but the rest of her remains a potential courtesan.

Parenthetically, it is interesting to observe "skirt work" at meetings at which men and women work together. Most of the women, at one time or another, embarrassed by stares and glances, try to work their short skirts to cover their knees and manipulate the slits so they do not reveal calf. But the simple fact is that women get sexual attention without trying. Men stare; when women stare back they risk angering the men or advertising themselves as wanton.

Games. Men appear to have rules when they compete with each other, although anyone who has played football knows that face masking and holding are infractions only when called. In fact, the rules of "survival of the fittest" prevail in most encounters between males. One of the interesting features of male relationships is the tendency of men to form teams. Every man (*Loving and Living,* Phillips & Goodall, 1983) wants to be the most valuable player on the winning team.

Women never compete with men. The women players have their own leagues and never move up from the minors. Men, who cannot be counted upon to play fair with each other, cannot be expected to play fair with potential victims. Women who expect a fair shake are a couple of maraschinos short of a sundae.

The accomplishments of women are subject to systematic verbal debasement. If they tilt as well as a man, it is regarded as a fluke or "not bad–for a girl." Even those rare few women whose expertise is acknowledged are not welcome at court. (Scarlett O'Hara embarrassed her husband by adding up a long column of numbers in her head–and in public.) Admitting a woman's accomplishments makes it all the more urgent for the male to advance his at her expense.

It is easy to turn Freudian here and talk about castration. Men often do as a defense, claiming that women who do well only do so as a means of castration. It is humiliating to admit needing a woman as an ally and even more humiliating to be in debt to one. A survey of case histories done a decade ago indicates that mediocre men actually protect themselves by making sexual advances on competent females. By distracting their attention from work to the sexual arena (where the rules are stacked toward the males), the women are handicapped in competition. What is unthinkable for mediocre males is to concede the equality of the other gender (in this case, regarded as a subspecies). Powerful and successful men can afford to do so condescendingly because of their skill and control, but often men who concede female equality do so to win the confidence of the females in order to secure sexual favors.

In any case, it is extraordinarily difficult for women to keep men's attention off of their body parts and on work. Given that sex is a natural, biological activity, it is not altogether desirable that they do so. Thus, they are caught in a bind, because if they admit their own biology they concede defeat in most vocational competitions.

Information Systems. Women learn what is expected of them from covert information systems. Often, what the boss says aloud is contradicted by the silent system. The boss is required to conform to public codes of decency–in public. Thus, he may deny being sexist and even speak strongly against it on formal occasions, but the "scuttlebutt" may be just the opposite. Attention to scuttlebutt is important. In *The Court Jester*, Danny Kaye had to keep in mind the information that "the chalice from the palace has the pellet with the poison while the flagon with the dragon has the brew that is true." The public information was that both vessels (including the vessel with the pestle) had wine in them. The covert information carries the truth, and failure to attend to it means death. This is known as the "Borgia Gambit."

Often, nobles had others do their talking for them. The vizier or other major courtier might carry unpleasant messages. This is equally true today; underlings often convey messages quietly. David Riesman (*The Lonely Crowd*, 1950) refers to "inside dopesters." In *Community Power Structures* (1953), Floyd Hunter refers to a group known as "knowledgeables." They are present in all organizations, and they do the work that is required of them. The town crier, in medieval times, carried the official news, but the peasants understood what the truth was. (Robin Hood told them! He is long dead.) What makes life even more perilous for women is that they are often excluded from the information networks and consequently only know what is official. This makes them susceptible to blindsiding.

Thus, the most important communication is the informal talk that links individuals and enables them to share important information such as how to stay out of trouble and how to get ahead. Older lackeys learn how to stay out of trouble. Observing their example and listening to their stories can stand a newcomer in good stead. In every court, there were courtiers and lackeys who did not grovel, who knew how to avoid the wrath of the noble and get the most out of the system. Some even had the head man's "ear." These were the important people who had learned the proper balance of presence and absence to avoid harassment. They survived and prospered and rose to power like Robert Graves's Claudius. (This may not fully apply to women until they become "of a certain age," however, and are no longer considered prime sexual conquests. This is known as "growing on the job.")

Women's Rules. We make metaphors about "noble self" or "other voices" and afford ostensible identity to those who did not have it. Carol Gilligan (1982) tries to establish that women have "different ethical rules." Her book generated a theology, that men and women live by different rules. But Gilligan never proved her "women's rules" were anything more than "the game" as played by powerless people. Henley (1977) offered "post oppression theory," as an explanation. Neither dealt with sexual harassment per se. Both books made the best-seller list but did little to improve the strategic position of women. Furthermore, now we have Robert Bly (1990) and his "men's movement," replete with hairy savages and wounded children, the pounding of tomtoms and running around nude and screaming. This, presumably, confirms male identity, male privileges, and, of course, male superiority. Take that, Betty Friedan (1963)!

Actually, women who attain power play the game by men's rules and do it very well. In medieval times, new nobles got a coat of arms. Today, members of excluded groups get the trappings of office when admitted to power. In the sense of Quintilian's *imitatio,* women emulated the men they replaced and most did it well. They become competitive and exclude the powerless, often other women. Ardrey (1966) and others note the process of older females abusing younger and weaker women exactly like males. These routines are characteristic of acculturation in exclusively female occupations such as nursing or flight attendants. Skill and special knowledge offers no protection for the woman from depredations by her own gender. That is why so many women claim to prefer male bosses.

Fighting Back. In the medieval court, direct confrontation was dangerous. Sellout was possible, but traitors were killed. There were few successful rebellions in the medieval court; even fewer in contemporary corporations. Rebellions and takeovers led to new tyrannies. The French Revolution overthrew the nobility but brought Napoleon; the Mensheviks in Russia gave way to the Bolsheviks. Corporate takeovers merely change the color of the brass; the privilege of harassment remains, although the names of the cast may be changed. Women are advised today to fight back; to let the perpetrator know the behavior is offensive. Most males will not be put off by this kind of challenge. ("Aha, you little vixen!" they will shout.) Men are always on the winning side. It is facile to say men do not know what they are doing is wrong and merely need to be informed. They know perfectly well it is wrong, and they enjoy it. It is in their genes. Males and females are animals and the dance of sex is primal. Thus, despite the offensiveness of some acts, most women prefer silence and avoidance to facing the public humiliation of accusation and a legal defense which they are likely to lose.

Avoidance (chastity) is somewhat more effective, but it costs women some freedom of movement. Men, in fact, may interpret avoidance behavior as being coy. Furthermore, overcoming resistance is part of the game for men. Among animals, alphas seek power in order to get females. Sexual access is the reason why men seek money. With it, men can purchase cars and clothes to impress females exactly as a peacock spreads his tale or a mandrill displays his purple behind. Forcing women to submit is man's greatest game.

It is interesting, however, as Desmond Morris (1967) noted, that when animals fight, the winner does not kill the loser. Rather, he makes the loser present himself in a sexual position. He is then pardoned and sent on his way (although Zuckerman [1932] noted, monkeys in captivity will commit homosexual rape on their defeated victim). We have yet to examine the metaphor of man as an ordinary animal devoid of soul. It would violate the religious principles of social science. But the men and women of the Middle Ages understood it well and fairly.

The Legal System. The legal system holds no promise either. One theme in medieval stories was the miraculous intervention of some prince or duke to bring star-crossed lovers together and punish the seducer. The question always was: How do you get access to the duke? In corporate America it is hard to reach a person with sufficient power to intervene, unless appellate jurisdictions are provided. Men can get to the top by using their mentors. Women, however, must have patrons and they must usually pay for them. Getting to the top is not in their job description, and attempts to bypass a link on the chain of command means sudden economic death. You get fired! That is, she gets fired! He is terminated, deselected, or put on a different career track.

When legal remedies are available, the burden of proof falls on the female. Men are presumed innocent until the preponderance of the evidence shows otherwise. When overt acts are spelled out and made grounds for dismissal, women have a chance. When left loosely defined, as they are in fact and in most academic essays, males invariably win in the formal combat in the court. The Smith case has clearly established that point. The weight of the evidence was not sufficient for conviction and that was that. The message to women was, "Why bother?"

One could squeal—if the offense was serious enough and the person who committed it important enough. The story could be sold to a periodical for a one-time fee. But the whistle blower blows the whistle on herself, too. One woman's chance to blow the whistle is another man's chance to cover up. The cards are stacked from the beginning.

Rebellion. Sometimes an underling comes into possession of a vital secret, like how to burrow into the palace or how the new software works. These secrets can be sold. Betrayal, however, is not a solution, it is a rebellion. It is done for revenge or money. It is rarely done for advancement, for no one will trust a person who sells out. They will buy the secret, but they will not hire the salesperson. After all, if she sold out once, she could do it again.

Changing sides within the organization does not work. If your boss loses, you go down with him. If your boss wins, he can hardly concede that you were responsible for his victory. The most valuable warriors get no patent of land, no payoff. They remain women. Furthermore, conspiracy is a difficult thing to manage. It is hard to know whom to trust. Men have formed tight little secret societies. Women have their secrets, but they have not institutionalized them. Masons may not be very important any more, but their secrets remain secret. NOW members can't even keep their sexual proclivities under their hats.

It is important for women to identify whom to trust in the case of conspiracy. In many cases, the person who appears to be on the same level is slightly higher because of his or her willingness to report secrets to the person in charge. Conspiracies usually fail, and the weaker conspirators take the punishment. Secretaries take the rap for their bosses; or men keep their mouths shut in exchange for sexual favors. Women do not have the physical or political power to topple the walls of the Bastille. Just as a single rooster can keep order in a barnyard full of hens, the "boss" in the corporation controls the "chicks" and "foxes."

Sabotage. Sabotage can sometimes be fun. Planting viruses in computer systems or fouling up the phone circuits can be discommoding and expensive, but the problem with sabotage is that it is nothing more than a nuisance unless someone knows why it is being done. There's the rub—when she blows her cover she is washed up at the company and probably everywhere else. Back in medieval times, she would lose her head. It happened to Anne Boleyn because she couldn't conceive a boy, and she was the queen. Of course, she was mother to Elizabeth I.

Rumors. Spreading stories is another effective device. Expert storytellers never make up stories. They preface their remarks with disclaimers like, "what if . . . " (as in, what if the boss and Gloria were having an affair) or "I heard somewhere that . . . " (as in I heard Gloria is on the take.) The person who hears the stories will transmit them. Once a story goes beyond the second person, however, disclaimers cannot quell it. It becomes institutionalized, details are added, and it takes on a life of its own. The object of the story has to deal with it. Stories add up to reputation. The stain will stay on Thomas throughout his sojourn in public life. That much, Hill accomplished. But, sadly enough, she, too, is stained and probably disqualified from public life.

Camelot fell because of the rumors about Lancelot and the boss's wife. Despite his reputation as a loyal lover (with Elaine), Lancelot was sullied and Galahad had first track on the grail. Galahad's "strength was as the strength of ten, because his heart was pure," which simply meant he was a better killer because he did not have nocturnal emissions (credits to Maurice Samuel [1950] for the preceding line), or diurnal, either. The point was he had the best reputation so he got the grail. In present-day terms, grail = promotion or election. (No one really knows what Bill Clinton and Gennifer Flowers did.) But storytelling, in the final analysis, is also nothing more than catharsis.

Poison and Futility. Some Borgia women used poison. Others were used as tokens for the complex intermarriages out of which medieval empires were built. Those endowed by God with rights of inheritance had a modicum of clout, although no say in with whom they bedded. But "you've come a long way, baby," and all women are compelled to be eligible (except, of course, those who are unattractive). Prudence dictates that one must not let the natural need for catharsis impede victory. The question is, how do the powerless get power when their identity is synonymous with futility and they cannot change their identity? Revenge is sweet, but impractical.

So, women remain powerless. Like all powerless people, they are interchangeable and devoid of identity. They are known mainly by their sexuality; in that sense, they are described by Ben Franklin's admonition that "in the dark, all cats are grey." The courtiers had no trouble finding sex partners. If one woman wouldn't play, she could be killed or banished, or better yet, imprisoned, tortured, and raped. There were dozens of others who "knew" the rules and would play. Their present-day equivalents are the groupies that lined up for Wilt Chamberlin and Geraldo Rivera. Magic Johnson is honored for testing HIV positive, while Kimberly Bergalis dies an ignominious death.

WOMEN AS A MIDDLE CLASS

We have not talked at all about the growth of the middle class which offers some small defense. Consider, for example, the situation of the Jew in the Middle Ages. Because the church forbade loaning money at interest, Christians were required to turn to Jews for cash. This system worked well for Jews who got paid back and knew "when to walk away and knew when to run." The other Jews were killed. When the coupons were due, the men with the swords appeared. In Russia and Poland, Jews were used as safety valves. Whenever the nobles felt threatened, they called a pogrom to divert the energy of the peasants.

The artisans and artists were a bit more fortunate. Because they could not be forced to perform, they were protected and rewarded economically, if not with political power. This is a possible role for women. In fact, the increase in the number of single-parent households headed by women indicate that there is a considerable movement of female independent artisans toward the middle class. On the other hand, there is no evidence that the middle class is free of harassment; and most of the women, denied child care payments by their husbands, simply remain poor. The "Mr. Goodbar" theory of male/female relationships argues that any female out alone in public has only one thing on her mind. The acquittal in the Smith case recently upheld the theory that the legal system remains the defender of the accused. We have gone in a gigantic circle. The very patents of freedom that enabled women to aspire to equity imprisons them because of the ease with which crimes against them can be concealed or defended.

Women, of course, once partially empowered, can play St. Georgina (or Karen Silkwood and have Cher for a sidekick). They can find dragons. They can rise and assault the system; "woman" the barricades as it were. The feudal system is not without dangers. Knights can overthrow. Nobles can conspire with artisans as in the Magna Carta and demand concessions from the king. Women can conspire and control as in the case of Lysistrata or Nancy Reagan, or countless Agatha Christie stories in which the murderer was a female acting in the model of Lucrezia Borgia. The artisans and members of the middle class have power in numbers as well. The American, French, and Russian revolutions were hardly risings of the downtrodden masses (at least at the outset). The middle class developed out of people with technical and financial skills. For a time, they stood apart from the nobility because of the rarity of their services. Eventually, they sought their share of power and initiated governmental change which rapidly turned to revolution, terror, and dictatorship. This characterized both the French and Russian revolutions. The so-called "American revolution" was actually a rebellion of middle class against middle class. The middle class has the peculiar characteristic of creating its own hierarchy and nobility, a process which is clearly going on in the women's movement. The recent descriptions of the warfare at the 1991 Modern Language Association (MLA) meetings graphically illustrate this point.

Contemporary labor unions emulated guilds, although the decline of skilled labor has proliferated new vassals and opened boundless opportunities at the bottom for women. On the other hand, women in unions, although blatantly pestered by wolf whistles and obscene comments, actually enjoy more equity at fornication than they do as vassals within the corporation. Among equals, they are permitted to initiate seductions and ward off advances without fear of economic repercussions.

In lower socioeconomic areas, women are still constant victims. They are sexually available, some because they buy into the system which makes them sexual pawns. Medieval times were a bit closer to primal conditions. People were well aware of basic needs, the urgency to stay alive, the drive for raw sex, and they made arrangements for it. It did not matter to them whose rights they violated. In fact, the whole notion of rights is a relatively late development. Moreover, rights do not exist for a great many women. Brutalizing women is a fact of life in the lower socioeconomic classes (and a covert fact in the middle class and above). Despite our thin veneer of civilization, women are still victims, much more so than blacks, as witnessed by how Wilt Chamberlain and Magic Johnson became heroes by virtue of their athletic and sexual prowess. The women with whom they scored are as important as the baskets they scored.

Today, those women who buy into the norms operate on a variety of levels. Some become highly paid courtesans in exchange for public display. We call them entertainers. Aspirants parade in decolletage and high-cut bathing suits and are judged like cattle at livestock competitions. They put money in the bank (if they are smart) or buy real estate to sustain themselves in their old age, and some of them reverse the tables by buying young men for sexual use and by harassing their own subordinates. (The editor-in-chief of the magazine on *Anything But Love* is a good example, albeit a caricature.)

Further, there is powerful pressure among women, imposed especially by the church, that kirche, kuchen, und kinder is still the guiding principle. Spouse bashing, abandonment, and social isolation are accepted as normal usufruct of the natural law that governs the system of relationships between men and women. Small wonder that women in the workplace are vulnerable to imposition and depredation. There is further pressure imposed by the propaganda from female writers about "biological clocks," the importance of keeping house, and other arguments designed to keep women in their place. Said Kipling (1892), "who has children in the cradle had best be at peace with the world." The maternal capability of the female also keeps her preoccupied and reduces her power to fight back. (This is not the place to discuss it, but "biological clock" talk is another confession of political and personal weakness.)

The "beauty trap" is a special form of pressure. The culture imposes the demand that women be sexually attractive. Males are honestly presented with the paradox of neatly coiffed and carefully garbed women, equipped by their designers to emphasize their sexual parts. Women are on display, whether they have anything for sale or not. They are involuntary courtesans. It is also noteworthy that so many flower children remember the free sex of Woodstock more than the principles of the Port Huron statement. The sexual revolution succeeded because it was to the advantage of men. It led to elimination of alimony laws in many states and it emboldened some women who became more available. (Drug use remains, too, but that is an economic issue. Who remembers the political principles?)

All of these forces create the superwoman cliché. Women try to conform to traditional standards of motherhood and contemporary standards of corporate success. They often hold themselves culpable if they do not succeed at both, while men are not held responsible for similar success at fathering and vocational skill. This social mythology forces women into a position of guilt, in which they accept their harassment as part of "the process." In medieval days, it was only necessary for a woman to play one role.

SUCKING UP AND ADVERTISING: THE NORMAL SURVIVAL ALTERNATIVES

There is an old Yiddish word, "schmeichling," which means what it sounds. "Sycophancy" would be the appropriate euphemism. It is crucial to learn how to do it. It was the mainstay of survival at court. The idea was to use the softer inartistic proofs of flattery and euphuism to soothe the nobles into quiescence. By presenting the appearance of availability and compliance a courtier could avoid challenges and perils. In exactly the same way, the employee of the corporation can avoid harassment merely by sacrificing ego. (It is actually a small price. One can go home and be oneself. The cost is that the employee suffers by being unable to find fulfillment, and the company suffers by losing the employee's best efforts.)

Skill at "sucking up" is crucial. It is the ultimate defense mechanism for both males and females. The female who learns how to handle it may be asked to make the coffee, but rarely gets chased around the table. The male who does it is often a candidate for promotion. Please note the difference in consequences. Administrators are notoriously poor judges of talent. They award the appearance of talent, but rarely try to confirm it. They reward claims of success, often without validation.

The person who does not suck up gets harassed or fired. Males are regarded as stubborn, truculent, rebellious. Women are regarded as bitches. Often the person who does not suck up regards the need to suck up as harassment. Survival in the organization, as at court, means learning a method of sucking up that is not so demeaning as to be intolerable. Make no mistake, sucking up is as important to survival today as it was in the medieval court. Even the most democratic of bosses demand it.

The *second* most important method of sucking up is doing the job well. Most important is *talking* about doing the job well. Often bosses and nobles cannot tell the difference between the two. As long as you *are seen* as vital to the organization, you are rewarded. You are not expendable. Women who are hyper and dedicated (and who wear glasses and frumpy clothes and who come early and work late and who say "yessir" a lot) are usually not victims.

Administrators merely want to feel the job is being done well, just as the king wanted to know all was well in the kingdom. Whoever brings good news is rewarded; the bearer of bad news is customarily killed. Consequently, talking about "it" may be more important than doing "it." (This is especially true when bosses talk about the women they have had. Their accounts are always questionable. They do not receive tokens with every successful conquest.)

Gilbert and Sullivan (1887) summed it up:

If you wish in the world to advance,
And your fortunes, you're bound to enhance,
You must stir it and stump it,
And sound your own trumpet,
Or, trust me, you haven't a chance.
    -RUDDIGORE (Green, 1941, p. 544)

Richard Armour (1958, p. 58) said it another way:

The codfish lays a million eggs, the little hen but one,
But the codfish doesn't cackle, to tell us what she's done.
So we despise the codfish, while the little hen we prize,
Which indicates to thoughtful minds, it pays to advertise.

Almost as effective as talk about performance is talk about future plans for performance. There are bosses and nobles who believe the promise as fact. "I will slay the dragon" is a safe way to rise in the hierarchy, at least until the dragon presents itself. Often, this never happens. (FYI: There are no dragons.) Protecting the boss from predicted catastrophe is a powerful method of sucking up to authority and making yourself indispensable. Say something impossible is going to happen and take credit for preventing it–the secret of success.

Add to this method of rising in the corporation the trite and commonplace inartistic proofs, such as financial bribes ("I can get it for you wholesale"), oaths of allegiance, sexual promises or favors (without delivery), cajoleries and flatteries, spurious camaraderie, and networking with family and friends. It is very useful, for example, to befriend the boss's spouse. (This sometimes failed with the nobility since the duchess was often a victim of the axe. One must be sure that the relationship is solid between the boss and spouse before attempting to influence said spouse, unless one wants to testify in the divorce case and take the attendant risks.) Invitations to family events (weddings, bar mitzvahs, and the like) are not so effective, although center-court seats for the Lakers or fifth-row center seats for a sellout show are compelling persuasion.

Invitations to quiet cocktails after work could be declined on the grounds of a "herpes flareup" or start of the "monthlies" whenever possible. In fact, one female middle management member testified her defense against harassment was a self-started rumor about her nonexistent herpes. Chastity belts were a medieval technique of protecting women by insuring fidelity. Women never selected them in self-defense. We have not yet thought of a contemporary equivalent, but they might be a defense. You don't harass if you can't consummate.

We should add that Murphy's Laws must be heeded. Within them lies potential protections against harassment. Also, females are admonished to avoid males who claim to be feminists and who rail against harassment. "Methinks he doth protest too much." Maurice Samuel (1950) pointed out that in *Gunga Din*, Kipling offered the line, "though I've belted you and flayed you, by the living God that made you, you're a better man than I am, Gunga Din." This means, of course, that pukka sahib will continue belting and flaying poor Gunga, just so he can have these noble moments of self-abnegation. Beware the man who betrays his own kind.

Finally, and on a practical level, in a day of AIDS and other perils, we recommend a formal system of "informed consent." Forms can be issued, somewhat like living wills, with questions like, "You may wink at me," "You may admire my clothing," "I will flirt with you," "Intercourse can be negotiated." The form should also include space for a medical report. Only HIV-negatives can be eligible. The forms should be executed formally and notarized and the attendant warnings taken seriously.

We have reached a point where the absurdity of the remedies seems to lighten the severity of the offense. Our point is that sexual harassment is a real and natural condition, a deterrent to the effective operation of an organization, and more than just an historical artifact. Since it is so close to the biologically primal, it is hard to rationalize out of existence; since it is so ephemeral, it is hard to interpret; and since it is so hard to identify, it is hard to penalize. At the moment, awareness, caution, a repertoire of strategic moves, and the ability to think quickly and move rapidly are the only defenses a female has.

In an article in the December 1991 *Harper's*, Professor Louis Menand (1991) notes that discussions about the abstract rights of women and consideration of issues such as harassment and acquaintance rape provide a laboratory for consideration of these issues. It is interesting to note the self conscious attention universities have paid to these issues, while taking very little note of reality. A reply to that article by a recent college graduate takes note of the fact that the steps taken by administrations toward political correctness have the effect of trying to knock down a mountain of marshmallow with a BB gun (our metaphor, not hers...we are deconstructing).

At some point, females might get themselves together and bring about retribution. They are a majority. Males might do well to tend to the job. While they are out merrily a-harassing, they have female competitors who are moving up and passing them by minding their own business and doing it well. A female biogeneticist pointed out that males are not necessary for females to become impregnated. Given parthenogenesis, the present-day victims may well become the only occupants of the planet in time. In the meantime, women will continue to be victims of insincere promises by men who profess support for female causes and will be regularly disappointed by the failure of the laws they trust to protect them in both their vocational and private lives.

REFERENCES

Anonymous. (1968). *A man with a maid.* New York: Grove Weidenfeld. (Original work privately published 1884)

Ardrey, R. (1966). *The territorial imperative.* New York: Atheneum.

Armour, R. W. (1958). *Nights with armour.* New York: McGraw-Hill.

Becker, E. (1968). *The structure of evil.* New York: G. Braziller.

Bly, R. (1990). *Iron John: A book about men.* Reading, MA: Addison-Wesley.

Brown, H. G. (1983). *Sex and the office.* New York: Avon.

Castiglione, B. (1900). *The book of the courtier* (Sir T. Hoby, Trans.). London: D. Nutt. (Reprinted from the *edition princeps* of 1561)

Dershowitz, A. M. (1991). *Chutzpah*. Boston: Little, Brown.

Eco, U. (1983). *The name of the rose* (W. Weaver, Trans.). San Diego: Harcourt Brace Jovanovich.

Friedan, B. (1963). *The feminine mystique*. New York: Norton.

Gilbert, W. S., Sir, & Sullivan, A. S., Sir. (1941). Ruddigore: or, The witch's curse. In Martyn Green (Ed.), *Martyn Green's treasury of Gilbert & Sullivan* (pp. 499-625). New York: Simon & Schuster. (First production 1887)

Gilligan, C. (1982). *In a different voice*. Cambridge, MA: Harvard University Press.

Graves, R. (1948). *The white goddess* (1st ed.). New York: Creative Age Press.

Henley, N. M. (1977). *Body politics: Power, sex, and nonverbal communication*. Englewood Cliffs, NJ: Prentice-Hall.

Hickson, M., III, Grierson, R. D., & Linder, B. C. (1990, October). A communication model of sexual harassment. *Association for Communication Administration Bulletin*, No. 74, 22-33.

Hughes, T. (1911). *Tom Brown's school days*. London: Harper & Bros.

Hunter, F. (1953). *Community power structure*. Chapel Hill, NC: University of North Carolina Press.

Kipling, R. (1892). *Barrack-room ballads and other verses*. London: Methuen.

Lyly, J. (1902). *The complete works of John Lyly* (R. W. Bond, Ed.). Oxford: Clarendon.

Machiavelli, N. (1897). *The prince* (2nd ed., N. H. Thompson, Trans.). Oxford: Clarendon.

Menand, L. (1991, December). What is the university for? *Harper's*, pp. 47-57.

Morris, D. (1967). *The naked ape*. New York: McGraw-Hill.

Phillips, G. M., & Goodall, L. G., Jr. (1983). *Loving and living*. Englewood Cliffs, NJ: Prentice-Hall.

Post, E. (1975). *The new Emily Post's etiquette*. New York: Funk & Wagnalls.

Reage, P. (pseud.). (1965). *Story of O*. New York: Grove Press.

Riesman, D. (1950). *The lonely crowd*. New Haven, CT: Yale University Press.

Samuel, M. (1950). *The gentleman and the Jew*. New York: Knopf.

Wilson, E. O. (1978). *On human nature*. Cambridge: Harvard University Press.

Zuckerman, S., Sir. (1932). *The social life of monkeys and apes* (1st ed.). London: K. Paul, Trench, Trubner & Co.

Chapter 17

Promoting a Sociocultural Evolutionary Approach to Preventing Sexual Harassment: Metacommunication and Cultural Adaptation

Gary L. Kreps
Northern Illinois University
DeKalb, IL

THE PROBLEM

Sexual harassment is a serious organizational problem that not only dehumanizes those who are harassed, but inevitably negatively influences the effectiveness of organizing activities and diminishes the quality of work life for organization members. It clearly causes personal and professional harm to the targets of harassment. It promotes distrust and hostility between those individuals who are the initiators and targets of sexual harassment, between those who are accused of harassment and their co-workers who level accusations, as well as between those who side with these different parties to sexual harassment. This distrust and hostility is clearly illustrated in the case studies of sexual harassment provided by Lenny Shedletsky (in Chapter 5) and Mark Braun (in Chapter 6). Such distrust and hostility ultimately leads to the creation of defensive organizational climates, in which the working relationships (and levels of cooperation) between organization members deteriorate (Kreps, 1990). Sexual harassment also distracts organization members from the accomplishment of important organizational goals, irrevocably decreasing both the quality of organizational life and the productivity of organizational activities.

Sexual harassment is an organizationally repugnant pattern of behavior. Yet, as many of the previous chapters in this book (such as Rebecca Leonard and her colleagues in Chapter 11, Mary Gill in Chapter 10, and Robin Clair in Chapter 13) clearly illustrate, sexual harassment is a pervasive problem in modern organizational life. Recent revelations about the 1991 meeting of the U.S. Navy's Tailhook Association of aviators at a Las Vegas hotel, for example, at which at least 26 women, more than half of them Navy officers, were pushed along a gauntlet of drunken male officers who groped, disrobed, and sexually abused them, illustrate the insensitivity and utter disregard of the rights of women that exist in modern organizational life. The fact that Navy administrators tried to ignore the problem and resisted taking disciplinary actions against the officers who participated in this ritual of collectively expressed sexual harassment provides clear evidence of the institutionalization of sexual abuse in organizations. The fact that cases of blatant sexual harassment and abuse such as the incidents that occurred at the Tailhook meeting happen at all is shocking, but the failure of formal organizational leaders to take quick and decisive disciplinary actions in response to such incidents is morally unacceptable because it tacitly condones such behavior and even encourages future expressions of sexual harassment

Organizational responses to sexual harassment that do not clearly demonstrate disapproval of such actions are irresponsible. Leaders must communicate to organization members in no uncertain terms that sexual harassment will not be tolerated and will be dealt with severely. Organizational failures to swiftly and forcefully respond to situations of sexual harassment exacerbate the problem by encouraging organization members to underestimate both the seriousness of sexual harassment and the harm such behavior causes. This concluding chapter argues that to eradicate sexual harassment in organizational life, the repugnance and unacceptability of such behaviors most be powerfully communicated to organization members through formal and informal communication channels. Such communication will help to establish, implement, and reinforce cultural norms prohibiting sexually harassing behavior in organizations.

SEXUAL HARASSMENT AND CULTURE

Current employment and labor laws (as evidenced by Ramona Paetzold and Anne O'Leary-Kelly in Chapter 4 suggest that organization members have the right to expect ethical treatment in their work organizations. Yet, this right depends upon the willingness and abilities of all organization members to live up to their responsibilities to communicate ethically with others. Sexual harassment is both unprofessional and unethical. It violates several primary expectations for the ways organization members expect to be treated. The expression of sexual harassment is disrespectful, unjust, and causes unwarranted harm to organization members (Kreps, 1986). Those who harass others are organizational bullies who abuse their authority, disregard their organizational responsibilities, and violate legal and moral standards for behavior.

Kay Payne (in Chapter 9) describes sexual harassment as an expression of power and domination in organizational life. Gerald Phillips and Susan Jarboe go even further than Kay Payne when they suggest (in Chapter 17) that sexual harassment is an inevitable consequence of men's primitive urges to establish power and gain sexual gratification. While the logic or their argument, which traces the historical and phylogenetic bases of sexual harassment, is compelling, it also overstates the omnipotence and irreversibility of such base desires as influences on human behavior. Sexual harassment is not an inevitable consequence of sexual politics, power inequities, or unrestrained libidos. Mature human beings have the ability to overcome primitive urges to act in inappropriate or irresponsible ways. People have the ability to rise above their natural inclinations, by learning how to act in accordance with cultural expectations. Mature individuals direct their behaviors to comply with culturally approved standards for "correct" behavior. Since sexual harassment is a primitive and immature pattern of behavior that violates the rights and expectations of others, those that engage in such behaviors must be taught to "grow up" and communicate more appropriately with their organizational colleagues.

The key question is whether sexual harassment is a pattern of behavior that is influenced more by nature (primal urges) or by nurture (cultural learning). The numerous incidents of sexual harassment in modern organizational life suggest that in current practice harassers are more influenced by their primitive natural inclinations than they are by cultural nurturing that discourages such behavior. Cultures must do more to outlaw sexual harassment, and do a better job of nurturing organization members to avoid engaging in sexually harassing behaviors.

Sociocultural evolutionary theory suggests that human beings have developed the ability to survive by joining together in social groupings (cultures) and collectively developing strategies for responding to social pressures (Campbell, 1965). Groups evolve cultural norms to guide the selection of adaptive behaviors for members to adopt to meet changing needs and constraints. Cultural membership can be conceptualized as an educational process used to help members learn the rules for appropriate behavior. Cultures teach their members through socialization processes to refine their behaviors to meet accepted standards of ethics and civility. Cultural acceptance depends upon adherence to important cultural rules and violations of these rules are not tolerated. To eliminate sexual harassment, socialization processes must be used to teach organization members that such behaviors are serious violations of cultural standards.

Cultural norms are rules that guide member behaviors by designating the boundaries of acceptable interpersonal interaction. Norms are taught to members through metacommunicative processes that reinforce culturally approved behavior and punish those who break cultural rules, socializing members to behave in prescribed ways. Metacommunication is a specialized form of feedback, feedback about communicative behaviors, through which established members of cultures tell neophyte members "how things are done around here" (Kreps, 1990). If newcomers follow cultural norms, they are warmly accepted into the culture; if they violate the norms, they are rejected and ostracized.

The more central a norm is to a culture, the more explicitly it is communicated to members, and the more strongly it is upheld (Garfinkle, 1964). It is very dangerous for organization members to violate central cultural norms, since they risk the scorn and disdain of all other members of the culture who expect these norms to be upheld. Peripheral norms are not explicitly communicated and the violation of these norms, while not approved, are often tolerated within organizations. The pervasive expression of sexual harassment in organizational life suggests that in many organizations there are only peripheral norms condemning such behavior.

IDEOLOGICAL CHANGE AND THE PREVENTION OF SEXUAL HARASSMENT

For too long sexual harassment has not been taken seriously in organizations by many organization members, especially men. It has been winked at and laughed at and joked about. There has been a "nonconscious ideology" that has made sexual harassment invisible for many years; this ideology viewed sexually harassing behaviors as natural, harmless, and playful interactions between men and women (Bem, 1970). It was assumed that this is the way things are; such behaviors were a natural part of organizational life. Men who engage in what is clearly sexually harassing behaviors often frame their actions as jokes or expressions of their appreciation for the attractiveness of the women they are harassing. Many others in organizations perceive these actions similarly. For example, some people may think it is harmless for men to whistle at attractive women or pinch these women's buttocks. These behaviors are too often seen as innocent flirtations. As Hal Witteman illustrates (in Chapter 3), sexually harassing behaviors are often cast as organizational romance. Jill Axelrod shows (in Chapter 7) how these stereotypic assumptions about flirtatious behavior are reinforced in popular media, such as movies.

Erroneous assumptions that frame sexual harassment as innocent flirtations are encouraged by cultural ideologies that stereotypically portray women as inferior to men and that view women as sexual playtoys for men (Bem, 1970). Communication must be used to raise public consciousness about the nonconscious ideologies that denigrate women and encourage sexual harassment. Julia Wood (in Chapter 2) clearly illustrates this issue of raising public consciousness when she discusses the importance of naming sexual harassment. Communication should be used to call attention to the repugnance of sexually harassing behavior, thereby socially legitimating condemnation of sexual harassment. Such communication must clearly and forcefully debunk the stereotypic and misleading assumptions fostered by the nonconscious ideologies that underlie sexual harassment.

The public charges of sexual harassment against Clarence Thomas by Anita Hill that were so dramatically portrayed on national television during the Senate confirmation hearings of Mr. Thomas' appointment to the Supreme Court may serve as a critical event in eliminating sexual harassment in organizational life, because it raised public consciousness and awareness of the issue of sexual harassment. This incident put sexual harassment in the public spotlight. It set the agenda for examining sexual harassment by making sexual harassment an acceptable topic for public and private conversation and debate. The conversations about sexual harassment that evolved from the public hearings are extremely educational. In many cases the hidden rage that those who had been targets of harassment had harbored over the years came spilling forth in conversations between friends, colleagues, and family members in living rooms, bars, kitchens, and offices across the country. The stereotypic assumptions (based upon nonconscious ideologies) about the extent, impact, causes, and remedies for sexual harassment were made explicit. These assumptions could now be challenged and argued in both public and private forums. Furthermore, the reality of sexual harassment in modern organizational life could no longer be ignored. When Anita Hill bared her soul to the world and charged Clarence Thomas with sexual harassment, she legitimated the experiences of all others who had been targets of harassment and gave them license to speak their minds.

USING METACOMMUNICATION TO RESPOND TO SEXUAL HARASSMENT

Gerald Phillips and Susan Jarboe (in Chapter 17) not only suggest that sexual harassment is inevitable (a contention rebutted earlier in this chapter), but also suggest that the best strategies women can use to avoid being sexually harassed is to grovel and ingratiate themselves to potential harassers, referring to these strategies as "sycophancy and servitude." Sycophancy and servitude do not seem to be very effective strategies for avoiding sexual harassment. They are also sexist, offensive, and degrading recommendations to make to women. Ingratiating strategies such as sycophancy and servitude provide little long-term benefits in the struggle to prevent and eliminate sexually harassing behaviors in organizations. They are merely short-term survival tactics that undermine the integrity of women and perpetuate the nonconscious ideologies about women's lack of status that legitimate sexual harassment. These suggestions are tantamount to telling people who are oppressed (such as Jews, African-Americans, or homosexuals) that their best strategy for confronting oppression is to ingratiate themselves to and grovel before bigots that persecute them. How do you think a survivor of the concentration camps at Auschwitz would respond to the suggestion that sycophancy is the best strategy for avoiding Nazi persecution? A powerful lesson learned during World War II was that giving in to and making concessions to tyrants like Hitler only encouraged oppression by demonstrating weakness. Similarly, sycophancy and servitude are strategies that will work to encourage the bullies who are the perpetrators of sexual harassment, not discourage them.

Metacommunication (providing feedback about the acceptability of specific communication behaviors) is the strategy suggested here for confronting sexual harassment. Metacommunication may not always result in immediate or painless solutions to sexual harassment, but such communication will promote long-term cultural changes in the ways sexual harassment will be perceived and responded to in organizational life. Those who are subjected to sexual harassment are encouraged to clearly and directly express their outrage at such treatment. They should let it be known that they will not tolerate such behavior. Sexual harassment has to be clearly recognized as a serious violation of central cultural norms if it is to be eliminated in organizational life. Metacommunicative messages can provide organization members with continuous unanimous support within their organization and within the larger relevant environment for behaving in ways that are not sexually harassing. Correspondingly, metacommunicative messages can provide unanimous condemnation for those who engage in sexually harassing behaviors.

Metacommunicative messages should be directed to the initiators of sexual harassment and to relevant others within the organization to identify and condemn expressions of sexual harassment. Formal and informal leaders should be informed about incidents of sexual harassment. They must be told how offensive and unacceptable such behaviors are. Others within the organization should also be informed so they can provide public support for the targets of harassment and public condemnation for perpetrators of harassment. By using metacommunication to bring incidents of sexual harassment to light, organization members can raise public consciousness about sexual harassment, encourage disciplinary actions to be taken against harassers, and discourage the expression of sexually harassing behaviors in organizational life. Unethical behaviors, such as sexual harassment, are more likely to occur in the dark than they are in the light of public scrutiny.

If internal audiences within the organization are not responsive to feedback about instances of harassment, it may be necessary to metacommunicate with key individuals within the organization's relevant environment, such as representatives of regulatory agencies, professional associations, accrediting bodies, and the press. At Dartmouth University, for example, the names of men who female students claimed had engaged in date rape were published and disseminated on campus to let these men know that their actions would not go unnoticed and to increase awareness on campus of the widespread occurrence of such sexual abuses. While such public "outings" of those accused of date rape may have caused unwarranted suffering by those who may have been falsely accused, it provided a forum for women to express their discontent with abusive behavior, fostered attention to the issue of date rape, and encouraged the development of organizational policies to prevent such abuses in the future. Public attention to cases of sexual harassment, such as in the Tailhook meeting incident (discussed earlier in this chapter) and in the Fallongate incident (described by Mark Braun in Chapter 6), can foster public support for those who are harassed and condemnation for those who engage in harassment, leading to individual changes and organizational changes to prevent sexual harassment.

Metacommunicative messages are powerful influences on behavior that can influence and change even entrenched habitual behaviors. For example, there has been a dramatic change in attitudes and behaviors about public smoking of tobacco products in the U.S.A. over the last decade that is largely attributable to metacommunicative messages that let smokers know that smoking in public is unacceptable. Ten years ago smoking in public was an uncontested right (nonconscious ideology) of every smoker. Slowly but surely, health promotion specialists (such as C. Everett Koop, the former Surgeon General) used communication to raise public consciousness about the risks of smoking and second-hand smoke. They encouraged health care systems, planning commissions, industries, businesses, restaurants, and schools to develop and implement local smoking control ordinances and work-site smoking control policies. They also empowered individuals to let smokers know that smoking in public is unacceptable. The combination of individual, organizational, and government support for "smoke-free" workplaces and public places provided a multilevel battery of metacommunicative messages to smokers about acceptable behavior. Similarly, metacommunication about sexual harassment from individual, organizational, and government sources can discourage sexual harassment in organizational life.

Strategies for interpersonal, organizational, and governmental communication to confront and prevent sexual harassment are described in the chapters of this book. Mary Helen Brown illustrates (in Chapter 8) how women can provide interpersonal support and guidance for responding to sexual harassment. Kay Payne (in Chapter 9), Judy Bowker (in Chapter 12), Robin Clair and her colleagues (in Chapter 13), and Vince Waldron and his colleagues (in Chapter 14) examine the use of interpersonal strategies to confront sexual harassment. Kathleen Galvin (in Chapter 15) and Cynthia Berryman-Fink (in Chapter 16) describe organizational training programs that can discourage sexual harassment. Furthermore, (in Chapter 4) Ramona Paetzold and Anne O'Leary-Kelly describe government support for discouraging sexual harassment through laws that condemn such behavior. Sexual harassment can be eradicated as a major problem of organizational life by strategically utilizing multiple channels of communication to raise public consciousness about the repugnance of such behaviors, to legitimate the plight of those who are targets of sexual harassment, to denigrate those who engage in harassing behaviors, and to help develop strong cultural norms that condemn sexual harassment and educate organization members to refrain from such unethical and harmful behaviors.

REFERENCES

Bem, D.J. (1970). *Beliefs, attitudes, and human affairs.*Belmont, CA: Brooks/Cole Publishing.

Campbell, D. T. (1965). Variations and selective retention in socio-cultural evolution. In H. R. Barringer, G. I. Blanksten, & R.W. Mack (Eds.), *Social change in developing areas: A reinterpretation of evolutionary theory.* Cambridge, MA: Schenkman.

Garfinkle, H. (1964). The routine grounds of everyday activities. *Social Problems, 11,* 225-249.

Kreps, G. L. (1986). Ethical dimensions of organizational communication. In W. Hamel (Ed.), *Proceedings of the association of human resources management and organizational behavior, national conference* (pp. 285-289). Virginia Beach, VA: Maximillian Press.

Kreps, G. L. (1990). *Organizational communication: Theory and practice* (2nd ed.). White Plains, NY: Longman.

▼ Author Index

▼ Subject Index